# GunDigest® Book of
# CLASSIC AMERICAN
# COMBAT
# RIFLES

edited by Terry Wieland

Published by

Gun Digest® Books, an imprint of F+W Media, Inc.
Krause Publications • 700 East State Street • Iola, WI 54990-0001
715-445-2214 • 888-457-2873
www.krausebooks.com

To order books or other products call toll-free 1-800-258-0929
or visit us online at www.krausebooks.com, www.gundigeststore.com
or www.Shop.Collect.com

Cover photography courtesy Chip Morton Photography, morton.chip@gmail.com,
www.chipmortonphoto.com, 951-699-7873

ISBN-13: 978-1-4402-3015-8
ISBN-10: 1-4402-3015-3

Cover Design by Tom Nelsen
Designed by Dave Hauser
Edited by Corrina Peterson and Terry Wieland

Printed in the United States of America

# Contents

# Introduction

## Welcome to the *Gun Digest Book of Classic American Combat Rifles*

No country in the world owes as much to the rifle as the United States. The rifle brought victory in the War of Independence, held the country together through a devastating Civil War, won the West, and made America a great power through the 20th century.

In many ways, America's combat rifles — firearms purchased by the government, and issued to our troops — tell the story of the country itself. At any given time, the rifles used by the U.S. Army, Navy, and Marines reflect America's progress toward technological and industrial might.

Today, there is more interest than ever before in the rifles Americans have used in combat throughout our 235-year history. We have rifles in use in historical reenactments of Revolutionary and Civil War battles, period rifles used in cowboy-action competitions, the current interest in the AR-15 platform as a hunting, defense, and target-shooting rifle for civilians, and, of course, the continued activity of arms collectors at all levels.

Since its first issue in 1944, the study of America's combat rifles has been a major part of *Gun Digest*. We have published articles on the romance, design, performance, historical and technical significance, and — of course — the shortcomings of the many rifles which have been used by American troops in battle.

Most shooters recognize names like Springfield, Garand, ArmaLite, Sharps, and Spencer. But those are only the rifles that made it to the top and stayed there. Many other rifle designs were tested and adopted by the U.S. military, only to see limited use in action before sliding into historical oblivion. Other patterns bridged gaps between major technological advances.

One thing all of these rifles have in common is that, at their time, they were tre-

mendously important to the men who used them, and they are all part of the history of the American combat rifle.

In this volume, we have gathered the best articles on American combat rifles published by *Gun Digest* during the last 66 years. Like GD itself, they are quite varied; some are historical accounts by academics in the field; others are first-hand looks by soldiers who used the rifles in combat. To us, one of the most interesting aspects of compiling a book like this is not only the many different points of view, but the chronological view points — for example, looking at the rifles of World War II just as that war was ending and without the benefit of historical perspective and distant hindsight.

The history of *Gun Digest* extends back to a time when men living, shooting, and writing about it were personally acquainted with soldiers who lived through everything from the Civil War to the two World Wars, and could recount their experiences first hand. This gives the *Gun Digest Book of Classic American Combat Rifles* a different flavor than we would find in even the most comprehensive history written by one author.

Here, we have articles by some of the best-known and respected writers working in the field during the second half of the 20th century. On the Springfield rifle, we have Col. Townsend Whelen and Lt. Col. William S. Brophy, Jr.; on the rifles of World War II, Charles T. Haven, the noted Colt historian and technician at Johnson Automatics; on the M14, John Lachuk, one of the acknowledged fathers of the .44 Magnum.

From 1946, when he became editor, until 1984, when he retired, John T. Amber guided the editorial fortunes of *Gun Digest* with the enthusiasm of a shooter, the intense interest of an historian, and the editorial rigor of the best editor ever to work in the firearms field. Amber was interested in every aspect of firearms, but he loved rifles the best; he was escpecially interested in those little-explored nooks and crannies of rifle history.

When a writer came to Amber with an idea, he was given a forum and as much space as he needed to tell the story — provided the story was worth telling. When the manuscript was submitted, Amber then applied standards of accuracy worthy of a college thesis. As a result, much of the material that appeared during his tenure could be reproduced, without apology, in a professional technical journal.

Even after John Amber's retirement, having an article published in *Gun Digest* remained a goal that writers, both professional and amateur, regarded as a mark of having arrived as a gun writer. Both Amber's demanding ways, and the professional commitment of his writers, is reflected in the articles published here.

Almost as interesting as what we have included is what was not covered in the pages of *Gun Digest*. By and large, Amber did not assign topics to writers; writers came to him with ideas, and Amber either approved them or not. This left his subject matter at the mercy of the interests of his writers, and this in turn was dictated by their own experience and the attractions of the rifles themselves.

The short-lived M14, for example, warrants only one article. For years, it was viewed in military terms as a stop-gap between the Garand and the AR-15; today, the virtues of the M14 are more widely recognized (as witness the success of Ruger's Mini-14, a small rifle modeled on its action.) Similarly, there is little on the trapdoor Springfield, which is now enjoying renewed interest on several different levels.

One reason for this is that Amber was dealing with an annual publication. He was not — and did not want to be — in competition with more frequent periodicals such as the NRA magazines. He preferred to devote his editorial space to subjects that were not being covered elsewhere, including arcane and under-appreciated designs such as the Hall rifle, the Whitworth, or the rifles of James Paris Lee.

If a writer wanted to deal with a more main-stream topic that was already widely covered elsewhere, he needed to come up with a unique angle in order to interest John Amber. The result is a substantial body of firearms literature that concentrates on the obscure corners of firearms history, or gives radical views of more familiar topics.

For example, James Paris Lee is regarded by some as a second-tier rifle designer, none of whose designs made it to the big time as an American combat rifle. Amber's view (and that of writers Larry Sterrett and John Wallace) is that Lee was far ahead of his time, and both he and his designs deserve more recognition than they receive.

Lee qualified for this book (barely) by the fact that the U.S. Navy adopted his rifle and 6mm cartridge, albeit briefly, and we have reprinted three articles that both give Lee his due and are excellent examples of the scope and quality of *Gun Digest* articles over the past 66 years. It is this willingness to look beyond the obvious that made *Gun Digest* what it is, and gives this collection of articles a unique historical perspective on that subject of endless fascination, the American combat rifle.

*Terry Wieland, Editor*

# Muskets, Powder and Patriots

The firearms used in the Revolution were of many types and of highly mixed ancestry, yet they served the patriots adequately, if not well, in their struggle to victory.

▌ M. L. Brown

The fabled "long rifle" was a novelty in the eastern colonies. In July, 1775, amazed patriots at Cambridge, Mass., watched in awe as one company of frontier riflemen placed all its shots in a 7-inch target at 250 yards — or so the story goes! Credit: Department of the Army.

GRIM-VISAGED Massachusetts Militia from Acton, Carlisle, Chelmsford, Concord and Lincoln nervously fingered loaded muskets on the muster field beyond Concord town. A dark column of smoke suddenly smudged the clear morning sky above the tiny Middlesex village and, as if on signal, determined patriots marched in double file toward the ominous beacon. Leading the van was taciturn Acton gunsmith Capt. Isaac Davis, and when his small band of citizen-soldiers approached "… the rude bridge that arched the flood …" they were met by a thunderous volley of musketry from three companies of British light infantry. Davis was killed instantly, the first patriot officer to fall in battle. It was April 19, 1775, and an infant nation saw birth in the bloody throes of revolution.

Gen. George Washington faced many difficulties throughout the Revolution, among them critical shortages of artillery, small arms and gunpowder. He triumpted, accepting Lord Corn-wallis' surrender at Yorktown, 19 October 1781. Credit: Library of Congress.

Craftsmen, farmers, frontiersmen; mariners, merchants, statesmen and scholars rallied to that clarion call of freedom and they would desperately need vast quantities of arms and munitions to meet the insatiable demands of the arduous struggle ahead. As early as 1750 Parliament attempted to curtail colonial iron production and discouraged other American enterprise, yet despite severe restrictions iron production flourished clandestinely. An adequate supply of iron was available throughout the war, although the vagaries of combat often made procurement difficult while inflation escalated prices.

In 1774, as relations between stern Mother England and her recalcitrant child rapidly deteriorated, Parliament placed an embargo on all firearms exported to the colonies and, on 1 September, Gen.

Thomas Gage, Royal Governor of Massachusetts, confiscated the gunpowder stored in the public magazine at Charlestown and brought from Cambridge two fieldpieces to strengthen defenses at Boston. Aggrieved patriots retaliated when on 13 December they seized British gunpowder at Fort William and Mary.

Two months before Longfellow's immortal farmers "… fired the shot heard round the world …," Massachusetts organized Committees of Safety, which were soon emulated elsewhere. The committees were empowered to mobilize the militia, confiscate military stores, encourage the expansion of domestic arms-making and procure arms and munitions from domestic and foreign sources either by contract or purchase from available supplies.

It has been estimated that at the outset of the Revolution only a third of the firearms in the colonies were of domestic origin while lead, essential for casting projectiles, was almost exclusively imported, as were prime gunflints; each was discovered to be in short supply after hostilities commenced. The shortage of gunpowder was even more acute, and a usually optimistic George Washington was forced to admit that "Our situation in the article of powder is much more alarming than I had the most distinct idea of."

Under British rule militia service was compulsory for all able males between 16 and 65. Although most colonists were prosperous enough to own firearms, and

were required by Crown regulations to possess a musket and accouterments suitable for military use, they were poorly trained and equipped in comparison to British regulars. Familiarity with firearms doubtlessly sustained patriot efforts early in the conflict and, when integrated with the iron discipline hammered out by Baron von Steuben at Valley Forge in the harsh winter of 1777-78, welded the battered rebels into a more formidable foe.

## Variety of Arms

Throughout the war Pvt. Yankee Doodle, of necessity, embraced virtually anything that would shoot. This was early indicated by a Pennsylvania Council of Safety report that in several units up to seven types of ammunition was required for the variety of arms in use, while at Valley Forge a perturbed Von Steuben complained that "muskets, carbines, fowling pieces, and rifles were found in the same company." American, British, Dutch, French, Hessian, Prussian and Scottish arms all found their way into patriot hands by various means, quantity generally prevailing over quality, though early in the Revolution British arms predominated; many of these were seized by patriot forces at the outset. To these were added a number of French arms, captured relics of the French and Indian War (1754-63).

The large caliber, single-shot, muzzle-loading, smoothbore flintlock musket was the mainstay of the 18th century weapons system, and in the colonies it was often used for hunting as well as military service. Its combat effectiveness was enhanced by the bayonet, and it was frequently loaded with ball or shot or a combination there-of.

The average musket had an effective range of 80 to 90 yards and, in the hands of seasoned troops using paper cartridges containing both powder and ball, could be loaded, primed and fired four to five times a minute, while the heavy lead ball inflicted a devastating wound. Excavations of various Revolutionary War encampments and battlegrounds have uncovered musket balls of both British and patriot origin bearing obvious mutilations — some with nails driven through them- doubtlessly calculated to inflict more horrible wounds.

Lack of ranging power and low accuracy had little bearing on the effectiveness of the musket, for military tactics of that era were based on a massed volume of fire delivered at close quarters. Troops were trained to point rather than aim, firing in unison on command, and speed in loading was the essential factor. Theoretically 500 men could in 20 to 25 seconds, deliver 1,000 rounds into enemy ranks at less than 100 yards and, on the heels of the final volley, came the spirited dash with the bayonet executing even more carnage. That mortal men faced such murderous fire and the cold steel that followed is difficult to comprehend in this Nuclear Age; that they did it so regularly is astonishing.

The gradually emerging American rifle performed a minor role in the Revolution despite popular concepts to the contrary. Until the conflict began the rifle was virtually unknown to colonists in the coastal settlements and few American victories can be exclusively attributed to patriot riflemen. The rifle was primarily the weapon of the sniper, forager, picket and skirmisher, having little success except on the frontier. There it was used advantageously in the sanguinary Indian-fighting campaigns by skilled woodsmen accustomed to that deceitful type of warfare.

Highly accurate up to 200 yards, as many British officers and artillerymen belatedly discovered, the American rifle nevertheless had two distinct disadvantages when used as orthodox tactics demanded. The tight-fitting, patched ball, requisite for range and accuracy, made it more difficult and slower to load than the musket — riflemen delivering about three shots a minute — and the absence of a bayonet dictated by its less rugged design and construction often proved disastrous. That was the case at Princeton, 3 January 1777, when Hugh Mercer's Virginia riflemen were shredded by the 17th Leicesters and 55th Borderers.

Pistols were used extensively in the Revolution. Basically cavalry and naval weapons, these single-shot, muzzle-loading arms were used at short range. Generally carried by officers, they were issued to enlisted men in some units of the British Army. Many were fitted with left-side hook, attached to the sideplate, to prevent slipping when thrust into the sash or belt. Horsemen generally carried a pair of pistols in specially designed cloth or leather holsters with a brass muzzle cap. The holsters were joined by a wide leather band and slung across the saddle pommel. Some were ornately decorated.

Martial pistols were rather cumbrous, having massive butts serving as bludgeons after the initial shot. John Paul Jones, spirited captain of the *Bonhomme Richard*, used his pistols in a somewhat unorthodox fashion during the epic struggle with the *Serapis* on 23 September 1779. Angered by a gunner's cowardice, Jones threw both of his pistols at him, one of them fracturing his skull!

In addition to the various types of muskets, rifles and pistols in patriot ranks there were carbines, commonly called musketoons, wall guns and special-purpose weapons such as signal pistols and grenade-launching muskets. Carbines served both cavalry and artillery, those of the former having a sidebar and ring for attachment to a shoulder belt. Most were 10 to 12 inches shorter than the average musket, many of them made by shortening damaged musket barrels. Contemporary authors often used the word "musketoon" as a synonym for carbine or to denote a martial blunderbuss. The latter was widely used on both land and at sea to repel boarders and to defend narrow passages such as bridges, fords, doorways, barricades and staircases. The *amusette*, known variously as the wall or swivel gun, also saw sea and land service. Considerably larger than the common musket, weighing up to 50 pounds and firing up to a 2-inch ball or shot, the amusette incorporated a swivel attached to the forestock which was mounted on the walls of forts and other embrasures. Despite its weight it was a portable weapon and often substi-

Washington's Chief of Artillery, Maj. Gen. Henry Knox (1750–1806), reached patriots surrounding Boston in January, 1776, with a vital cargo of heavy ordnance, gunflints and lead from Fort Ticonderoga, subsequently forcing the British to evacuate the port. Credit: Library of Congress.

tuted for light artillery, especially on the frontier where rough terrain often made it difficult to transport heavy ordnance. Some specimens were rifled.

Until the beginning of the War of Independence Massachusetts was the hub of colonial arms-making, producing more firearms than the remaining colonies combined. Rifle-making, however, centered in southeastern Pennsylvania and, because of the variety of arms made by Pennsylvania riflesmiths during the conflict, the Lancaster area became famous as the "Arsenal of America." When war began arms-making facilities were expanded and new installations built in most of the colonies; however, the southern colonies made fewer firearms due to shortages of skilled labor and the minimal development of natural resources, yet this was offset by the vast quantities of arms and munitions entering southern ports from abroad.

Unfortunately there is no complete record of the hundreds of gunsmiths actively engaged in fabricating arms for the various Committees of Safety, the Continental Congress or the infant states, and space limitations preclude listing all known makers in the text. The gunsmiths were an integral part of the socio-economic life of the colonies; most were respected community members and many were sedulous civic and military leaders. Whatever his ability and experience, the gunsmith was a skilled craftsman, either learning the trade through an exacting apprenticeship-often a maximum of seven years' duration-or under the tutelage of his father or a relative, for gunsmithing was not only a trade, but an art passed on from one generation to the next.

## Gunsmiths of the Revolution

Many 18th century American gunsmiths could trace their ancestry to English arms-makers of the early colonial era. Such was Gen. Seth Pomeroy, gunsmith and French and Indian War veteran, who fought as a private at Bunker (Breed's) Hill. Pomeroy died, age 71, at Peekskill, N.Y., 19 February 1777, on his way to join Washington in New Jersey. He was the grandson of gunsmith Eltweed Pomeroy who in 1630 came to the Bay Colony from Devonshire, England, siring a family of arms-makers active until 1849.

It was a patriot gunsmith who first learned of British intentions to march on Lexington and Concord to confiscate public arms and munitions stored there. Known simply as "Jasper," his shop located in Hatter's Square, Boston, he warned

the Committee of Safety which promptly sent post riders William Dawes and Paul Revere to arouse the militia on the eve of that fateful day in American history.

Innumerable gunsmiths served as armorers in the militia and Continental Army; so many in fact that Congress requested they be exempt from military service because their technical skills were vital to the war effort. Richard Falley of West-field was the first official armorer for the Massachusetts Bay Colony and John Fitch, who in 1769 established a gunsmithery on King Street in Trenton, New Jersey Colony, served as an armorer and lieutenant in the Continental Army. Fitch made muskets for the N.J. Militia until burned out by the Redcoats in 1776. One of history's tragic figures, he is now best remembered for his pioneering efforts in the application of steam power to sailing vessels.

One of the most prominent Massachusetts gunsmiths active during the Revolution was Hugh Orr. Born in Scotland, 2 January 1715, Orr immigrated in 1737, settling at Easton, Pa. He moved, a year later, to Bridgwater, Mass. An experienced gun-and — locksmith, he established a scythe and axe works featuring the first trip-hammer forge in New England. In 1748 he made 500 muskets for the Massachusetts Militia, most of these taken from Castle William by the British when on 17 March 1776 they evacuated Boston. Shortly after the war began Orr erected a foundry, casting both brass and iron cannon while also making large quantities of ammunition. He died at Bridgewater, 6 Dec. 1798.

Another active and eminent maker of firearms for the patriot cause was William Henry. Born in West Caln Township, Pennsylvania Colony, 19 May 1729, Henry was apprenticed to Lancaster riflemaker Mathew Roeser and from 1755 to 1760 was chief armorer to the Pennsylvania forces in the French and Indian

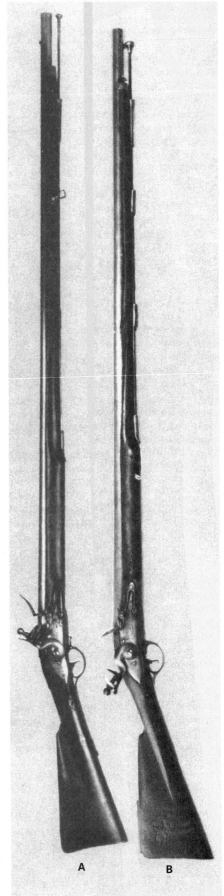

(A) John Churchill, Duke of Marlborough, introduced the 1st pattern "Brown Bess" infantry musket ca. 1714. This specimen, made by Jordan of London in 1747, probably served in the French and Indian War. "US" mark is visible on the lockplate. Credit: West Point Museum.

(B) Committee of Safety musket made by Henry Watkeys, New Windsor, Ulster Co., N.Y. (fl. 1770–80). Watkeys and Robert Boyd contracted for 1,000 muskets at £ 3–15s each for the N.Y. Colony on 13 June 1775. Stock is branded "N-Y REG." Credit: Smithsonian Institution.

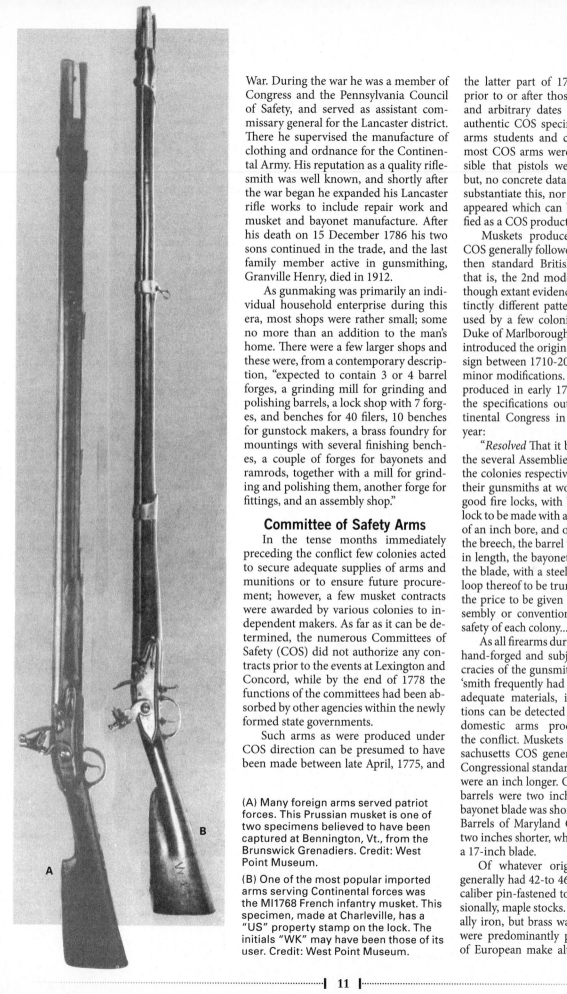

War. During the war he was a member of Congress and the Pennsylvania Council of Safety, and served as assistant commissary general for the Lancaster district. There he supervised the manufacture of clothing and ordnance for the Continental Army. His reputation as a quality riflesmith was well known, and shortly after the war began he expanded his Lancaster rifle works to include repair work and musket and bayonet manufacture. After his death on 15 December 1786 his two sons continued in the trade, and the last family member active in gunsmithing, Granville Henry, died in 1912.

As gunmaking was primarily an individual household enterprise during this era, most shops were rather small; some no more than an addition to the man's home. There were a few larger shops and these were, from a contemporary description, "expected to contain 3 or 4 barrel forges, a grinding mill for grinding and polishing barrels, a lock shop with 7 forges, and benches for 40 filers, 10 benches for gunstock makers, a brass foundry for mountings with several finishing benches, a couple of forges for bayonets and ramrods, together with a mill for grinding and polishing them, another forge for fittings, and an assembly shop."

## Committee of Safety Arms

In the tense months immediately preceding the conflict few colonies acted to secure adequate supplies of arms and munitions or to ensure future procurement; however, a few musket contracts were awarded by various colonies to independent makers. As far as it can be determined, the numerous Committees of Safety (COS) did not authorize any contracts prior to the events at Lexington and Concord, while by the end of 1778 the functions of the committees had been absorbed by other agencies within the newly formed state governments.

Such arms as were produced under COS direction can be presumed to have been made between late April, 1775, and the latter part of 1778. Firearms made prior to or after those rather ambiguous and arbitrary dates are not considered authentic COS specimens by discerning arms students and collectors. Although most COS arms were muskets it is possible that pistols were also contracted, but, no concrete data have been found to substantiate this, nor have any handguns appeared which can be definitely identified as a COS product.

Muskets produced for the various COS generally followed the pattern of the then standard British infantry musket, that is, the 2nd model "Brown Bess" although extant evidence indicates that distinctly different patterns may have been used by a few colonies. John Churchill, Duke of Marlborough, is thought to have introduced the original "Brown Bess" design between 1710-20, and it saw several minor modifications. Most COS muskets produced in early 1775 closely followed the specifications outlined by the Continental Congress in November of that year:

"*Resolved* That it be recommended to the several Assemblies or conventions of the colonies respectively, to set and keep their gunsmiths at work, to manufacture good fire locks, with bayonets; each firelock to be made with a good bridle lock, ¾ of an inch bore, and of good substance at the breech, the barrel to be 3 feet 8 inches in length, the bayonet to be 18 inches in the blade, with a steel ramrod, the upper loop thereof to be trumpet mouthed: that the price to be given be fixed by the Assembly or convention, or committee of safety of each colony...."

As all firearms during this period were hand-forged and subject to the idiosyncracies of the gunsmith, and because the 'smith frequently had difficulty obtaining adequate materials, innumerable variations can be detected in the character of domestic arms produced throughout the conflict. Muskets made for the Massachusetts COS generally conformed to Congressional standards although barrels were an inch longer. Connecticut musket barrels were two inches longer and the bayonet blade was shortened to 14 inches. Barrels of Maryland COS muskets were two inches shorter, while the bayonet had a 17-inch blade.

Of whatever origin, COS muskets generally had 42-to 46-inch barrels of 75 caliber pin-fastened to walnut and, occasionally, maple stocks. Furniture was usually iron, but brass was also used. Locks were predominantly pre-war English or of European make although some were

(A) Many foreign arms served patriot forces. This Prussian musket is one of two specimens believed to have been captured at Bennington, Vt., from the Brunswick Grenadiers. Credit: West Point Museum.

(B) One of the most popular imported arms serving Continental forces was the MI1768 French infantry musket. This specimen, made at Charleville, has a "US" property stamp on the lock. The initials "WK" may have been those of its user. Credit: West Point Museum.

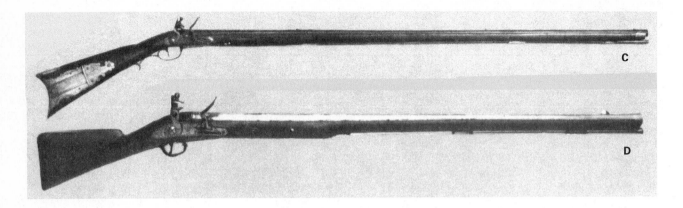

C

D

(C) A prime example of the American rifle-smith's craft is this "Kentucky" rifle made by Henry Albright of Lancaster, Pa., ca. 1770. Contrary to popular concepts, rifles performed a minor role in the Revolution. Credit: The Metropolitan Museum of Art. Gift of Winfrid Wood, 1956.

(D) This full-stocked British Tower-marked wall gun with belled muzzle weighed nearly 25 lbs., with an over-all length of 72¾ . Bore was nearly an inch in diameter. Credit: Smithsonian Institute.

of domestic origin. Double-bridle types were ordinarily specified, but, single-bridle types were substituted when necessity dictated. Sling swivels were common on army muskets although conspicuously absent on naval models which were usually kept in racks aboard ship, and the barrels of navy models were up to 10 inches shorter; this made it easier for marines and sailors to load when in the rigging or atop masts. The musket in the famed Minuteman statue at Lexington, Mass., is a typical navy specimen.

Massachusetts COS arms-makers were paid £ 3 each for muskets complete with iron ramrod and bayonet, that is, a stand, shortly after the war began. During this early period the average cost of a stand was $12.50, although inflation escalated prices as the war continued. A letter from a group of Lancaster riflesmiths to the Pennsylvania COS on 16 March 1776 commented that "… We are apprehensive of meeting with many obstacles in making … a new contract. Our workmen universally complain that the sums already fixed are inadequate to their Labours; that the Sacrifice they made in *quitting their rifle business** is greater than they can well bear without some equivalent. … they cannot in Justice to their families, provide the muskets and bayonets at a less

*Italics supplied. MLB.

sum than £ 4 10s or £ 4 15s. We are very sensible that their observations … are not without foundation …." Fiscal as well as labor and material procurement problems would plague patriot gunsmiths throughout the war.

## Marks and Stamps

The often repeated assertion that patriot gunsmiths refused to mark their products, fearing British reprisals, is not substantiated by fact. Most COS muskets were signed by the maker and displayed in various forms the mark of the colony as well. Connecticut required that muskets be "… marked with the name or initial letters of the maker's name." The letters "CR" and the Rhode Island coat of arms appears on all arms purchased by that colony, while Massachusetts ordered that its muskets be stamped with the letters "MB" (Massachusetts Bay). Other markings are also found on arms used or produced by the various colonies, including captured and imported specimens.

In Pennsylvania alone COS contracts accounted for 4,500 muskets, most of these produced by gunsmiths in 11 countries between October, 1775, and April, 1776. While COS arms were generally contracted from independent gunsmiths, many colonies established and operated their own arms-making facilities. Peter DeHaven supervised musket production at the State Gun Factory in Philadelphia and, to prevent capture the works was moved to French Creek near Valley Forge in December, 1776; thence for the same reason to Hummels Town in September, 1777. The factory was dismantled and sold in 1778. The Pennsylvania State Gun Repair Shop was founded at Allentown on 26 September 1777 with James Walsh as superintendent. On 11 May 1778 Walsh reported that 800 complete muskets were available and 150 more were in the assembly stage.

In neighboring Maryland the State

Gun Lock Factory was established at Frederick in 1777 with Charles Beatty, James Johnson and John Hanson named commissioners. Samuel Boone, nephew or brother to the famed Daniel, managed the works and on 17 June was directed to deliver 110 gunlocks to musket-maker Nicholas White. This installation was sold in November,1778.

The Hunter Iron Works, operated by James Hunter on the Rappahannock near Falmouth, Va., was purchased by the colony in June, 1775. Known thereafter as Rappahannock Forge, the works produced muskets, pistols and wall guns for the Virginia Militia and may have made pistols for sale elsewhere as indicated by one specimen marked "CP" (Commonwealth of Pennsylvania) on the lockplate. Operations ceased in 1781. Located at nearby Fredericksburg was the Virginia State Gun Factory established by an act of the assembly on 4 July 1775 and supervised by Col. Fielding Lewis and Maj. Charles Dick. Producing muskets and bayonets, the works closed late in 1783.

Ordnance facilities were also established by the North Carolina Colony early in the war. The Charlottesville Rifle Works produced rifles, muskets and pistols for the militia in 1775-76, while at Halifax the North Carolina Gun Works, founded in 1776, made muskets under the supervision of James Ransom who served as Master Armorer there until 1778.

The Continental Congress also evinced interest in arms manufacture, and on 23 February 1776 appointed a committee to "contract for the making of muskets and bayonets for the use of the United Colonies …." On 8 March a $10,000 appropriation was authorized, while on 23 May the committee directed the manager of the "continental factory of firearms at Lancaster, and the manager of the gunlock factory at Trenton to deliver … all muskets and gunlocks … for the more expeditious arming of the continental battalion …."

Muskets and rifles and perhaps pistols were contracted under Congressional auspices, but because of a large inventory of serviceable weapons few Continental arms contracts were made after 1778. Also noteworthy is that many state installations halted production in that year. However, thousands of arms were refurbished at the Congressional arms repair shop at Carlisle, Pa., and at Springfield, Mass.; the latter facility was established at Gen. Washington's behest in 1777 as an arsenal and powder magazine, but was subsequently expanded to include repair work and the manufacture of cartridges and gun carriages.

### Musket Patterns

Continental muskets were apparently not patterned after the 2nd model "Brown Bess," for Congress furnished contractors with pattern pieces, which would otherwise have been unnecessary since most gunsmiths were familiar with the British musket. What patterns were used is not indicated by any extant documentation. The arms produced for the Continental Army were stamped with the maker's name or initials only, but, it was determined that a more distinctive mark of public ownership was necessary because such arms were frequently stolen and later sold. After repeated and generally unsuccessful attempts to halt this nefarious trade Congress, adopting the recommendation of the Commissary General of Military Stores, declared on 24 February 1777 that:

"… the several States … take the most effectual steps for collecting from the inhabitants, not in actual service, all Continental arms, and give notice of the number … to General Washington.

"That all arms or accoutrements, belonging to the United States shall be stamped or marked with the words 'UNITED STATES:' all arms already made to be stamped upon such parts as will receive the impression, and those hereafter to be manufactured, to be stamped with the said words on every part comprising the stand; and all arms and accoutrements so stamped or marked shall be taken wherever found for the use of the States, excepting they shall be in the hands of those actually in Continental service.

"That it be recommended to the legislatures of the several States to enact proper laws for the punishment of those who shall unlawfully take, secrete, refuse or neglect to deliver, any Continental arms or accoutrements which they may have in their possession."

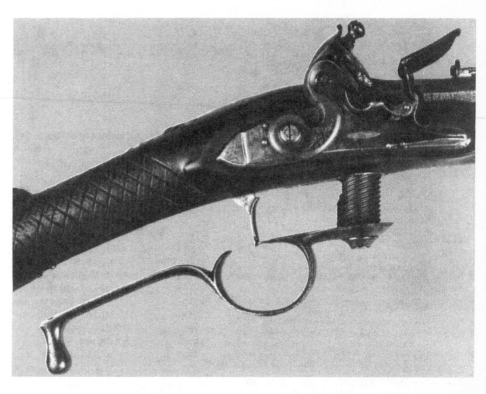

To this was added a suggestion by Brig. Gen. Alexander McDou-gall, writing to Gen. Washington on 12 April 1777, that all barrels and locks be stamped and all stocks branded with the words "UNITED STATES." That this was found acceptable can be seen on many Revolutionary War arms with "U. STATES" burned into the stock. Noteworthy is that such markings were also abbreviated to "US," while state and COS arms were also branded on the stock with appropriate letters.

As most COS muskets were made early in the war, few survived the vicissitudes of battle, while time and cannibalization contributed to the scarcity of the remainder. Continental and imported arms fared little better. When hostilities terminated, Congress, in a rare spate of gratitude, voted the patriots their arms as a farewell gift. While some were doubtlessly kept by those weary, intrepid veterans, many were sold to defray travel expenses home, for the magnanimous Congress that presented them their weapons had frequently neglected to feed, clothe, shelter and pay them during the war.

### Colonial Rifles

The American rifle, termed variously the "Kentucky" or "Pennsylvania-Kentucky" rifle, slowly evolved from the shorter, more massive Jager rifle brought to the colonies around 1710 by German and Swiss immigrants setting in the Lancaster region of southeastern Pennsyl-

Rotating the trigger guard a full-turn opened the breech of the Ferguson rifle. The ball, followed by the powder, was inserted into the opening atop the breech. The rotating breech plug provided an excellent gas seal and also sheared the excess powder. Credit: West Point Museum.

vania. Just prior to the Revolution the American rifle entered its second phase of development and at this point had nearly attained the pinnacle of perfection.

Congress, by the Act of June 14, 1775, authorized 10 companies of riflemen, two each from Maryland and Virginia and 6 from Pennsylvania, and while the war stimulated the demand for rifles and production increased it was often at the expense of quality. Although many riflesmiths were engaged in producing muskets, others continued to make rifles either on a contract or individual basis. There were about three to five hundred riflesmiths in the colonies when hostilities commenced, the majority in Pennsylvania; others were located in Maryland, Virginia and the Carolinas. A few of the most prominent artisans were Henry Albright, Peter Angstadt, John Beck and Peter Humberger, Sr., all from Lancaster, Pa.; William GraefF of Reading, Pa., and Abraham Morrow of Philadelphia, who had a U.S. contract for flintlock rifles.

While there is no such thing as a typical American rifle, for no two were made

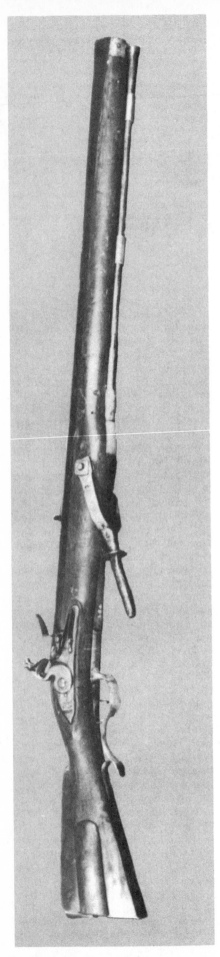

exactly alike, the rifles of this period illustrated similar characteristics, and were atypical of those produced after the war. The average specimen displayed a generally unmarked, hand-forged lock somewhat inferior to English or French flintlock mechanisms, and a rather straight, heavy stock with a slight drop. A patchbox was located on the right side of the stock, usually fitted with a hinged brass cover and sideplates although sliding wood covers are noted. Barrels were fully octagonal, about 42 to 48 inches long and of 45 to 50 caliber. The barrel was held to the stock by round pins and a screw passing through the barrel tang. Both front and rear sights were laterally adjustable, and an iron ramrod was provided; most furniture was brass. Innumerable variations in design and ornamentation are the rule.

Despite continuous but at times sporadic domestic production, the bulk of the shoulder and hand arms in patriot ranks during the latter part of the war were of European origin. Of these the regulation French infantry musket was commonly encountered, and it has been estimated that at least 102,-000 French long arms were imported between 1776 and 1781. These ranged in character from the obsolete M1718 to the M1768, although the M1763 infantry musket predominated.

## The Blockade Guns

Benjamin Franklin, serving as one of the American commissioners to France, reported in April, 1777, that "… We have purchased 80,-000 fusils, a number of pistols, etc., of which the enclosed is on account, for 220,000 livres. They were King's arms and second-hand, but so many … are unused and exceptionally good that we esteem it a great bargain if only half of them should arrive."

Franklin's enthusiasm was matched by his proverbial thrift, for the purchase of French muskets at an average of $5.00 each was a boon when compared to domestic prices. In June, 1777, Continental forces received an unexpected gift of 250 M1763 muskets from the Marquis de Lafayette who joined the patriot cause.

Numerous modifications marked the evolution of the French infantry musket. The popular M1768 later served as the

This rifled wall gun was made at Rappahannock Forge in 1776 and is one of four surviving the ravages of time. It fired a 6-oz. ball of about 1.25 caliber and had an effective range of 1,000 yards. Note sliding wood cover on patchbox. Credit: West Point Museum.

pattern for the first (M1795) U.S. martial musket.* It was considered superior to the "Brown Bess" due to its slender profile, excellent balance, reinforced cock, banded barrel and greater range. Over-all length was 59⅞ inches with a round, 69 caliber barrel of 44¾ inches. The walnut stock was fixed to the barrel by three spring-held iron bands; the upper band fitted with a brass blade front sight and the center band with a sling swivel. Excepting the sight, all metal parts were iron, finished bright. The flashpan was detachable from the lockplate and the lower sling swivel was attached to the trigger guard.

Like other French arms the M1768 carried such armory markings as *CHARLEVILLE* in script, surmounted by a *D* topped with a star; *MANUF ROYAL de ST. ETIENNE* with a crowned *HB*; and *MAUBEUGE* with a crowned *H* above, all appearing on the lock. Variations of the *US* stamp is often seen on the lock, barrel tang or barrel, while stocks were frequently branded *U. STATES*. In many instances these *US* markings were crudely executed, indicating that the responsible facilities had not received official dies.

Available records show that French arms shipments began in early February, 1776, when Connecticut received 3,000 assorted muskets, and continued until August, 1781, when the *Resolute* delivered 16,800 long arms to Boston. Through the efforts of Silas Deane, another American agent in France, and the support of Pierre Garon de Beaumarchais, a dummy corporation known as Roderique Hortalez et Cie was organized in May, 1776, to channel arms, munitions and other war materials to the beleaguered patriots. Hortalez was active until late 1778 when France, declaring war on England, obviated the necessity for subterfuge.

Ten ships were dispatched by Hortalez either directly to the colonies or the French West Indies ports, where vital cargoes were transferred to American vessels, mainly privateers. Only one of the 10 ships was intercepted by the British. First to arrive was the brig *Mercury* out of Nantes. In April, 1777, she made Portsmouth, N.H., unloading 364 cases of arms (11,987 muskets), 1,000 barrels of gunpowder, 11,000 gunflints, large supplies of shoes and clothing, and reported that no less than 34 other ships were clearing French ports for the colonies. Another vessel, the *Flamand*, docked at

---

*Many arms historians have confused the M1768 with the M1763; the latter was equipped with a long ramrod spring between the two upper bands, a larger lock and different bands. See The American Rifleman, Vol. 115, No. 7., p. 19.

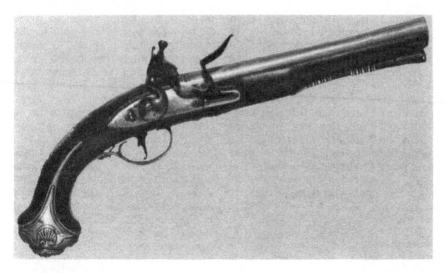

This handsome English flintlock holster pistol was made ca. 1772. Pistols of this type were commonly carried by British and patriot officers. Credit: The Metropolitan Museum of Art. Rogers Fund, 1948.

Portsmouth on 1 December with 3,000 muskets and 1,100 carbines.

Pliarne, Penet et Cie, also a French subsidized firm, sent arms and munitions to the colonies in concert with a subsidiary, James Gruel & Co. Muskets purchased from these firms were of poor quality, made at Liege. The industrious Dutch were also active in the brisk, profitable arms trade, shipping large numbers of quality muskets either directly to Massachusetts or via St. Eustatius in the Dutch West Indies. These arms are believed to have been contracted from reliable makers by Franklin, representing Massachusetts, and extant examples are marked *THONE, AMSTERDAM* on the lock-plate and bear Amsterdam proof marks on the barrels of 65 caliber secured by three brass bands; the upper band distinguished by its 8-inch length.

Captured Hessian muskets were also employed by patriot forces, their characteristics varying considerably because of the different types supplied to the Hessian auxiliaries supporting the British Army. Extant specimens have brass furniture whether barrels are banded or pin-fastened, and all have elliptical brass front sights either attached to the barrel or upper band. The round barrel is 41 to 44 inches long and of 75 to 80 caliber. Lockplates are blunt at the rear and the frizzen is identified by its square top. Stocks are heavy with a massive butt and high comb. Raised carvings around the mountings are characteristic. Most were inferior to the English, Dutch, French and American muskets.

Hessian rifles also appeared in the colonies. Limited in number, they were short, heavy arms with octagonal barrels of 28 to 30 inches. Caliber ranged from 60 to 70. The stock was rather cumbrous

with a massive butt incorporating a patch box with sliding wood cover and the forearm extended to the muzzle. Furniture was usually brass. Hessian rifles compared favorably to American in range and accuracy.

English rifles also served in the Revolution. These unique arms, invented by Maj. Patrick Ferguson, were the first flintlock breechloaders adopted for military use by any nation. In all probability less than 300 saw service, mostly by Loyalist riflemen recruited by the inventor. Aware of prior developments in breechloading systems, Ferguson produced a more practical version scaled to the dimensions of the standard Brown Bess. Both officer's and enlisted men's models were made. The rifle weighed 7.5 pounds and the enlisted model was of 58 caliber. Barrels ranged from 34 to 36 inches long, rifled with 8 grooves. It could be loaded and fired five to six times a minute and was accurate up to 300 yards. Traditional military resistance to new concepts dimmed Ferguson's hopes for the future of his invention, and his death at King's Mountain sealed the fate of his rifle. If the British had adopted the accurate, fast-firing rifle on a large scale the American colonies might never have won their independence. (See the Gun Digest, 1959, p. 53.)

## The Patriots' Pistols

As a rule American martial pistols followed the British pattern. Those produced at Rappahannock Forge bore an exact resemblance to the new model British martial pistols appearing in 1760. They were marked *RAPa FORGE* on the lock-plate and had heavier brass furniture than most domestically made pistols. Both old and new model British martial pistols served in patriot ranks, many of them captured

at the outset of hostilities.

Adopted about 1714, old model British martial pistols were relics of King George's War (1744-48) and the French and Indian conflict. They had round, 12-inch barrels of about 60 caliber, pin-fastened to the walnut stock, with additional support provided by the breech-plug tang screw. The convex iron sideplate, lockplate and brass furniture resembled that of the 1st model Brown Bess musket. The bulbous butt was capped with brass as was the wooden ramrod. Most were engraved with the letters *GR* (George Rex), in script, surmounted by a crown in the center of the lock-plate, while behind the cock the word *TOWER* appeared in a vertical arc. The broad arrow ordnance stamp, denoting Crown ownership, also appeared on the lock, while barrels displayed either London or Birmingham proofmarks. Some specimens have only the maker's name and date on the lockplate.

The new model British martial pistol was somewhat shorter and stronger, having a 9-inch round barrel of 69 caliber. Some of the brass furniture was eliminated or redesigned. The sideplate and lockplate were flat with stamped rather than engraved markings. Navy models incorporated a belt hook and retained the longer barrel of the old model. Both types were profusely copied by patriot gunsmiths.

The various Highland regiments serving the British in America were the only units in which all enlisted men were issued pistols. These unusual arms were of all-metal construction. Officer's models were primarily holster pistols, made exclusively of iron and highly ornamented, often heavily chiseled and inlaid with precious metals, while enlisted men's models were of iron with a brass stock. Ramrods of both were iron, and the soldier's type was equipped with a belt hook. Those made before 1758 were marked *HR* (Highland Regiment), those thereafter *RHR* (Royal Highland Regiment). Most were made in Scotland prior to 1762 when Birmingham and London emerged as production centers.

Highland pistols had no trigger guards or sights and all displayed button-type triggers. The lock internally resembled the so-called English dog lock, popular a century earlier, as there was no half-cock position and the sear acted laterally, protruding through the lockplate. Barrels were round of between seven and eight inches while caliber fluctuated from 55 to 57. Both types illustrated kidney-shaped, heart-shaped or fish-tailed butts, with officer's models often terminating in a ramshorn design. A removable knob, located in the center of the butt, served as a combination oiler/vent pick.

John Waters of London and Birmingham produced many plain Highland pistols, some with London proofmarks on the barrel. Another maker, Isaac Bissel of Birmingham, made officer's models characterized by a ramshorn butt with an oval petal grip design and channeled cock pin, oiler/vent pick and button trigger. Highland pistols display a wide range of ornamentation, and variations in design are common.

France, largest European supplier of muskets to patriot forces, also provided a large number of pistols. However, no accurate or complete record exists which can verify the precise number or type. Most were martial specimens. Both army and navy patterns of 1763 were popular, featuring round, 9-inch barrels of 67 caliber, held in a walnut stock by a tang screw and long, double band at the muzzle held by a retaining spring. The lock resembled that of the M1763 infantry musket with a reinforced cock and iron pan. The furniture of the army model was iron and that of the navy model brass. Each had a button-head iron ramrod, and most were produced at St. Etienne.

In 1776 France adopted a new pattern martial pistol which differed radically from the M1763. The M1776 first appeared in 1777 in both army and navy models. Each was of 69 caliber with a 7.5-inch barrel, tapering toward the muzzle. Navy models were provided with a belt hook. Frames were brass and the brass pan was integral. The cock, frizzen and ramrod were iron. There was no fore-stock or sights. The butt curved sharply, supported by an iron backstrap and terminated with a brass cap. Arsenal marks appeared in an arc under the cock and the stock was stamped with an inspector's mark and date. The M1777 French martial pistol served as a pattern for the first U.S. martial pistol (M1799).

The few German pistols used in the Revolution varied considerably in character and were generally inferior to other imported and domestic pistols. They commonly had brass furniture and pin-fastened, round iron barrels of 75 caliber.

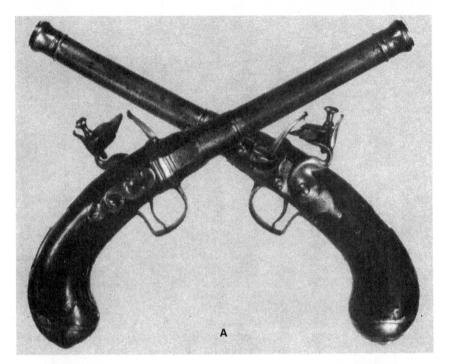

**A**

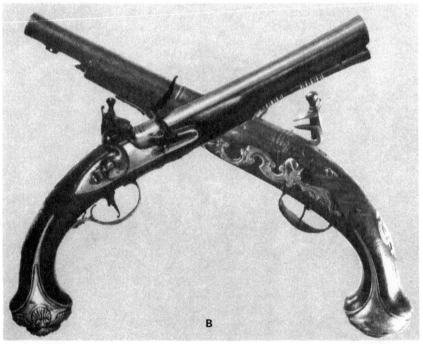

**B**

On some models the iron ramrod was attached to the barrel by a swivel. These pistols, normally fitted with a brass front sight, had a reinforced, convex cock and were bought by American agents in the various German states and Holland.

An undetermined number of Prussian pistols, mostly old and unserviceable, found their way into patriot hands. Many were bought by representatives of the Virginia Colony. Barrels were round, 11¾ inches long and pin-fastened to

(A) These somewhat battered pistols, made at Rappahannock Forge, were patterned after the British martial pistol of 1760. Rappahannock Forge pistols were generally of better quality than most domestic handguns. Credit: Smithsonian Institution.

(B) Early type Queen Anne "turn-off" screw-barreled pistols by Cornforth of London (ll. 1760-90). Cannon-shaped barrels distinguish these popular pistols and many appeared in the colonies, serving as the pattern for the "Kentucky" pistols emerging ca. 1740. Credit: Smithsonian Institution.

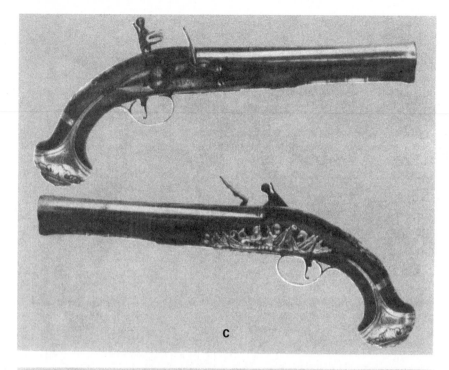

C

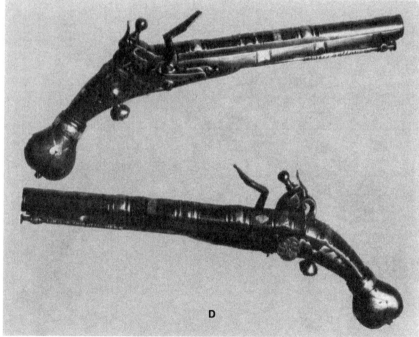

D

Of better quality than German or Prussian pistols were those provided by the Dutch. Most are stamped *THONE, AMSTERDAM* in two lines on the lockplate. Both army and navy models were bought, the latter displaying a belt hook. Each had a 10-inch, round, pin-fastened barrel of about 69 caliber, iron ramrod, brass blade front sight and notch-type rear sight. The cock was convex and the pan brass. There was no sideplate. The stock had a bulbous butt minus a cap, while the fore-end was capped with brass.

In addition to the various types of martial pistols used in the Revolution there were numerous non-martial types of domestic and foreign origin. Most were of British make, and highly popular was the Queen Anne screw-barrel or so-called "turn-off" pistol. Early models (c. 1740) had the cock situated on the right side of the gun, but after about 1760 the cock was centrally hung. Over-all length was about 11.5 inches, and the round, cannon-shaped barrel was of about 60 caliber. Loading was accomplished by unscrewing the barrel, pouring the powder into the chamber, placing the ball atop the charge and replacing the barrel. Those made for cavalry use often had a short chain attached to the barrel and breech to prevent loss when loading. Range and accuracy were superior to the average pistol as there was virtually no gas leakage around the ball, and in rifled specimens accuracy was extremely good. Many of these and other personal pistols were exquisitely ornamented.

Colonial riflesmiths produced pistols similar in character to the Queen Anne type while retaining features common to the American rifle. These so-called "Kentucky" pistols, made prior to and during the Revolution, differed in many respects from later specimens. The earliest known type dates from about 1740. Most reflected the Queen Anne barrel style although all were loaded at the muzzle and the majority were smoothbores. Caliber varied from 36 to 50, and barrel length ranged between 7.5 and 9.5 inches. Both brass and iron pin-fastened barrels are encountered, while brass and coin silver were generally used for furniture and ornamentation. Stocks normally extended the full length of the barrel although some were half-stocked and most had birdshead grips. Figured maple was favored for stocking, but cherry and walnut were also used, while ramrods were often made of hickory tipped with brass or silver. Specimens are found with and without sights; the sights patterned after the rifle type.

(C) All-metal pistols such as this ornate pair were carried by officers of the Scots Highland regiments. Knob in center of heart-shaped butt is attached to combination vent pick/oiler. Credit: The Metropolitan Museum of Art. Gift of Mrs. Elizabeth Cameron Blanchard, in memory of her husband, J. Osgood Blanchard, 1916.

(D) George Washington's silver-mounted, brass-barreled pistols were made by Hawkins of London (fl. 1750-75). Over-all length 13½", 8" barrels of 66 caliber. Washington is said to have owned at least 50 firearms. Credit: West Point Museum.

the stock. All had brass front sights, and some displayed a rudimentary rear sight consisting of a shallow notch filed into the breech plug tang. Furniture was of brass, and the stock was characterized by a heavy buttcap and fore-end cap. The lock and sideplate were flat, and there was no ramrod. Proofmarks were found on the trigger guard and barrel while the royal cipher appeared on the buttcap. Some are marked *POTZDAMMAGAZIN* (Potsdam Arsenal) on the lockplate.

Imported locks were generally used, and markings varied considerably; some specimens have different names or initials on the lock and barrel, for even during this early period specialization in arms-making was apparent. The craftsmanship displayed on these often elegant pistols was decidedly superior to that found on most domestic specimens of the period.

## The Gunpowder Shortage

With the commencement of hostilities gunpowder was everywhere lacking. Restrictions by Parliament, difficulty in procuring the ingredients in sufficient quantity, and the superiority of English gunpowder all contributed to the decline of domestic powder making. While charcoal was abundant, sulfur was exclusively imported and saltpeter production disturbingly irregular. The powder seized at Fort William and Mary in 1774 had served the patriots at Bunker Hill, but one reason for the American withdrawal was a dire powder shortage.

In July, 1775, patriot forces ringed Boston, outnumbering the Redcoats two to one, yet Washington had neither enough artillery nor powder to oust the British. Young Henry Knox, affable and brilliant Boston bookseller who became Washington's chief of artillery, proposed a wild scheme whereby captured ordnance at Fort Ticonderoga could be transported to Dorchester Heights above Boston. Despite protests Knox left in November and found at the fort 78 serviceable pieces of ordnance and 30,000 gunflints in addition to 2,300 pounds of lead. By boat, sledge, wagon, determination and pure guts he shepherded the vital cargo across frozen rivers, snow-capped mountains and frigid wilderness in the dead of winter to Boston, 300 miles distant. Arriving with 55 assorted cannon, mortars and howitzers in January, 1776, he was delighted to discover that the capture of the British supply ship *Nancy* had provided the powder for his guns.

Shortly after the war began most of the colonies took steps to rectify the powder shortage, and mills sprang up on various locations. Oswell Eve ran a powder mill at Frankford, Pa., and it was probably there that Paul Revere studied the manufacture of powder, erecting a mill near Boston after the war. Two other mills were situated near Eve's works and another was located in Dauphin County.

Numerous complaints concerning the quality of Eve's gunpowder reached Congress and, on 7 June 1776, a committee was appointed to investigate. On 28 August the committee suggested that inspectors be assigned to the various mills with orders to mark every acceptable keg of powder with the letters *USA*. This was the first use of the marking subsequently applied to all U.S. arms and other ordnance material.

In 1780 a powder mill was constructed near Washington's winter headquarters at Morristown, N.J., concealed in the deep woods. Saltpeter for this facility was provided by the local populace, probably from natural deposits although possibly from artificial niter beds produced by soaking the earth with human urine rich in nitrate.

The estimable victory of patriot riflemen at King's Mountain on 7 October 1780 was substantially assisted by 500 pounds of gunpowder donated to the cause by Mary Patton who, in the absence of her husband serving in the army, operated a powder mill in Tennessee. It was an expensive gift, for at that time powder was selling for a dollar per pound.

The scarcity of gunpowder on the

French Cavalry M1777 pistol differed radically from most handguns of the Revolutionary War era. The 7.5" round barrel was cased in a brass housing supporting the lock and iron ramrod. The pistol served as a pattern for the first U.S. martial pistol, the North & Cheney of 1799. Credit: West Point Museum

frontier was even more crucial, for it was there that a thin, buckskin-clad line valiantly withstood the savagery of Indian attacks promoted by the British, who supplied their numerous Indian allies with arms and munitions throughout the war. A frontier settlement obliged to defend itself expended more powder in an hour than would have been used in a year of hunting. Despite the powder shortage the generally outnumbered frontiersmen miraculously prevented British-led Indian marauders from penetrating the populous coastal settlements and harassing Washington's weary Continentals.

Patriot frontiersmen went to great lengths and took considerable risks in procuring adequate supplies of gunpowder. In 1775 George Rogers Clark persuaded Virginia authorities to part with 500 pounds of powder for the defense of Kentucky. Second Lieutenant William Linn and 15 volunteers left Fort Pitt in July, 1776, for New Orleans, where the officially neutral Spanish covertly sold powder to American agents. Linn procured 98 barrels-nearly five tons-and began the hazardous 2,000-mile return trip, eluding both British and Indians to arrive at Wheeling on 2 May 1777, just in time to meet the summer threat of Indian attacks. His party had been gone 11 months. Clark also took advantage of Spanish co-operation, and gunpowder from New Orleans bolstered his chance for victory when, in the summer of 1778, he invaded Illinois, capturing Kaskaskia and Vincennes.

Although domestic powder-making increased as the war progressed, American powder was never made in sufficient quantity to supply patriot forces, nor was it comparable to English, French or Spanish powder in quality. Due primarily to the advancements in chemistry achieved by Antoine Laurent Lavoisier (1743-94), French gunpowder was superior to any produced in the world at the time of the Revolution, and it has been estimated that French gunpowder fulfilled 80 percent of patriot requirements. Much of it reached the colonies through the efforts of Hortalez et Cie.

The road from

Lexington to Yorktown was a long and bloody road. The American War of Independence was won not only by the inordinate courage displayed on the grim field of combat, but by the simple determination and singular purpose of a united people working toward a common goal. The contribution to victory generated by the many who left bloody footprints in the snow and survived by gnawing the bark from frozen trees was no more vital than what was given by the many who toiled long hours in the blazing heat of the barrel forge or sat hunched over a filer's bench.

## Bibliography

### Primary Sources

Carey, A. Merwyn. *American Firearms Makers*. New York: Thomas Y. Crowell, 1953.

Chapel, Charles Edward. *Guns of the Old West*. New York: Coward-McCann, Inc., 1961.

Gardner, Robert. *Small Arms Makers*. New York: Bonanza Books, 1962.

Gluckman, Arcadi. *United States Martial Pistols and Revolvers*. Harrisburg, Pa.: The Stackpole Co., 1956. __.*United States Muskets, Rifles and Carbines*. Buffalo, N.Y.: Otto Ulbrich Co., Inc., 1948.

Kauffman, Henry J. *Early American Gunsmiths*. New York: Bramhall House, 1952.

__*The Pennsylvania-Kentucky Rifle*. Harrisburg, Pa.: The Stackpole Co., 1960.

Peterson, Harold L. *Arms and Armor in Colonial America*. New York: Bramhall House, 1956.

Russell, Carl P. *Guns on the Early Frontiers*. New York: Bonanza Books, 1957.

### Secondary Sources

Lancaster, Bruce and Plumb, J. H. *The American Heritage Book of the Revolution*. New York: The American Heritage Publishing Co., 1958.

Martin, Joseph Plumb (Scheer, George F., ed.). *Private Yankee Doodle*. New York: Little, Brown & Co., 1962.

Miller, John C. *The First Frontier: Life in Colonial America*. New York: Dell Publ. Co., Inc., 1966.

Perry, Clay. "Big Guns for Washington," *The American Heritage Reader*. New York: Dell Publ. Co., Inc., 1956.

Peterson, Harold L., ed. *Encyclopedia of Firearms*. New York: E. P. Dutton & Co., 1964.

Scheer, George F. and Rankin, Hugh. *Rebels and Redcoats*. New York: World Publ. Co., 1957.

Van Every, Dale. *A Company of Heroes*. New York: Wm. Morrow & Co., 1962.

Woodward, Wm. *The Way Our People Lived*. New York: Liveright Publ. Corp, 1944.

### Periodicals

*The American Rifleman*, The National Rifle Assn., of America, Washington, D.C.

*Gun Digest*, Digest Books, Inc., Northfield, Ill.

*Guns & Ammo*, Petersen Publ. Co., Los Angeles, Cal.

Patriot victory at Trenton, 26 December 1776, succeeded in reviving American morale and prompted French, Spanish and Dutch assistance in procuring additional troops and arms. Credit: Department of the Army.

Gun Digest

13th Annual Edition 1959
edited by John T. Amber

# Breechloaders in the Revolution

Ferguson's rifle – and his rifling – were years ahead of their day.

■ Jac Weller

LIEUT-COLONEL
Pat. Ferguson

Killed at King's Mountain

SOUTH CAROLINA

7th Oct. 1780

Patrick Ferguson, a wax bust now owned by Keith Neal, noted arms expert, and the author of *Spanish Guns*.

P AT FERGUSON'S rifle was capable of delivering aimed fire at 220 yards. The usual smoothbore musket of that era couldn't hit a man-sized target at 50 yards more than once in three shots. The Ferguson rifle was a breechloader and could be fired seven times in 60 seconds, even while the filer was prone. These things were a century ahead of their time. Although Ferguson's rifles were used successfully in the American Revolution, they were never adopted either in the British or American armies. Few regular infantry soldiers were armed with rifles before 1850; breechloaders weren't introduced successfully until almost a hundred years after Ferguson's death.

The story of the Ferguson rifle begins with the young British officer's service on the European continent in the early 1760's. He saw a good deal of fighting; a few of the German allies were armed with ponderous rifles. Ferguson was wounded and came home to his native Scottish highlands to recuperate; he had a passion for deer stalking and accurate fire. He experimented with all rifles then known.

In 1768, Ferguson, a captain at 24, went out to join his new regiment, the 70th Foot, then stationed in the West Indies. The British position in these islands at that time was anything but secure. Both Spain and France had larger areas, populations, and garrisons. Even on the individual Carribean islands held by Britain, there was frequently opposition from the natives.

reinforcements if you find you need them. Take a few days to get your bearings, and then let me hear what you propose."

Ferguson, accompanied by a sergeant and his own servant with a second rifle, made his first reconnaissance that very evening. Tobago was not unlike the Scottish highlands, save for the tropical vegetation. A single excursion gave the young captain an idea.

With the aid of his company sergeant, he picked eight men and rearmed them for the job at hand.

Ferguson had brought with him eleven cased sporting rifles, no two of which were exactly alike. With these, he made his selected squad into marksmen in less than ten days, firing up some 40 pounds of powder and 250 pounds of lead. The sergeant and the new men couldn't shoot

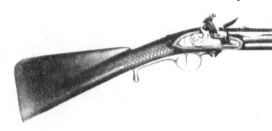

Three views of the Ferguson rifle in sporting version, made by D. Egg of London. Note sliding bayonet, and that multi-thread breech-plug is without vertical slots to help carry off powder fouling.

Ferguson was assigned to the hal fof the 70th stationed on Tobago Island. His servant hadn't even unpacked his clothing and small arsenal of sporting arms when the major in command gave his latest replacement officer a tough assignment. This island, like several others, was inhabited by Black Caribs, descendants from the original Caribs living on the islands at the time of European discovery and black slaves who had escaped from the plantations. These people had given the British garrison on Tobago a great deal of trouble. They were fierce and utterly hostile; there was some reason to believe that occasionally they reverted to cannibalism. Because of their knowledge of the island and their agility and swiftness of foot over the mountainous terrain, they were extremely hard to catch. Further, they had firearms and ammunition supplied by the French. Chasing these men with a company of infantry in full uniform and armed with smoothbore, muzzleloading muskets was futile, and costly in British lives.

"Your first assignment, Captain Ferguson, will be to bring these Black Caribs under control," the major said. "There aren't more than 200 men and boys, but regular tactics have been of little use against them. According to your record, you have skill and experience in stalking. I warn you, however, that this game shoots back."

"What force will I have at my disposal, Major?

"Your own company and

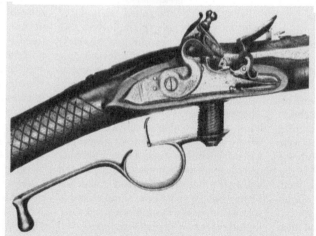

as well as Ferguson, or his old Highland body servant, but they were incomparably better with their new rifles than any soldiers armed with smoothbore muskets.

Once his squad could shoot, Ferguson went to work on their equipment. Heavy packs, sometimes carried even in combat in those days, were discarded. Red coats, white leather belts, white breeches, and all polished articles were left behind. Ferguson took his squad out into the mountainous country in the drab clothing of the hunting field. He taught them tactics based in part on his deer stalking experience. They soon became active and resourceful.

The very first morning of active operations, the Black Caribs, accustomed to the range of the Brown Bess muskets, gave Ferguson's men nine shots at from 150 to 200 yards. They scored two certain kills. The next day they did even better.

Within a week, Ferguson was penetrating into the very heart of the mountainous island. The enemy, which had been so formidable against formal, slow-moving British Redcoats armed with smoothbore muskets, proved less numerous than was supposed. Even though they far outnumbered Ferguson's squad, they lacked the discipline to press home an attack against his deadly aimed fire. The British commander managed to avoid hand-to-hand fighting by keeping, where possible, to the very crags and rocks where the natives had formerly performed to their best advantage.

Within a month of the young captain's arrival, the Black Caribs were disarmed and peaceful, all at a cost of two men wounded by the enemy and one killed when he fell off a cliff. Even the Caribs lost only a dozen or so; their confidence in themselves was broken by being suddenly out-climbed, out-stalked, and out-shot by the same men they had come to despise.

For almost six years, Ferguson continued in the West Indies, save for a short assignment in Nova Scotia and a rather extended visit to New England. He became an expert at fighting in the West Indies, even on islands where the Black Caribs were far more numerous than on Tobago. His knowledge and his ability to train light infantry for such warfare were used frequently. On Saint Vincent Island, in 1773 and 1774, there was a full scale small war against several thousand of these Caribs who had been supplied with arms and military advisers by the French.

Ferguson, and a special light infantry corps he commanded, performed brilliantly. The British forces were completely victorious and at relatively small cost to themselves.

## Development of the Ferguson Rifle

When Ferguson returned to Britain in 1774, he had very definite ideas about the rifle that now bears his name. While in the West Indies, he had ordered certain special rifles made according to his developing experience. Of these early rifles used against the Black Caribs, an English breechloader was the best. By means of a wrench, a plug could be unscrewed from out the top of the barrel, exposing the chamber for loading. It shot extremely well, since its oversize ball completely sealed the bore and fitted the grooves of the rifling completely. However, it was slow and complicated to load.

The London gunmaker, Durs Egg, had made several rifles for Ferguson in 1770 with a breechplug unscrewing towards the bottom. In these the plug was attached rigidly to the trigger guard, which served instead of a separate wrench. This rifle was a tremendous improvement, but twelve turns of the trigger guard were required to completely uncover the chamber. Further, the threads of the long plug fouled badly; only half a dozen shots were possible before cleaning of the breech was necessary.

Ferguson had ideas to remedy both these defects. He planned to use a multiple-thread breech and plug. Instead of turning a single-pitch threaded plug twelve times, he was going to turn a ten- or twelve-pitch threaded plug once. The only catch was the possibility that the gun-makers of that era could not make a tight multi-pitch thread.

A refinement of Ferguson's design was an arrangement for interrupting the threads on the breechplug in such a way that fouling which collected on the threads would be forced into these interruptions and dropped out of the bottom of the gun after each opening.

## Trials in the Highlands

So confident was Ferguson of the practicality of his new weapon that he ordered a dozen of a military type stocked to within a few inches of the muzzle and equipped with special bayonets. Somehow, the gunmakers solved the problem of producing tight multi-pitch threads. When the rifles were ready, Ferguson went personally to London and brought them back to Aberdeenshire. He and his original servant, now more of an assistant, tested these in all sorts of ways.

Mere stalking excellence was now not enough. These rifles were shorter and lighter than the Brown Bess. They balanced superbly and were easily carried in difficult country. They were hard-hitting and probably the most accurate weapons made until that time. But the two problems Ferguson was most anxious to solve were ease and speed of loading.

Tests proved these new rifles to shoot faster by far than any other rifles ever made; soon both men could get off more aimed shots than even the best drilled soldiers could fire from smoothbore muskets with undersize bullets. They were so easy to load, for at least a score of rounds after a complete cleaning, that *any* man could do it while lying flat on the ground, a feat approached by only a very few skillful men with muzzleloaders.

Ferguson now recruited ten militiamen, mostly his father's employees, and trained them in the handling of the rifles. Since there were no Black Caribs at hand, he took his small force out to shoot game. A casual witness would have thought Britain invaded. Ferguson's men would advance in open order and then suddenly let go with a volume of fire worthy of a whole company. The enemy, however, was usually only a mass of driven rabbits, extremely plentiful in parts of the Highlands. The twelve-man squad could fire better than 70 shots in a minute. Ferguson's last doubts as to his rifles and their usefulness in war were now at rest.

## Trial in Combat

Ferguson demonstrated his rifle before the King and his senior officers. A squad of men from one of the Guards regiments was trained quickly to handle these weapons. The results were truly remarkable both as to accuracy and ease and speed of loading.

The top British brass were sold on the Ferguson rifle idea. They had seen with their own eyes what could be done; they knew Captain Ferguson's record against the Black Caribs. An order for 300 rifles was placed with Durs Egg and William Hunt in the summer of 1776. A corps organization, to consist of both infantry and dragoons, was tentatively set up for use in the war in America. However, the manufacturing of these arms delayed Ferguson's departure; he arrived in New York with his orders for the special corps and the weapons to arm them in the spring of 1777.

The select corps, consisting of a few men from many British regular regiments, was trained carefully by Ferguson. This was the first group of native Britons ever trained as riflemen, although units of American colonial riflemen and the German Jagers had been used in the British Army for some time.

Ferguson's Corps led one of the two British columns in the actions that culminated in the Battle of Brandywine. So well did they do their job in the final stages of the approach that the British line troops moved through broken country already cleared of all opposition right up to the American position. In this advance guard fighting, the easy loading of the Ferguson rifle, even from a prone position, was of great value.

Just before the battle, in the woods south of Brandy-wine Creek, George Washington and a single aide appeared less than 60 yards from Ferguson and some of his men. Even though Ferguson obviously believed in aimed fire, he refused to allow his men to shoot the two unidentified officers or fire himself. He even refused to allow a sergeant to kill Washington's horse. He felt it unsporting to take advantage of the ill luck of the two, then, unidentified officers. Apparently, there was an interval of about thirty seconds before Washington put spurs to his horse.

Ferguson's corps accomplished its mission and probably inflicted a fair number of casualties on the Americans, while losing only two men wounded themselves. Unfortunately, one of these was Ferguson.

During Ferguson's time in the hospital, Sir William Howe broke up the Rifle Corps and returned the men to their old regiments. He ordered the Ferguson rifles to be returned to "store" and had the men re-issued Brown Bess muskets. Howe was never favorably disposed toward Ferguson's rifle, probably because they had been approved on "orders from home."

## Ferguson's American Corps

When Ferguson came out of the hospital with a permanently stiff right elbow, he found his command gone, his special rifles either lost or in storage and his own regiment at Halifax in Nova Scotia. However, with characteristic ability, ambition and cheerfulness, he set about making himself useful. His elbow, healed but forever set at an angle of about 90°, allowed him sufficient use

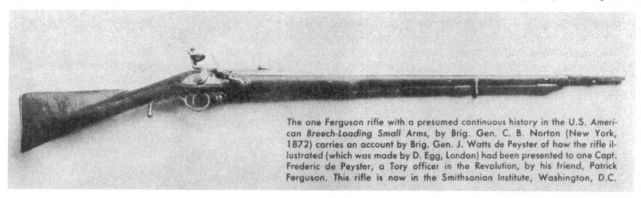

The one Ferguson rifle with a presumed continuous history in the U.S. *American Breech-Loading Small Arms*, by Brig. Gen. C. B. Norton (New York, 1872) carries an account by Brig. Gen. J. Watts de Peyster of how the rifle illustrated (which was made by D. Egg, London) had been presented to one Capt. Frederic de Peyster, a Tory officer in the Revolution, by his friend, Patrick Ferguson. This rifle is now in the Smithsonian Institute, Washington, D.C.

of the arm to handle a rifle tolerably with practice. He learned to handle both a sword and pistol with his left hand. He served at the Battle of Monmouth as an aide.

Once the British Army was back in New York, Howe had no intention of wasting the obvious talents of the young Scots captain. He called Ferguson in and offered him command of a corps of American Loyalists who were to be enlisted, paid, and trained as regulars rather than militia. Ferguson was to have charge of the recruiting and arming of these; some were to be dragoons.

Ferguson accepted immediately and soon found himself back training new men in his way of fighting. These men from New York, New Jersey, and Connecticut learned quickly to handle his rifles, of which, perhaps, 200 remained — possibly, far fewer than that. He soon had his men ready for active duty.

In the eighteen months that followed the Battle of Monmouth, Ferguson built himself a reputation for sagacity, daring and strategic ability. He commanded the army portion of a successful amphibious attack on a privateer base. He surprised and defeated Pulaski's Legion. He held the fortifications at Verplanck's Point even after the sister fortress across the river at Stony Point fell to Wayne's Light Infantry. He reoccupied, refortified, and held Stony Point.

## Southern Campaign

Early in 1780 Major Ferguson and his Corps of Provincial Regulars were ordered south to take part in the British southern campaign, now about to start in earnest. It was thought that the abundant Loyalist sentiment, particularly in Georgia and the Carolinas, would aid in swinging the tide towards the British Government. Ferguson landed at Savannah and marched inland to Augusta. A portion of the Corps was now mounted. Their service around Augusta was short; they were ordered to join the main British army, which was advancing on Charleston, still in American hands.

The Corps performed with credit in the fighting that led up to the fall of Charleston. Ferguson was again wounded this time in the left arm, but recovered. After Charleston fell, the stage was set for Ferguson's last and greatest performance; the part he was called on to play required every bit of his military and political ability.

Ferguson, now with the rank of lieutenant colonel, was dispatched on 22 June, 1780, with his Corps (numbering about 200) to the back country of South Carolina. He made the village of Ninety-Six his headquarters. For three and a half months he did one of the outstanding jobs in the Revolution for the British side. He showed a considerable grasp of conditions in this country and a flair for appealing to people on a personal basis. He could sit down and talk to Americans in a way unique among British officers. Much of this hill country had been settled only a few years before by Scottish highlanders — from regiments disbanded at the end of the Seven Years War — on land given to them by the Crown. As a Highlander himself, he was instantly popular with these men.

## Command in the Hill Country

However, he was almost equally popular with the other sections of the hill country population. He was modest and seemed younger than his 36 years. Not imposing in looks or actions, he was strikingly handsome with a courteous, unostentatious manner. He signed some of his proclamations simply, "Pat Ferguson." Somehow, all recognized his keen logical mind and, what was far rarer, his fairness and kindness even to the families of those in arms against him. The people found him a first-rate soldier, a superb shot and a regular guy. He was clean in mind and language. He tried to prevent thievery and the like, which had become almost universal with both sides in the South late in the Revolution. On several occasions, he paid damages from his own pocket to people injured by his soldiers. Ferguson was so infuriated in one instance by the behavior of some of Tarleton's Tory dragoons that he was with difficulty restrained from hanging them on the spot, even though he was not their commander.

Ferguson enlisted, organized and trained an army of some 2,500 Tory militia, although it wasn't practical to have them all under arms at one time. He restored the King's authority over large stretches of back country. However, his very success roused the patriots against him. Ferguson's oral messages to the "overmountain" men were twisted into insults. American riflemen from western North Carolina, Virginia, and what is now Tennessee, rose as never before. They hemmed-in Ferguson and a portion of his army at King's Mountain.

## Final Defeat

Ferguson's position on 7 October, 1780, was on top of a small wooded hill about 600 yards long by less than 50 yards wide in most places. His forces were utterly defeated and he himself killed by American backwoods riflemen in one of the strangest actions ever fought. Ferguson, with about 1,000 of his Tory militia and some 130 provincial regulars, was overwhelmed by a slightly smaller number of hunter-backwoodsmen who surrounded his men and shot them down Indian fashion. These mountain men, commanded by nine different independent officers, volunteered for the sole and specific purpose of "catching and killing" Ferguson. Their movements were determined by a council of their officers. Somehow, this council managed to accomplish its purpose exactly. After winning the battle, they divided the spoils, and went back to their homes.

There was no battle ever fought in warfare where aimed fire was of more importance. The mountain riflemen had no semblance of drill or order. They had no intention of awaiting a charge by Ferguson's bayonet-wielding infantry. They took shelter as best they could. They pressed in from all sides, up the difficult slopes. When attacked in one sector, they gave ground there, but pressed in everywhere else. They held Ferguson inside this fluid line and exposed themselves little as they fired from behind trees and boulders. They riddled the British formations with their accurate fire.

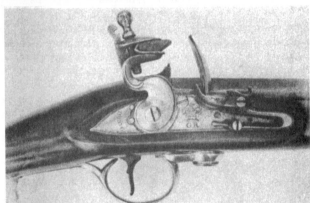

Ferguson's forces could make no effective defense against this form of attack. His provincial regulars were in part armed with his superb rifles; however, he needed these very men to spearhead each of his bayonet charges. He couldn't order his riflemen to take cover and fight as he had taught them without leaving the Tory militia with no stiffening for their formations. Ferguson gambled that solidarity and the bayonet would be victorious. He lost.

The backwoods riflemen shot dead 157 loyalists and wounded as many more, while suffering only 90 casualties, both killed and wounded. Ferguson, who during the entire action exposed himself recklessly, seemed to bear a charmed life; he rode from one Tory command to another, everywhere heartening his men for the fight. Suddenly, his luck ran out. In the space of a few seconds, while leading one last charge, he was hit by seven bullets. After Ferguson fell, the remaining British forces surrendered.

The Whigs in this section were near complete defeat before the battle; this victory restored the situation. The Tories of the South never really dared to assert themselves again. Cornwallis abandoned his invasion of North Carolina temporarily. The next time he moved north, it was but to surrender finally at Yorktown. King's Mountain was the Saratoga of the South.

These now famous weapons were praised by all who saw them. Too far ahead of their time, perhaps, both in design and mechanical details of construction, the Ferguson rifle probably wasn't practical mechanically when invented, or for years later. Even in Britain, which then led the world in gunmaking skill, there wasn't enough capacity to turn out the multi-pitch threads required in the breech mechanism with sufficient nicety for sealing off the powder gases. At least 100,000 weapons would have been required to arm the British forces. The entire capacity of the gun-makers in England to produce these intricate threads was probably less than one per cent of this.

We shouldn't compare the Ferguson to the NATO rifle. But when seen alongside its contemporaries, which were both muzzleloading and smoothbore, they are truly remarkable. They were the first standard military weapons to be capable of delivering aimed fire. For accuracy, they were at least the equal of the far

Above — Ferguson rifle made by Durs Egg of London, one of England's best gun craftsmen. The ten-thread breechplug is slotted to help carry powder fouling away. One turn up or down closed and opened the breech for loading. Now owned by the author, this specimen was bought in North Carolina around 1900, carried to England and returned here recently.

Above — Ferguson rifle, also with a ten-thread breechplug, made by Wm. Hunt of London about 1 776. In W. Keith Neal's collection.

more delicate, less powerful, American or "Kentucky" rifle which was privately produced and completely nonstandard. The Ferguson rifle could deliver aimed fire in larger volume than the finest trained men with smoothbore muskets could shoot at random. Ferguson's rifle could deliver at least three shots for every shot fired by any other rifle; it would probably deliver at least six times as many rounds as the usual American rifle of the Revolution.

## Ferguson the Man

In one of his last letters Ferguson said, "One cannot control the length of his life, but he can decide how it shall be spent." He seems to have lived by this; he was a scholar, a gentleman, and a soldier. He eternally refuted the statement sometimes heard that a soldier cannot also be a sensitive, humane individual.

Ferguson was an enemy and defended a way of life that we in America didn't want; however, he understood us better than any other British officer. He also understood the theory and practice of fighting with a rifle as well as any man who ever lived. We can admire now his skill, his ability, and his courage. After all, we beat him at his own game.

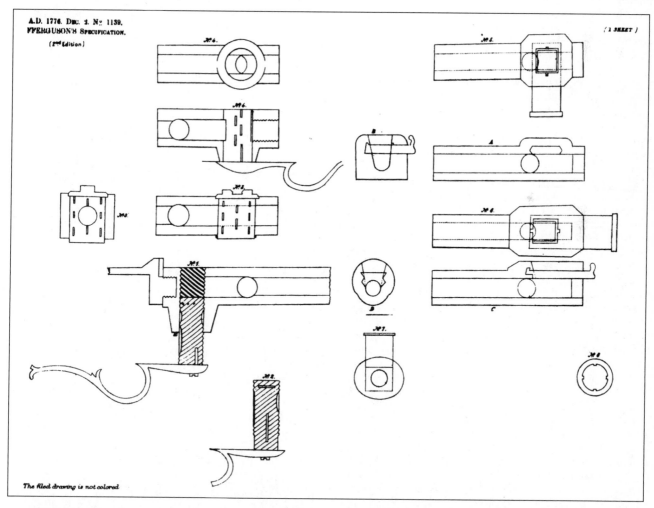

Ferguson's 1776 English Patent. Figs. 1 and 2 show the design found in Ferguson rifles, but the inventor also included other breechloading plug forms, such as the sliding and rotating types seen in Figs. 3 through 7. Note Fig. 8, showing a 4-groove barrel in section. Could anything be mors like modern rifling? His patent specification reads, in part: "...the projections formed in the ball by the cut of the rifle being twice as large as they commonly are, will not be liable to strip." Ferguson's rifling was not to see general use until some 80 years later, when W. E. Metford, great English engineer and rifleman, developed the groove form we know as Enfield rifling today — indistinguishable from Ferguson's!

1998

# The Mississippi Rifle

A watershed design in military history. ▮ Edward R. Crews

**Gun Digest**

1998 / 52nd Annual Edition

© The complete gun book, comprehensive and detailed, for all shooters — hunters, handgunners, collectors, handloaders and law enforcement officers.

Edited by
Ken Warner

Many a Confederate carried a U.S. Rifle Model of 1841 to his big war — it was a very serious weapon. (Virginia Historical Society photo)

THE MEN OF the 1st Mississippi Regiment watched the Mexican cavalry advance toward them. The enemy horse soldiers looked like an overwhelming force, but they had to be stopped. If not, Gen. Zachary Taylor's tiny American Army deep in Mexico near a hacienda named Buena Vista would be crushed.

The task of holding the American line at the Battle of Buena Vista rested mainly with Col. Jefferson Davis, his Mississippi troops and their rifles.

It was the second time that day — February 23, 1847 — that the Army's fate lay with this unit. Earlier, a 4500-man Mexican assault force broke another American unit and threatened to flank Taylor's Army. Davis recognized the danger immediately. He ordered his 370 volunteers to attack. His men stopped the Mexicans and then pushed them back.

Now, the American Army again was in danger. And, again, Davis and his soldiers stood at the key point on the battle line. That so much depended on these men and their weapons was a bit ironic.

Months earlier, when Davis was outfitting his regiment for service in the Mexican War, top Army brass opposed his idea to arm an entire regiment with rifles. Senior officers believed that the U.S. Army of 1846 would get the mass firepower it needed from standard-issue smoothbore flintlock muskets. Davis disagreed. He probably would have conceded that the flintlocks offered comparatively high rates of fire. However, they were cumbersome and finicky (particularly in wet weather), and their range and accuracy were exceedingly poor.

Even freshly minted West Point lieutenants knew the flintlock's shortcomings. Ulysses S. Grant, who served in the Mexican War as a twenty-three-year-old junior officer with the 4th Infantry Regiment, said of the smoothbores: "At the distance of a few hundred yards, a man might fire at you all day without your finding it out."

Unlike some officers, Davis recognized that a major revolution had occurred in small arms technology. And he wanted to take advantage of it. Thanks to a major breakthrough in musket ignition systems, the rifle was becoming a practical infantry arm, offering outstanding range, power and battlefield reliability.

Davis' decision to arm the 1st Mississippi with rifles would receive a severe test at Buena Vista. Failure could mean defeat and death; success could change warfare forever.

Prior to the Mexican War, smoothbore advocates could argue that the flintlock had served the Republic well in the Revolutionary War, the War of 1812 and on the frontier. To fire this musket, a soldier loaded his weapon with blackpowder and a round ball. The two were seated at the breech using a ramrod. The musket's external hammer held a piece of flint. When the trigger was pulled, the hammer fell from its fully cocked position. The flint struck an upright piece of metal, called a frizzen. This striking action created sparks, which fell into a small pan containing a priming charge. That charge burned through a hole in the barrel to ignite the main charge, thus firing the musket.

Military flintlocks typically were smoothbores. Range accordingly was limited. A soldier might hit an individual at 80 yards and a tightly packed military unit at 100 yards. Infantry tactics dictated by this weapon's technology were simple. Commanders massed large bodies of troops. These units were marched within range of the enemy. Once there, the troops would fire as rapidly as possible. The idea was to smother the enemy with a high volume of fire. When they were weakened and demoralized, an attack was made with the bayonet. Battered forces usually either stood and fought to the death or ran. If they took the latter course, they faced the possibility of being pursued by saber-wielding cavalry.

Like all military weapons from all periods, the smoothbore flintlock offered a mix of advantages, disadvantages and compromises. On the plus side, it could be loaded and fired rapidly. The British army during the American Revolution expected troops to fire fifteen rounds in 3.75 minutes. Recruits could master the weapon in a comparatively short time. The weapon also was proven in battle, and its tactical deployment was understood perfectly by officers. On the minus side, the flintlock ignition system often failed to work properly. Some historians estimate that even under ideal conditions it misfired 20 percent of the time. Rain, sleet and snow could prevent any use of this long arm.

Interest in developing a better ignition system became widespread near the close of the 18th century. Various inventors began to experiment with different explosive compounds, searching for something that would be both reliable and easy to use.

The ignition problem largely was solved about 1816 by Joshua Shaw with the creation of a reliable percussion cap. Some historians identify Shaw as a British painter or an American sailing captain. But whatever his true vocation, he built on the work of earlier inventors to create an ignition system that is the great-grandfather of that used for weapons today. Shaw took a small metal cap and filled it with fulminate of mercury, a highly explosive substance. The cap was placed over a nipple that led directly into a musket's breech, where the main charge sat. When the hammer fell on the cap, the resulting small explosion fired the main charge. The cap and nipple arrangement thus replaced the flintlock's flint, priming pan, frizzen and priming charge. Not only was the percussion cap easy to use, it also allowed for quicker loading and proved much more reliable in bad weather.

Army Ordnance (but not all commanders) embraced the percussion cap and the rifled musket in 1841 when it accepted the U.S. Rifle, Model 1841, caliber 54. To load it, soldiers were issued a paper cartridge, which they bit open. They then poured the powder down the barrel and seated a patched round ball atop the powder with a ramrod. A good shot could hit a man-sized target at 300 to 400 yards with this weapon.

The rifle was about 49 inches long, had a 33-inch barrel and weighed almost 10 pounds. The firearm featured a patch box in the stock. Fit and finish were superb. The rifle's lines were pleasing, and one can look at this musket today and arguably call it the most handsome weapon ever issued to American troops. Its only shortcoming was the absence of a bayonet lug.

Although designated the Model 1841, the rifle preferred by Jeff Davis would not get a significant combat trial until the Mexican War began in 1846. This conflict largely was about territory. The United States wanted to expand westward into large land tracts claimed by Mexico. The American government had offered to purchase a great deal of property. Mexico, however, said no. Tensions heightened in the 1840s until March, 1846, when U.S. President James K. Polk sent Zachary Taylor with a 3000-man force toward an area near the Rio Grande claimed by both nations.

Southern sentiment was strongly in favor of the conflict. Accordingly, the call for volunteers to fight was enthusiastically greeted in Mississippi. The state was authorized to raise one infantry regiment. Competition to enlist was keen. Davis, a West Pointer turned civilian, was chosen to serve as colonel of the unit, which was formed officially on June 16. As mentioned earlier, Davis demanded his men carry rifles and got these weapons after a fight with Army commanders.

The road to Buena Vista was long for Davis and his men. They arrived in the theater of operations in July and fought in the Battle of Monterey in September. The 1st Mississippi was serving with Taylor when he took Saltillo in November and Victoria in December.

Along with the rest of Taylor's command, Davis and his men found themselves in a dangerous position in January.

Through captured documents, Mexican General Antonio Lopez de Santa Anna learned that the U.S. Army was stripping Taylor of troops and sending them to another force commanded by Winfield Scott. Santa Anna decided to attack Taylor in his weakened state and then move to crush Scott.

Taylor and Santa Anna met at the Battle of Buena Vista. Santa Anna's plan was simple but sound: Turn the American left flank and destroy Taylor's Army.

The Mexican commander opened the fight with a diversionary strike at the well-emplaced American right flank. Then, he sent the main assault force to strike the left and head for the Saltillo Road. The main force smashed an American infantry regiment, forced another into disorganized retreat and scattered yet another cavalry unit.

It was at this point that Davis reached the battlefield and sent the 1st Mississippi into the attack. After halting the Mexican advance and silencing enemy

cavalry firing on his rear, Davis waited for reinforcements. They arrived in the form of one cannon and the 3rd Indiana Infantry Regiment.

Davis' force didn't have to wait long for an enemy response. Santa Anna sent another cavalry force to try and punch through to the American rear. The conventional means for infantry to repel a cavalry attack was to form a square and use a bristling fence of bayonets on rifles to keep the horses at bay. Tested and proven, this formation was useless to the 1st Mississippi because their rifles had no bayonet attachments. Davis would need to do something else.

He quickly formed the two regiments into a V. The Mississippians formed the northern wing; the Indianians formed the southern one. The field gun was placed with Davis' regiment.

The Mexican cavalry began its advance. Davis ordered all the men to hold fire until he gave the command. The battlefield became quiet. When the enemy was within about 100 yards, the Americans opened fire. The result was devastating.

Men and horses fell. A retreat ensued. The Mississippi sharpshooters again had played a key role in saving the day. Davis' men would be called on again later in the day to fight the determined Mexicans. Though badly battered, Taylor's force was safe when night fell.

Santa Anna eventually retreated, having failed to crush Taylor, who would contribute little more to the conflict, but would use his reputation established there to run for president and make it.

The 1st Mississippi's performance at the Battle of Buena Vista vindicated Davis' belief in the percussion rifled musket, establishing it firmly in the Army as a reliable weapon. It also gave the weapon a new name — the Mississippi Rifle — in honor of the regiment that saved the American Army.

Buena Vista was the last pitched battle that Davis' unit fought. During the next few weeks, the regiment would serve as an anti-guerrilla force charged with keeping American supply lines open. In May, Davis and his men headed home. They reached Vicksburg in June and received an enthusiastic heroes' welcome before being mustered out of service. Mississippi's legislature gave them their now-famous rifles as a token of honor and respect.

His Mexican War service made Davis a national figure. He became a U.S. senator from Mississippi shortly after returning home. During his service in Washington, D.C., Davis naturally carved out a niche as an expert on military matters. He served on the Senate's Military Affairs Committee and as President Franklin Pierce's secretary of war. Some historians believe that Davis was the most able administrator ever to hold that post.

Secretary of War Davis naturally

A believer in the new tactics of the rifle, Jefferson Davis covered himself and the rifle he chose for his regiment with enough glory to take him to high office in two nations — the U.S.A. and the C.S.A. (Virginia Historical Society photo)

The flintlock musket had been the Queen of Battles before the rifle, none more royal than the Brown Bess of England. (Colonial Williamsburg Foundation photo)

showed a strong interest in weapons. He pushed for the widespread use of percussion rifles, supported adoption of the Minié ball (a rifle bullet that did not need a patch and was the primary infantry projectile of the Civil War) and directed the conversion of smoothbore flintlocks to rifled percussion arms. He also followed closely the developments in breech-loading rifles.

Through the years from 1847 to 1860, Davis also acted as a spokesman for the South as regional relations worsened in the United States. This, plus his military reputation and knowledge, made him a logical choice to serve as president of the Confederacy when the Southern states seceded.

During the Civil War, Davis sent thousands of Southern troops into battle with percussion rifles firing Minié balls. The Civil War was the first time in history that this sort of accurate firepower was widely in the hands of ordinary foot soldiers.

Both Union and Confederate soldiers would carry the Mississippi Rifle into battle. It would have a special place in the hearts of Southern soldiers. Many of these weapons had been rebored to 58-caliber in 1855 and could use the Minié ball.

The U.S. Army gradually shifted to breechloaders in the post-war years. The Mississippi Rifle and other muzzleloaders disappeared from the Army's inventory. However, many Civil War veterans knew the value of a reliable firearm and carried surplus Model 1841s with them to tame the American West.

The Mississippi Rifle was an important transitional weapon in American military history. Well-made and reliable, it signaled the arrival of a new technology and a profound change in combat that still can be felt to this day.

# The Guns of John Brown

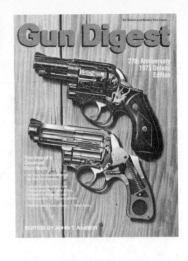

Some believed him a saint, others said he was Satan, this fierce guerrilla leader they called "Osawatomie" Brown. Whichever, he fought to abolish slavery years before the Civil War — and paid with his life. These are the weapons he used in "bleeding Kansas" and at Harpers Ferry.

❚ Louis W. Steinwedel

John Brown, the popular image. This old Currier & Ives pictures Brown as he appeared to the Northern public — the popular martyr, a near saint against a background of almost classic symbolism.

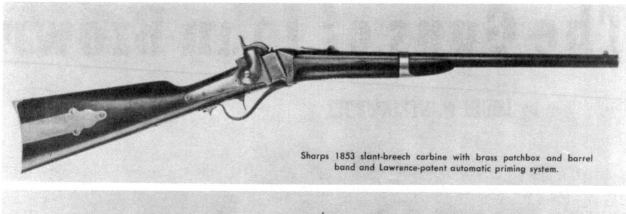

Sharps 1853 slant-breech carbine with brass patchbox and barrel band and Lawrence-patent automatic priming system.

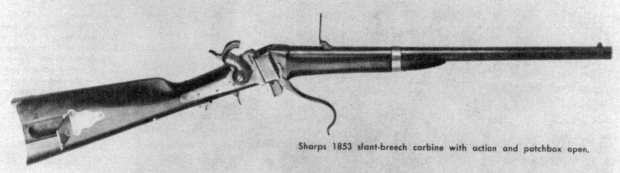

Sharps 1853 slant-breech carbine with action and patchbox open.

IRONY AND contradiction are often the warp and woof of history, but there are enough unnatural measures of the unknown in the lurid story of John Brown to spin many a tale weird enough even for modern television. Most of these are best left to the historian, psychologist or armchair thinker to ponder, but at least one of the curious circumstances of Brown's bloody career is of interest to gun collectors — how Brown came to defy Virginia, the Union and the world with 200 of the best rifles money could buy and an equal number of probably the worst revolvers.

The so-called "John Brown Sharps rifle" is fairly well known to collectors, the slant-breech model of 1853 with brass patchbox in the buttstock and brass barrel band and buttplate. The raiders' guns were not, as some people apparently still believe, the similar but more modern vertical breech model 1859 Sharps which appeared the same year as the storied seizure of the Federal armory at Harpers Ferry. Less well known to collectors are two other facets of the fanatic's armament: his long standing personal association and preference for Christian Sharps' advanced rifles and his extremely unlikely supply of sidearms.

John Brown bought his first Sharps rifle in 1848, the first year of the gun's introduction, and became — in his own way — one of the first boosters of this re-markable breechloader. For some reason known only to Brown, he wanted this personal gun unmarked, and that was the way he got this potent, accurate arm that served him well through the years of border war in "bleeding Kansas." The Sharps was the ideal weapon for the early day guerrilla warfare that he and his free-soilers waged and perfected in Kansas. Settlers backed by fiery New England abolitionists and opposed by equally determined Southerners anxious to replant slavery to fresh Western soil bled along with Kansas through the 1850s on a miniature Civil War battleground.

Determined that the advocates of slavery in the West would do the bulk of the bleeding, Henry Ward Beecher and other less vitriolic New Englanders sent the best guns they could buy to be sure that their version of right was backed by a sufficient supply of might. Crates of sparkling blue, brass, and casehardened Sharps breechloaders sallied forth secretly from their native New England with the incongruous deception "Bibles" neatly blackened on their white pine sides. Beecher (along with his sister Harriet Beecher Stowe, authoress of *Uncle Tom's Cabin*), shouldered probably more personal liability for the Civil War than any other one man, possibly even more than Brown himself. He got a little extra claim to fame when his Sharps rifles blazed their way across the Kansas prairie nicknamed "Beecher's Bi-bles." It was altogether fitting.

## Brown's Personal Revolver

John Brown's personal sidearm through much of the Kansas bloodletting was the perfect complement to the advanced rifle he carried — an 1851 Colt Navy 36, recognized from the Barbary Coast to Balaclava as the best friend a man could have in his holster. Of graceful lines, beautifully balanced and comparatively light for its day, the Navy was patently impressive, either coming out of leather at full speed or simply lying at rest on the green felt of a gaming table. How Brown got his Navy Colt, the fifty-one thousand and tenth to be made, and how he parted with it is another ironic twist to the Brown legend.

William F. Amy, a canny Kansas politician and abolitionist, eyeing the bearded fanatic's devotion to the cause with appreciation, strategically chose to overlook the more disagreeable facets of Brown's quixotic personality. Amy believed that this ardent fighter in Kansas' "holy war" should be materially rewarded with a token and, fittingly, gave him a gun. Amy chose the best, the long barreled Colt Navy 36, plain finished except for the usual naval battle scene rolled onto the cylinder. Brown accepted it and conscientiously carried it in Kansas. For two years it became a witness to the most Inquisition-like page in American history.

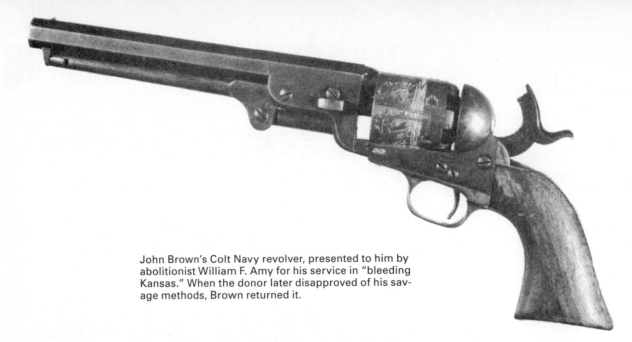

John Brown's Colt Navy revolver, presented to him by abolitionist William F. Amy for his service in "bleeding Kansas." When the donor later disapproved of his savage methods, Brown returned it.

"Osawatomie" Brown, as he liked to be called, after the best known site of the Kansas conflicts, was a psychologically fascinating man. He was burdened with precious few scruples over murder on the coldest terms when it furthered his cause, or even over feeding his sons to his hopeless ambitions at Harpers Ferry, yet he was meticulously honest. Eventually Brown's bloody Biblical-like vengeance mercilessly visited upon the "offenders" sickened even the devoutly abolitionist Arny. When Brown learned that he had fallen from favor in the mind of the donor of his revolver, he reasoned that the gift was conditional and that he no longer had any right to it. Accordingly, W.F. Amy promptly received from Brown one Colt's Navy 36, serial number 51010. However, the slim Colt had apparently been to Brown's liking since he soon acquired another one, with his own cash no doubt. Such a gun, or at least the remains of one, was found in the aftermath of the Harpers Ferry debacle in 1859, though not used there. Its barrel was sent to Hartford as a souvenir for Samuel Colt.

By the middle of 1856 a shaky peace had descended upon Kansas. At this time, however, a shipment of 200 more Sharps 1853 carbines was on the way from Massachusetts, creating a situation not far removed from the Russian missiles-in-Cuba crisis of about a century hence. The New England financiers of the "Kansas Crisis" began to fear that Federal military authorities in Kansas might take a dim view of the presence of this many rifles considerably superior to their own. Also, with the usual ingrained Yankee regard for hard cash, there was an investment of some $5500 to protect.

### Brown Gets Rifles

So, the Sharps shipment was secretly diverted to a depot at Tabor, Iowa. The attempt at secrecy did not of course include so trusted a warrior as John Brown. That, as history shows was a mistake, because the power inherent in 200 superb rifles was simply too much for the Kansas guerrilla, who saw bigger things in the wind to resist. It did not take much persuasion for Brown to get possession of the guns with the stipulation that he sell them privately and distribute the proceeds as relief funds. Brown did nothing so charitable, and the Sharps carbine showed up three years later on the rented Kennedy farm a few miles from the U.S. Armory at Harpers Ferry. Osawatomie Brown was apparently willing to compromise even his lofty principles about rightful possession when the "cause" stood to profit by an abuse of the Eighth Commandment.

The fast, accurate, easy handling Sharps served Brown astonishingly well in his otherwise botched raid at Harpers Ferry, permitting seventeen men to, as Henry Ward Beecher phrased it in a sarcastic sermon, "overawe a town of two thousand brave Virginians and hold them captive until the sun had gone laughing twice around the globe."

The Sharps was a splendid weapon, but the revolvers which Brown carried East stood in stark contrast to it. These were tiny 31-caliber revolvers made by the Massachusetts Arms Co. for the firm of Wesson & Leavitt. Some 200 of these handguns, complete with such accouterments as flasks, nipple wrenches and bullet moulds, had originally been sold to Boston abolitionist George L. Stearns. Through some espionage they ended up in the hands of John Brown in Iowa in 1857, and they too made it to the Kennedy farm in Maryland two years later.

This Massachusetts Arms Co. revolv-er was about as far as you could get from John Brown's hefty Navy Colt, and a highly unlikely nominee for the quasi — military foray on the banks of the Potomac. It was chosen, apparently for financial reasons; these 31-caliber jobs cost only $6.50 complete with accessories while a Navy Colt cost roughly double that — and was worth more.

The Massachusetts revolvers were unusual in concept and appearance, not unlike some of the very early attempts at revolving repeaters. With the exception of a topstrap over the cylinder which served to hold the cylinder pin and barrel to the rest of the parts, the gun appeared almost frame — less, like a dueling or target pistol

John Brown, the private image. This rare, unbearded view of Brown was regarded as his best picture by the family. He appears less ferocious than usual here, but the cold and expressionless eyes are the perfect symbol of his character.

with a cylinder added as an after-thought. The revolver's only touch with the times was its Maynard automatictape primer which was intended to eliminate the necessity of a separate percussion cap for each shot. The system had been invented in 1845 by a Washington dentist named Edward Maynard and enjoyed a measure of popularity by the 1850s, particularly when adapted to the muzzle-loading military musket.

The Maynard system was simple. When the hammer of the gun was cocked a small arm pushed up the end of a coil of waterproofed paper containing small fulminate charges, almost exactly the same as toy caps for children's cap pistols. On musket conversions the original percussion nipple was retained, so ordinary copper caps could be used in a pinch. However, the Maynard adaptation to the revolvers which Brown's men used completely did away with the usual nipples at the rear of the cylinder. Instead, the roll of caps was fed to a single nipple mounted in the frame which communicated the flash of the cap explosion through a tiny vent in the rear of each chamber in the cylinder. This was one of those ideas which look great on paper but which have a way of turning out to be unmitigated disasters.

It is understatement to say that the Maynard system was not noted for its reliability. Despite its claim to waterproof caps, a Maynard equipped gun often would not fire during damp weather. During such conditions, the militiaman could slip an old-fashioned copper cap on the nipple of his musket and be sure of a kick when he pulled the trigger, but the Maynard priming system was exclusively and forever married to the Massachusetts Arms revolver. Having the ignition system reach the powder chambers by a small vent hole was a throwback to the flintlock, and had the same problem of black powder residue fouling the vent after the first or second firing. These two factors combined made the Massachusetts Arms revolver dependable for little more than casual Sunday afternoon shooting, yet fate capriciously sent it along on one of history's boldest expeditions.

By another quirk, fate chose a U.S. colonel named Robert E. Lee to yank Brown from his makeshift fortress with the gracefully arched windows and the top-heavy looking cupola. The breaching of the armory firehouse took only three sweeps of the minute hand of Colonel Lee's big gold watch, but it quickly became popular history that is still providing fodder for movie and television screens.

The whole thing was a holiday in the

1853 Sharps and stocked Colt Navy carried by John Brown, Jr. The Collins cavalry officer's saber was presented to Brown, Jr., by his Civil War regiment. Wooden canteen was the senior Brown's.

picturesque Virginia hills and it did not take the revelers long to locate the bulk of Brown's private arsenal at the rented Kennedy farm a few miles away in Maryland. One of the regiments at the farm, the "Baltimore Greys," did not consider it unprofessional to re-appropriate some of the expensive abolitionist carbines as spoils of war.

## Collector's Sharps

Fortunately for history, one of the shiny brass-bound Sharps carbines found its way into the hands of Colonel A. P. Shutt, commander of the 6th Regiment of Maryland Volunteers. In civilian life Shutt worked for the Baltimore & Ohio Railroad and was in Harpers Ferry mainly to protect company property from the gun-toting mobs that had swarmed in for the carnival and free whisky. The colonel was one of the few recipients of Brown's guns that sensed a bit of drama about it rather than a simple windfall of a good gun. He gave the unused carbine to his son and the lid of the inlaid brass patchbox was later engraved: "Captured from insurgents at Harpers Ferry, Va. October 18, 1859 by Col. A. P. Shutt and presented to his son Augustus J.C.L. Shutt." Today, the gun belongs to the Maryland Historical Society. It is the most authentic of the extremely few Brown guns and relics that survived the years after the raid. Its serial number is 15864.

Officially, 102 Sharps carbines and an equal number of Massachusetts Arms revolvers were removed from Brown's rented base of operations, so apparently the better part of a hundred of each were carried off by enterprising souvenir seekers. Some

of the other remnants of Brown's shattered dream of a slave rebellion included 23,000 percussion caps and 100,000 percussion pistol caps, ten kegs of powder, plus spears, pikes, and assorted martial hardware with which Brown had planned to arm the slaves which never rose to follow him. The guns were removed to the Federal arsenal, where they were appropriated once again when the town later was captured by the Confederacy and — the greatest irony of al l— the guns for John Brown's "holy war" vanished into the ranks of the rebel cavalry.

The scene of the raid seemed to suffer a fate under Brown's curse which no other piece of American territory has ever had to endure. Like some little European border town, with spectacular Rhineland-like scenery to complete the comparison, Harpers Ferry was alternately shelled by armies as they advanced, pillaged of its machinery while they were there and burned as they retreated, until by the end of the war it literally ceased to exist. Years later the ghost of Osawatomie Brown seemed to still haunt the spot with a vengeance as the usually placid Potomac swallowed it.

• • •

John Brown was a saint or a satan, generally depending on which side of the Mason-Dixon line the opinion originated, but there is no argument that he was an enigma, a strange blend of idealism and savagery, something mysteriously apart from the ordinary mould of men — and that the exotic about him extended even down unto his armament.

# "The Minié Rifle"

■ E. F. Donnelly

JUST OUTSIDE the little town of Gettysburg on a hot July afternoon in 1863, some 15,000 crack Confederate infantrymen of General Lee's command moved out from their positions on Seminary Ridge. Forming into three main attack groups or divisions, the men started off across the open fields towards the gentle slopes of Cemetery Hill. Their objective was to take that hill and the jumping-off hour had arrived. In a day before dog tags were issued to soldiers, many of these men had scribbled their names and home towns on scraps of paper and thrust them into pockets. There was a nervous checking of cartridge boxes and other equipment as they surveyed the distance they'd have to traverse before closing with the enemy. 1100 to 1400 yards separated the three divisions from the quiet Federal lines on Cemetery Hill, and no one was more aware of the distance involved than these waiting men, many of whom were about to die. Already a few ranging shells from the Federal batteries had burst in and about the gray lines, when at last the word was given to move forward. With heads bent as though walking in a strong gale, they weathered an ever increasing barrage of shot and shell flung at them from batteries already thought silenced until a moment before. Torrents of grape and canister tore through the ordered ranks, but then, closing with their objective, they hurled themselves on the waiting lines of Yankees dug in along the ridge.

Ironically, hung on the cemetery gate about which a portion of the Yankee lines were formed, was a sign which read, "All persons found using firearms on these grounds will be prosecuted to the full extent of the law." With utter disregard for the law, however, the blue-clad troopers poured such a storm of musketry into the oncoming Rebels that, within an hour, the

massive assault was stopped. Crushed and beaten, the survivors of that great action known as "Pickett's Charge" sullenly fell back to the shelter of their own lines. With a gallantry unsurpassed in the history of warfare, the Rebels had marked the trail of their three pronged attack with some ten thousand casualties.

What type of weapons had caused the valiant South to sustain such a horrific loss in one hour of attack? A loss which is shocking, even when compared to the great battles of the world's two most recent wars.

This awful carnage was not accomplished with the aid of machine gun, atomic cannon or fighter-bomber, for such items were yet to be developed. No, the weapons in the hands of the Blue and Gray on that hot afternoon so long ago were such simple little arms as the Springfield and Enfield rifle-muskets, rifled and smoothbore artillery pieces, Colt's and Remington revolvers, and the inevitable bayonet. Antiquated weapons to be sure. Yet with such outmoded weapons, Americans of more than than ninety years ago managed to inflict almost one million casualties on each other in a war which still stands as the most costly to American lives. The military experts list many reasons for the terrible death rate between 1861 and 1865, but the fact remains that the war was primarily an infantry affair. Despite grape, canister, shot and shell; disease, improper camp sanitation and lack of medical skill; the greatest single killer in that war was the Springfield rifle-musket. This weapon, sometimes known as the "Minié" rifle, was the principal shoulder arm used by the Civil War soldier. Without becoming either too technical or involved in explanation, this article will describe some of the characteristics of that weapon.

The great bellow of Civil War cannon is mostly stilled these days, except for those rare occasions when Hollywood calls for its services, but the bark of the muzzle-loading Springfield rifle can still be heard in many parts of the country. Gun collectors and shooters are now finding the old Springfields both enjoyable and economical to fire, and as a result, gun stores, collectors' meetings and old attics are being scoured in an effort to locate more of the old charcoal burners. Public interest even extends to the Camp Perry National Rifle Matches, where one of the non-scoring events consists of an exhibition of shooting with the service muzzle loader of the 1860's. A couple of years ago, to the surprise of many of the spectators present, the muskets shot exceptionally well. This,

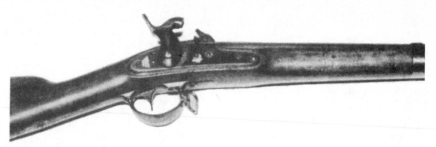

U.S. Model 1842 Percussion Musket, 69 caliber smoothbore. Barrel, 42", total length without bayonet 57.8". Weight with bayonet 9.8 lbs. Walnut stock. Front sight is a brass knife blade attached to top barrel band. Spread eagle on lockplate looks back toward hammer. Arsenal name and year of manufacture is stamped on lockplate just to rear of hammer. Breech end of barrel is marked with a V.P., an eagle's head and the year. This musket, manufactured at both the Springfield and Harper's Ferry Arsenals, was the first issue musket ever made on the completely interchangeable plan. Discontinued in 1855, it was the last of the government's smoothbores, while also the first of the percussion muskets. Many of this model were rifled just prior to the Civil War. (This musket property of Rock Island Arsenal Museum.)

U.S. Model 1855 Rifle-Musket, 58 caliber. Barrel length 39¾", total length without bayonet 58½". Weight with bayonet 9.75 lbs. Walnut stock. Markings: a spread eagle on the Maynard tapebox cover; "U.S. Springfield" or "Harper's Ferry" and the year of manufacture on the lockplate; a V.P. with an eagle head on the breech of barrel. The most noticeable feature is the Maynard Patent Priming Device of the lockplate. Barrel retaining bands are flat and held in place with band springs. The cone seat has a clean-out screw, used in cleaning out the barrel vent. This model may be found with an adjustable slide-type rear sight or with the typical two-leaf rear sight so common to Civil War muskets. (This musket property of R.I.A. Museum.)

U.S. Model 1864 Rifle-Musket, 58 caliber. Barrel, 40", total length without bayonet 56". Weight without bayonet 8.6 lbs. In this model there is a change in the cone seat, which had been accomplished in the 1863 model. However, the most obvious change in the '63 and '64 models is in the shape of the hammer. (Musket shown is property of the writer.)

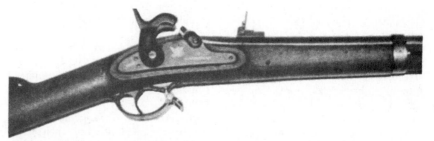

Special Model 1861 Rifle-Musket, 58 caliber. Sometimes referred to as the Colt Pattern or Special Model 1861 Musket, this weapon was manufactured for the government by the Colt's Patent Fire Arms Mfg. Co., Inc., the Lamson, Goodnow & Yale Co. of Windsor, Vt., and the Amoskeag Mfg. Co., of Manchester, N.H. Barrel length and twist of rifling same as the 1855 and 1861 models. Except for the trigger guard assembly and rear sight, parts made for this model will not interchange with the other issue muskets of the period. The hammer shape is noticeably different than the 1861 model. (This musket is the property of the writer.)

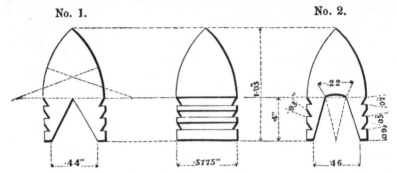

No. 1.                    No. 2.

Weight of No. 1, 500 grains.    Weight of No. 2, 450 grains.
Weight of powder, 60 grains.    Weight of powder, 40 grains.
No. 1, section of musket ball.
No. 2, section of pistol-carbine ball.
Both balls have the same exterior.

of itself, is an indication as to how short-lived is the human memory. A generation ago, our grandfathers could have told many a story testifying as to the deadly effectiveness of their old Minié rifles.

By a strange quirk of fate, it is interesting to note, the Springfield 58 caliber Rifle-Musket, Model of 1855, was approved for the general use of the Army by the then Secretary of War, one Jefferson Davis. In a letter to the Chief of Ordnance in the summer of '55, Davis approved and recommended changes proposed for the service musket by the Army Ordnance Board. The musket preceding the new 1855 model had been the regulation shoulder weapon of the Army from 1842, and held the rather unusual position of having been the first percussion arm to be adopted for the service and at the same time being the last of the smoothbore muskets. This big weapon fired a 69 caliber lead ball in a manner hardly to be described as accurate; but in spite of its erring ways, the services clung to the old musket with that affection borne of long familiarity.

To equip the entire Army with a rifled arm stirred up quite a controversy in the War Department of the 1850's. Actually, small units of the U.S. Army had been equipped with flintlock and percussion rifles from the very beginning of our history, but the principal arm of the infantry had always been the smoothbore musket. There was no doubt as to which was the most accurate, but with the black powder then in use, the smoothbore musket was much easier to load and fire than the rifle. The latter, requiring a tightly fitted patched ball which was difficult to ram down a fouled and dirty bore, took roughly twice as long to load as the inaccurate smoothbore. The proposed reduction in bore size created an additional furor.

Many of the veteran officers and enlisted men, schooled in the use of the 69 caliber smoothbore, felt that to reduce the caliber to 58 would leave the soldier with such a "small bored" weapon that he would no longer be able to, make "good Indians out of bad ones." Those of us who have been in the service in recent years know that the 50 caliber machine gun bullet is a slug to be reckoned with, yet our gentle ancestors were afraid that a 58 caliber bullet would fail to stop an Indian. In spite of the objections raised by the diehards, however, the proposed changes were made, the caliber reduced to 58. The length of the infantry musket's barrel was set at forty inches, and it was to be rifled. It was decided, in fact, that all future mus-

kets would be rifled to make use of the newly developed Minié ball, a recent hollow-based importation from France.

This Minié ball or bullet, an adaptation of the original bullet developed by Captain Minié of the French Army, was as much an outstanding innovation to the military of the 1850's as is the guided missile and atomic weapon of today. For the first time since the invention of black gunpowder, the Minié ball's accuracy placed the infantrymen more on an even footing when facing artillery fire. By the same token, the artilleryman found that he must either move back out of range of the enemy's aimed rifle fire, or else die fighting his guns. Prior to this, when facing the smoothbore musket or even such rifled arms that used a patched round ball, the enemy soldier or artilleryman hit by deliberate aim at much over one hundred yards was an unlucky individual indeed. However, with the adoption of the Minié ball, conventional warfare underwent some drastic changes. Aimed effective rifle fire was increased by two hundred yards, but what was probably of greater importance, the soldier had at last been given an arm which inspired him with confidence. If he took good aim, he could score a hit.

The military muzzle loader had just about reached perfection in the late '50's and early '60's, but its full development could not have been attained without the Minié ball. This fact was quickly realized by the Army's Ordnance Board, after it had experimented with the French projectile. Adapting the original projectile to its own needs, the Ordnance Board reached the following conclusions: first, by using the elongated, undersized ball, the muzzle loading rifle could be loaded and fired almost continuously, without stopping to

clean out a barrel fouled and caked with burnt powder residue. Expanded upon firing, the self cleaning Minié would push the residue from preceding shots out the barrel ahead of itself. Secondly, the expansion of its hollow base, forming nearly a perfect bore seal, resulted in a better utilization of the propelling gases and also gave greatly increased accuracy. This in contrast to the loose fitting round balls of former times, which had lost much of their range and accuracy by permitting the propellant gases to escape up the bore.

With the addition of Dr. Maynard's patent primer tape device, which speeded up the process of loading, the U.S. Rifle-Musket of 1855 was certainly the fastest loading, if not one of the world's best muzzle loading weapons. Jefferson Davis played his small part in approving the weapon that would help destroy the Confederacy, yet to be born.

During the first ten years after its adoption, the new 58 caliber weapon was modified and again remodified to meet those various needs of the services, needs that only active field use can discover and develop in any type of Army equipment. Basically and ballistically, it was the same weapon, although the government identified it by the year such changes were made, e.g., the Model 1855, the Special Model 1861, the models of 1863 and 1864. The rifle-musket was manufactured both with and without Maynard's patent priming device. It was put out with barrel lengths from 33 inches to 40; sometimes as a carbine, other times as a rifle. During the war years, the North found that its government arsenals could not even begin to supply enough rifles to meet the needs of an ever increasing armed force; to meet this demand, contracts were

# CARTRIDGE FOR EXPANDING BALLS

**FULLSIZE FOR NEW MUSKET**

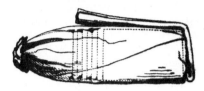

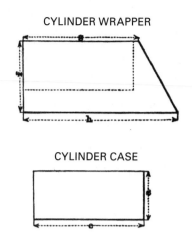

CYLINDER WRAPPER

CYLINDER CASE

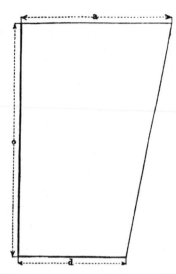

OUTER WRAPPER

given to private arms manufacturers. As a result, arms collectors will find Civil War period muskets made not only at the Springfield Arsenal but also by Colt's, Remington, Whitney, Savage, Norwich Arms Company, and a host of others too numerous to mention here. (See C. Fuller's The Rifled Musket, described fully in the book review pages.) Without attempting to discuss the various modifications of the original weapon, let us select one item, an 1863 Springfield.

The '63 model rifle-musket had a long slim barrel some 39¾ inches long, rifled with three shallow grooves, the twist having a uniform pitch of one complete turn in six feet. It was bound to its walnut stock with three iron barrel bands. Its lock, trigger guard, bands, and in fact the barrel itself, were all finished bright. The "bright" finish of the weapon shows what complete disregard our Ordnance then had for what is now known as good camouflage discipline. A column of infantry marching along on a clear day could usually be seen for miles, the sun reflecting merrily off the bright and shiny barrels of scores of muskets. Mounted atop this gay and gleaming barrel was a two-leaf rear sight, quite common to the Civil War musket. With both leaves down the piece was sighted in for one hundred yards; one raised leaf gave a 300-yard sighting, the other 500. Could they hit anything with those three- and five-hundred yard sights? They could indeed, but more about that later.

It had been found from experience that the 1855 model, when fitted with the Maynard device, a mechanism quite similar to a toy repeating cap pistol, was not as reliable as was first anticipated. After receiving many complaints from soldiers in the field, the Models 1861, 1862 and all the later versions were again fitted with the older, simpler type lock, one similar

to that used on the 1842 musket. If that seems like progress in reverse, possibly it was. However, reliability of functioning was a compelling requirement, not always to be had with the Maynard mechanism. Under ideal conditions Maynard's device functioned quite well; as the hammer was pulled back a capsule of mercury fulminate automatically appeared over the nipple. Unfortunately, conditions and field use developed unexpected quirks in the mechanism and it was dropped from further use. Once again the soldier was required to place each percussion cap in position with his fingers. Naturally this method was slower but, on the other hand, it was a more reliable way to insure the rifle going off when desired.

That "going off or ignition system of a percussion musket is simplicity itself. The percussion cap bears the same relationship to the loaded rifle as the spark plug does to the automobile cylinder loaded with gasoline vapor. Screwed into the breech end of the barrel at the right side is a "cone" or "nipple," whose axis is pointed upward and rearward. Drilled through the center of this nipple is a channel leading directly into the barrel, while the upper opening of the nipple is positioned just beneath the descending hammer. To fire such a piece, one rammed powder and ball down the barrel, then slipped a percussion cap over the nipple. Pulling the trigger caused the hammer to strike the cap, which, exploding, flashed its fire into the main charge.

In spite of its length (58½ inches), the weight of the rifle with bayonet attached came to just 9¾ pounds. Compared with the familiar Garand M1 of today's Army, the tip of the muzzleloader's bayonet was about on a par with a tall man's head. Ballisti-cally the rifle-musket was a short range weapon, and on paper its velocity

and stopping power are almost laughable. Laughable, that is, if one considers the terrible losses at Antietam, Cold Harbor and Spotsylvania a subject for merriment. To understand the lethal potentialities of the musket, one must again consider the Minié ball used in it.

A charge of sixty grains of black powder drove the 500-gr. hollow-based Minié out of the muzzle at a velocity of 950 feet per second; extremely slow when compared to the M1 rifle's 2800 feet per second. In spite of its slow speed, however, the lumbering Minié ball was a mean killer. Wounds made by it were particularly destructive because the bullet was given to tumbling end over end in its passage through the body. Joints and bone tissue struck by it were almost always shattered beyond any hope of healing, and unless the poor unfortunate so wounded died at once, he was usually subjected to the added misery of a battlefield amputation. If his wounds didn't kill him, the amputation or resulting infection usually did.

The ability of the rifle-musket to deliver this deadly missile to a given target was quite acceptable for the day and age. While not comparable to some of the contemporary sporting or target rifles, its accuracy was sufficient to enable the shooter to hit a target the size of a man on horseback at a full six hundred yards. Old Ordnance records list the musket's capabilities as follows: Its heavy bullet could penetrate four inches of soft pine at 1000 yards. When fired from machine rest, the musket was expected to place all of its bullets in a four-inch circle at 100 yards, in an eleven-inch bull at 333 yards, and into a 27-inch bull at 500 yards. Altogether the combination of rifle and bullet gave quite respectable accuracy. As for accuracy, possibly the reader may recall how proficient he became with the smoothbored air gun of his boyhood, assuming, of course, that he was lucky enough to own one. Remembering that, one can readily see how deadly proficient Billy Yank and Johnny Reb became in the use of this long slim rifle-musket. As contemporary Ordnance reports indicate, however, not all of the soldiers used their muskets with either proficiency or as the regulations prescribed. For example, in the excitement of battle an inexperienced soldier might insert his paper-wrapped cartridge into the barrel upside down, the powder on top! He might fail to tear the cartridge open before ramming it home. He might load his musket properly, then forget to prime it with a percussion cap. He might think that he had fired the piece and then ram another load down atop the first load. He might correctly load, but then forget to remove his ramrod. The latter mistake often resulted in the interesting phenomenon of a ramrod flashing through the air like a silver arrow. The soldier might just finish loading his piece and then before getting a chance to fire it, become a casualty himself. As often happened, another soldier might come along, pick up the same gun and ram one more charge down the long bore. In any of these events the musket so treated either failed to fire or fired so poorly as to be worthless.

Old Ordnance records again provide an interesting commentary on the ease with which even the best of military muzzleloaders could be temporarily put out of action. Reports tell us that of the 37,574 stand of muskets listed as battlefield pickups after Gettysburg, some 24,000 were loaded. Of this number 6,000 had one load each; 12,000 had two loads each; 5,999 had from three to ten loads each; and one barrel contained twenty-three loads. After these figures were released even the most stanch adherents of the muzzleloader agreed that it just had to go. We couldn't effect the change while actively engaged in a war, however, and so the adoption of an efficient breechloader was delayed until after the war.

To give the modern infantryman a notion of how well off he is with his semi-automatic rifle, just consider all the motions that Billy Yank or Johnny Reb had to go through before he was ready to deliver that fatal Minié ball. These will be the typical motions of the soldier as he loaded and fired at will — as opposed to the methodical motions employed when firing by volleys at a given command. Let's assume that the soldier has just fired his piece. As the considerable puff of white smoke drifts away, the soldier brings the

rifle down from his shoulder and pulls the big hammer back to its half cock position. (Some veteran soldiers maintained that the hammer should not be pulled back, but should be left closed, as is the damper on a stove.) He reaches back into his leather cartridge box and brings out a paper wrapped cartridge; a unit containing both powder and Minié ball. The soldier brings the cartridge up to his mouth and tears it open with his teeth. He then pours the powder down the barrel, squeezes the bullet out of the paper tube and inserts it into the muzzle. He next draws the ramrod from its groove underneath the barrel, and in two or three strokes, rams the ball down on top of the powder. Sometimes he uses the cartridge paper as wadding and rams it down on the powder, too, at other times he throws it away. If he's pressed for time, as during an attack, he just bites the cartridge so that it's at least partly open, rams it down the bore, and trusts to luck that it will go off. Crouched behind that fence or tree, our soldier doesn't even bother returning his ramrod to its place beneath the barrel. For the sake of speed, he thrusts it into the ground at his feet, where it will be handy for the next shot. As the last act of loading his piece, the soldier reaches into the cap box attached to his belt, pulls out one percussion cap, places it on the nipple of his musket, then draws the big hammer back to full cock. He's now cocked, primed, and ready for another target.

Reports tell us that some veteran infantrymen became so expert at reloading that two or three shots a minute were not considered exceptional for the times. Reports also mention that after a few volleys on the battlefield the smoke from the thousands of muskets would become so dense that the troops would be unable to see each other until the wind had cleared the smoke away. This is pure conjecture, of course, but possibly the casualty rates in a typical Civil War fire fight can be

tied in with the difficulty the soldiers had in reloading their muskets. After going through the entire wearisome process of loading they were going to try to make every shot count, if at all possible.

No discussion of the rifle-musket would be complete without pointing out some of the more interesting uses to which the weapon was put. For example, the weapon was often used as a fairly effective shotgun. With its slow twist rifling, the musket did not disperse a load of shot

| PRINCIPAL DIMENSIONS, WEIGHTS, ETC., OF SMALL ARMS. | | | | | | |
|---|---|---|---|---|---|---|
| Dimensions. | Rifle muskets. | | | Rifles. | | Pistol carbine. |
| | 1822. | 1840. | 1855. | 1841. | 1855. | 1855. |
| | Inches. | Inches. | Inches. | Inches. | Inches. | Inches. |
| Barrel.. Diameter of bore ............. | 0.69 | 0.69 | 0.58 | 0.58 | 0.58 | 0.58 |
| Variation allowed, more...... | 0.015 | 0.015 | 0.0025 | 0.0025 | 0.0025 | 0.0025 |
| Diameter at muzzle... ...... | 0.82 | 0.85 | 0.78 | 0.90 | 0.90 | 0.82 |
| Diam'r at breech between flats. | 1.25 | 1.25 | 1.14 | 1.15 | 1.14 | 1. |
| Length without breech screw. | 42. | 42. | 40. | 33. | 33. | 12. |
| Bayonet.—Length of blade............ | 16. | 18. | 18. | 21.7 | 21.7 | ...... |
| Ramrod.—Length ............ | 41.96 | 41.70 | 39.60 | 33.00 | 33.00 | 12. |
| Arm comp'te. Length without bayonet....... | 57.64 | 57.80 | 55.85 | 48.8 | 49.3 | 17.6 |
| With bayonet fixed........... | 73.64 | 75.80 | 73.85 | 71.3 | 71.3 | ...... |
| With butt-piece............ | ...... | ...... | ...... | ...... | ...... | 28.2 |
| Grooves Number..................... | 3 | 3 | 3 | 3 | 3 | 3 |
| Twist ... ............... | 6. | 6. | 6. | 6. | 6. | 4. |
| Width ...................... | 0.36 | 0.36 | 0.30 | 0.30 | 0.30 | 0.30 |
| Depth at muzzle............. | .005 | .005 | .005 | .005 | .005 | .005 |
| Depth at breech............. | .015 | .015 | .015 | .013 | .013 | .008 |
| WEIGHTS. | Lbs. | Lbs. | Lbs. | Lbs. | Lbs. | Lbs. |
| Barrel, without breech screw.......... | 4. | 4.19 | 4.28 | 4.8 | 4.8 | 1.4 |
| Lock, with side screws................. | * 95 | .95 | .81 | .55 | .81 | .6 |
| Bayonet ....................... | 0.73 | 0.64 | .72 | 3.05 | 3 05 | ...... |
| Arm comp'te. Without bayonet............. | 9.06 | 9.51 | 9.18 | 9.68 | 9.93 | 3.56 |
| With bayonet................. | 9.82 | 10.15 | 9.90 | 12.72 | 12.98 | ...... |
| With butt-piece............. | ...... | ...... | ...... | ...... | ...... | 5.09 |

\* Maynard primer.

as readily as a modern rifle's rapid twist will do; shot loads were frequently substituted for the service round. If so used, with a little luck, Johnny or Billy might then proceed to toast a duck or a rabbit on the end of that old reliable all-purpose ramrod.

Another specialized load for the old gun consisted of a lighter 300-gr. bullet which, backed up by 100 grains of black powder, attained a speed close to 1800 feet per second. A fairly hot load indeed, and supposedly used by sharpshooters only. Another special bullet was issued on occasion and this one might truly be termed an explosive bullet. Something akin to the Minié ball, this nasty little number contained a three-second time fuse and a small portion of fulminate. Developed by a chap named Gardiner, this bullet was supposed to be fired into the enemy's artillery caissons. Judging from the number of blown up caissons in any given battle of the Civil War, it is fairly safe to assume that not all of them were blown up by counter battery fire. Possibly the little explosive bullets did their intended work after all.

There were other muzzleloading shoulder weapons in considerable use throughout the war, but the majority of them were roughly in the same category as the Springfield when it came to celerity of fire, accuracy, and range. Possibly the best known of these weapons was the English 577-caliber Enfield rifle-musket. These were brought into the South by means of fast Confederate blockade runners, and were greatly in demand by the Confederate who was probably still toting his Grandpap's War-of-1812 flintlock. The Whitworth sharpshooters rifle, another English import, was never brought into the conflict in any great numbers, but was one of the most highly prized because of its exceptional accuracy. The 54 and 58 caliber Harpers Ferry rifles, a product of the U.S. government arsenal of the same name, were also found in considerable quantities on both sides of the lines. The U.S. 1842 models were also brought out of retirement and issued for use, along with thousands of other muskets (both foreign and domestic) that should have long before been relegated to the scrap heap. For example, the Federal government purchased thousands of Austrian muskets; a fair percentage of these were of such poor and antiquated quality that, in at least one instance, Federal soldiers staged a minor mutiny rather than accept them. In the Confederate Army, the constant shortage of weapons caused the use of any and all weapons that could be scraped from the arsenals and attics of the South. They used flintlocks, converted flintlocks, shotguns, sporting rifles, and what-ever arms could be captured from the Yankees; many were captured, never doubt it. They even turned to the manufacture of weapons, and the few made were good. Only the lack of raw materials stopped production in quantity. At times Johnny captured new breechloaders from the Yanks, but because he could not make the special ammunition they required, or else lacked the parts to repair the weapons, he deliberately remade them into muzzleloaders. Johnny was resourceful when it came to weapons, and in his capable hands they all performed quite well.

There are many of the old rifle-muskets still about, and if found to be in good condition, there is no reason why they shouldn't be fired. Bullet moulds, powder and percussion caps are available from many sources in this country, and one can fire these old timers today about as inexpensively as a 22 rifle. When using the rifle-musket, as well as any other muzzle-loader, always remember that the old weapons were built to handle black powder only. Black powder is safe to use in any of them, but modern smokeless powder will almost invariably blow them apart. In addition to the danger of using the wrong powder, there are also such factors as metal fatigue and rust. Before firing any muzzleloader, if you have even the slightest doubt about the strength of the barrel, have the weapon checked by a competent gunsmith.

It's been nearly a hundred years since the days of our last muzzle loading rifle. It was rugged, sufficiently accurate, and easily mass produced. It served its purpose well when the chips were down. Nothing better can be said of any weapon.

# The Whitworth Rifle
## a great milestone in rifle history

The first comprehensive and critical review of a famous rifle, the result of the author's deep and diligent research. Fully illustrated.

▊ DeWitt Bailey II

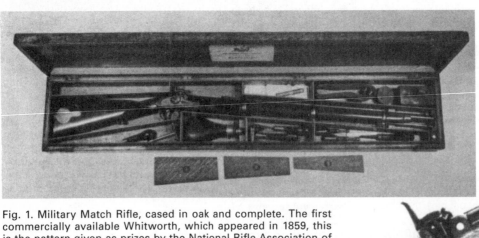

Fig. 1. Military Match Rifle, cased in oak and complete. The first commercially available Whitworth, which appeared in 1859, this is the pattern given as prizes by the National Rifle Association of Great Britain in 1860, 1861 and 1862. This type was also given as a prize by many Volunteer units and civic organizations during those years. Note that the case is unlined. The round capbox, the lock and breech design, the smooth-headed ramrod and stock design are characteristic of this model. Courtesy E. J. Burton.

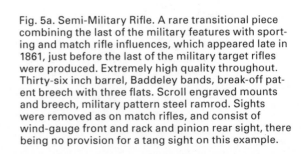

Fig. 5a. Semi-Military Rifle. A rare transitional piece combining the last of the military features with sporting and match rifle influences, which appeared late in 1861, just before the last of the military target rifles were produced. Extremely high quality throughout. Thirty-six inch barrel, Baddeley bands, break-off patent breech with three flats. Scroll engraved mounts and breech, military pattern steel ramrod. Sights were removed as on match rifles, and consist of wind-gauge front and rack and pinion rear sight, there being no provision for a tang sight on this example.

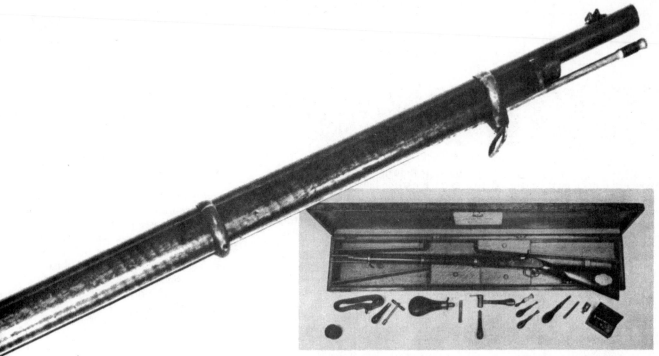

Fig. 2. Military Match Rifle, a reverse view of fig. 1, with contents displayed. Implements are, from left – cap tin, sling, punch for pushing bullet from mould, combination tool, German-silver topped leather covered flask, WHitworth patent cartridge, conical mould and base plug, lock brush, hammer face cleaner, nipple cleaner, screwdriver, torque bar, oil bottle, japanned tin for holding wads and other small pieces. Courtesy F. J. Burton.

JOSEPH WHITWORTH began his career as a toolmaker in Manchester in 1833. He died in January, 1887, with a world-wide reputation as the most eminent producer and designer of precision machine tools. The standards set by his machines are still current today. His standardization of screw threads, dating from the 1840s, still stands.

Problems with the production and performance of the Pattern 1853 Enfield rifle musket, the absence of standardization of tools and gauges, the problem of supply in the face of the Crimean War and its extraordinary demands, led the British government to call upon Whitworth in 1854 to suggest remedies to existing difficulties. Whitworth's exhibits at the Great Exhibition of 1851 had won his international acclaim, and as the nation's most outstanding engineer and machine tool manufacturer it was natural that he should be selected to investigate the standardization and mass-production possibilites of the Enfield works.

In 1854 Joseph Whitworth was not well acquainted with the manufacture of small arms, and in order to familiarize himself with the processes and practices involved he visited most of England's leading gunmakers. His basic conclusion from these visits was that gunmakers proceeded upon little if any actual proven theories, but rather from hit-and-miss experiments and methods learned during their apprenticeships. From this it followed that there was no rational explanation for the irregularities in the performance of the Pattern 1853 Enfield; before Whitworth would undertake to criticize this particular weapon he felt it necessary to establish in his own mind just what the perfect form of rifled small arm should be. From the experiments he conducted to find the answer to this question came the Whitworth rifle and the heavy ordnance so well known, at least in name, to arms collectors today.

It appeared to Whitworth that both the caliber and barrel dimensions of the Pattern 1953 Enfield had been chosen by arbitrary and unscientific methods. It was obvious to him as well that the problems encountered in its performance were due to inaccuracies in the interior of the barrels, possibly even in their basic construction. Whitworth explained his views to the government and offered, if the government would pay his expenses, to conduct a series of tests to determine the best form of small arm for military service. He refused to accept any salary for his work.

In the early stages of his work, Whitworth experimented with a wide variety of rifling twists, calibers, barrel lengths and metals, reaching such extremes as a 20-inch barrel with a twist of one turn in one inch. Whitworth had apparently not examined any other than the standard Enfield 577-caliber barrels, but had seen a polygonally-rifled barrel designed by Isabard Brunel and constructed by Westley Richards. Richards and Whitworth worked closely together during the early stages of Whitworth's work, and much of Whitworth's knowledge of the firearms trade must have been gained from Westley Richards. It was not until the end of 1856 that Whitworth appears to have settled on a design for his rifle; its first official tests came in April, 1857. From

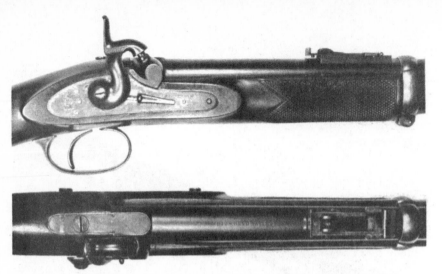

Fig. 3. Military Target Rifle, breech closeup. Note the Enfield style snail, with underside overhanging lockplate, Whitworth trademark on tail of plate, sliding safety bolt and typical WHITWORTH marking above bolt. The rear sight is an early pattern before the rack-and-pinion type was adopted; many of this model are found refitted with a rack-and-pinion sight of an early type. Hammer, trigger guard and trigger, checkering pattern and form of breech (note patent breech but absence of hook breech) are typical of this model. Courtesy E.J. Burton.

this time onwards, the now-familiar hexagonal bore, with a twist of one turn in 20 inches, seems to have been the standard in Whitworth rifles. The tests of 1857 and 1858 proved the far superior accuracy of Whitworth's system against that of the 577 Enfield (which were rifled with three lands and grooves having a twist of one turn in 78 inches, with the depth of rifling gradually decreasing from the breech to the muzzle), but as accuracy was but one of the criteria to be considered in the acceptance of any system for military use, the basic issues were far from solved. Such questions as fouling, tendency to missfire, ease of handling, manufacture of ammunition suitable for military conditions, costs of manufacturing — all seemed to create some doubts in the minds of the investigating committee members. In addition, a small-bore Enfield had performed very nearly as well as the Whitworth rifle, and there was some question whether Whitworth's system might be the only answer.

The Crimean War had been weathered, the national emergency was over, and thoughts of economy were again uppermost in the minds of the government. By 1859 the whole project had been narrowed down to two basic problems. First, would other manufacturers be able to produce the standard of precision required to manufacture Whitworth rifles in some future emergency, if they were to be produced on a large scale? Secondly, Whitworth still asked £10 per rifle for 1,000 or 1,200 rifles, while the Pattern 1853 rifle musket cost £3.5.1 from contractors or £1.19.8 from Enfield ($48.00 for the Whitworth as against $15.44 and $8.48 for the

Pattern 1853 Enfield). Economy won the day and the question of Whitworth vs. Enfield was dropped. It was at this point that Whitworth turned his energies to heavy ordnance rifled upon his hexagonal principle. During the next 5 years a nationwide controversy developed as to the comparative merits of the Whitworth and Armstrong systems. During the Civil War the Confederacy purchased a number of Whitworth field guns and naval cannons in breech-loading and muzzle-loading styles; the Confederate ironclad ram *Stonewall* was armed with two of Whitworth's heavy naval guns.

Concurrently with the military experiments being conducted on behalf of the government, an increased interest in rifle shooting was developing among civilians, culminating in what was termed the "Volunteer Movement." The political friction between England and France present in the 1850s had increased after the conclusion of the Crimean War (in which the two countries had been allied) largely because of the expansionist tendencies of Napoleon III, and the discovery that the Orsini bomb plot against Napoleon had been planned and developed in England. The always invasion-conscious British public, egged on by a ubiquitous and inflammatory press, increasingly clamored for protective measures against possible French invasion.

In 1859 the parliamentary act authorizing the raising and equipping of volunteer corps to fight on English soil, in case of invasion — which had been passed in the Napoleonic Wars period — was regenerated. A rapid rise in the number of rifle companies throughout England resulted.

As of January 1st, 1860, one hundred per cent of such troops would be equipped at government expense if the necessary conditions were met. It soon became obvious that a national organization devoted to the development of accurate rifle shooting was highly desirable, and the National Rifle Association of Great Britain came into being in November, 1859. The first meeting was held at the beginning of July, 1860.

### First Whitworths

At this meeting Queen Victoria fired the opening shot with a Whitworth rifle mounted on a rest. For the next 8 years the Whitworth rifle, in various models, was always among the top contenders for honors at British rifle matches.

Aside from the rifles themselves, the initiative of Joseph Whitworth in creating a superbly accurate rifle (for its time) spurred other gunmakers and inventors into action. The result was a profusion of rifling systems, mostly based on the basic Whitworth principles of a 451-caliber bore with a twist of one turn in 20 inches, firing a 530-gr. bullet. The fact that a number of these systems ultimately succeeded in out-shooting the Whitworth in competition does not detract from the significance of Whitworth's contribution in establishing the basic knowledge, and in taking the first positive steps towards a formerly un-thought of degree of both range and accuracy in military and civilian marksmanship.

In the spring of 1860 experimental rifles were again ordered from Whitworth, but the trials were not actually held until mid-1861. Further trials were held in 1862, and both proved beyond any doubt the superiority of "small bore" (.451" as opposed to .577") weapons so far as accuracy was concerned. Other small bore rifles were tested during these trials, but Whitworth's proved the best of the lot. The Ordnance Select Committee, in charge of the trials, had stressed the importance of putting the rifles into the hands of troops to determine their performance under field conditions. It was with this factor in mind that 1,000 rifles were ordered in May, 1862. As these rifles gave no initial indications of the problems which later developed, a further 8,000 rifles of a slightly different pattern were ordered in 1863. These were issued on a trial basis to a number of British Army units in England and on foreign duty. Despite the official adoption of the Snider breech-loading system in 1865, many of these Whitworth muzzleloaders were still in the hands of troops as late as 1867. Whitworth rifles continued to be used in the firing for the Queen's Prize at Wimbledon through 1870.

To bring his rifling system to the broader attention of the general shooting public, Whitworth entered the commercial market in mid-1859, hoping that success among sportsmen and Volunteers would induce the government to take up the matter of his rifles again. The advent of the National Rifle Association was a Godsend to Whitworth insofar as his civilian market was concerned, for the majority of the prize rifles awarded at N.R.A. meetings for the remainder of the muzzle-loading era were Whitworths.

In 1860 a retailing company known as the Whitworth Rifle Company set up offices at 51, Sackville Street, Manchester. Shortly after receiving the order for 1,000 rifles in May, 1862 (it turned out that only a part of these rifles were produced by Whitworth, aside from the barrels), the firm name was changed to the Manchester Ordnance & Rifle Company, an obvious indication that Whitworth was now actively engaged in the production of cannon. By 1865 the addresses of the Manchester Ordnance & Rifle Company and Joseph Whitworth & Company are combined, indicating that the market in both rifles and heavy ordnance was sufficiently diminished that the operation could be combined under one roof. There is, in fact, considerable doubt that the small arms made with Whitworth's rifling were actually fabricated at any Whitworth works. The barrels were probably the only part of the rifles actually made by the Whitworth firm. In the case of the Pattern 1863 Short Rifles Whitworth made but 1,803 of the 8,203 barrels supplied.

### The Various Models

The rapid rise of the Volunteer movement and Whitworth's desire to keep his rifling system before the eyes of military men brought about the introduction of what was to become the most common of non-military Whitworths — the *military target rifle*. The earliest form of this rifle made its appearance in the summer of 1859, but it would seem that by the time of the formation of the National Rifle Association, and its first meeting in July of 1860, certain modifications and improvements had taken place to produce the rifle in its best-known form (figs. 1, 2 and 3). This is the rifle used in most small bore competitions at Wimbledon, and the rifle which was presented to Queen's Prize winners and numerous runners-up, as well as for other competitions. Many were presented by various organizations, both

civil and military, to members of Volunteer units who had won local or regional competitions. Whitworth thus received a large measure of "free" advertising through the Kingdom.

In basic outline the military target rifle resembles the Pattern 1853 Enfield, but the refinements are legion and the contours more elegant. Some early examples have 33-inch barrels, presumably to conform more closely to the Pattern 1860 Short Rifle, then the standard issue for rifle companies and for sergeants of line regiments. Three barrel bands of normal Enfield clamping pattern hold the barrel to the full length forearm. The steel ram-road is similar to the Enfield, having a slotted head but lacking the concentric rings of the Enfield. Most rifles have a patent breech, but there is no false breech; the tang screw must be removed to take the barrel from the stock. The patent breech is recessed on the left in the manner of contemporary sporting arms, but the tang and snail closely resemble the Enfield; the snail slightly overhangs the lockplate, and generally has borderline engraving (fig.

3). The lock-plate is of Enfield pattern but smaller, and the hammer is a compromise between the heavy military and lighter sporting patterns, generally having Enfield-pattern border engraving. There is a sliding safety bolt forward of the hammer, and two lock screws hold the lock to the stock; Enfield pattern screw cups support the screws on the left of the stock.

The stock is of dark walnut, some examples having fine contrasting colors. It is fitted with steel furniture throughout, consisting of a forearm cap of Enfield pattern, trigger guard similar to the Enfield, round capbox, and Enfield-pattern buttplate. Sling swivels are mounted on the upper barrel band and through the rear of the trigger guard strap. The wrist and forearm are checkered, the diamonds large and coarse compared to later models, but quite typical of contemporary Volunteer rifles. The furniture, excepting the color case-hardened cap-box, is heat-blued.

The sights of the military target rifle present something of a confusing study to the arms collector. As they went from the works the sights were relatively plain,

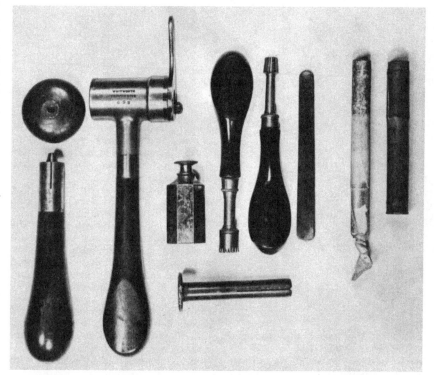

Fig. 4. Typical Whitworth accessories found with military target rifles. Left to right — wooden knob (above) screws onto steel ramrod to aid in loading; base plug for conical bronze one-piece bullet mould; bullet mould with typical Whitworth markings; octagonal steel oil bottle; nipple cleaner; hammer face cleaner; torque bar which fits through slot in head of rod to give a better grip when cleaning or extracting a ball; military Whitworth cartridge; Whitworth's Patent "trap door" cartridge, with military load of 70 grains of black powder and a 530-gr. bullet. Horizontal item at bottom center is hollow bore protector, used when loading and cleaning. Courtesy E.J. Burton.

but because they were the "first of the breed" they later underwent, in many cases, considerable alteration at the hands of not only gunsmith and individual owners, but from the Whitworth firm itself. The original rear sight consisted of a long leaf with platinum-lined notch and slide, graduated to 4° on the left side and 1,000 yards on the right side, both on the bottom of the leaf. There were a number of minor variations in the sight bed; some were virtually flat, or with very slight elevators on either side, while others have one or two distinct steps to the elevators. The front sight was a windage-adjustable blade, a small screw in the center of the front face of the sight base allowing for adjustment.

The great popularity of the Whitworth rifle and its extensive use at N.R.A. meetings led shortly to a refinement of the sighting equipment, and a hooded front sight with pin-ball post replacing the earlier blade. The famous "rack & pinion" rear sight so often seen on Whitworth rifles was patented by Whitworth and Hulse on August 2, 1861, along with a hooded front sight and a combination tool. Whether the sights were actually being produced before the patent was taken out is questionable, but by 1862 the Whitworth Rifle Company was notifying dealers that they would re-equip any of their rifles with the new "Patent Sights," re-finish the barrel, and shoot the barrel with the new sights, for £3,10.0 ($16.80 in 1860 dollars). A large number of the military target rifles are found with this new set of sights, which were fitted at the Whitworth works (or at the works of some gunmakers hired

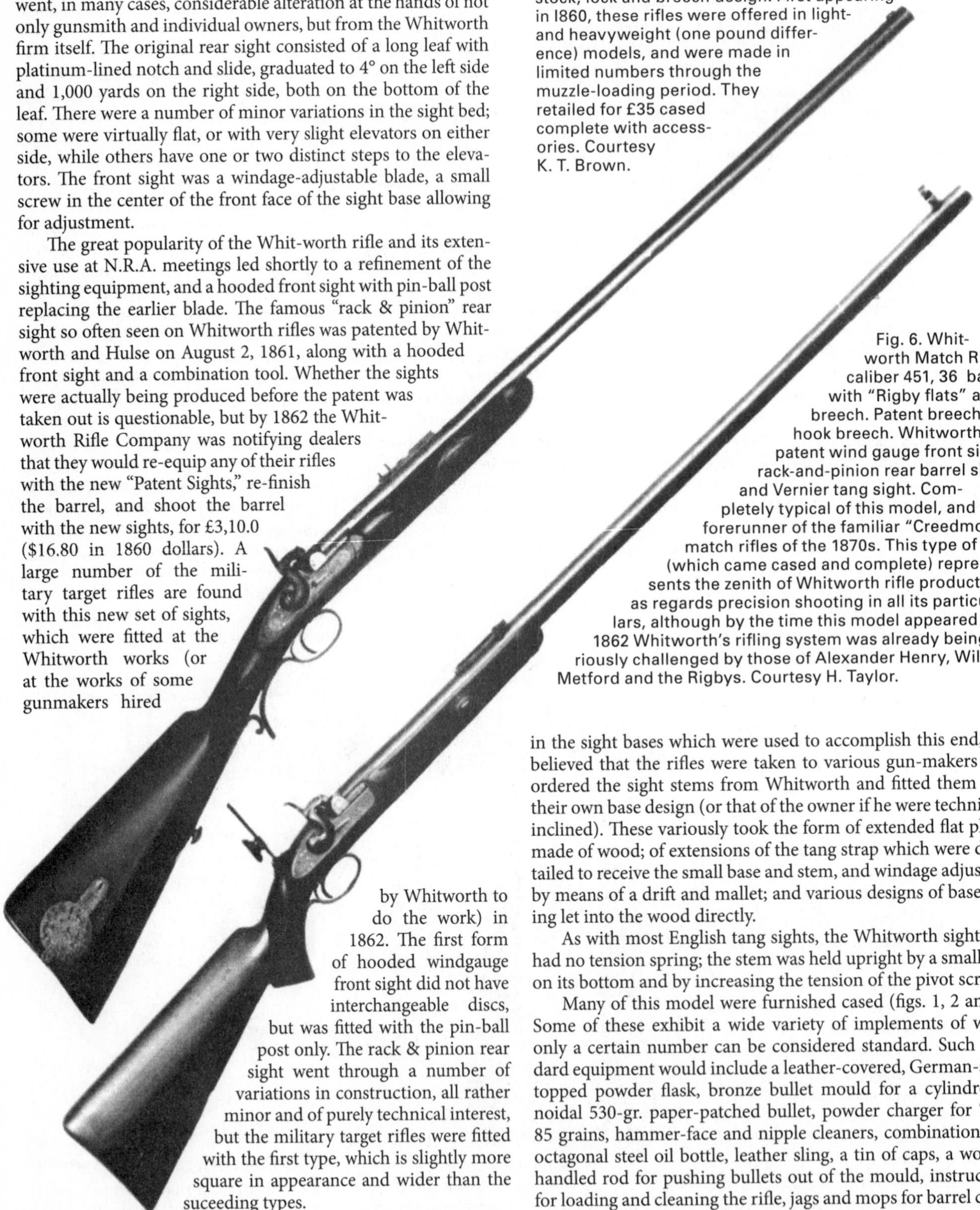

Fig. 5. Early Sporting Rifle with spur guard and 30 barrel. "Cape" rear sight, windage-adjustable "Express" front sights are typical, as are stock, lock and breech design. First appearing in 1860, these rifles were offered in light- and heavyweight (one pound difference) models, and were made in limited numbers through the muzzle-loading period. They retailed for £35 cased complete with accessories. Courtesy K. T. Brown.

Fig. 6. Whitworth Match Rifle, caliber 451, 36 barrel with "Rigby flats" at breech. Patent breech, hook breech. Whitworth's patent wind gauge front sight, rack-and-pinion rear barrel sight and Vernier tang sight. Completely typical of this model, and the forerunner of the familiar "Creedmoor" match rifles of the 1870s. This type of rifle (which came cased and complete) represents the zenith of Whitworth rifle production as regards precision shooting in all its particulars, although by the time this model appeared in 1862 Whitworth's rifling system was already seriously challenged by those of Alexander Henry, William Metford and the Rigbys. Courtesy H. Taylor.

by Whitworth to do the work) in 1862. The first form of hooded windgauge front sight did not have interchangeable discs, but was fitted with the pin-ball post only. The rack & pinion rear sight went through a number of variations in construction, all rather minor and of purely technical interest, but the military target rifles were fitted with the first type, which is slightly more square in appearance and wider than the succeeding types.

The third variation in the sighting equipment of the military target rifle was the fitting of a tang sight. Originally this did not form a part of the sighting equipment, but with the introduction of finer sights on Whitworth rifles, there apparently arose a desire on the part of owners of earlier rifles to have this refinement. In view of the complete lack of uniformity

in the sight bases which were used to accomplish this end, it is believed that the rifles were taken to various gun-makers who ordered the sight stems from Whitworth and fitted them with their own base design (or that of the owner if he were technically inclined). These variously took the form of extended flat planes made of wood; of extensions of the tang strap which were dovetailed to receive the small base and stem, and windage adjustable by means of a drift and mallet; and various designs of bases being let into the wood directly.

As with most English tang sights, the Whitworth sight base had no tension spring; the stem was held upright by a small stud on its bottom and by increasing the tension of the pivot screw.

Many of this model were furnished cased (figs. 1, 2 and 4). Some of these exhibit a wide variety of implements of which only a certain number can be considered standard. Such standard equipment would include a leather-covered, German-silver topped powder flask, bronze bullet mould for a cylindro-conoidal 530-gr. paper-patched bullet, powder charger for 70 or 85 grains, hammer-face and nipple cleaners, combination tool, octagonal steel oil bottle, leather sling, a tin of caps, a wooden handled rod for pushing bullets out of the mould, instructions for loading and cleaning the rifle, jags and mops for barrel cleaning, grease wads (generally hexagonal in form), and a wooden knob with threaded brass center which screwed onto the end of the ramrod to aid in loading, spare platinum-lined nipples and a screwdriver. Items which may be considered as optional in Whitworth cased sets of this and other models would include a bullet swage, a lock brush, packets of hexagonal bullets, a brass muzzle protector for use in loading; a torque bar which fitted through the slotted head of the ramrod to aid in cleaning the barrel, removing bullets when they had been seated without powder, "bad" loads, and so forth; powder chargers which screw on the end of the ramrod to place the entire charge in the breech, patch paper, patent cartridges, mainspring vise, a ball puller and a tompion or muzzle stopper. Sporting and purely target models also included loading rods and short starters, and a double-ended rod having at one end a Whit-worth hexagonal scraper and at the other a brass charger to breech-position the entire powder charge.

The military target rifle sold for £20 ($96 in 1860 dollars) or £25 ($120 in 1860 dollars) cased complete. The cases were of oak, with varnished finish in natural color, and were unlined (figs. 1 and 2).

Concurrently with the introduction of the military target rifle, Withworth made his bid for the deer-stalking market with the introduction of a Sporting Rifle in the summer of 1859. They appear to have enjoyed but limited sale right through to 1866, judging from a study of serial numbers and markings. Despite the relatively long period of production — so far as Whitworth rifles are concerned — these sporting rifles are among the rarest of Whitworths (aside from the experimental models), since Whitworth production seems to have been very largely taken up with military and semi-military style rifles. This emphasis is, of course, quite nat-

ural, since it was the military authorities that Whitworth was primarily interested in impressing.

Whitworth's sporting rifles were very similar to the usual British sporting rifles of the mid-19th century except that they were made only with full round barrels rather than the normal octagon type. They are fitted with a hook or break-off breech, a patent breech design internally, and the snail has a platinum plug. The barrels are blued, the patent breech color case-hardened. The early sporters have 30" barrels, while later rifles have varying lengths down to 28½ inches; 30 inches appears to have been the standard. Another feature typical of the early sporting rifles is the use of a spur trigger guard (fig. 5) rather than a pistol grip stock; the latter feature is found on a few of the later sporting rifles. The furniture, of blued steel, is of typical shotgun pattern, and finally engraved with scroll work and animals. The round capbox is typical. Stocks were of highly polished fine-grained walnut often showing beautiful color contrasts.

The sights of the sporting rifle as they left the works consisted of a long bead "express" front sight which was windage adjustable, and a "Cape" style leaf rear sight having separate leaves folding into the base for 100 and 200 yards, plus a long leaf, with a slide hinged forward of the short leaves, for 300, 400 and 500 yards.

Sporting rifles appear to have been sold only as complete cased sets, as there is no provision for a ramrod on the pro-

duction model. This item was included in the set and carried by the gentleman-sportsman's keeper or bearer. The rifles were offered in "heavy" and "light" weights, 7½ and 6½ pounds respectively. A complete cased outfit consisting of the rifle, "mahogany case, with leather covering … bullet mould, powder flask, 300 rounds of ammunition and a full set of apparatus," sold for £35 ($168 in 1860 U.S. dollars) in either weight.

The continuing growth in popularity of rifle shooting, and the expanding program of the National Rifle Association encouraged Whitworth to further refine and upgrade the appearance of his military target rifles, and the result was the semi-military rifle (fig. 5a), combination of military and sporting features, designed for long range target shooting.

These were first marketed in the late fall of 1861; they appear from the first to have been but a transitional piece. In terms of serial numbers these rifles occur for a brief period just prior to the appearance of the military target rifles with 36" barrels and Baddeley bands. They ceased to be produced about the time the Match Rifle was introduced in the spring of 1862. In point of sales, however, it appears that the supply of military target rifles continued to be sold concurrently with the semi-military rifle. All of the latter type thus far noted are highly finished arms, all having at least some scroll and floral engraving on the locks and mounts, and very fine checkering. Although obviously

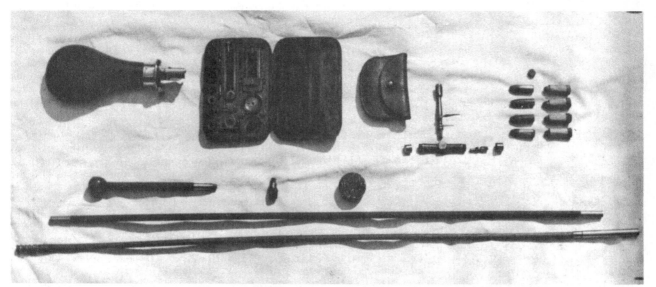

Fig. 7. Whitworth Match Rifle accessories. From left — Patent-top leather covered flask calibrated for two brands of powder; sight case holding wind gauge front, rack-and-pinion rear, and Vernier tang sights, with 8 interchangeable front sight discs, sight-adjusting key, two peep cups (one missing); wallet for small spare parts; combination tool, disassembled; Whitworth hexagonal bullets in various stages from naked to fully cased with wads attached; short starter; hexagonal bore mop; cap tin; loading-cleaning rod; double-ended rod with Whitworth hexagonal scraper on left and charger for placing powder in breech of barrel on right. Courtesy H. Taylor.

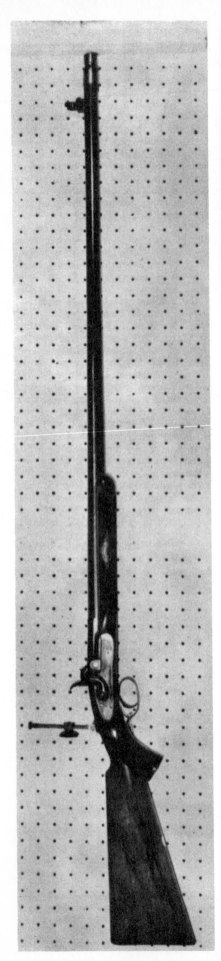

intended as presentation-grade weapons, only a very few of them carry inscriptions or plaques.

The barrel of the semi-military rifle, 36 inches long rather than the 33 inches of the earlier model, is fitted with a sporting pattern breech having three "Rigby" flats and a hook breech. The side of the snail has a platinum plug, and the left side of the patent breech is recessed deeply as on other high-grade sporting arms of the period. The barrel is held to the full length stock with three barrel bands of the type patented by Major J.F.L. Baddeley, R.A., on May 10th, 1861. These bands have smooth outer contours with the screw heads recessed into the band to avoid catching on clothing. The military form of steel ramrod is retained, but of the usual Enfield pattern having both a slotted head and concentric rings, reduced in size to fit 45 caliber. The stock tip remains of the Enfield pattern, but here the military features of the rifle end; the remainder are of a sporting design.

The lock of the semi-military rifle is of the same pattern as the sporting rifle (fig. 5a), but the engraving is not quite as lavish on most examples known. The sliding safety bolt is forward of the hammer, and there is only one lock screw, having a plain circular cup supporting it on the left side of the stock. The tumbler is detented, and rifle rather than musket nipples are used. Those examples known bear the mark WITHWORTH RIFLE CO MANCHESTER on the lower edge of the plate.

The stock is of fine-grained walnut with a lighter color and better contrast than previous models, with a highly polished oil-varnish finish. The checkering is of fine quality and execution. The fore-end is longer between the lock and lover barrel band and displays a greater expanse

of checkering. The furniture is heat-blued throughout and, excepting the stock tip, is of the type found on sporting rifles of the period. The trigger guard has a long checkered spur which acts as a pistol grip, the forward finial being in the form of a round pineapple. The buttplate has a short ornamental top tang, but the two screws securing it to the stock are both on the face of the plate. The capbox is omitted on this model, as on the majority of 36-inch barreled military target rifles.

The sights of this model are virtually identical with those of the match rifle which succeeded it, except that not all semi-military rifles are fitted for tang sights. The front sight, of the Whitworth patent variety, was furnished with at least 8 interchangeable discs of varying types. It was adjustable for windage, a thumb screw entering from the right side. One variation has the discs removable by the use of another thumb screw, while the other makes use of a square key fitting into a flush screw. The windage adjustment screw is also found in these two styles. The rear sight is of rack and pinion style. When a tang sight is present it is of the standard type found on the match rifle (fig. 6).

Judging from the serial numbers there were probably less than 100 of the semi-military rifles produced before Whitworth, in the spring of 1862, abandoned the military style with the introduction of his match rifle. The style of this rifle is what is generally known in the United States as a "Creed-moor" rifle, as it is identical in profile to the Rigby rifles used by the Irish teams at the International Matches held at Creedmoor, New York, beginning in 1874.

The match rifle has a 36-inch full round barrel, with the same patent breech

Fig. 8. Probably made in the mid- or late 1860s, the 36″ round barrel having the three barrel flats usually found on Rigby target rifles. The center or top flat is engraved METFORD'S PATENT 948. GEORGE GIBBS, 29, CORN STREET, BRISTOL, is engraved ahead of the Metford markings, on the top center of the barrel. The case-colored lockplate is marked GEORGE GIBBS also. The nipple boss carries a platinum plug. • The Gibbs serial number, 9764, appears on the trigger guard rear tang. • The Vernier tang sight is calibrated to 4 degrees, in increments of 10 minutes, with **Rad. 37.8** (for the distance between this sight and the front sight) hand engraved on a strip of platinum inlaid into one side of the staff. The front sight is adjustable for windage, takes various discs. • The hard rubber grip cap is fluted in a sunburst design, the hard rubber buttplate grooved crosswise. The fore-end tip is of buffalo horn. • The muzzle has a small pin at its top to take the bayonet-locking slot of the 1¾ long false muzzle. The false muzzle, not common on British match rifles, is rifled with 5 lands, these about the width of the grooves, right hand twist of about one in 30 . This is not Metford's celebrated segmental rifling, but rather his first patented system. It looks much like modern rifling — aside from land width. • The rifle weighs an even 9 lbs. without false muzzle. John Amber's coll.

design and lock as on the semi-military rifle (fig. 6). There is no provision for a ramrod, and the barrel is held to the half-stock by a single wedge or key surrounded by oval steel escutcheons on both sides of the stock. The stock tip is of black horn, as is the grip cap. There is no capbox. The stock is of full pistol grip type, with finely checkered wrist and fore-end. There is an initial plate set into the stock to the rear of the pistol grip. The wood used on match rifles is dark and straight-grained, as was typical on target arms to avoid possible warping.

The sights (fig. 7) consist of the Whitworth patent windgauge front sight, on many rifles the rack and pinion rear barrel sight, and the Whitworth Vernier tang sight. A rear barrel sight is not present on all rifles of this model.

Match rifles were furnished fully cased with loading and cleaning accessories and ammunition. Figs. 6 and 7 show an unusually complete outfit in superb condition. It should be noted that such articles as powder flasks and combination tools and, in fact, all accessories save the bullet moulds (which were not included in target outfits since extruded bullets were considered necessary to first-class accuracy at long range), were not made by Whitworths but were purchased from various contractors in such implements. The great majority are very similar to one another and it is obvious that these tools

were purchased in quantity batches, and that the same contractors were patronized for succeeding purchases; it is not correct, however, to expect one set of implements to be identical to those in another similar cased set. Target Rifles are the only sets in which packets of patched hexagonal bullets should be considered standard rather than optional equipment.

Fig. 8 shows a fine match rifle made by one of Whitworth's chief rivals in the later period. The Gibbs-Metford rifle pictured is described in detail in the caption accompanying it.

At this point in the chronological examination of the various Whitworth models we turn from the best quality target rifle and revert to an issue military rifle: the Pattern 1862 Whitworth Rifle. It was for this rifle that an order of 1,000 stand was placed in May, 1862, but from existing examples it is clear that Whitworth did not manufacture anything close to the total numbers, he may not even have supplied all of the barrels. This rifle is, in fact, correctly termed an *En-field-Whitworth*, as they were set up at the Royal Small Arms Factory at Enfield Lock. There are, however, a number of examples known with commercial markings, (fig. 9) which differ from the issue piece in minor aspects.

The *Pattern 1862 Whitworth* has a 36-inch iron barrel of the usual 451-caliber and rifling characteristics, the barrel being secured by three Bad-deley-pattern barrel bands. As it was made at Enfield, all parts are interchangeable, and in addition all parts excepting the ramrod, stock tip and two forward barrel bands will interchange with the *Pattern 1860 Short*

*Rifle* (so far as lock and furniture are concerned). The Pattern 1862 was intended to conform as closely as possible to the issue *Pattern 1853 Rifle Musket*, and the barrel takes the same bayonet. The front sight is of similar design, while the rear sight is basically similar but adapted for the use of either cylindrical or hexagonal bullets, the latter graduations extending for another 100 yards.

These rifles apparently met with considerable approval upon being issued to various regiments, and it was decided to equip a larger number of troops with the small bore rifle for extensive trials. The result was the *Pattern 1863 Whitworth Short Rifle*. It was decided to use steel rather than iron for the barrels of this model, and in order to keep the weight within limits the barrel length was reduced to 33 inches, thus making it officially a "Short Rifle" even though it was fitted with three barrel bands rather than the normal two. The sword bayonet fastens to the upper barrel band rather than to a standard on the barrel, as it was considered too difficult to weld a sword bar to a steel barrel. This same welding problem caused the snail to be made integral with the barrel, rather than separately as was the normal practice when using iron barrels.

The *Pattern 1863 Whitworth Short Rifle* (fig. 10) is again an "Enfield-Whitworth" even though Whitworth actually finished up 100 of these rifles at Manchester. The steel barrels were obtained from four different contractors, including Whitworth, who supplied 1,497 barrels which bore normal Whitworth serial numbers beneath the barrel as well as the date of setting up.

Fig. 9. Pattern 1862 Whitworth military rifle, a prototype made at Manchester with commercial markings and non-standard trigger guard. The issue model, of which 1,000 were made at Enfield, has normal Enfield trigger guard and lock markings. Standard Enfield pattern ramrod. 36" barrel with three Baddeley barrel bands. Tower of London collection, British Crown copyright.

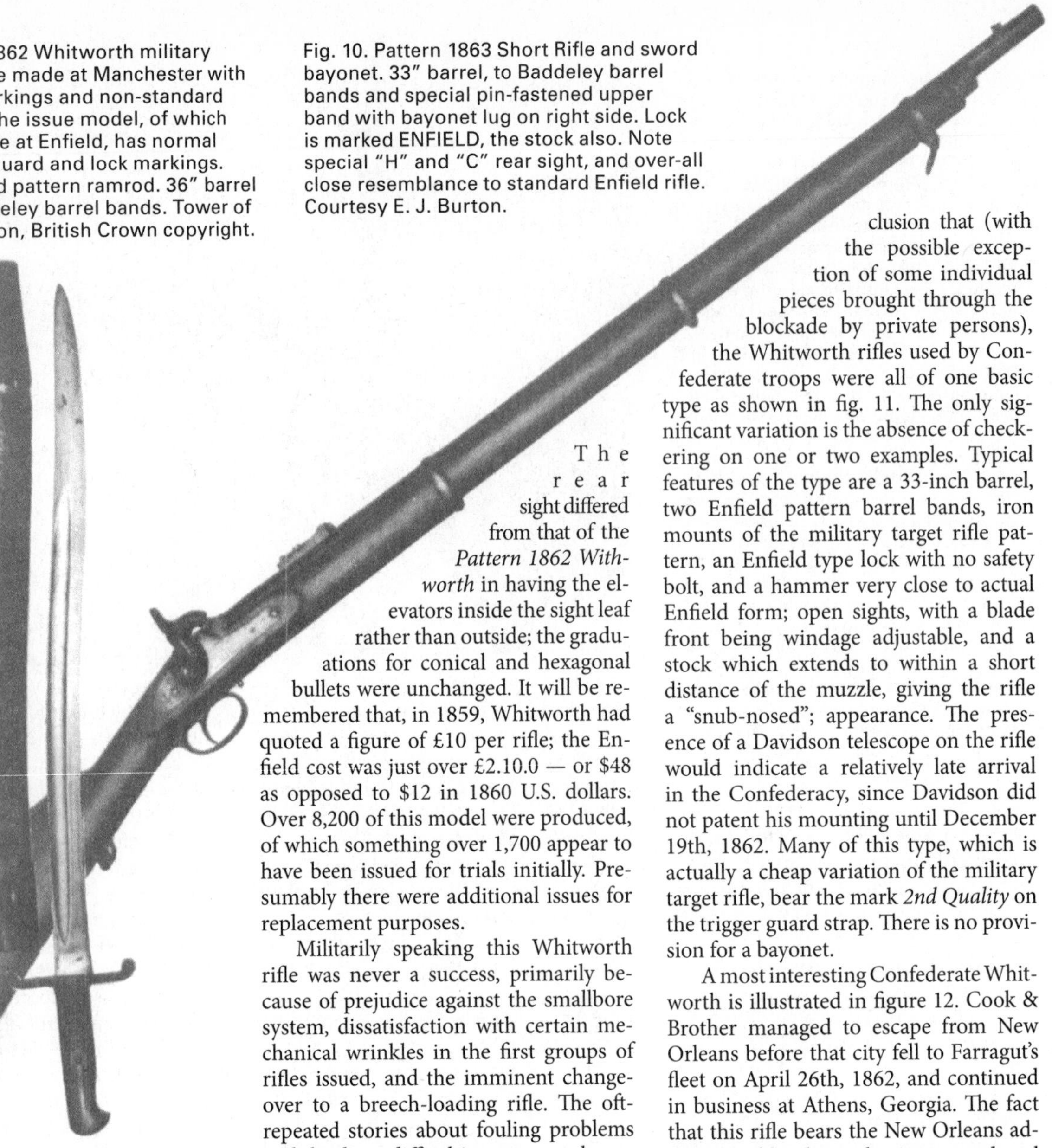

Fig. 10. Pattern 1863 Short Rifle and sword bayonet. 33" barrel, to Baddeley barrel bands and special pin-fastened upper band with bayonet lug on right side. Lock is marked ENFIELD, the stock also. Note special "H" and "C" rear sight, and over-all close resemblance to standard Enfield rifle. Courtesy E. J. Burton.

The rear sight differed from that of the *Pattern 1862 Whitworth* in having the elevators inside the sight leaf rather than outside; the graduations for conical and hexagonal bullets were unchanged. It will be remembered that, in 1859, Whitworth had quoted a figure of £10 per rifle; the Enfield cost was just over £2.10.0 — or $48 as opposed to $12 in 1860 U.S. dollars. Over 8,200 of this model were produced, of which something over 1,700 appear to have been issued for trials initially. Presumably there were additional issues for replacement purposes.

Militarily speaking this Whitworth rifle was never a success, primarily because of prejudice against the smallbore system, dissatisfaction with certain mechanical wrinkles in the first groups of rifles issued, and the imminent changeover to a breech-loading rifle. The oft-repeated stories about fouling problems and loading difficulties are not borne out by the official reports on the trials of these rifles. Aside from obviously prejudiced exceptions the rifles were highly praised on these points from such unlikely areas as India and South Africa. It does not appear that hexagonal ammunition was ever issued in quantity with the military rifles, and in general the troops got on well with them. However, their marksmanship does not appear to have markedly improved over that obtaining with the 577 En-fields, which is rather surprising.

## The Confederate Whitworth

The actual *extent* to which Whitworth rifles were used by Confederate troops during the Civil War is still conjectural, but examination of those rifles known to have been used or at least owned by Confederate personnel, and consideration of their serial numbers, has led to the con-clusion that (with the possible exception of some individual pieces brought through the blockade by private persons), the Whitworth rifles used by Confederate troops were all of one basic type as shown in fig. 11. The only significant variation is the absence of checkering on one or two examples. Typical features of the type are a 33-inch barrel, two Enfield pattern barrel bands, iron mounts of the military target rifle pattern, an Enfield type lock with no safety bolt, and a hammer very close to actual Enfield form; open sights, with a blade front being windage adjustable, and a stock which extends to within a short distance of the muzzle, giving the rifle a "snub-nosed"; appearance. The presence of a Davidson telescope on the rifle would indicate a relatively late arrival in the Confederacy, since Davidson did not patent his mounting until December 19th, 1862. Many of this type, which is actually a cheap variation of the military target rifle, bear the mark *2nd Quality* on the trigger guard strap. There is no provision for a bayonet.

A most interesting Confederate Whitworth is illustrated in figure 12. Cook & Brother managed to escape from New Orleans before that city fell to Farragut's fleet on April 26th, 1862, and continued in business at Athens, Georgia. The fact that this rifle bears the New Orleans address would indicate that it was produced and purchased prior to the fall of New Orleans to Federal forces; this, coupled with the high serial number for the Confederate type (C575) indicates that most of the Whitworth rifles used by the Confederates were manufactured prior to the spring of 1862 — wwhich coincides neatly with already established serial ranges and dates. The rifle itself is typical of the type, but it lacks the checkering found on the majority of this pattern.

## Later Production

Taken as a whole, civilian Whitworth rifle production tapered off sharply after 1862; while a steady trickle of match rifles and sporting rifles appears to have been turned out during the period 1862–1865, the major part of Whitworth's efforts during this period seems to have been devoted to the production of heavy ordnance, government trials of his rifling system in both ordnance and small arms, and his machine-tool business. Small arms production as such seems to have been secondary to those other considerations. It is, however, during this later period that some of the most interesting of Whitworth's rifles, including the 30-caliber sporting rifle, 568-caliber semi-military rifle, and double-barreled sporting rifle were made, all on a very limited basis which might reasonably be called — with the possible exception of the double barreled rifles — experimental production.

The single barreled sporting rifles produced in this later period generally have full pistol grip stocks, as opposed to the earlier rifles with spur trigger guards, and some of the later rifles lack capboxes.

The double-barreled sporting rifles generally have barrels varying from 24 inches to 28 inches, the majority being about 26 inches long. The barrel group is one piece of steel, into which both bores have been drilled, a feature which Whitworth patented in June, 1857. The half-length stocks have a full pistol grip, two pipes for the ramrod, no capbox, and a black horn cap on the pistol grip. The low bead express front sights have windage adjustment, while the rear sights use a series of flip-up leaves for 100 to 500 yards. The locks have sliding safety bolts forward of the hammers.

## Whitworth Production and Serial Numbers

If it is accepted that there are no significant gaps in the indicated serial number ranges of Whitworth rifles, the total number produced with commercial markings would be about 5,000 of all styles, including the early rifles and BSA-marked rifles with Whit-worth-serialed barrels, but excluding the greater part of 1,000 *Pattern 1862 Military Rifles* and all but 1,600 of the 8,200 *Pattern 1863 Short Rifles*; both of these were assembled at Enfield and bear Enfield marks. If these last are included, a grand total of approximately 13,400 Whitworth muzzle loading rifles were

produced from all sources. Those rifles produced under license from Whitworth by such makers as Bissell, Beasley Brothers, and McCririck — which did purport to be honest imitations of Whitworth's rifling — are not included, and would increase the total somewhat.

From a study of existing rifles and fragmentary records, it appears that the serial numbering of Whitworth rifles from their first production in 1857 through the end of the muzzle-loading era and into the breech-loading period proceeded on a regular chronological basis. Having commenced with the number 1, the initial series continued through to 1,000, and then re-commenced with a letter prefix and proceeded through a series of these prefixes as follows:

1 — 1000: first production, 1857 through mid-1860.

B1 — B999: mid-1860 through late 1861.

C1 — C999: late 1861 through mid-1862. If gaps exist it will be in this series.

D1 — D999: spring 1862 to early 1863.

E1 — E999: early 1863 into mid-1864, primarily Pattern 1863 Military Rifles.

F1 — F700: mid-1864 through 1865; after F700 some breechloaders appear in regular numerical order. BSA-marked rifles also occur in this series.

Although there are still some unanswered questions regarding the connections between the Whitworth firm and the Birmingham Small Arms Company, it is clear that Whitworth offered to supply the gun trade with their barrels, in either finished or semifinished state, the latter being rifled only. In 1866 B.S.A. had used Whitworth barrels on their rifles for the N.R.A. and other standard Short Rifle patterns are known with B.S.A. markings and Whitworth serial-numbered barrels; in addition several match rifles of Whitworth profile and rifling have been reported with B.S.A. markings. It is obvious that B.S.A. purchased a batch of barrels from Whitworth in various states of com-

pletion and applied them to a small group of rifles of the several popular styles, in the 1865–66 period.

## Whitworth Markings

With the conspicuous exception of those experimental rifles made throughout the entire production period of Whitworth muzzle-loading rifles, a study of the markings on the rifles relates directly to the serial numbers, and makes the assignment of a production date relatively easy. The early Whitworth rifles, made prior to 1860, bear a variety of non-standard marks, but as most of these include a date on the lockplate, the problem is greatly simplified. There are some individual instances, however, where the date is misleadingly late for the rest of the rifle. Lockplates on these early rifles generally bear the mark WHITWORTH PATENT, plus the serial number and Birmingham proof marks. The lockplate is marked, forward of the hammer and above the safety bolt WITHWORTH 1860 in two lines, or simply WHITWORTH. To the rear of the hammer appears the Whitworth crest (a crowned wheatsheaf), a W sometimes appearing beneath the wheatsheaf. The great majority of locks used on Whitworth rifles, even some of the plain military rifles, were made by Joseph Brazier of Wolverhampton; this is shown in some form generally on the inside of the lockplate. This may be his initials — *JB* or *IB* — to the most elaborate form noted so far: *JOSEPH BRAZIER ASHES*, the latter word being the name of Brazier's works.

At the very end of the production period for military target rifles (during which time the "Second Quality" rifles of this type were being made), the lock markings change to WHITWORTH RIFLE Co. MANCHESTER, with the Whitworth crest behind the hammer. This mark continues in use, along with the WHITWORTH PATENT marking on the breech of the barrel, through the period of the semi-military rifle and the early production of the match rifle.

Fig. 11. A Confederate Whitworth with 33 barrel. Except for the Davidson telescope, in typical side mount, the rifle seems a standard Confederate Whitworth in all features. Some are without checkering. Note snub-nosed appearance, two Enfield barrel bands, and early-pattern adjustable open sights. Enfield-pattern lock. Courtesy Tennessee State Museum.

The long Vernier-system folding tang sight is engraved on the rear of the staff, T. MURCOTT GUNMAKER (on one side), with 68 HAYMARKET LONDON N° 509 on the other.

The picture of the muzzle area shows the deep chamfering of the hexagonal rifling and the form of the slotted steel ramrod.

The 33″ barrel is full round, shows double Birmingham proof marks, the serial number 937, and is marked WHITWORTH PATENT at the top rear.

The walnut stock shows good figure, and is coarsely checkered at wrist and ahead of the lockplate. Weight of the Whitworth rifle shown is 9½ pounds. John Amber's collection.

This 451 caliber Whitworth rifle was probably made in mid-1860 in view of the style of markings on the lockplate — WHITWORTH RIFLE C° MANCHESTER — and the serial number 937, without letter prefix, on the barrel. The rear barrel sight is of the Vernier type (double pinions and pinion bar are missing); the front sight dove-tail base once held a globe or hooded sight container with windage control knob, these also gone. These sights were added later, perhaps, by Whitworth, using the style patented by Whitworth and Hulse in late 1861. The right side of the rear barrel sight base is marked WHITWORTH/RIFLE Co. PATENT, while the top of the folding leaf is graduated on the right side 1 through 12 for 100 to 1200 yards; the left side is marked 10, 20, 30 and 40 for minutes of angle.

Shortly before the conclusion of the C-prefix serial number range, the lock marks change to MANCHESTER ORDNANCE & RIFLE Co.; and this marking continues through the D- and E- or F-prefix serial ranges, being found almost entirely on Pattern 1862 and 1863 military rifles, and on match rifles. The WHITWORTH PATENT mark on the breech of the barrel is retained, as is the Whitworth crest to the rear of the hammer, with and without the W beneath.

The Pattern 1862 Rifle and the Pattern 1863 Short Rifles made at Enfield bear standard Enfield markings for the period; the date is stamped over ENFIELD forward of the hammer, and a crowned *VR* on the tail of the lockplate. The barrel breeches of both military models bear the mark WHITWORTH PATENT. Where the barrels were supplied by the Whitworth firm a normal D-, E- or F- prefix serial number will appear on the underside of the barrel, generally accompanied by a figure such as 6/63, indicating that the rifle was set up in June, 1863.

In the later production period there was considerable mixing of markings, particularly on sights and sight parts. It is not uncommon that a rifle bearing MANCHESTER ORDNANCE & RIFLE CO. markings on the lock will have WHITWORTH RIFLE Co. on the sight base of the rear barrel sight and the stem of the Vernier tang sight. Similarly, a few rifles bearing THE WHITWORTH COMPANY LIMITED on the lockplate will have MANCHESTER ORDNANCE & RIFLE CO. on the above-mentioned sight parts.

In the final production period of Whitworth muzzle-loading rifles, the lock and barrel markings change almost entirely. The Whitworth crest is the only hold-over from previous patterns. The lock markings in the very high E-prefix serial range and throughout the F-prefix range read THE WHITWORTH COMPANY LIMITED, while the markings on the barrel are changed to WHITWORTH MANCHESTER in a circle or oval form. Some of the very last Whitworth muzzleloaders have J. WHITWORTH & Co. Manchester on the lockplate. As this was the firm name of Whitworth's machine tool business, this would seem to indicate nearly the end of Whitworth's production of firearms. An early breech-loading double rifle by Whitworth is marked in a similar manner, with the trade label of the case reading "JOSEPH WHITWORTH & COMPANY Patentees and Manufacturers of WHITWORTH RIFLED ORDNANCE, SMALL ARMS & SPORTING GUNS. General Machine and Tool Manufacturers. Works, Chorlton Street, Manchester, London Office, 28, Pall Mall, S.W." This rifle follows closely upon the serial number of the last muzzleloaders, and there is no evidence at present known to prove that production of breechloaders was long continued.

Whitworth's essay into the field of small arms seems never to have gone beyond the scientific and theoretical stage in his own mind. Commercially speaking very little was done by Whitworth to advance the sales of his rifles. Contemporary literature on the topic is noticeable by its scarcity, advertising nil. The success of this rifling system and the presentation of so many of his earlier rifles as prizes went far towards advertising, but quite clearly the rifles themselves were only a vehicle for his system, and a bid for government work. It is curious that while Whitworth's reputation for the introduction of standardization in mechanical and industrial processes is so great, his rifles were no better in construction than any other eminent gunmaker of the time: the parts will not interchange in any respect. Some sights will, by pure luck, fit more than one rifle, but lock parts and furniture all exhibit minor variations to a degree precluding interchangeability. Those military rifles made at Enfield upon Whitworth's system will, of course, interchange to conform to government standard, as will other Enfield rifles made after 1858. All major parts appear to have been obtained through the gun trade, Whitworth manufacturing the barrels only (even this point remains controversial), and the rifles were set up at one point following the normal procedures of the time. Although Whitworth took out several patents dealing with small arms and their appurtenances between 1854 and 1865, very few of the items covered appear to have been produced or used. Even implements peculiar to Whitworth rifles (such as the patent combination tool and hexagonal wad punches appear to have been made in lots by more than one contractor, and there are consequently very few accessories which can positively be labelled as "Whitworth tools," as will be noted in the illustrations.

The place of the Whitworth rifle in the history of rifled longarms and ballistic history is of paramount importance. Sir Joseph Whitworth (he was made a baronet in 1869), through analytical study which had never before been applied to the science of firearms design, demonstrated what could be done with elongated projectiles and precision machining; so well did he succeed in his efforts that he spurred the entire British gun trade into a period of experimental production

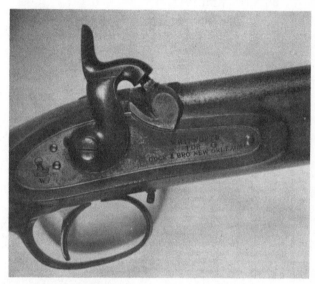

Fig. 12. Confederate-marked Whitworth, possibly unique. Made for Cook & Brother before they evacuated New Orleans in April, 1862. The crowned wheatsheaf on the lockplate's tail is a Whitworth trademark. Courtesy Weller & Duffy Ltd.

the likes of which had not been previously witnessed. As a result of the standards for accuracy set by Whitworth's rifles, other gunmakers tried system after system — there were at least two dozen, all primarily variations of the basic Whitworth system of 45-caliber barrels with a twist of one turn in 20 inches and polygonal rifling — to equal or excel the Whitworth. This led to the ultimate development of such systems as those of William Metford and Alexander Henry, which led the world not only in civilian shooting but in military marksmanship and long range accuracy well into the 20th century.

The writer wishes to express his sincere gratitude to Dr. C. H. Roads for permission to use certain facts and figures concerning the experimental and military Whitworth rifles, contained in his superb volume, *The British Soldier's Firearm, 1850–1864*, and to those gentlemen who kindly furnished photographs of rifles in their collections.

# Spencer's Great '7-Shooter

■ Norman B. Wiltsey

TWENTY-one-year-old Christopher Spencer was working at Colt's in Hartford, Connecticut, when the idea of his repeating rifle occurred to his fertile brain. The year was 1854. While several repeating rifles were already on the market, including Colt's revolving - cylinder percussion rifle, Spencer envisioned a repeating rifle of a daringly different type, one that used metallic cartridges. As there was no such rifle in existence at the time, he had nothing to work with but his keen imagination and the gunsmithing that was in his blood. His grandfather, Josiah Hollister, had been an armorer with the Continental Army in the Revolution and, over the years, had imbued young Chris with an enthusiasm for firearms — his skills, too, he had passed on to his eager grandson.

"Don't be afeared to take a chance on somethin' new," the ancient craftsman had told Chris. So, in 1855, Spencer followed his grandfather's advice, quitting Colt's and going to work at the Cheney Silk Mills in Manchester. Here he was invited to work out his "somethin' new" in the plant machine shop — on his own time, of course.

The going was painfully slow. Spencer's spare time for the next several years was spent in making drawings, then various parts of the projected rifle in wood. Finally he was ready to construct his model — Josiah Hollister would have been proud of it. It was so smoothly assembled that Chris and his employers were sure it would work; sure Chris had developed a weapon that would be invaluable to the nation as it moved inevitably toward the holocaust of approaching war.

## Spencer's Patent

On March 6, 1860, U. S. Patent 27,393 was granted to C. M. Spencer. The exact wording of the application read as follows:

"My invention consists of an improved mode of locking the movable breech of a breech-loading firearm whereby it is easily opened and closed and very firmly

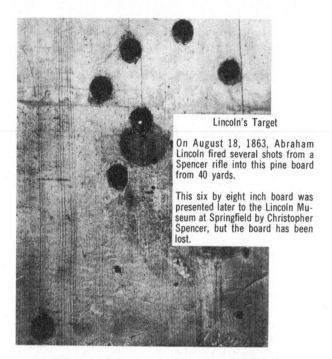

**Lincoln's Target**

On August 18, 1863, Abraham Lincoln fired several shots from a Spencer rifle into this pine board from 40 yards.

This six by eight inch board was presented later to the Lincoln Museum at Springfield by Christopher Spencer, but the board has been lost.

secured in place during the explosion of the charge. It also consists of certain contrivances for operating in combination with a movable breech for the purpose of withdrawing the cases of the exploded cartridges from the chamber of the barrel and for conducting new cartridges thereinto from a magazine located in the stock."

Briefly, Spencer's revolutionary new repeater was a 7-shot lever action arm; the tubular magazine with in the stock loaded from a trap in the buttplate. J. O. Buckeridge, author of the documentary story of the Spencer, *Lincoln's Choice* [1], describes the action in these words: "... The breech-block, a quarter-circle of steel with a groove on top, was hinged to the box-like frame by a screw at its lower front corner. Whenever the block was lowered by the lever attached to it, a heavy coil spring in the magazine pushed a cartridge onto the groove. The groove served as a cartridge carrier or track. The single motion of raising the lever eased the cartridge into the rear of the barrel and closed the breech. All that remained was to cock the ham-

mer and pull the trigger. A flick of the lever opened the breech, ejected the empty, and lined up a fresh cartridge."

The Spencer's magazine, being within the stock, could not be damaged if the weapon was dropped or accidentally struck against a rock or tree — most important, neither could the copper-cased cartridges. The finger lever served also as a trigger guard; in the patent drawings, a spring-catch locked the lever against accidental opening, but Civil War Spencers do not have this feature. The early Hartford-made smaller Spencers, however, do have a spring that keeps the lever closed, though the patent drawing catch was not fitted. Aside from its unorthodox appearance, the main disadvantage of the new rifle was the awkward fact that it was slow to load — one cartridge at a time. This serious drawback was later corrected with the introduction of Blakeslee's patent cartridge box. This handy device carried ten tubes of cartridges, each tube holding seven cartridges and each tube loadable as a unit.

While Spencer's rifle-design was

ready for the Union forces at the outbreak of the Civil War in April of 1861, it still required refining and revision for mass production.* The problem was to convince the top brass of its practical value. Any inventor who has ever tried to convince high government officials of the value of anything really new can readily appreciate how great was Spencer's problem. Yet, insurmountable as it seemed, it had to be faced. Backed by his friend and partner Charles Cheney, Chris screwed his courage up to invade official Washington.

Gideon Welles, Secretary of the Navy, was a friend and neighbor of Cheney's. This fact helped set up an interview with the busy Secretary. The result was a test of Spencer's repeater at the Washington Navy Yard in June, 1861.

Spencer, as per the rigid conditions of the test, fired his rifle 250 times without cleaning the barrel, on two successive days. The weapon's calculated rate of fire was 15 shots per minute, but Chris exceeded his own estimate by getting off 21 rounds per minute. The Navy officers present were vastly impressed. Commander (later Rear Admiral) John A. Dahlgren, inventor of the famous Dahlgren naval cannon, was so enthusiastic over the Spencer that Capt. Andrew A. Harwood, then Chief of Navy Ordnance, ordered 700 Spencers.

Lincoln visited the Navy Yard the following day, but whether he saw the Spencer then or a short time later is not clear. Bruce (*Lincoln and the Tools of War*) says that Lincoln fired the Spencer carbine some short time later, emptying two magazines-ful into a piece of paper at a "few score feet." Lincoln had whittled a front sight out of wood, one he felt to be an improvement, and used this carved foresight on the Spencer that late evening in

---

[1] Harrisburg, Pa., 1956.

*Spencer had considerable difficulty in living up to his later contracts because of production problems; some of them, certainly, because Spencer himself pressed for numerous changes and modifications in his design.

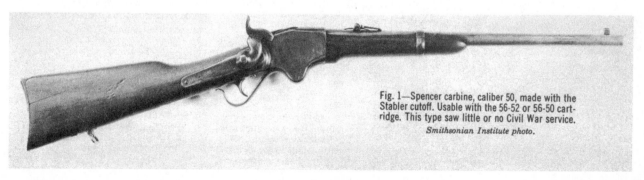

Fig. 1—Spencer carbine, caliber 50, made with the Stabler cutoff. Usable with the 56-52 or 56-50 cartridge. This type saw little or no Civil War service.
*Smithsonian Institute photo.*

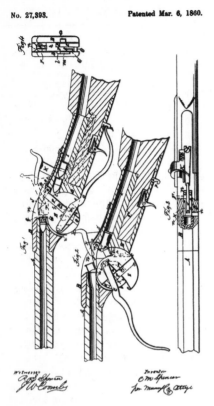

C. M. SPENCER.
Magazine Gun.

No. 27,393.     Patented Mar. 6, 1860.

Fig. 2 — Spencer's original patent, No. 27,393, issued March 6, 1860. Note "M", sawblade cartridge extractor and "p", lever lock, neither of which is found on Civil War Spencers. The saw-edge extractor, however, is used on the early Hartford-made smaller Spencers.

Washington.

(It has not been possible to document this alleged earlier meeting of Lincoln and Spencer, or of Lincoln's shooting the Spencer in 1861. Spencer left no record of such a meeting, whereas he did, as we shall see, record in detail his later meeting with the President in 1863.)

Captain A. B. Dyer, of Army Ordnance (later Brig. Gen. Dyer and Chief of Ordnance), tested the new rifle further at Fortress Monroe, Virginia, in August of 1861.

"I fired in all some 80 times," he reported. "The loaded piece was laid on the ground and covered well with sand to see what would be the effect of getting sand into the joints. No clogging or other injurious effects appeared to have been produced. The lock and lower part of the barrel were then covered with salt water and left exposed for 24 hours. The rifle was then loaded and fired without difficulty ... I regard it as one of the very best breech-loading arms that I have ever seen."

## The Small Spencers

Nowhere, however, in his report did Captain Dyer designate the caliber of this original Spencer. There is no doubt that it was handmade.

This rifle used in the Navy trials may well have been, in fact, *a 36 caliber rimfire.* Spencer's early rifles, made prior to his contract-arms production in Boston, were *smaller* (about three-fourths the scale of the Civil War weapon) and of 36 rimfire caliber. Three of these smaller Spencers are in the Winchester collection and another, serial number 13, is illustrated in fig. 5.

The small Spencers are marked C. M. SPENCER/HARTFORD, CT./PATd MAR. 6, 1860, in a style suggesting hand-stamping. Spencer lived in nearby South Manchester. The stamping on production Spencers of Boston manufacture is: SPENCER REPEATING-/RIFLE CO. BOSTON, MASS./PATd. MAR. 6, 1860.

These smaller 7-shooters are also distinguished by their cartridge extractor; on these models this is a saw-toothed segment riding in a slot in the bottom of the chamber.

As the lever is dropped, the rounded edge of the breechblock carries this saw-edge back, thus catching the rim of the cartridge and pulling it from the chamber.

Further evidence that these smaller 7-shooters were indeed the type used in early (1861) tests is given

Fig. 3 — This drawing of the Spencer 7-shooter, published in the "Scientific American" for January 25,1862, shows modifications over Spencer's original patent design — note extractor (c) pivoted at the left side, the absence of a locking catch for the lever and the single-finger loop of the lever, identical with the loop on the 38 rimfire smaller Spencers.

by Capt. Dyer. He wrote, following his severe tests of the Spencer, that the only improvement he "could suggest was to make the extracting *ratchet* of tempered steel to reduce wear."*

## Spencer Calibers

Most writers have designated the Spencer arms and ammunition used in the Civil *War* as caliber 56-52, but no less an authority than Col. B. R. Lewis (U.S.A., Ret'd.), author of *Small Arms and Ammunition in the United States Service*, had this to say in a letter to the editor dated January 4, 1961:

"Those dimensions (bullet size, bore diameter and chamber size) for the 56-56 Spencer were: .55", .52" and .564". The cartridge measured .56" and was nearly a straight case. Spencer used cal. 52 barrels because Sharps made them for him ... There were other Sharps parts used in the early Spencers also."

"The 56-56 was *the* cartridge used in the Civil War Spencers. The 56-50 was the "ideal" cartridge worked up at Springfield but adopted too late to make much difference in the War, though a lot of that size was bought (and became surplus right after). About 1866-67 Spencer improved the 56-50 a bit by removing the excessive crimp and giving it a slight bottleneck. This was called the 56-52, and was interchangeable in 56-52 and 56-50 rifles, both of which had a .50" barrel diameter. Spencer never promoted the 56-50 commercially, and the Army never used the 56-52 cartridge. So — the CW Spencers were 56-56, the tail-end of the War M1865 Spencers the 56-50, and that size continuing in the postwar years with cal. 50 Spencers. The 56-52 was strictly a sporting cartridge but usable in the 56-50 arms."

Buckeridge mentions also that the Sharps Rifle Company "gaveSpencer a barrel and a few common parts," to help out in the construction of his first model, but does not name the caliber. Philip B. Sharpe, in *The Rifle in America*, states that the original Spencer "was turned out in caliber .52 using the standard No. 56 rimfire cartridge which by 1867 was called the .56-56" and goes on to say: "This particular rifle in the hands of collectors (sic) is fitted with a Sharps rear sight bearing the markings R. F. Lawrence Pat. Feb. 15, 1859, and was probably made in the Sharps factory from Sharps rifle parts. It may have been one of his (Spencer's) experimental jobs before he got into actual production.

Mrs. Charles F. Taylor, daughter of the

---

*Bruce, op cit.

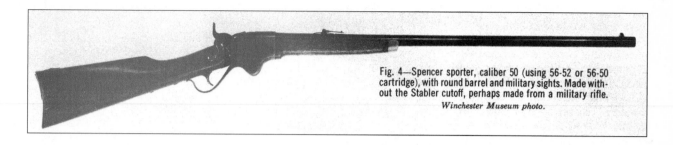

Fig. 4—Spencer sporter, caliber 50 (using 56-52 or 56-50 cartridge), with round barrel and military sights. Made without the Stabler cutoff, perhaps made from a military rifle.
*Winchester Museum photo.*

inventor, has no idea of the whereabouts of the original model and doubts that it exists. If it is indeed "in the hands of collectors," firearms historians would be grateful if the owner or owners of it would make public a detailed description of it, including the caliber.

Winston Churchill called the Civil War "the last gentleman's war." That it may have been, but it was also the first modern war. The camera, the telegraph, and — most important of all to the ruthless concept of total destruction of enemy manpower — the repeating rifle; all made their debut in this most costly in numbers of casualties of all American wars. Three repeating rifles were used in varying numbers by the Northern troops; the Colt, the Henry, and Chris Spencer's 7-shooter. Of the three, the Spencer was finally judged to be the best by both field and staff officers. But it did not win the confidence it merited from the top military brass until the war was half-over. The Navy accepted the 7-shooter at once, following the rigid tests given the weapon by Captain Dyer, but the great contract with the Army that Spencer had hoped for since he assembled his first successful model took two years to accomplish.

## Ripley Rejects the Spencer

Just why this was so is clouded in mystery, but it is known that Brigadier General James W. Ripley, Chief of Army Ordnance until after Gettysburg, rejected the odd-looking repeater without giving it a second look. Ripley was "old Army" in every reactionary sense of the word, favoring muzzle-loaders for Federal troops and even advocating the use of smoothbores over the rifled musket. To Ripley's scornful refusal to see any merit in a weapon he scathingly termed a "new-fangled jimcrack" may be credited the fact that Spencers did not get into the hands of Northern soldiers in large quantity until after his replacement as Chief of Army Ordnance.

Despite Ripley, Spencer sought the President's help, and on December 26, 1861, Lincoln instructed General Ri-

ple to order 10,000 Spencer rifles. The Spencer-Cheney group accepted this first sizable order on the last day of 1861.

Had the 7-shooter been adopted for general Army use earlier in 1861 — and furnished in really large numbers — there can be no doubt that the war would have been measurably shortened and many thousands of lives saved.

This bitter fact is even harder to to understand when one realizes that the Federal troops were outgunned by the small arms of the Confederacy all through the first two years of the war. Old flintlock muskets converted to percussion comprised the arms of whole Northern regiments. Many cavalry regiments were armed with nothing but sabers and huge smoothbore horse pistols. Conversely, the largely rural South sent troops into the field armed with rifles they had used since boyhood. These men, crack shots for the most part, represent one reason for the disproportionately large casualties suffered by the North in the early battles of the war. The other reason was the sheer timidity and inefficiency of Union generals. Disgusted with their leaders, doubly disgusted with muzzle-loading muskets that required nine separate, distinct and dangerously time-consuming operations to load and fire, it is a marvel that Northern troops did not desert in droves instead of driblets.

Gradually, armament conditions improved as the appalling Federal casualty lists soared. The Government bought 90,000 Sharps breechloaders, nearly 2000 Henry 16-shot repeaters, and a few thousand Colt's revolving percussion rifles and Berdan telescopic rifles. Bedeviled buyers from Army Ordnance went abroad to purchase 500,000 British Enfield muzzle-loaders, similar in effectiveness to the hopelessly outdated Springfields; picked up another half-million inferior Belgian and Austrian muskets. Small wonder that the angry Colonel of a New York regiment called his poorly trained city boys "poor, damned, doomed devils!" upon receipt of such wretched arms.

All this time, Chris Spencer and his

associates were frantically trying to get Army Ordnance experts to at least try his seven-shooter — to no avail! There was, however, one ray of hope to the young inventor. While the pompous "Colonel Blimps" of the War Department followed General Ripley's lead and professed to see no merit in the new repeater, the officers in the field exhibited keen interest. Colonel C. P. Kingsbury demonstrated the rifle to General-in-Chief McClellan in the fall of 1861, and subsequent tests by a special Army board appointed by McClellan — which included an officer from the Ordnance Department — brought a recommendation that the light Spencer carbine be issued "in limited numbers" to mounted troops in the field for trial. There is no evidence to indicate that the report got beyond the waste-basket in General Ripley's office.

But Spencer was not one to give up in face of repeated rebuffs. Working through his friend Cheney, Chris again enlisted the aid of the Secretary of the Navy, Gideon Welles. The Secretary, in turn, deftly tossed the ball to James G. Blaine, Speak-

Christopher Miner Spencer (June 20, 1833 - January 14, 1922) when he was 30 years old. Photo courtesy Mrs. C. F. Taylor (Vesta Spencer), daughter of the great inventor.

er of the House of Representatives and a New Englander himself. The result of the maneuvering was a meeting between Spencer, Blaine and Welles late in 1861, and an order by the Secretary of the Navy for 10,000 7-shooters *for the Army!* Obviously Secretary Welles took a calculated risk of official censure in placing the order for a branch of the Service other than the Navy, but he cagily minimized the risk by prevailing upon the Assistant Secretary of War Thomas A. Scott to share the responsibility by counter-signing the paper. As we have seen above, Lincoln insisted that Ripley confirm this order.

The 6th Michigan Cavalry, Col. James H. Kidd commanding, was one of the first Federal units to be armed with the 7-shooter out of this lot of 10,000 manufactured at the Boston factory in 1862. None were delivered until the close of 1862.

"… If the entire army had been supplied with it the war would not have lasted 90 days," was Col. Kidd's glowing estimate of the effectivness of the Spencer.

The first skirmish in Chris Spencer's frustrating battle to get his rifle recognized and accepted by the Army had been won. Yet Army Ordnance remained adamant, blocking his efforts to see President Lincoln and to demonstrate the new repeater to him personally. Not until after Gettysburg, in which three Spencer-armed regiments provided the winning edge for the hard-pressed Northern forces, was the inventor able to arrange a meeting with Lincoln.

Blakeslee's patent loading tubes for the Spencer repeater. Ten tubes, each holding seven cartridges, were carried in this tin-wood-leather box.

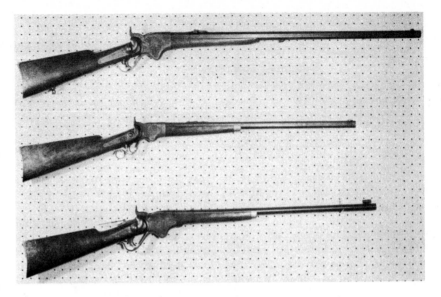

Fig. 5 — Three Spencer sporters. Top — full octagon bbl. is 32" long, cal. 56-46, 5-groove rifling makes one turn in 26", right twist. Length overall, 48¾", serial no. 34198. Wt., 12 lbs. Because of the 5-groove bbl., and the existence of the sling-ring base on this rifle, it is doubtful that the Spencer Co. made it.

Middle — Spencer sporting rifle in the early small-action form, doubtless made prior to any production arms. The octagon-top receiver is marked C. M. SPENCER/HARTFORD, CT./PATd. MAR. 6, 1860, in three lines. The full octagon bbl. is 24" long, and is without marks. Caliber is 36 (approx. groove dimension); five-land rifling, lands about half the groove width, rate of twist one turn in 44 inches, right hand. The action of this early specimen, numbered 13, is 27/16" deep compared to the production Spencer's depth of 33/16". The central saw-edge extractor, part of Spencer's original patent, is found in this sporter. Length over-all, 40 5/8"; wt., 8 lbs.

Lower-Full round bbl. is 25 7/8" long, rifled with 6 grooves making one turn in 30", right twist. A simple (non-graduated) folding tang sight, and a globe front sight are fitted. Serial no. 8386 appears on the top tang and underneath the bbl. Number 7 also is seen underneath the bbl., and in several places on the action parts. An unusual feature is a push-forward set-trigger, seemingly original. Length over-all, 42½";wt., 9½ lbs.

## Spencers in Action

It is, of course, impossible here to cover every Civil War engagement in which the Spencer played an important role; highlights only may be noted. The bloody battle of Antietam was the grim theater for the initial appearance of the 7-shooter in American land warfare. Sergeant Lombard, 1st Massachusetts Cavalry, fired the first shots from a Spencer on the day of the great battle, September 17, 1862. This weapon, handmade by Chris Spencer, had been presented to Sergeant Lombard by the inventor early in the same month, when the 1st Massachusetts had been camped near Washington.

Both the Blue and the Gray lost heavily in the indecisive battle of Antietam, but the Federal troops stopped Lee's first attempt to invade the North. General Lee would not try again until the climactic battle of Gettysburg marked the high tide of Southern military fortunes the following summer.

In the winter of 1862–1863, Spencer roamed the Western front of the war, doggedly trying to sell his improved repeater* to individual commanders. At Murfreesboro, Tennessee, the inventor demonstrated his repeater to General Rosecrans and his staff. Impressed, Rosecrans regretfully

---

*Incorporating extractor changes (see U. S. Patent 36062, issued to C. M. Spencer July 29, 1862).

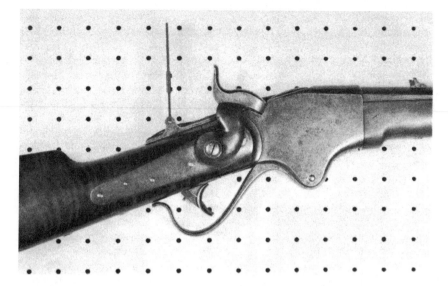

Fig. 6 — Close up of Spencer sporter number 8386 (pictured on these pages elsewhere), showing set trigger. Set-screw in rear of trigger adjusts weight of let-off pull.

informed Spencer that he could not obtain the approval of the War Department to arm his men with the new weapon. But Colonel John T. Wilder ordered 4000 of the 7-shooters for his own brigade.

Army Ordnance flatly refused to honor Colonel Wilder's order. Furious, Wilder asked his men if they would pay for the Spencers with their own money. The brigade voted "Yes" to a man. The Colonel endorsed their notes and made good on all losses incurred. Each rifle cost $35 and most of the men paid off their notes in full — if they lived through the heavy fighting that followed. The 4000 Spencers shipped to Wilder's men from the Boston factory upped the total to almost 10,000 7-shooters in action in the Western campaign in that memorable summer of 1863. On June 24, Wilder's cavalry won their immortal title of "The Lightning Brigade" when the flashing volleys of their deadly Spencers routed the Rebs from Hoover's Gap in the Cumberland Mountains, opening the way for the smashing Federal victory at Chickamauga a few weeks later.

The battle of Gettysburg found 3500 Spencers in the hands of Federal cavalrymen. Jeb Stuart's famous cavalry, 10,000 strong, clashed with the four regiments of the Michigan Brigade led by General Kilpatrick on June 30, 1863, at Hanover, 14 miles southeast of Gettysburg, to start the action. Flamboyant George Armstrong Custer, recently promoted to Brigadier General, was in the forefront of the fighting that historic day at Hanover. His Spencer-armed 5th and 6th Michigan

regiments, aided by the 1st West Virginia Cavalry, poured out such a volume of fire that Stuart's gray-clad legions were forced to swing wide of Lee's main army to Carlisle, 35 miles to the north.

Thus, on the eve of the crucial battle of the war, Lee was deprived of "the eyes of my army," dashing Stuart and his hard-riding, fanatically dedicated troopers. Stuart did not reach Gettysburg until the evening of July 2nd, too late for his weary cavalrymen to perhaps turn the tide for Lee and the Confederacy.

On July 3, the third and last day of the titanic struggle, the deadly Spencer played its usual role of "stopper," checking and finally shattering the stubborn Gray advance. The gallant Confederate soldier, with his archaic muzzle-loader, was now outclassed.

The crushing defeat at Gettysburg signalled the beginning of the end for the Confederacy. Yet there was much bitter fighting to come, and in most of it the Spencer-armed Northern regiments saw heavy and decisive action.

## Lincoln Shoots the Spencer

President Lincoln, through direct reports from the front, became keenly aware of Chris Spencer and his repeater after Gettysburg. Lincoln invited the inventor to bring his rifle to the White House for a personal demonstration.

The long overdue meeting took place on August 17, 1863. "I arrived at Washington on the morning of August 17th and went direct to the White House," wrote

Spencer in his carefully detailed account. "Presenting my credentials, the guard at the door showed me into the President's office. He was alone when I entered and appeared to be expecting me, as without a moment's delay he took the gun out of my hands, as soon as I removed it from its cloth covering. He examined it carefully and handled it like one familiar with firearms. He requested me to take it apart and show the 'inwardness of the thing' and was greatly impressed that all I needed was a screwdriver ..."

"President Lincoln then invited me to return at 2 p.m. the next day, saying, 'we will go out and see the thing shoot.' When I returned at the time designated I found the President standing, with his son, Robert, and an officer from the Navy, named Middleton, on the steps of the White House. As we walked toward the War Department, the President asked his son to go in and invite Secretary of War, Stanton, to join us and see the shooting.

"While we were waiting for him to return and during a lull in the conversation between Middleton and the President, I mustered up enough courage to ask Mr. Lincoln if it were not a great responsibility to govern such a vast country during the war. Turning toward me with a smile he said: 'It is a big chore with the kind of help I have...'"

"The four of us walked over to what is now Potomac Park, near where the Washington monument stands. The naval officer had picked up a smooth pine board, six inches wide and three feet long, for a target, and after making a small smudge at one end for a bullseye, it was set up against a tree. I slipped seven cartridges into the rifle and handed it to the President. Pacing off 40 yards he took his position "... President Lincoln fired his first shot. It was about six inches low. A second one struck the bullseye and the other five were close to it.

"'Now we will see the inventor try his luck!' remarked the President as he handed me the rifle. When the Naval officer reversed the target, I fired, beating him by a small margin. 'Well,' said President Lincoln, 'you are much younger than I am, have a better eye and steadier nerve.'"

"After we returned to the White House the Naval officer sawed off the end of the board which the President had used as a target, and handed it to me as a souvenir. Then I presented the rifle to President Lincoln, and he marched into the White House with it over his shoulder; I walked out of the gate with the target under my arm. In 1883, the target was sent to Springfield, Illinois (home town of Lincoln), to be placed in the collection of war relics there."

Spencer returned to the White House for another test of his rifle the next day. When he left, it was with the thrilling conviction that his long, frustrating ordeal was over — that President Lincoln himself liked his gun well enough to recommend it highly to Army Ordnance. The young inventor's intuition was correct. "After that," he wrote jubilantly, "we had more orders than we could fill, from the War Department as well as the Navy, for the rest of the war."

The deal was swiftly and efficiently expedited by Brigadier General George D. Ramsay, Lincoln's replacement of General Ripley as Chief of Army Ordnance. Ramsay warmly endorsed the rugged, long-range Spencer over the Colt and the Henry, calling the 7-shooter "the cheapest, most durable and efficient of any of these arms."

The first of the new shipments from the Spencer factory went to the Cavalry, and with the welcome receipt of these additional repeaters the Federal horsemen increased their newly won superiority over their Confederate counterparts. Acquisition of the new weapons by picked regiments of Northern infantry accelerated the Southern military decline. The staccato barking of the 7-shooters from the opposing Blue ranks quickly became a sinister symbol of destruction to the harried Confederates, still armed with muzzle-loaders.

## After Gettysburg

The Spencer thereby became a valuable weapon in psychological warfare, even though the fancy phrase had not yet been coined. Post-war statements by Confederate commanders disclosed that often the sound of rapid firing from the Union repeaters led them to the errone-ous conclusion that brigades instead of regiments of the enemy were moving against them, causing them to discard carefully laid battle plans and resort to hurried and often rash maneuvers. General Bragg, for example, at Chickamauga misinterpreted the tremendous volume of fire coming from five Indiana and Illinois Spencer-armed regiments as the steady volley-firing of an entire corps attacking his left flank. The error caused him to delay a planned wide-scale attack and undoubtedly cost him the battle.

What the unfortunate Federal soldier still lacking the 7-shooter thought of the weapon is revealed in a brief, poignant letter now reposing in the National Archives in Washington. Date-lined Chattanooga, Tenn., September 19, 1863, the first day of the battle of Chickamauga, it shows eloquently and a bit pathetically the hope of survival the new repeater meant to men facing the blazing hell of battle armed only with muzzle-loaders. The letter follows:

*Chattanooga, Tenn., Sept. 19, 1863*
*Spencer Repeating Rifle Company:*

Gentlemen: — I take liberty in writing and inquiring about your rifle as to the manufacturing prices, the number to be had, and the time they could be sent to us at Chattanooga. The whole regiment is willing to buy them and pay for them the next payday, as they will have four months pay coming to them, or the Colonel commanding the regiment would secure your pay; and I believe the whole of the 3rd Brigade of Sheridan's division would buy them if we could get them.

Yours respectfully,
John E. Ekstrand
*Regt. Ord. Sgt.,* 51st Illinois Volunteer Infantry, 3d Brigade, 3d Div., 20 A.C.

At Gettysburg, three Spencer-armed regiments had provided the winning punch for General Meade's Army of the Potomac; at Chickamauga, five Spencer-armed regiments did the same for the Blue.

In the bloody three-day melee of the Battle of the Wilderness, in early May of 1864, Grant's army boasted eleven regiments equipped with the deadly repeater. Without the 7-shooters it is extremely doubtful if the surrounded Federal troops could have burst out of the trap so expertly laid for them by Lee and Stuart. Advancing behind a lethal screen of fire from their Spencers, the Union horsemen drove Stuart back to the Po River, permitting the beleaguered Army of the Potomac to move out of the death trap of the Wilderness and on to Spottsylvania. There, on May 8th, the Federals, headed by the Spencer-armed cavalry, defeated Lee in another furious battle.

General Sheridan's great raid, clear around Lee's befuddled army, was the next move on Grant's relentless program of ceaseless hammering away at the enemy. 10,000 Northern cavalry, half of them armed with Spencers, met and defeated Stuart's forces in four major engagements during the hectic 16-day campaign. At Yellow Tavern, on May 11th, Jeb Stuart was mortally wounded, probably by Spencer-toting expert marksman John A. Huff, of Company E of the 5th Michigan Cavalry. Stuart's death, like that of General Jackson's the year before at Chancellorsville, was a stunning personal blow to

Fig. 7 — (Top) post-Civil War Spencer military rifle, caliber 50 (using the 56-52 or 56-50 cartridge), with the Stabler cut-off. Lower, Spencer carbine, chambered for the 56-56 cartridge. Below it lies the Spencer magazine tube. Photo courtesy the West Point Museum.

# SPENCER
## RIFLES AND CARBINES

Spencer models are difficult to classify, as L. D. Satterlee noted in his 2-part article in *The American Rifleman* for May 1 and 15, 1926. The list that follows leans heavily on that invaluable study, as well as on the same author's *A Catalog of Firearms For The Collector* (Detroit, 1927).

Rifles of 30" bbl. length and carbines with 22" bbls., both cal. 52 (bore 519"-20", grooves 537"- 38" taking the 56-56 Spencer cartridge of .885" length, using 42-grs. of powder (black) and a 362-gr. bullet of .540" diameter. These were all 6-grooved barrels, and all were made at Boston in the Chickering Piano Works at Tremont and Camden Streets. Early specimens had no serial num bers. Despite the order for 10,000 rifles given to Spencer on Dec. 26, 1861, none was delivered until Dec. 31,1862, nor were any of the 700 rifles ordered by the Navy earlier in 1861. Part of the delay was because of a design change, presumably the change over to the side position ex tractor (U.S. Patent 36062 of July 29, 1862, assigned to F. Cheney). During the period of non-delivery, Spencer's contract for 10,000 Army rifles was reduced to 7500. Deliveries by the Spencer Company continued up to June 20, 1863.

Following tests in May, 1863, Massachusetts ordered 2000 Spencer rifles, but the federal government was so anxious to have these that they were turned over to the U.S. on Oct. 2, 1863. Spencer then made 1868 rifles and 1176 carbines for Massachusetts, and again these were turned in to the U.S. on May 4 and May 9, 1864.

Meanwhile the U.S. had contracted for 11,000 carbines on July 13, 1863. 7000 only were delivered, from Oct. 3 to Dec. 31,1863, the rest cancelled. On Dec. 24,1863, another contract was given Spencer for 34,500 carbines. 7000 were delivered, from Jan. 20, 1864 to May 17, 1864, the balance cancelled.

On May 24, 1864, Spencer contracted to deliver as many carbines as he could up to Sept. 1, 1865. Between June 4, 1864 and August 31, 1865, 45,500 carbines were delivered.

Post-War carbines of 56-50 caliber. These were fitted with Stabler's cutoff (Edw. Stabler's U.S. Patent 46828 of May 14, 1865), and carried, generally, 20" bbls. 34,496 of this style, all with 3-groove bbls. (to conform to Army practices), and made by the Burnside Rifle Co., of Providence, R.I., were delivered to the U.S. between April 15, 1865 and October 31, 1865. This was in con formance with a contract given to Burnside on June 27, 1864. These are usually stamped "Model 1865."

The Spencer Co. delivered another 3000 of the 56-50 carbines between Dec. 13, 1865 and Jan. 1, 1866, these the same as the 56-50 carbines just described except that some had 22" bbls., and this lot of 3000 were made at the Boston works and so-stamped. Some are stamped "New Model" or "NM" on the barrel.

From about Nov. 1866 to Oct. 1867, Spencer con tinued to furnish 3-groove 50 cal. carbines and rifles (using the 52 cartridge or, as it was soon called, the 56-52. This dates the 56-52 load from about Nov. 1866. Military rifles of 3-groove form were also sold in this brief period (also using the 52 or 56-52 cartridge — Spencer never advertised the Army's 50 cal. cartridge), as were sporting rifles in 46 or 56-46 caliber. Spencer felt that the Army's 50 cal. cartridge had an excessive crimp, and the 56-52 was his re-design using a bottleneck form. L.D.S. wrote that "Serial numbers start from one (1) up to perhaps about 20,000."

From about October, 1867 to the last days of the Spencer Co. in Sept., 1869, Spencers were made with 6-groove bbls. These barrels were stamped "M-1865", "M-1867" and "N.M.," according to L.D.S. He also notes that the Spencer Co.'s Oct. 1867 catalog "mentions the 'Old Model,' 'Model 1865' and 'Model 1867'" and that serial numbers started over again.

Spencers above serial number 100,000 (states L.D.S.) are sometimes found with a cutoff that Spencer designed and patented (U.S. Patents 58737 and 58738 on Oct. 9, 1866), but that one could have this or the Stabler cutoff or none at all. Generally, Spencers with either cutoff are late specimens. The Spencer type cutoff attaches to the cartridge guide atop the action.

L.D.S. thought that a final Spencer Co. catalog may have been issued in Oct., 1868, and comments that advertising of Spencers in the *Army & Navy Journal* ceased with the Oct. 31, 1868 issue.

The *Boston Post* for Sept. 29, 1869, reported on the sale of Spencer's machinery the day before. $138,000 was realized, this in addition to whatever Winchester may have paid for the patent rights and stocks of firearms on hand. (See *Winchester*, pp. 58 and 398, by C. F. Williamson, Wash., D.C., 1952). C. M. Spencer, at the close of the Civil War, had left the Spencer Repeating Rifle Co., joining Sylvester Roper in the unsuccessful Roper revolving shotgun venture. In 1868 Spencer formed the Billings & Spencer Mfg. Co., with C. E. Billings.

On Dec. 11, 1869, the *Scientific American* advertised the sale by Winchester of 2000 Spencer military rifles, 30,000 Spencer carbines and 500 Spencer sporting rifles.

It is difficult to determine whether a given Spencer sporting rifle was actually made by the Spencer Co. or not — most such types do not carry any barrel stampings to indicate company manufacture. The years that followed the Spencer firm's dissolution saw many jobbers and dealers in firearms offering Spencer arms of all types, among them sporting rifles in various styles, treatments, barrel lengths, etc., and it is a fair assumption that some such "Spencer" sporters were made up by altering Spencer Civil War rifles and carbines.

Delving into Spencer's patents brought out a peculiar thing — U.S. Patent 45952, dated Jan. 17, 1865, covers the loading tube system used in the Spencers from his first handmade models on. The specifications describe the inner and outer tubes, the right-angled locking piece that pivots into position at the buttplate, etc., all features of Spencer arms from their inception, as far as we know.

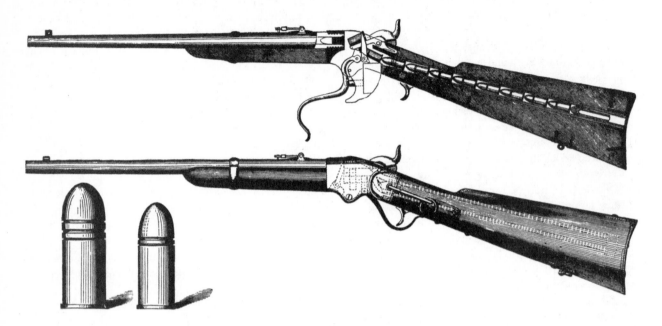

Fig. 8 — Spencer carbines illustrated in the 1866 Spencer catalog. Note that the Stabler cutoff is not shown. Spencer offered three basic models in this catalog — the Army and Navy rifles, with 30-inch barrels, a Cavalry carbine with 20-inch barrel, these in 56-50 caliber and with 3-groove bbls., and a basic sporting rifle with 26-inch octagon barrel in 56-46 caliber. Longer sporting barrels could be had, and other calibers.

General Lee and a disaster to the crumbling Confederacy.

Sheridan's cavalry sweep through the Shenandoah Valley of Virginia resulted in brilliant victories over the fading enemy at Winchester, Fisher's Hill and Cedar Creek in the month from September 19th to October 19th of 1864. 17 regiments armed with the Spencer provided overwhelming firepower against the opposing troops of Jubal Early.

Brigadier General Garrard's cavalry division, composed mostly of Spencer-armed regiments, spearheaded the 1864 Georgia campaign of Generals Sherman and Hooker. In the ruthless drive to Atlanta, the 7-shooter equipped units blasted a corridor through stubborn enemy resistance. Before the fall of Atlanta, Grant recalled nearly all of the Spencer-armed cavalry and turned it over to General Wilson for a swift move against the Confederate army under Hood.

The end came for the doomed Confederacy early in the spring of 1865. Sheridan, flushed with victory after victory over the hungry, exhausted, outgunned Southerners, led his 10,000 troopers — now almost entirely armed with Spencers — successfully against Lee in the battle of Five Forks, Virginia.

Richmond fell to Grant the next day, and the stolid victor moved at once to join forces with Sheridan. The juncture was effected on April 5.

The battle of Sailor's Creek, last major battle of the war, began April 6. Sergeant William O. Lee, Company M, 7th Cavalry of the Michigan Brigade, wrote of the end of hostilities in these graphic words:

"After standing 'to horse' all night in open order of column by squadrons, about four o'clock on the morning of the 9th, in the gray of dawn, a line of the enemy skirmishers was discovered advancing. The 7th was at once deployed and was soon hotly engaged. Under the steady stream of lead poured out by Spencer carbines, the advance of the enemy was checked, held for a time, and then forced slowly back."

"... As we emerged from the woods, Lee's whole army, deployed for action, came into view and our bugles were sounding the charge. Just at this juncture several horsemen emerged from the woods of the enemy's lines, the leader waving a white flag of truce."

## The War Ends

The guns fell silent; there remained but for Generals Grant and Lee to meet at the McLean house near the battlefield and sign the historic terms of surrender. Suddenly, stunningly, after four years of carnage and destruction, the Civil War was over.

Over 106,000 Spencers were contracted for by the war's end — 94,196 carbines and 12,471 rifles. Thousands more saw service, of course, counting the large number purchased by battle groups and individuals, and those that armed several volunteer and militia organizations.

The murder of President Lincoln by the crazed actor, John Wilkes Booth, on April 14th, 1865, not only robbed the nation of its great leader and the stricken South of its best friend, but also deprived the Spencer of its most influential backer. With Lincoln dead and Andrew Johnson in the White House, Army Ordnance quickly reverted to the single-shot Sharps and Springfield.

The bankrupt Spencer firm was sold at auction on September 28, 1869, to the Winchester Repeating Arms Co. 30,000 Spencers remaining in stock were bought by the Turkish Government; all other properties and assets went to Winchester.

By this one keen stroke of business, the Winchester Company eliminated its strongest competition. Even the name "Spencer" was dropped from all future firearms manufactured by the Winchester plant; yet the unique loading system of the Spencer was retained and utilized by Winchester when they produced the first self-loading rifle — the 1903 Model 22 caliber made famous by the great Texas marksman, Ad Topperwein.

After the loss of his rifle company, Christopher Spencer began manufacturing drop forgings and sewing machine shuttles. His invention of the world's first automatic screw machine stemmed directly from his work on the repeating rifle that so briefly bore his name. This ingenious machine — essential in the mass production of practically all metal items — ironically forms the only enduring monument to the inventive genius of Christopher Miner Spencer, who died in 1922 at the age of 89.

Ironic also is the fact that Custer, who won fame in the Civil War with his Spencer-armed cavalry, was an indirect casualty of the failure of the Army to continue using the Spencer.

Armed with the unreliable 45–70 Springfield carbine, more than 200 of Custer's 7th Cavalry, along with their yellow-haired leader, died battling 2000 Sioux warriors at the Little Bighorn, June 25,1876. Custer himself, openly scornful of the Springfield, went into his last battle armed with his 50–70 Remington Rolling Block Sporting Rifle. None knew better than weapons-expert Custer that the Springfield had a fatal weakness in the ejecting mechanism; the heads of the cartridges were apt to be pulled off by the extractors after the guns had been fired steadily for any length of firing time exceeding a few rounds. After the battle, some dead soldiers were found with jammed Springfields clutched in their hands.

The Spencer with the longest service appears to have been, from scanty available records, the Model 1867 Sporting Rifle, caliber 56-46. This weapon was in active service among hunters, especially in the West, many years after the other models were but fond memories or collectors' items.

Buffalo hunter Jim "Rawhide" Wilson, who cherished his 50-caliber Spencer sporter for nearly 40 years, was still killing bear, elk and muledeer with it in 1900.

Yet this was the same sturdy repeating rifle discarded by U. S. Army Ordnance in favor of the unreliable Springfield — a single-shot arm.

No wonder Chris Spencer complained of the density of "those Generals in Washington!"

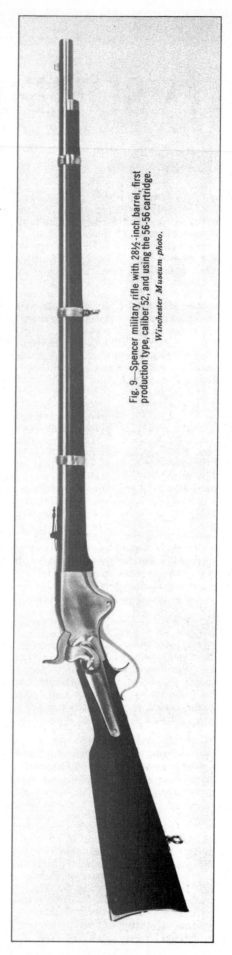

Fig. 9—Spencer military rifle with 28½-inch barrel, first production type, caliber 52, and using the 56-56 cartridge.
*Winchester Museum photo.*

# The Gettysburg Sharps

■ Paul A. Matthews

I T IS A MATTER OF HISTORY that the battle of Gettysburg stemmed the tide of the Confederate advance during the Civil War, but it is a matter of opinion as to what action turned the tide at Gettysburg. Some historians, and General Lee himself, claimed that Pickett's charge was a blunder. Others give full credit to Meade, who took command of the Federal troops on the eve of the battle, while soldiers in the ranks of the Confederacy said that "the damyankees have finally learned how to fight, ride, and shoot." Rifle-minded historians give credit to the accuracy, operation and fire power of the Sharps percussion breech-loading rifle.

Such credit is not unfounded. Lee was on an offensive action with 75,000 troops as opposed to Meade's 80,000. He had out-maneuvered Meade in the first two days of the fighting, and on the third day had him bottled up on ridges, ravines, and hills south of the town. Admittedly, he under-estimated the Federal artillery on Cemetery Ridge, but even so, Pickett's 15,000 men nearly carried the hill. Had General Longstreet, who was making a flanking movement around the Two Round Tops, not been

the same estimable position as our M1 Garand did in World War II. It was the first efficient, successful breech loader, and was the rifle for the infantry, being especially adapted for skirmish work and a high rapidity of fire when needed. It was far more accurate than the muskets carried by most of the troops, though not a target rifle capable of fine sniping work. Its breech-loading system allowed the infantryman to fire ten shots a minute from the prone position, whereas the musket users had to stand upright or nearly so when reloading — most undesirable and dangerous for the soldier anxious to be as small a target as possible.

The weight of the New Model 1863, eight and three-quarter pounds, was much less than that of the long smooth-bores, and its short overall length, even with a thirty inch barrel, gave the infantryman a light, handy weapon.

Sharps New Model 1863
percussion rifle.

delayed, he might easily have taken the Federal artillery from the rear and the history of Gettysburg and the Union would have been entirely different. General Longstreet and his 30,000 troops were held back forty minutes by a mere three hundred men, one hundred of which were from Col. Berdan's Sharpshooting Regiment and the others from the 3rd Maine Regiment. Berdan's men, armed with the Sharps rifle, fired about 9500 shots in a twenty minute barrage, at the same time sending word back to Meade to redeploy the troops defending the Round Tops.

Somewhere in that bloody three-day melee — possibly with Berdan on the reconnaissance, maybe with the 2nd U. S. Sharpshooters in the ravine between the Round Tops, or maybe farther north on Cemetery Ridge — was Samuel H. Williams of Company C, 171st Pennsylvania Volunteers. He was armed with a 52 caliber Sharps, New Model 1863, serial C,30303, a hundred paper or skin cartridges, and a bayonet.

The Sharps percussion rifle and carbine used in that war held

One of the principal defects of the early breechloaders, before the advent of brass cartridges, was gas escapage. In the 1863 Sharps, this is cut to a minimum by a deep counterbore in the face of the breechblock, into which is fitted a tapered, sliding faceplate, with a circular opening for the flash tube. On firing the rifle, the explosion exerts a thrust on the inside edge of the plate, driving it forward against the rear face of the barrel, thus sealing the chamber. Even so there is some leakage, and anyone attempting to fire an old Sharps should keep his arms covered and wear gloves. The first time I fired Pvt. William's rifle from the bench, I used a sling and kept my left hand well up on the fore-end, but my sister-in-law, who kept her hand back under the breech when she shot it, suffered blistering burns. Some gas also escapes around the top edge of the block, and on this particular rifle the lower face of the barrel is badly eroded, allowing most of the gas to go in that direction.

Coupled with the gas escapage is the sooty fouling common to all "charcoal" burners. When I first fired the Sharps, the breechblock refused to move when f started to reload. After tap-

Col. Berdan and "California Joe" from Berdan's United States Sharpshooters ... 1861–1865 by C. A. Stevens (St. Paul, Minn., 1892.)

ping lightly on the top of the block with a piece of brass and exerting pressure on the finger lever at the same time, the breech finally opened. As a preventive measure, I first tried greasing the face plate and rear barrel face with tallow. This helped to some degree. Then I tried water pump grease, and finally, after mixing powdered graphite with it, I had a suit able concoction. I also discovered that a small gob of grease on the inside edge of the chamber worked better yet as it blew out with the escaping gas, keeping the residue very soft. When the rifle was in new condition, and the moving parts highly polished, it was doubtless unnecessary to take these precautions each time the gun was fired.

Another advantage of the 1863 breech-loading percussion Sharps, especially from the infantryman's point of view, is the ease with which the breechblock can be removed for cleaning. On the right side of the receiver, just forward of the block mortice, is a spring loaded plunger that keeps the lever-pin from turning when the lever is operated. A small flange on the "arm" of the pin fits into a slot in the receiver, keeping the pin from falling out. When the infantryman wished to remove the breech-block, he depressed the plunger, swung the arm downward, and pulled out the pin. The breech-block then fell out and was easily cleaned. On the right side of the block is a lever-toggle-screw, and on the left side is the vent-cleaning screw.

As a safety measure, Mister Sharps put an "ear" on the upper right hand corner of the lock plate. This fits into the small curve of the hammer, keeping the latter from striking a cap when the breech is partially closed. A lever-spring snaps the lever to a closed position when the shooter brings it up within an inch of

the stock. Once closed, no amount of pressure on the breech-block will open it.

Coming close to making the Sharps a "repeater" is the pellet primer magazine in the lock plate. This could be charged with a tube of fifty of the Sharps pellet primers and then held in reserve for furious action (by Lawrence's patent cut-off) when the ordinary musket cap would be too slow to use. When necessary, such as it must have been at Cemetery Ridge, the cut-off plate was pulled back. This allowed a sliding plate, actuated by a cam on the inside face of the hammer, to push out a pellet synchronized with the hammer; the hammer hits the pellet as it flies over the nipple. (A quite nice job of timing). The pellets, actually thin wafers, were held in a vertical tube with a spring plunger forcing them upward where the plate could pick them up.

The bore diameter of Pvt. Williams' rifle measures .518 inches while the groove diameter is .529 inches, so I purchased the regular Lyman mould #533476, casting a hollow-base Minié-ball weighing 410 grains. I did not size any of the bullets, but merely dipped them in bullet lubricant and scraped off the excess. At first I made a number of paper cartridges using hard tracing paper as a wrapper and water-glass as glue along the sides. This combination worked very well. The water-glass hardens almost as fast as applied, and when the gun was fired there were no burning embers left in the chamber. For a powder charge I used 55 grains of duPont FG Black.

In order to make the paper cartridges, I first had a piece of steel four inches long turned to the .533 diameter of the bullet. Then, taking a piece of paper four inches long and wide enough

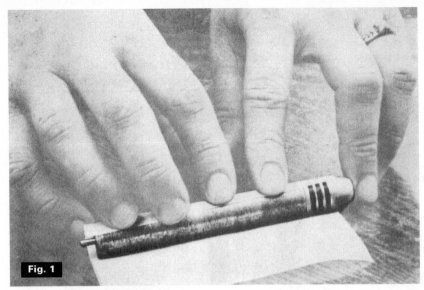

**Fig. 1**

## Preparing a Paper Cartridge

Fig. 1 — The first step in rolling a paper cartridge around a steel dowel and a lubricated Minié ball.

Fig. 2 — Gluing the top edge of the paper cartridge and along the side seam with water-glass.

Fig. 3 — Charging the cartridge with a scoop of FG black powder. The scoop has been filed off so as to hold 55 grains of powder.

Fig. 4 — Pinching the tube just behind the powder charge. The tail is then clipped to length and glued to the side of the cartridge.

Fig. 5 — The completed cartridge ready for use.

**Use nothing but black powder in the old percussion Sharps, and for your eyes' sake, wear a pair of shooting glasses — those escaping gasses are hot!**

Silver medal awarded to the Sharps Rifle Mfg. Co. in 1853 by the Massachusetts Charitable Mechanic Association.

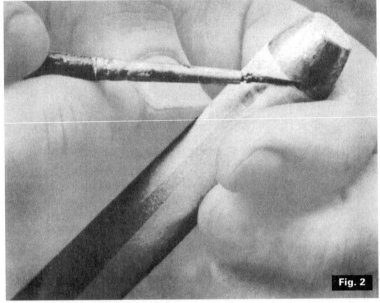

**Fig. 2**

A closeup shot of the lock plate showing the 'ear' that keeps the hammer from striking the nipple on a partially closed breech, and the vertical, spring-loaded plunger hole of the Sharps' primer pellet magazine.

to wrap around the steel twice, I laid it on the table, the long edge toward me. With the left hand, lay a bullet on the paper, just covering the grease grooves, and then place one end of the steel roller against the base of the bullet. Roll both tightly as a unit, then with a pointed brush run a small amount of water-glass around the top edge of the paper where the bullet protrudes, and down the side of the tube on the edge of the paper. It takes only a few seconds for the water-glass to harden and then the steel roller can be dropped out and the tube charged with powder. This leaves two or three inches of paper tube to be pinched flat, the outer edges folded inward, and then the flat tail folded across the base of the cartridge and up the side. Here again, I used water-glass to seal the tail and stick it to the side of the cartridge tube.

In loading the rifle with paper cartridges, I pulled the tail loose, pushed the cartridge into the chamber, and as the breech was closed, the face plate sheared off the excess paper, leaving the powder exposed to the flame of the cap. The Italian Fiocchi musket caps distributed by the Alcan Company gave plenty of hot flame and never once misfired.

Considering the sighting equipment of the old rifle — a low, narrow-bladed steel front sight and a V leaf rear sight — and the pitted breech end of the barrel, plus a trigger pull upwards wards of

demise of the company, the falling block design was picked up by other companies and is used to some extent today, as in the five inch anti-aircraft Naval rifles that so many of us became familiar with during World War II.

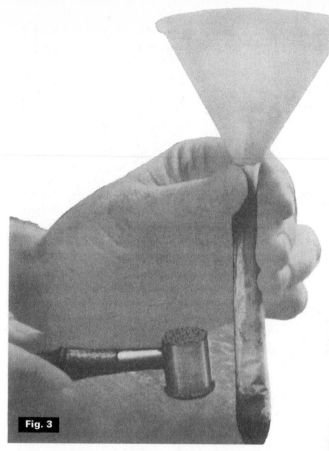

**Fig. 3**

†W. O. Smith in *The Sharps Rifle* (New York, 1943) writes, "The standard military bullet for the Sharps .54 caliber (sometimes designated .52 caliber) weighed about 475 grains ..." Later, "In 1860 the standard powder charge for the ... carbine was 50 grains, but some of the later cartridges were found to contain as much as 65 grains ..."

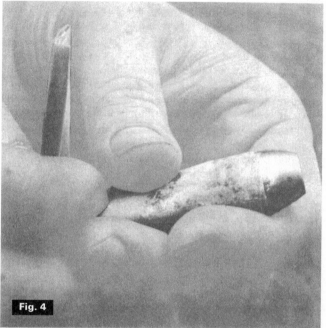

**Fig. 4**

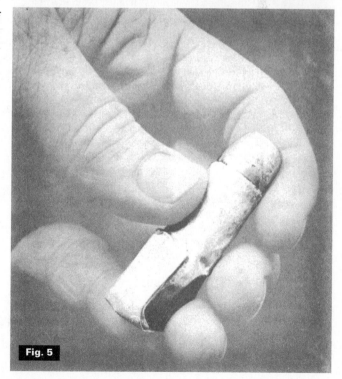

**Fig. 5**

six pounds, accuracy was not too bad. A ten shot group at 100 yards measured 7 inches vertically and 5½ inches horizontally, with the center of the group about ten inches below the point of aim. Six of the shots went into less than 3 inches. I also detected a slight tendency to tipping with the hollow-base bullet. Possibly I could have used a heavier charge, bringing the group closer to the point of aim, but dealing with an arm over ninety years old, I thought it better to be conservative.†

The success of the New Model 1863 was an outgrowth of several patents and changing designs. Christian Sharps' original patent granted in 1848 covered the sliding breechblock which in models 1851 through 1855 was of the slanting type. In the attempt to prevent gas escapage, these blocks were closely fitted in the receiver mortice, and some carried a fixed platinum ring more erosion resistant that the steel block.

Escaping gas was still a problem, however, and one H. Conant designed a sliding ring closely fitted into a counterbore. The explosion forced the ring forward, sealing the breech. In the 1859 model, R. S. Lawrence improved this by the addition of the sliding face plate described earlier, and this system was used in all subsequent percussion models.

All models following the 1855 model were also equipped with the Sharps automatic pellet primer magazine using the cut-off feature designed by Lawrence. Previous to this, the Maynard tape primer was used, while the models of 1852 and 1853 had the Sharps primer magazine without the cut-off.

It is interesting to note that the Confederacy made several versions of the Sharps carbine, some with parts that had been "borrowed" from the Federal Cavalry.

Though the Sharps was with us for all too brief a time (1848–1881), the company having been plagued with law suits, mortgages, and penalties for late deliveries, it helped bring to an end a muzzle-loading army and heralded the beginning of a new era in the history of firearms. In the years following the

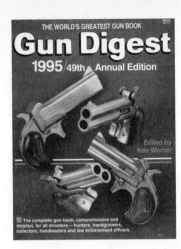

THE WORLD'S GREATEST GUN BOOK

**Gun Digest**
1995/49th Annual Edition

Edited by
Ken Warner

The complete gun book, comprehensive and detailed, for all shooters—hunters, handgunners, collectors, handloaders and law enforcement officers.

# Johnny Reb and His Guns

■ Edward R. Crews

**N**O JOHNNY REB manning the Confederate line at Mayre's Heights could be unimpressed at the spectacle before him. On an open plain between this high ground and the nearby town of Fredericksburg, Virginia, thousands of Federal troops were massing for an attack.

William M. Owen, a Confederate artillery officer, watched on December 13, 1862, as the enemy soldiers ran toward him behind unfurled battle-flags, chanting a deep-throated refrain — Hi! Hi! Hi! "How beautifully they came on," he wrote years later. "Their bright bayonets glistening in the sunlight made the line look like a huge serpent of blue and steel."

Union Major General Ambrose E. Burnside was hurling his Army of the Potomac against the Southern defenses. He wanted to rout General Robert E. Lee and his Army of Northern Virginia, and then march into Richmond about 50 miles south and end the war. Burnside had massed 27,000 men for the attack on Mayre's Heights; Lee had only 6000 defending it. Although Federal assaults earlier that day had failed elsewhere along Lee's line, Burnside hoped this attack would work.

The Union attack, however, was doomed to fail. Lee held a superb defensive position. Mayre's Heights commanded nearby terrain and was studded with artillery. At its base, a breast-high stone wall provided shelter for the Georgia infantrymen of Cobb's Brigade. Also, many of Lee's men had rifled muskets, the war's most common infantry weapon. A properly trained soldier could hit targets at 300 yards, firing three rounds a minute.

That so many of these weapons would be in Southern hands was a miracle. When the various states that comprised the Confederacy left the Union in 1860 and 1861, they had few modern military rifles. U.S. arsenals seized by the South held older, less-desirable guns. Plus, the South had virtually no rifle-making facilities. Perceptive Southern

Stonewall Jackson reviews his troops during his famous Valley Campaign of 1862. So much enemy equipment was captured that the Confederates found themselves well-armed when the fighting ended. This mural is in the gallery with the Southern gun collection. (Richard Cheek photo.)

◀ This unmarked Confederate rifle in the Springfield pattern is proof the South had an ordnance system. (Virginia Historical Society photo.

leaders knew that a Union naval blockade eventually could slow, and probably halt, imports. All these factors produced an ill-armed military.

"At the commencement of the war, the Southern army was as poorly armed as any body of men ever had been," wrote John H. Worsham of the 21st Virginia Infantry Regiment. "Using my own regiment as an example, one company of infantry had Springfield muskets, one had Enfields, one had Mississippi rifles, and the remainder had the old smoothbore flintlock musket that had been altered to a

percussion gun. The cavalry was so badly equipped that hardly a company was uniform. Some men had sabers and nothing more, some had double-barreled guns. Some had nothing but lances, and others had something of all. One man would have a saber, another a pistol, another a musket, and another a shotgun. Not half a dozen men in the company were armed alike."

That situation had changed dramatically by late 1862, as Burnside and his men learned at Fredericksburg.

Federal commanders initiated the attack around noon. Their men had to cross about 600 yards of open ground to reach the Confederate position. Union troops began taking casualties as soon as the advance started. When they were within 125 yards of the stone wall, Cobb's infantrymen shouldered their muskets.

"A few more paces onward and the Georgians in the road below us rose up, and, glancing an instant along their rifle barrels, let loose a storm of lead into the faces of the advanced brigade," Owen wrote. "This was too much; the column hesitated, and then, turning, took refuge behind the (nearby earthen) bank."

Burnside repeatedly sent assault waves against the enemy lines all day. Only the arrival of night ended the fighting. No Billy Yank came closer than fifty yards to the stone wall. Federal losses were 8000 compared to 1600 for the South.

Fredericksburg was a testament to the Army of the Potomac's courage. It also showed that the rifled musket was ending the sweeping, grand Napoleonic charge. This weapon represented a significant technological gain in warfare. It was powerful enough, accurate enough and had enough range to pound apart the most determined attack a foe could mount. The industrialized North could supply hundreds of thousands of these arms to its soldiers with comparative ease.

The agrarian South, however, faced staggering supply problems. Against all odds, the Confederacy did get sufficient modern arms to its troops. That required hard work, organization, improvisation and the talents of a remarkable man — Josiah Gorgas. Nobody in the Confederacy would do more to get rifles for Johnny Reb.

A Pennsylvanian, West Pointer and pre-war professional soldier, Gorgas became chief of Confederate ordnance early in the war. Before it ended, he would run thousands of guns through the Yankee blockade and build a Southern weapons industry from scratch. Southerners in 1861 might have gone to war with fowling pieces and old smoothbores, but by mid-1863, thanks to Gorgas, they generally had equipment that matched their Federal foes'. One Southern leader succinctly and accurately described his wartime achievements: "He created the ordnance department out of nothing."

Gorgas knew early on that the rifled musket would play a key role in the conflict, and the Confederacy would need large quantities of them. He also understood its capabilities. Compared to today's military rifles, the typical Civil War musket was heavy, big, cumbersome and fired a huge bullet, often more than half-an-inch in diameter. Such muskets required twenty steps to load. A soldier typically did this standing upright and holding his weapon in front of him with its butt on the ground. Ammunition came in paper cartridges that contained a bullet and a standard charge of blackpowder. Johnny Reb would bite off a cartridge end, pour the powder down the barrel, discard the paper, place the bullet in the muzzle and ram it to the breech using a ramrod carried in a channel beneath the barrel. The Civil War musket's ignition system relied on the percussion cap, a metal cap filled with fulminate of mercury. The system was reliable and could function in all weather conditions.

The same could not be said of the previous generation of military shoulder arms. The flintlock muzzleloader depended on a piece of flint striking a piece of metal to create a spark. Much could go wrong with this process, and damp powder doomed it. Knowing the flintlock's limitations, both Civil War armies eagerly embraced the percussion system.

Average Johnny Rebs and Billy Yanks in the infantry used the same weapons and used them the same way, both as individuals and as members of military units.

For much of the conflict, officers in blue and gray deployed troops in large, concentrated units that shot in volleys. This allowed commanders to mass fire and to control fire rates. The only way to move men into these combat formations was through standardized maneuvers, which explains why the 19th century American soldier spent much time drilling.

Although presented with a powerful, comparatively long-range weapon in the rifled musket, generals stuck with those formations and tactics appropriate to the short ranges and inaccuracy of the smoothbore era. Surprisingly enough, leading commanders on both sides failed to immediately grasp the rifle's destructive power. Not only did Burnside embrace the frontal assault at Fredericksburg, but so did Lee at Gettysburg, Ulysses S. Grant at Cold Harbor, and Confederate Lt. Gen. John B. Hood at Franklin, Tennessee. At all these places, the results were disastrous.

As the war progressed, however, the average soldier realized the value of entrenching. Southern infantrymen became adept at creating trenches and rifle pits whenever they stopped, using tin cups and plates as well as shovels to put a few inches of dirt between them and the enemy. The 1864–65 Petersburg campaign, in fact, was largely a fight between entrenched armies that knew a direct attack against such works was tantamount to suicide.

For the average Confederate soldier, combat was a terrifying experience. It also was hard work. To begin, loading the rifle was difficult. Even veteran soldiers could easily forget what they were doing in the heat of battle. Sometimes they loaded a bullet first, powder second, or jammed load after load down the barrel without capping the nipple. Blackpowder also quickly clogged musket barrels and wrapped the battlefield in clouds of dense smoke that made seeing targets difficult, if not impossible.

Johnny Reb also endured his rifle's hefty recoil. Sam Watkins, a Southern soldier, reported firing 120 rounds during the Battle of Kenesaw Mountain. Afterwards, his arm was battered and bruised. "My gun became so hot that frequently the powder would flash before I could ram home the ball," he wrote, "and I had frequently to exchange my gun for that of a dead colleague."

How good a shot was Johnny Reb? We'll probably never know. While the rifled musket could perform outstandingly, and many Southerners lived in a society that prized good guns and marksmanship, battle imposed great demands on the best of shots. The danger, excitement, loading process and smoke-covered battlefields made accurate shooting extraordinarily difficult. One historian has estimated that for every casualty produced, 200 rounds were fired. Others believe the figure to be much higher.

If the tactical implications of the rifled musket were sometimes imperfectly understood, its value as an improved shoulder arm was easily grasped. So Confederate officials knew that getting these weapons into Johnny Reb's hands was vital, and Confederate ordnance chief Gorgas energetically set to work on the problem from the war's start. He knew only three sources of supply existed: capture, import and Southern manufacture.

The Confederacy turned to capture first. As each Southern state left the Union, it seized any Federal arms held at arsenals or armories within its borders. The pickings were lean. These establishments did not have many modern arms. They mainly held older government

models of little value. Among these was the U.S. Model 1822 musket, a 69-caliber smoothbore. Many were converted from flintlock to percussion, but the improved ignition system did not compensate for their unrifled barrels. Their range and accuracy was limited. Hitting a specific target more than 100 yards away relied on luck as much as skill.

Once the fighting began in earnest, the Confederacy wasted little time in seizing modern Union weapons whenever they became available. Federal prisoners, battlefield gleanings and captured warehouses yielded first-class arms for the Cause.

As veteran Southern infantryman Worsham noted: "When Jackson's troops

marched from the Valley (of Virginia) for Richmond (in 1862) to join Lee in his attack on McClellan, they had captured enough arms from the enemy to replace all that was inferior; and after the battles around Richmond, all departments of Lee's army were as well armed."

Probably the most preferred capture from the Yankees was the 58-caliber Springfield, which came in several models. This rifled musket was superior and typical of its type. The weapon weighed roughly 9 pounds, was 58 inches long, and saw more service with the U.S. Army than any other rifle. Government and private armories produced hundreds of thousands during the war.

Also especially desired by Johnny Reb

Anthony Sydnor Barksdale (1841–1923) of Charlotte County posed with his rifle for this ambrotype (ambrotypes are reversed photos), taken in 1861 when Barksdale was twenty. He served as a private in the 14th Virginia Infantry Regiment and later transferred to Edward R. Young's battery in Mosely's Battalion. Captured in Petersburg in 1865, he was a prisoner of war at Point Lookout for several months. (Virginia Historical Society photo.)

was the U.S. Model 1841. It was first issued in 54-caliber, but many were altered to 58-caliber, and a fair number came into Confederate hands through Federal arsenals in Southern states. This weapon was commonly known as the "Mississippi rifle," from its Mexican War service with Mississippi volunteers commanded by Jefferson Davis.

Confederates also were delighted to get their hands on Federal breechloaders like the Sharps and Spencer. Both represented significant gains in rates of fire and ease of loading.

To load the Sharps, a 52-caliber breechloader, the soldier pulled down the trigger guard. This caused the breechblock to drop and opened the chamber into which was inserted a linen or paper cartridge filled with powder and a bullet. The Sharp's rate of fire was three times that of a musket.

The Spencer fired metallic cartridges. Its tubular magazine in the buttstock held seven rounds. A skilled operator could fire twenty-one rounds per minute. Unfortunately for the South, captured Spencers suffered from an ammunition shortage as the Confederate industry frequently was incapable of meeting cartridge needs created by the weapon's firepower abilities.

Though infantrymen seldom carried revolvers, the Confederate cavalry loved them, especially captured Colts. These were Northern-made, but saw widespread use in both armies. Six-shooters in 36- and 44-calibers, their cylinders could be loaded with paper, foil or sheepskin cartridges, or loose powder and ball. Ignition

required a percussion cap on each nipple at each chamber.

Imports were another vital source of armaments. Europe eagerly provided guns to both sides. Southern weapons had to come through the Federal blockade, and a surprisingly large volume made the trip.

Europe offered some superlative weapons and some junk. Particularly despised by Johnny Reb were rifles made in Austria and Belgium. Unwieldy, inaccurate and unreliable, they were dead last on his wish list.

The most desired import was the 577-caliber Enfield. A British-made musket, the Enfield was rugged and accurate. The Enfields came in several styles, including a carbine. Southern cavalry was particularly attached to the latter, even though as a muzzleloader it lacked the rapid-fire quality of Union repeaters. Another popular and well-crafted British import was the 44-caliber Kerr revolver.

Great Britain also supplied some of the war's best sharpshooter rifles: the 44-caliber Kerr and 45-caliber Whitworth. Southern marksmen treasured these guns, which enabled them to hit targets at 1000 yards. The most famous long-range shooting incident of the war occurred on May 9, 1864, during the Battle of Spotsylvania.

Several Southern marksmen are given credit for what happened, but it is impossible to know who did the shooting. One version of the incident comes from Captain William C. Dunlop who commanded the sharpshooters of McGowan's Brigade. This Confederate unit was ordered to

move ahead of the main body of Southern troops to scout for Federals that day. Dunlop concealed his men in position along a ridge where they could see the Union VI Corps deploying on a distant hill. Immediately, Dunlop's men began firing with telling effect.

Among Dunlop's troops was a Private Benjamin Powell of South Carolina, who carried a Whitworth that day and was looking for important targets. One soon presented itself. Powell could see a Yank officer moving along the enemy firing line, giving commands and viewing the field through binoculars. His behavior and the staff trailing behind him suggested this was an important man.

Powell decided to shoot him. The round traveled 800 yards and struck General John Sedgwick, the corp commander, in the left cheek, killing him. Only moments earlier, the general had tried to calm his troops who were agitated by the sniper fire. They "couldn't hit an elephant at this distance," he said seconds before he died.

One of the most intriguing weapons that made it through the Union's naval blockade was the Le Mat revolver, which could fire nine 41-caliber rounds from its main barrel plus buckshot from a shorter one. (Oddly enough, its main barrel's caliber is variously reported as ranging from 40- to 42-caliber.) The idea for this monster came from Jean Alexander Francois Le Mat, a New Orleans doctor. Once the Confederacy accepted his pistol, the doctor headed for France where it was produced. A carbine model also was developed.

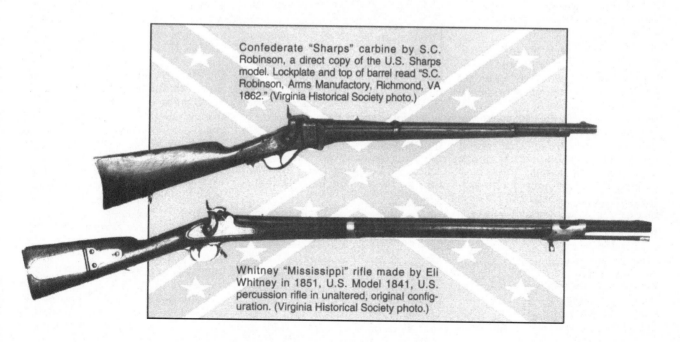

Confederate "Sharps" carbine by S.C. Robinson, a direct copy of the U.S. Sharps model. Lockplate and top of barrel read "S.C. Robinson, Arms Manufactory, Richmond, VA 1862." (Virginia Historical Society photo.)

Whitney "Mississippi" rifle made by Eli Whitney in 1851, U.S. Model 1841, U.S. percussion rifle in unaltered, original configuration. (Virginia Historical Society photo.)

The last source of weapons was from within the Confederacy. Given the virtually non-existent manufacturing base there, Gorgas achieved astonishing results, creating government armories as well as inspiring various private firms to enter the armaments field.

The best Southern-made weapons came from government operations in Richmond and Fayetteville, North Carolina. Early in the war, the Confederacy captured Federal gun-making equipment at Harper's Ferry. This was used at both Confederate plants to produce 58-caliber muskets, known as Richmond and Fayetteville rifles.

These two factories were not the only source of "home-grown" weapons. Other production facilities sprang up in Georgia, Louisiana, South Carolina, Mississippi, Texas and Alabama. Quality and volume varied greatly from factory to factory, as the case of the Confederate "Sharps" proved. These were versions of the Sharps carbine Model 1855, made by the Richmond firm of S.C. Robinson Arms Manufacturing Company. Forty were sent for field-testing to the 4th Virginia Cavalry Regiment in the spring of 1863. The gun was not a success. Reportedly seven of nine burst during firing. Furious, an officer of the regiment, Lieutenant N.D. Morris, fired off a letter to a newspaper, *The Richmond Whig*, which ran a story on the weapons under the headline "An Outrage."

"The lieutenant suggests," ran the article, "that the manufacturers of these arms be sent to the field where they can be furnished with Yankee sabres, while the iron they are wasting can be used for farming implements!"

Ordnance officials rushed to defend the producers and the carbines, suggesting the soldiers using the weapons had not been trained properly, but the bad reputation stuck. Captain W.S. Downer, superintendent of the Richmond armory, also reported to Gorgas that somebody should remind the letter-writing lieutenant about army procedures. "I would also suggest that Lieut. N.D. Morris, of Capt. McKinney's Co., 4th Va. Cavalry, be notified to communicate with the Department through his proper officers, rather than through the columns of a newspaper."

Besides government plants, private firms got involved in weapons production. For example, Davis and Bozeman of Coosa County, Alabama, made 58-caliber rifles. J.&F. Garrett Co. of Greensboro, North Carolina, produced the 52-caliber Tarpley carbine, the only breech-loading

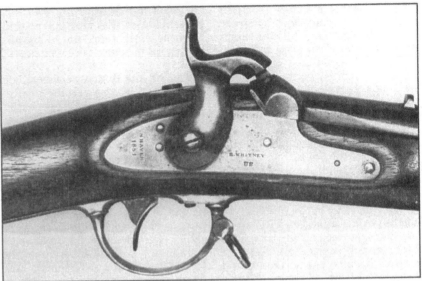

Whether marked "U.S.," like this Whitney Mississippi Rifle (above) or "RICHMOND, VA," as it says on the Robinson Sharpe (below), the Rebs used them all. (Virginia Historical Society photos)

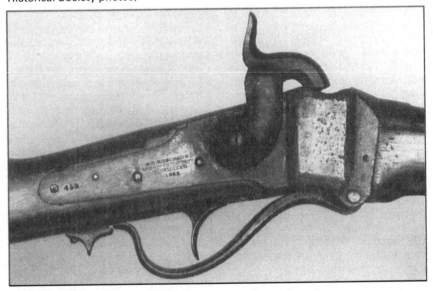

gun patented, manufactured and offered for general sale in the Confederacy.

Private industry made its biggest contribution to weapons production by making pistols. When the war began, the Confederacy had no revolver manufacturers within its borders. But wartime entrepreneurs appeared like Spiller and Burr, Griswold and Gunnison, and Leech & Rigdon.

Many entrepreneurs found that making weapons for the South was a difficult business indeed. Consider the story of Charles Rigdon, for example, a Southern sympathizer who lived in St. Louis. He moved to Memphis when the war started and formed a partnership with Thomas Leech to make swords. Advancing Union armies forced the pair to move to Columbus, Mississippi, and then to Greensboro, Georgia, where they made 36-caliber revolvers, which were copies of Colt's pistols. The partnership eventually collapsed. Leech kept making revolvers in Greensboro. Rigdon opened a new pistol firm in Augusta, Georgia — Rigdon, Ansley & Co. — that operated until the war's end. Interestingly enough, Samuel Colt sued the company for illegal use of his revolver patents.

One non-issue weapon that came from private manufacturers was the shotgun. Often brought from home, shotguns were popular among certain Confederate cavalry units, particularly in the Western Theater. Shotguns had limited range, limited tactical value and took a long time to load. But at close quarters they were

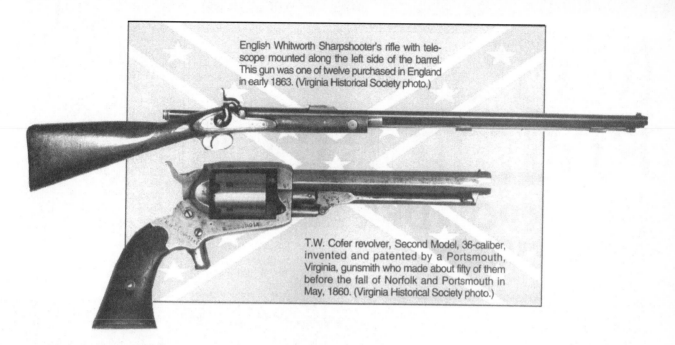

English Whitworth Sharpshooter's rifle with tele-scope mounted along the left side of the barrel. This gun was one of twelve purchased in England in early 1863. (Virginia Historical Society photo.)

T.W. Cofer revolver, Second Model, 36-caliber, invented and patented by a Portsmouth, Virginia, gunsmith who made about fifty of them before the fall of Norfolk and Portsmouth in May, 1860. (Virginia Historical Society photo.)

devastating. The 8th Texas Cavalry, better known as Terry's Texas Rangers, were particularly fond of scatterguns. During the Southern retreat from the Battle of Shiloh, this unit used these weapons effectively. Ordered to charge Union infantry pursuing the Southern army, the Texans swept forward, halted about twenty steps from the Federal line and fired their shotguns. Each barrel was loaded with fifteen to twenty buckshot. The Federal pursuit fell apart and a retreat ensued. The Texans then put their shotguns aside and pursued the enemy on horseback, firing their revolvers.

Much of the success of Southern weapon production came from the use of slave labor. African-Americans worked in armories and played a key role in the armament industry's labor force. For instance, the Georgia pistol firm of Columbus Fire Arms Manufacturing Co. hired forty-three blacks in 1862 and aggressively tried to find more during the rest of the war.

For blacks, working in weapons production was a mixed bag. It often meant separation from loved ones, hard work, long hours and daily rations of bacon and cornmeal. However, the work gave them valuable skills and provided an unprecedented degree of freedom.

Although the Confederacy ultimately lost the war, it did not do so due to a lack of weapons and ammunition. Granted, the Southern ordnance system had flaws. Armies in the East tended to be better supplied than those in the West. Units in either theater, even late in the war, might carry a hodgepodge of weapons, mostly rifled muskets but sometimes smooth-bores, and this variety made ammunition re-supply a headache. Some of the Southern-made rifles and pistols did not meet the standards of Northern or British factories, but on balance Gorgas did a remarkable job.

One anecdote makes the point. When Lee surrendered at Appomattox in 1865, his army was small, sick, ill-clad and poorly fed. However, most men were armed and, on average, each carried seventy-five rounds of ammunition.

Today, Confederate guns are scarce and costly. But the interested student of Civil War firearms can see one of the world's best collections of Southern weapons at the Virginia Historical Society in Richmond. The society owns an extraordinary collection of rifles, pistols, swords, belt-plates and buttons given to it in 1948 by Richard D. Steuart, a Baltimore newspaperman who had two grandfathers and nine uncles who served the Confederate cause. For many years, the collection was displayed to feature the weapons themselves as artifacts and objects of interest.

In 1993, the Virginia Historical Society decided to display its collection in an innovative way. The weapons were moved into a gallery decorated with life-sized murals of Civil War battle scenes. The new display uses the guns to tell the story of how the South armed itself. For the neophyte or life-long scholar of the conflict, the new display is entertaining and informative — you can *see* Johnny Reb and his guns.

For more information on the society and its collections, write: Virginia Historical Society, P.O. Box 7311, Richmond, VA 23221-0311 or call 804-358-4901.

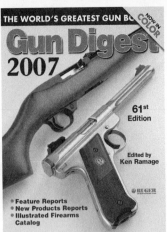

# Military Rolling Rifles
## of the Rarest Kind

■ George J. Layman

This close-up of the Edward Paget-manufactured military rolling block for the Austrian government with the hammer cocked, shows the spring-charged safety stopper in the frontal position.

*The Remington Rolling Block Rifle became an immediate favorite with many of the world's armies and was manufactured under license and modified by a variety of countries.*

The story of the Remington rolling block is well known to arms students throughout the world. However, several variations produced in limited numbers are relatively unknown. Herewith, a short overview on the development of the world's greatest single-shot military rifle.

In 1864–65 chief engineer Joseph Rider of the E. Remington and Sons Arms Co. was tasked to redesign and improve the Leonard Geiger breech-loading design. Geiger, a native of Hudson, NY, received his first patent (#37,501) on January 27, 1863; it was reissued in April 17, 1866, whereupon Rider refined the action even further. The complete redesign strengthened the earlier Remington "split breech" action purchased by the government at the end of the Civil War. The split-breech action was based upon the earlier 1864 patent, having its hammer fit between a weaker, slotted, breechblock that was compatible only with low pressure copper-cased cartridges such as the 46 or 56 Spencer rimfire. The new

1866 patent allowed Rider to improve the breechblock by forming it from a solid billet of steel drilled for a firing pin channel. The breechblock's solid crescent contour rolled beneath the hammer's crescent cut for loading and extracting a spent case. It was the strongest system known that could handle the largest blackpowder cartridges to arrive in the coming decades. The term "rolling block" became the action's sobriquet for eternity. Because the government's budget was strained by the war, and because there was a surplus

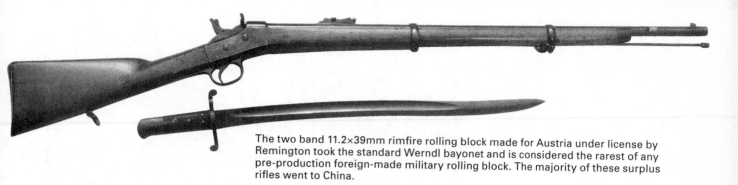

The two band 11.2×39mm rimfire rolling block made for Austria under license by Remington took the standard Werndl bayonet and is considered the rarest of any pre-production foreign-made military rolling block. The majority of these surplus rifles went to China.

of ordnance of all categories, many previously active arms suppliers to the War Department went out of business.

Remington saw this coming and was certain that, unless they quickly found some new business, they would be bankrupt like so many of the other wartime arms manufacturers. Seeking a market for the new rolling block rifle, in the summer of 1866 brother Samuel departed for Europe to demonstrate the qualities of the improved Remington rolling block Rifle. It proved a worthwhile journey; ordnance inspectors from Europe and the Middle East were present for Sam Remington's many hands-on demonstrations of the strength, reliability and rapidity of fire of the new Remington breechloader. Spain, Denmark, Sweden, Egypt, Austria — and a host of other countries — were immediately sold on the remarkable design of the new American breechloader. Once it was awarded a gold medal at the Paris Exposition of 1867, success was at hand.

## The Austro-Hungarian Model Of 1866

The Austro-Hungarian delegation became the first nation to obtain licensing rights to produce the rolling block in Vienna. The reason behind such a hasty arrangement was that Austria knew it would soon be at war with Prussia. Upon the particulars being worked out, the Austrian Emperor called on an English firearms engineer, Edward Paget, to come

to Vienna to oversee production. After Archduke Wilhelm's special commission concurred the rolling block would be an ideal breechloading arm for his military and police forces, Austria paid Remington the license fees to produce the rifle, and Paget began work immediately. According to an article in a British publication, *The Engineer*, dated 27 July 1866, the Emperor of Austria was said to contract with Paget to produce 6,000 rolling-block breechloaders; a later published source stated the number was 15,000.

In any event, Paget cleverly incorporated a number of changes on the Austrian 11.2 × 39.7Rmm rimfire rolling-block Rifle not found on the American-made versions. First, hammer and breechblock pins were retained by individual screws in lieu of the standard Remington "button" plate. Second, a spring-charged, hammer-shaped, "safety stopper" mechanism was cut into the center of the hammer. Unless both the stopper and hammer were simultaneously thumbed to the rear, the hammer could not be cocked. This modification prevented the hammer from automatically opening if a faulty cartridge exploded — which could possibly cock the hammer, slamming the breech block open and sending gases into the shooter's face. The chance of this occurring was very remote when using solid-head centerfire cases but, using the earlier thin copper rimfire cartridge it was a possibility. Single-shot author James J. Grant once credited the Swedes and Norwegians with the safety stopper device; later disproved when I finally obtained one of these rare military rolling-block Rifles.

The Austrian Model of 1866, produced in Europe, should be acknowledged as the first (albeit small) foreign contract obtained by Sam Remington before he departed from the continent. My specimen (s/n #1952) displays other unusual features such as a non-Remington oval-shaped trigger guard, a unique stock comb contour and a three-screw buttplate. Overall quality is quite acceptable, and the Rifle is marked on the left frame ED. A. PAGET, WIEN J. Only 2000 pieces are said to have been completed by Paget when production was halted following the 1866–67 Austrian debacle with the Prussians at Koniggratz.

The Austrian 4th Battalion and the 21st Jager Battalion were selected to conduct the field trials of the new rolling block. The snag that derailed this rolling block design was the issue of nationalism, as the Austrian press hammered the government for considering a foreign design. Between this and the Prussian troubles, the rolling block lost out to Joseph Werndl's system, which Austria finally chose as the national military arm.

Today, the Austrian Edward Paget-made rolling block is indeed the rarest of any Remington-sanctioned foreign prototype/limited production in existence. For years, many rolling-block students were left wondering about the disposition of the remaining 2000 arms. I discovered the majority of remaining surplus Paget-made Austrian rolling blocks ended up in Korea and China; surviving examples have been uncovered with Chinese/ Korean character cartouches on the buttstock. It is believed they were disposed of through a European version of an American Hartley and Graham military-surplus operation.

Evidence indicates they could have been used by Korean hostiles and their Chinese allies, who repelled the U.S. landing expeditions from the USS Colorado in 1871 during the battles at Kanghwa Island, Korea.

All the Austrian rolling blocks were marked ED.A PAGET WIEN 3. Serial numbers were located on the bayonet lug. Note the breech block and hammer pins are screw-retained, something the Swedes later copied.

The left frame of the 1868/74 Norwegian rolling-block rifle made at Konigsberg is one of the most well-inspected Scandinavian military rolling blocks to be found. The markings include the manufactured ate, serial number and inspectors' markings — even the screws are numbered. The production precision clearly shows it was made for a special purpose, perhaps for rifle competition.

The rear sight, calibrated in "Alens," is itself serial-numbered to the rifle.

## The Danish Model 1867/ 96/ 05 Carbine

In 1867, Denmark became the first quantity purchaser of the Remington rolling-block action, making it their official service arm. Contracting with Remington for 42,000 Rifles and 1800 carbines, the Danes received permission to begin domestic production in 1869. When, decades later, Denmark began to upgrade their older equipment, one of the most radically modified rolling blocks is unquestionably the Danish Model 1867/96/05 *Rytterkarabin* (cavalry carbine). This ultra-rare carbine is chambered for the 11.35×45Rmm Danish Remington carbine centerfire cartridge, which replaced the 11.7×42R rimfire version (for carbines) some years earlier. Beyond seeing one of these in the Copenhagen Arsenal display in 1968, I hadn't seen one in the United States until 1996. A Danish-American acquaintance brought one to this country in the 1950s and eventually sold it to me after several years of pestering. It is the first — and only — one I have seen in the Lower 48.

For years the Danes had experimented with manufacturing special-purpose rifles and carbines based on the rolling-block action. The 67/96/05 carbines were shortened to an overall length of 35.5 inches and were simply modified from the older 1867 Danish Bagladeriffels (infantry rifles) with worn barrels and other defects.

My Model 1867/96/05 was discovered with tang markings of E. Remington and Son indicating its action was from one the original rifles purchased

back in 1867. The 67/96/05's designation is derived from the official nomenclature being the Model 1867; '1896' indicated its sling swivels were repositioned, and the regraduation of the rear sight changed from the earlier Danish "Alen" to meters.

The modification of 1905, however, gave the carbine its most radical physical modification. The comb of the buttstock was laterally cut from the thumb rest on back and drilled to hold ten cartridges, thus increasing the soldier's basic ammunition load. Further, a hinged spring-tensioned aluminum cover and base plate kept the cartridges in place. A leather liner pinned inside the cover kept the cartridges silent when they hit against the cover.

Another interesting feature was the rounded, protruding knob installed on the left side of the frame, which served in place of a saddle ring.

With its "mushroom"-style head that fit into a clip spring on the saddle, it somewhat resembled the swiveling concept of the "Bridgeport Device" experimented with on Colt single-action revolvers for the U.S. Army.

The 67/96/05 cavalry carbine was fitted with conventional sling swivels with the rear swivel being angled on the right wrist, and had lightly-rounded finger grooves on the forend. All in all, it made

Having the entire comb of the stock stripped flat and drilled to hold ten cartridges beneath a spring-charged aluminum cover is indeed a radical addition.

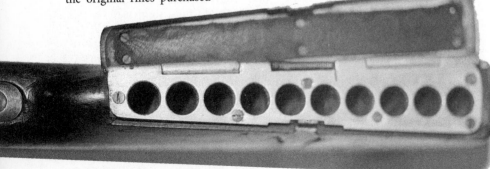

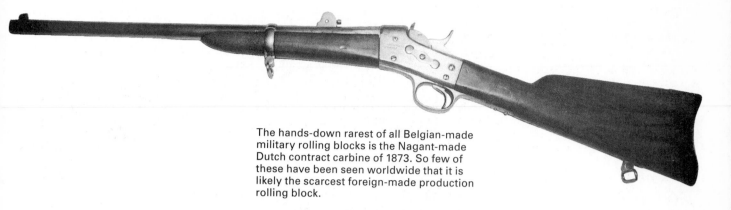

The hands-down rarest of all Belgian-made military rolling blocks is the Nagant-made Dutch contract carbine of 1873. So few of these have been seen worldwide that it is likely the scarcest foreign-made production rolling block.

for a very slick-looking carbine that appears about as far as one could go in modernizing the rolling block. The one feature it lacked was a buttplate.

The total number of 1867/96/05 modified carbines is estimated at 3000. Regarding Danish carbine production as a whole, 2500 Engineer carbines of the Model 1867 were delivered to the army, of which 1950 were altered to centerfire.

With substantial quantities of earlier rimfire ammunition in reserve stocks, a fair number of rimfire rolling-block carbines were left. Thus, breechblocks on some carbines were drilled with two firing pin channels — rim- or centerfire — allowing the firing pin to be moved to either position, depending on the ammunition issued.

Between 1872 and 1883, some 3078 carbines identical to the Engineer Model (with sling swivels on forend and lower buttstock) were received by the Danish navy (Marinen). The only distinguishing feature of service affiliation was the army or navy brass regimental or service disc in the buttstock. One of the reasons for the Danish military carbine upgrade of 1905 was to cover the shortage of 8mm Danish Model 1889 Krag bolt-action rifles. Interestingly, the Model 67/96/05 11.7mm centerfire carbines remained in active service with the regular army until 1914.

### The Norwegian 1868/74 Konigsberg Rolling Block Rifle

Another very rare Scandinavian copy of the rolling block made under license was the 1868/74 infantry rifle manufactured at Konigsberg, Norway in 12.11mm Norway/Sweden rimfire. This particular example differs from the typical Swedish-made versions as it has a 38 ½-inch barrel. This Rifle shows the highest quality of workmanship and attention to detail in every single part: the frame, barrel, rear sight, the three barrel bands and all other

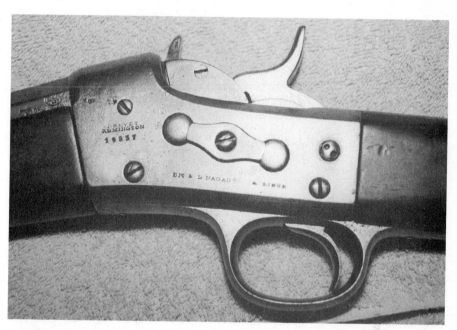

These right and left close-ups of the Nagant Dutch carbine show well-defined markings that identify it. The left frame side (top) has BREVETTE REMINGTON (Remington copy) over the company's master rolling block serial number. The pentagonal barrel flat shows still more inspectors' stampings.

A full-length view of my Chinese rimfire carbine has nowhere near the graceful lines of the Nagant-made Dutch contract carbine and seems to have been produced in the shortest amount of time possible.

components were serial-numbered. My specimen is s/n 31559 and is marked 1876 indicating continuous serial numbers on all Konigsberg-made rolling blocks regardless of special or standard issue; otherwise, many more of these unique M1868/74 rifles would be in circulation. I believe it was specially-made as a military match rifle due to the overabundance of inspectors' cartouches and overall precise fit. The Konigsberg arsenal produced thousands of rolling blocks for the Swedish crown, but this high quality example does not compare to the usual Konigsberg-produced rolling-block infantry Rifles with dates from 1875 to 1878 that I have observed. Whatever the case, this configuration is truly one to watch for.

## The Belgian Nagant Model 1873 Dutch Carbine

Two of Europe's most prolific arms manufacturers from Belgium were Emil & L. Nagant and August Francotte, both of whom had amicable relations with the Remington company in Ilion, New York. By the early 1870s, Remington found it had to work 24-hour shifts to keep up with orders from Spain, Latin America, Egypt and beyond. To meet production deadlines, the system of granting manufacturing rights to reliable, high-quality foreign arms manufacturing companies proved a profitable venture. Remington, though not receiving a full price for each Rifle, would receive a healthy royalty for each unit

manufactured under license.

Francotte produced rolling-block Rifles and carbines to help fill the large Egyptian order, and independently took orders for Uruguay and El Salvador for a two-band musketoon in 43 Spanish. Nagant also produced an order of two-band musketoons for Tunisia that had a crescent moon inlaid into the stock, with fleur-de-lis designs in the body of the crescent.

The aforementioned Francotte and Nagant rolling blocks are genuine scarcities, but the real prize among Belgian-made rolling blocks are those of the 1873 Dutch carbine contract made by Nagant. These are so difficult to uncover that ten years ago they could bring $1000 in Europe alone. Holland, though adopting the Beaumont Rifle in 1870, issued its Snider conversions to the home guard and some colonial troops, then in 1873 decided to also adopt a Remington rolling-block carbine to be made under license by Nagant. It would be chambered for the 11.3×45R or 11mm Dutch Remington centerfire cartridge. The Nagant-made rolling-block carbines served three purposes: to arm the cavalry, engineers, and gendarmerie (national police or gendarmes).

The variation shown is part of the collection of Tom Jackson of Kingman, Arizona. I have never owned a Nagant Dutch rolling-block carbine and have heard rumors from Europe that, during the Nazi occupation of Holland, even antiquated Dutch firearms were destroyed or dumped at sea by the Germans to keep them from the resistance groups. If true,

this could explain the worldwide rarity of these carbines. The thoroughness of the inspectors' markings on Jackson's Dutch carbine are indicative of the quality Nagant demanded on production that directly represented the Remington company. The left frame is marked Brevette Remington, or "Remington copy," with the number 19337 beneath. This is a "tracking serial number," indicating the total of rolling-block rifle actions the Nagant firm produced for royalty accounting purposes for Remington. Em. & L. Nagant markings are also present with the Liege ELG definitive proof on the barrel. The 1873 on the rear of barrel is the model year number and the 1877 on the buttplate is the year of manufacture. The D 565 appears to be the Nagant in-house serial number of how many carbines were produced on the contract so far. The circular Nagant cartouche on the right butt is very clear and it is obvious this carbine is in near excellent condition and obviously did not live a hard life. It can only be estimated that possibly 2000 to 4000 carbines were produced, conjecture based on military and police population size of the day. I have viewed rare photographs of the capitulation of the Dutch East Indies to the Japanese in World War II that show Dutch colonial police throwing what appeared to be rolling block-type carbines into an arms cache of all varieties of captured weapons. Thus it may be that numerous obsolete Dutch weapons, including Nagant-made carbines, were lost as a result of hostilities with Japan.

## A Mysterious Chinese Rolling Block Carbine

Rolling block usage in Asia has traditionally been confined to China and Korea. Partial records indicate that, in 1874, Remington received a rather dubious order for 144,000 rolling-block rifles. I have examined Chinese copies of the rolling block, none of which had any Remington or U.S. markings. Some of these were the surplus Austrian rolling blocks made by Edward Paget as discussed previously,

With the action open one can see the early grooved channeled breech block was utilized. The million dollar question which evades explanation up to now is who was the Belgian company involved in setting up this operation in China to build these carbines? Also, did the Chinese build these independently upon their departure?

and were strictly a surplus purchase without any connection to Remington.

The second copies I examined were a rifle and a carbine, the latter of which I now own. The carbine is a mysterious piece, without markings aside from the number 21 and two Chinese characters — all other major components have the Chinese character of the number ten "+" which is shaped like a cross. Chambered for an unknown 11mm rimfire cartridge, the carbine appears to be of Belgian design with a Springfield-style muzzleloading rear sight (possibly U.S. surplus or replicated production). Other features include a brass buttplate and a circular channel drilled horizontally through the center of the stock evidently intended for some sort of sling attachment device. The barrel has an octagonal chamber and an offset witness mark to line up with the frame. I purchased this carbine from a WWII veteran who brought it back from Manchuria after his assignment involving releasing U.S. soldiers from Japanese captivity. He mentioned he saw many carbines and Rifles of this design at the Mukden, Manchuria arsenal.

Who assisted the Chinese in manufacturing these? If the tooling came from Belgium, it is odd that no Nagant or Francotte markings are present. Both these firms were known for their strict quality control, and the absence of even a token showing of inspector markings

is very odd. Another peculiar note: of all of the surplus military arms coming out of China in the last 20 years or more, not one Remington-marked rolling block has ever been imported. What became of the so-called order of 144,000 rolling blocks? I feel there was a secret (at least at present) arrangement wherein China made an agreement with Remington to produce the arms either in China proper, or in Belgium for subsequent export to the Chinese mainland — or perhaps vice-versa. From a professional viewpoint, after having examined over a thousand foreign- and domestic-made Remington military rolling blocks, the theory of tooling and machinery being shipped to China and the arms subsequently manufactured there, under Belgian supervision, seems the most feasible scenario. Given the warlord system of the day, foreign inspector or manufacturers markings may have been purposely omitted since countless warring factions may have had their arms produced on the identical Belgian equipment overseen by

the same inspectors!

There have been at least two known sales of Chinese-made rolling-block rifles having this carbine's characteristics (excepting the drilled stock channel). They were sold by Kristopher Gasior, a dealer of rare and unusual military rolling blocks (www.Collectiblefirearms.com). The Chinese-made rolling-block rifles were definitely produced under trained Belgian supervision and — so far — have been two-band military rifles with a cleaning rod and a unique elevated rear sight almost eight inches from the receiver ring! Indeed a peculiar arrangement. Caliber of these Rifles appears very similar to that of a 50–70 rimfire cartridge. Regarding the carbine, I know of only one other example — it is in a Massachusetts collection and an exact clone of my carbine. Parts are completely interchangeable, but are marked with the Chinese character number of 216. Perhaps in the future, a long-forgotten arsenal — akin to the recent find of thousands of arms in Nepal's Lag-

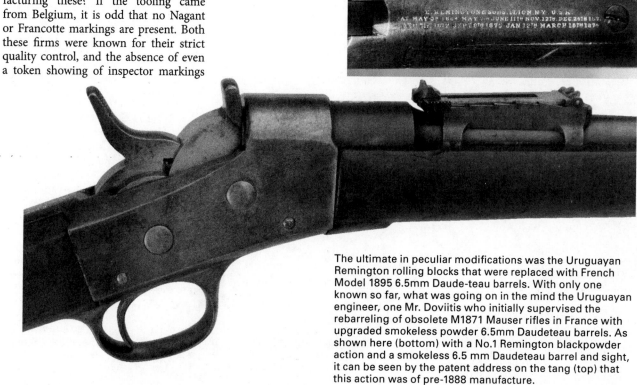

The ultimate in peculiar modifications was the Uruguayan Remington rolling blocks that were replaced with French Model 1895 6.5mm Daude-teau barrels. With only one known so far, what was going on in the mind the Uruguayan engineer, one Mr. Doviitis who initially supervised the rebarreling of obsolete M1871 Mauser rifles in France with upgraded smokeless powder 6.5mm Daudeteau barrels. As shown here (bottom) with a No.1 Remington blackpowder action and a smokeless 6.5 mm Daudeteau barrel and sight, it can be seen by the patent address on the tang (top) that this action was of pre-1888 manufacture.

an Silekhana palace — will be revealed on the Chinese mainland. For now, the so-called Chinese contract of Remington's mysterious "144,000" is a rolling-block version of lost treasure.

## The Uruguayan 6.5 Daudeteau/Doviitis Rolling Block Rifle

One nation that earnestly favored the rolling block system was the South American Republic of Uruguay. Whether made by Remington, Francotte or Nagant, they were probably the most prolific customers for this single-shot Rifle of any country south of the border. The Uruguayan military first purchased several thousand Remington rolling-block Rifles and carbines in 1880 in 43 Spanish, which was the standard chambering of nearly all Latin American countries that were rolling block-equipped. About that same year, Uruguay contracted with August Francotte of Belgium for approximately 2500–3000 two-band artillery musketoons, which are usually found marked "Republica Oriental," the early name for Uruguay.

Since Uruguay was populated by many German, Italian and other European immigrants, there was an ample population of educated machinists on hand, to include former European arms craftsmen. There is a great deal of evidence that they were conducting experiments on rolling block and other existing weapon systems.

Several years ago I obtained a particularly unusual and so far one-of-a-kind specimen, once owned by the late author Jerry Janzen, was obtained by the author several years ago. This Remington rolling-block action was fitted with what is known as the 6.5mm Mauser-Doviitis barrel, one of the great enigmas of foreign converted rolling-block actions. In the 1890s, a mysterious Uruguayan engineer named Dovitiis was tasked by his government to take an unknown number of surplus German Mauser Infanterie Gewehr Model 1871 bolt-action rifles and have them reworked by the French Societe Francaise des Armes Portatives of St. Denis in Paris (abbreviated S.F.A.P / St. Denis). Dovitiis is said to have supervised the installation of new French-made barrels chambered for the 6.5 × 53mm Daudeteau No.12 caliber to replace the old German 11mm (43 Mauser) tubes on the 71 Mauser actions (these barrels came from the now very rare Model 1895 Daudeteau Rifle sold to Uruguay, El Salvador and Portugal). No one ever seemed to find a record for this order, though many felt it was an interim purchase by the Uruguayan government to supplement its army's M1893 or M1895 Mauser rifles. Another rumor is they were intended to arm rebel factions in one of the Uruguayan states in the outback.

In any case, the arms were shipped from Antwerp, Belgium to Montevideo, Uruguay. A later rumor circulated that quantities of rolling-block actions were soon after being rebarreled in Montevideo arsenal, also with Dovitiis in charge of the operation. Whether intended to serve as government training arms or to supply the army (or rebels?) is unknown.

Up to this point, only a single specimen of the 6.5mm Daudeteau-chambered military rolling block is known to me. The late Mr. Janzen may have obtained this rifle on a trip to Uruguay, but no such record exists. If quantities were reworked and clandestinely issued to rebels, or other factions, perhaps none ever returned to be imported through legal means and could likely have been discarded by insurgents in the jungle outback after the ammunition became obsolete. My specimen is in superb condition.

The barrel is clearly marked with the SFAP ST. DENIS scroll behind the original banded ramp rear sight for the 6.5 mm Daudeteau rifle cartridge. The two-band forend has the French 1895 bayonet lug beneath the front sight band, along with the peculiar cleaning rod mounted offset to the right side. I have requested information regarding this Rifle and the Dovitiis connection but to this day however, the Uruguayan government is still secretive of disclosing even 19th century military information because of their past troubles with the 1970s Tupamaro rebels, off-shoots of another era. It would indeed be nice to see another specimen offered not only for sale but to simply compare and examine.

## The U.S. Model 1870 Uruguayan-Honduran Carbine Conversion

The Uruguayan-Honduran carbine conversion is a true 19th century multi-national rolling-block carbine that started life as the U.S. Navy Model 1870 rifle, purchased by the Navy and made under contract at the Springfield Armory. Almost 10,000 of these two-band rifles with Remington-marked actions, several thousand had the rear sight installed closer to the receiver ring than specified, and were subsequently rejected by government inspectors. Though another 10,000 were assembled properly for the Navy,

Unknown until the 1960s, the Canadian purchase of 60 Whitney carbines to arm the Montreal police department was exposed in a 1965 article in a Canadian arms journal. For years American collectors believed it was merely a rumor.

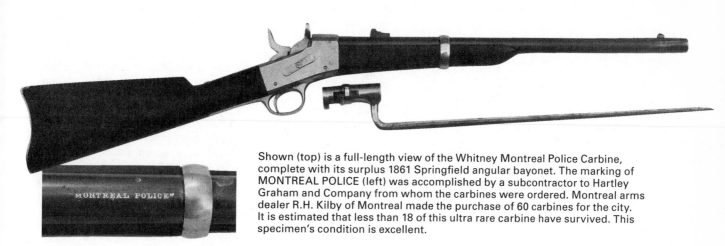

Shown (top) is a full-length view of the Whitney Montreal Police Carbine, complete with its surplus 1861 Springfield angular bayonet. The marking of MONTREAL POLICE (left) was accomplished by a subcontractor to Hartley Graham and Company from whom the carbines were ordered. Montreal arms dealer R.H. Kilby of Montreal made the purchase of 60 carbines for the city. It is estimated that less than 18 of this ultra rare carbine have survived. This specimen's condition is excellent.

many believe this first batch was purposely assembled incorrectly and was nothing more than a ploy to allow American surplus arms dealers to buy them and re-sell them to the French, who were clamoring for military Rifles during the Franco-Prussian War.

This clandestine act of "back-door" diplomacy actually succeeded, but the French ultimately lost the war in 1870.

The Hartley and Graham Company is believed to have bought them from the U.S. government at a bargain price, subsequently reselling them to France. Then, after buying the Rifles back from France, advertised them as "Franco-Prussian War Surplus," selling them for a profit yet again! Prime markets for such sales were Central and South America, where a ready market existed for rolling-block rifles. Many times, a country's numerous rival political groups would buy their ordnance from the same dealer — such as Hartley & Graham — who could care less which side was right. It was all about money. Uruguay, in 1873–75, again ordered some 2500 rolling blocks from Hartley & Graham, advertised as surplus 1870 Navy rolling blocks in 50–70 Govt. that had been repurchased from the French. The Uruguayans requested the Rifles to be re-barreled to 43 Spanish and shortened to carbine length, and fitted with a saddle ring and staple and carbine forend. These modifications would slightly raise the cost per cost of gun, but the contract with Hartley & Graham was nevertheless completed, and Uruguay received the delivery without a hitch. Upon receipt, all were inspected and stamped with the standard Uruguayan circular military cartouche on the left side of the stock with the date and EJERCITO URUGUAYO (Uruguayan Army). Interestingly, the button plate which held the breechblock and hammer pin in place was reversed to the right side

of the frame. The reversal button plate partially obscured the "giveaway origin" of the markings on the carbine actions — the U.S. Springfield 1870 marking and the American eagle motif.

Sometime in the mid-1880s, Uruguay sold a thousand or more of these carbines to Honduras as that rather poor nation could not afford to purchase new rifles from the United States. Over time, some of these carbines were captured by both Honduran rebel factions as well as El Salvadoran troops, and few have survived after years of hard service. My carbine was not terribly abused and its original Uruguayan cartouche is still noticeable. There is also a serial or rack number of "33" on the lower tang, which may be a Honduran addition since I once examined an identical specimen, imported from Uruguay, which lacked any numeration in this area. A "43 Span." stamping over the chamber is also present. Also, an E.H. is found stamped on the comb of the stock which appears to translate to Ejercito Honduras (Honduran Army). Very few of these have surfaced on the U.S. antique firearms market. But one thing is certain; they truly made money for their original American owners at least five times in their heyday!

Right up to the early 1910s, the M. Hartley Company of New York City (formerly Hartley and Graham) remained an agent for the Remington Arms Company, being redesignated as such after the Remington company was reorganized in 1888. As late as the 1900s, the Hartley Co. maintained an extensive inventory of out-of-production blackpowder-era rolling blocks and fulfilled countless orders for the poorer nations of Latin America who could not afford to arm all their soldiers with expensive Mauser bolt-action repeaters. Hartley and Co. produced hundreds of different unique military rolling blocks for numerous countries, which have often

been mistaken as genuine factory-correct Remington-made arms. This specimen of the Hartley & Graham-modified Model 1870 Navy rolling block sold to Uruguay, and then to Honduras, is a good example of how specially reworked rolling blocks confuse rolling block students as to being some sort of special-order contract made at the Remington factory. There are literally dozens of Hartley-converted rolling blocks: carbines with bayonet lugs or two-band full-stock carbines with a shortened cleaning rod, all going to Central or South American countries to arm both governments and rebel factions.

The 1870 Navy conversion sold to Uruguay should be considered among the most difficult to uncover, including those indigenously manufactured in a foreign arsenal under Remington license. Rest assured, many variations never before seen are waiting somewhere in the dark jungles of Latin America.

## Whitney Rolling Block Rarities

Along with E. Remington & Sons, the firm of the Whitney Arms Co. of New Haven, Conn. competed in manufacturing a rolling block-action rifle which resulted in two different types of actions offered at different periods of time. The earliest was the Whitney-Laidley patent breech-loading system; peculiar in that the breechblock and hammer components consisted of a five-piece assembly comprised of hammer, locking cam, thumb piece plate and breechblock. Its last patent was registered on July 16 1872. In production from 1871 to 1881, the first model action was eventually redesigned and "Remingtonized" to a less complicated system once the Remington patent expired. This allowed Whitney to closely copy its simpler competitor, resulting in an action more economical to manufacture.

The second model action was produced from 1881 until 1888 when the Whitney Firearms Company closed its doors, and was acquired by the Winchester Repeating Arms Co. Not having come close to the quantities of rolling-block Rifles Remington had churned out, Whitney military rolling-block rifles and carbines nevertheless had their following and, in their entirety, were exported outside the United States to countries primarily in Latin America. In nearly every case, those that returned to the U.S. surplus arms market in scanty numbers have been in conditions ranging from good to poor, indicating hard usage. To find any standard or special order Whitney military rolling-block rifle or carbine in excellent condition is truly sensational. Special production Whitney military rolling blocks for foreign customers have been almost non-existent in the past, but it is accurate to say that arms exporters Hartley and Graham made up at least some specially-modified Whitney rolling blocks for overseas buyers.

There is, however, at least one that was revealed by author Gordon Howard in a Canadian arms journal dated 1965. No one in the United States, including antique firearms expert Norm Flayderman, had ever seen the special Whitney Montreal Police Carbine until it was featured in the third edition of my book, The Military Remington Rolling Block Rifle (1998 Pioneer Press, Union City TN). Years ago, I heard from several Canadians that this arm existed, but had never owned an example until I purchased a single specimen from a Maine dealer/collector who began going on buying trips to Canada in the 1990s when our northern neighbor's government imposed draconian gun legislation. Many rarities were coming out of the woodwork as average Canadian citizens were frantically selling off their firearms, many of which were highly collectible.

The Whitney Montreal Police Carbine was a standard, first model Whitney military saddle ring carbine chambered in 433 Spanish Remington Carbine, a lighter-recoiling number than the full-blown 78-grain load of FFg of the standard 43 Spanish cartridge. The carbine was procured specifically for the city of Montreal in December of 1875 after the city police committee decided to pick out 50 men in the department and arm them with carbines in lieu of revolvers.

At the meeting on September 1, the police council stated…."the men shall be armed with carbines, as they are more useful than revolvers and that the number so armed be limited to sixty…" After $1330 was appropriated for the purchase, a Montreal arms agent named R.H. Kilby residing at Saint Catherine St. was to be the contact man for the procurement. Little is known whether Kilby or the Montreal city council specified details of the carbine regarding caliber, including the angular socket-type bayonets that accompanied all sixty pieces, which appear to have been surplus U.S. Springfield-style bayonets. It is generally felt that Kilby ordered the arms and had them stamped "Montreal Police" by Hartley and Graham Co. in New York City. In Gordon Johnson's article, he notes a former police lieutenant he interviewed believes the carbines were never fired except for brief training practice and were used as reserve weapons. In addition, the lieutenant stated that they were mostly used for escorting prisoners from the courthouse to Bordeaux Jail in the north end of Montreal city. All carbines had rack markings on the buttplate, with mine being #7. As with all Whitney rolling blocks, serial numbers are on the lower tang and, from all indications, they were not consecutively numbered.

In the early 1960s, a very small number of these carbines began to appear in Canada and were in from good to very good condition. The highest rack number known is #59, reported by Gordon Johnson. He also noted (in 1965) that no more than 18 to 20 carbines were said to exist. When they were withdrawn from service during World War I, they were stored in wooden cases in the basement of the Montreal Police School. Around 1923, a substantial number were destroyed or disassembled, and ammunition for the carbines was disposed of as late as 1961. The arms were supplied with a two-position carbine open and peep sight for 200 and 500 yards, and were finished in the white, aside from a blued barrel. Fortunately my specimen appears to have had little to no use — which explains its excellent condition. Only slight wear adjacent to the muzzle stems from bayonet installation and removal. For many years rumors circulated that rolling block firearms were being used in official military or police capacities in Canada, but no proof of this surfaced until the 1960s. The importance of the discovery of the Whitney Montreal Carbine caused it to be included as a special category of its own in the latest edition of FLAYDERMAN'S GUIDE TO ANTIQUE AMERICAN FIREARMS… AND THEIR VALUES.

Another extremely rare Whitney roll-ing block is a second model garden-variety three-band military rifle. What makes it special is that (a) it is one of the rare Mexican contract models and (b), its condition is almost at 90 percent, aside from a bullet hole in its stock indicating its violent past. Though the bullet took out a sizeable piece of walnut, especially at the exit, clear cartouches still remain on the wrist and other places. Whitney Rifles in 43 Spanish were ordered twice by Mexico, both orders being of the first and second models.

The rifle's fifth-generation owner, whose ancestors lived in California near the Mexican border, told me the Rifle was a participant — in the hands of Mexican bandits — in the second famous raid (the first being in 1875) on the "Old Stone" Trading Post in Campo, California in 1881. The trading-post workers won the shoot-outs and captured the Mexicans guns, a dozen or more Whitney rolling blocks recently stolen from a *Federale* arsenal in Mexico. This attests to the like-new condition with brilliant case colors, and the Mexican Sunburst and R.M. (Republic of Mexico) translating to *Republica Mexicana*.

Whitney Rifles in 43 Spanish were ordered twice by Mexico; both orders being of the first and second models.

## Remington-Made Rarities of both Black and Smokeless Powder Eras

Genuine Remington factory-made rolling-block military Rifles have their share of scarce models. One of the most elusive rolling blocks catalogued in 1870s and 1880s Remington factory literature is the Spanish Civil Guard Model, simply a two-band military rifle with a shorter 30-inch barrel. I've owned a meager total of four different Civil Guard models in the past 35 years: three from the Philippines and one from Costa Rica.

A most peculiar example I uncovered was found in Belize (the former British Honduras). I speculate it was part of a small lot ordered for Her Majesty's colonial militia in the late 1880s. The profusely British proof-marked Civil Guard Model is in 43 Spanish and has a tinned rear sight, a very peculiar addition. It is the second one from Belize that I have seen in "Del Norte" in about 20 years.

Well identified with numerous British proof marks, the Rifle has scattered pitting typical of the humid region; the bore however is surprisingly clean.

Why England ordered these in lieu of

issuing the standard British service arm, the Martini-Henry, is unknown. The only practical reason is that all British Honduras' neighboring countries used the 43 Spanish Remington rolling block. Thus perhaps the British reasoned from a logistical standpoint that if ammunition ran low during a skirmish with rebel or other forces from nearby Mexico or Guatemala, the interchangeable captured stocks of 43 Spanish cartridges could be utilized if required. Remember, no countries in that region used British Martini-Henry Rifles chambered for the 577/450 cartridge. Definitely a rare interesting rifle!

Another seldom-encountered military rolling-block rifle from that area of Central America, is from the post-1888 order from Guatemala. This period can be verified since the tangs on all these Rifles were marked REMINGTON ARMS COMPANY, indicating their manufacture followed the reorganization of E. Remington and Sons after that year. Fragmented records show that fewer than 2500 were exported to Guatemala between 1890 and 1894. Physical proof they were used to the extreme in that humid and politically violent country is obvious in that their condition ranged from fair to (barely) good. Their primary identifier was behind the rear sight, having the stamped metal displaying "EJERCITO GUATEMALA" (Guatemalan Army) which was often barely visible. The Guatemalan 43s usually ended up in the rebarreling vise to be converted, reblued, etc. into sporters at a time when military rolling blocks in less than new condition regardless of unusual markings, were looked upon as one step above scrap iron. I have found one intact, with markings, and in very good condition to boot. The Guatemalan army issue model is definitely one to watch for, but look closely for the markings as they are normally very faint.

On the opposite end of the beauty scale, Remington rolling blocks that were made as presentation pieces are in a one-of-a-kind category. One of the most beautiful blackpowder-era examples I had the chance to inspect was a fully engraved three-band rifle in 43 Spanish with a fancy silver inlay on the left side of the buttstock that was presented to a Spanish army general for the capture of Cuban insurrectionist D. Pedro Figueredo on August 10, 1870. The rifle was sold at auction in 2000 by J.C. Devine Auctioneers for well over $7500.

After 1896, the Remington rolling block entered the smokeless era. Examples considered antique scarcities, manufactured during this time frame (1896–1917), are primarily categorized by caliber and the presence of national crests. Since 7mm Mauser was the most widespread smokeless powder chambering in the Remington Model 1902, to discover one in 236 (6mm) Navy, 30–40 Krag and 7.65mm Mauser is so rare that they currently bring as much as $2500 to $3000 in good to excellent condition. The Remington Model 1897 rifles and carbines of the 1899–1900 Mexican contract, with the national crest stamped on the receiver ring, totaled 14,010 Rifles and carbines. Those that returned to the U.S. arms market in the 1960s were, for the most, in very sad shape. The majority of these hardened smokeless steel guns were rebarreled to modern calibers and given complete makeovers. A Mexican-marked Model 1897 Rifle or, especially, a carbine in very decent condition today is quite desirable and, price-wise, is a well above the 1962 price of $8.28! The condition of the crest is often the primary factor in determining desirability and price.

Aside from the Mexican contract model, the other crested military rolling block of the smokeless era are those of the El Salvador contract of 1902. These are even more difficult to discover because fewer were manufactured. Those that have been found are, on average, in rough and pitted condition. I've seen only one in very good condition in a private collection. The Salvadoran Model differs from the Mexican contract model not because it is a Model 1902, but because of an oversize upper handguard with a pronounced groove. Find one of these 7mm Rifles that worked the humid, wet jungles of El Salvador in excellent condition with a clean national crest, and you have one of the great prizes of the post-1900 era Remington military rolling block Rifles.

The very last Remington military rolling block of substantial number that closed out a 50-year era of steady production were those of the French contract of 1915–1916. It was basically a supplementary order to provide France with a single-shot Rifle in their national caliber of 8mm Lebel. This interim order gave Remington time to tool up for the standard Mannlicher-Berthier repeating bolt-action Rifle. The French purchased 100,291 rolling blocks in World War I, with most going to arm colonial forces from Morocco, Algeria and other colonies. The majority of these rifles saw very hard usage and, after

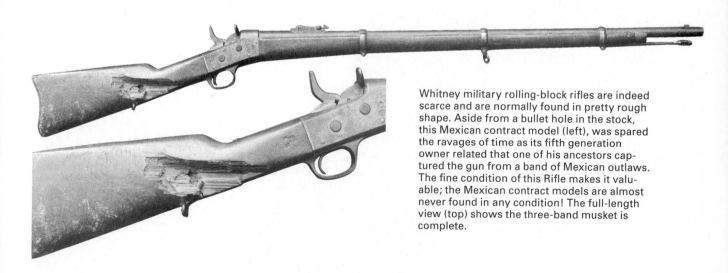

Whitney military rolling-block rifles are indeed scarce and are normally found in pretty rough shape. Aside from a bullet hole in the stock, this Mexican contract model (left), was spared the ravages of time as its fifth generation owner related that one of his ancestors captured the gun from a band of Mexican outlaws. The fine condition of this Rifle makes it valuable; the Mexican contract models are almost never found in any condition! The full-length view (top) shows the three-band musket is complete.

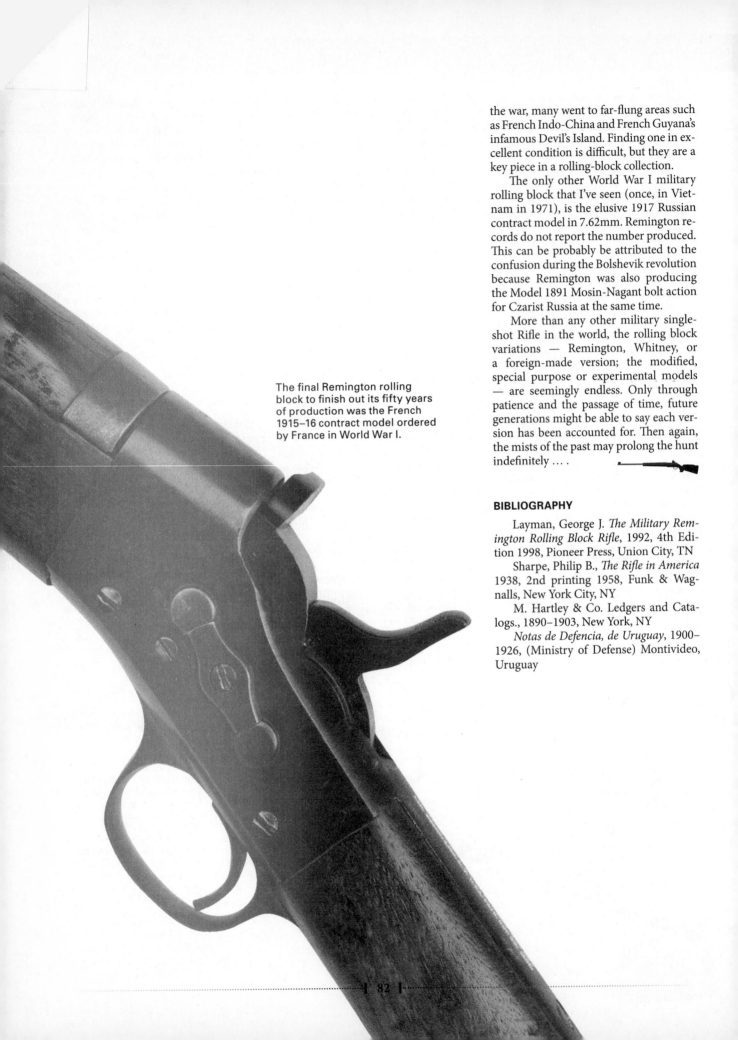

The final Remington rolling block to finish out its fifty years of production was the French 1915–16 contract model ordered by France in World War I.

the war, many went to far-flung areas such as French Indo-China and French Guyana's infamous Devil's Island. Finding one in excellent condition is difficult, but they are a key piece in a rolling-block collection.

The only other World War I military rolling block that I've seen (once, in Vietnam in 1971), is the elusive 1917 Russian contract model in 7.62mm. Remington records do not report the number produced. This can be probably be attributed to the confusion during the Bolshevik revolution because Remington was also producing the Model 1891 Mosin-Nagant bolt action for Czarist Russia at the same time.

More than any other military single-shot Rifle in the world, the rolling block variations — Remington, Whitney, or a foreign-made version; the modified, special purpose or experimental models — are seemingly endless. Only through patience and the passage of time, future generations might be able to say each version has been accounted for. Then again, the mists of the past may prolong the hunt indefinitely … .

### BIBLIOGRAPHY

Layman, George J. *The Military Remington Rolling Block Rifle*, 1992, 4th Edition 1998, Pioneer Press, Union City, TN

Sharpe, Philip B., *The Rifle in America* 1938, 2nd printing 1958, Funk & Wagnalls, New York City, NY

M. Hartley & Co. Ledgers and Catalogs., 1890–1903, New York, NY

*Notas de Defencia, de Uruguay*, 1900–1926, (Ministry of Defense) Montivideo, Uruguay

# Days of the Springfield

■ Col. Townsend Whelen

U.S. Springfield, Model 1903, with type "C" stock.

IN THE Spanish American War, 1898, our officers became rather dissatisfied with the Krag rifle performance compared with that of the 7mm Spanish Mauser. The Krag had a muzzle velocity of 2,000 feet per second and the cartridges had to be fed one at a time into the magazine. The Mauser shot a cartridge that had a muzzle velocity of 2,300 fps and thus a much flatter, hence longer danger space, and the magazine could be filled in one quick motion by means of a clip of five cartridges, thus giving much greater sustained fire; both very important features from a m ilitary point of view. The Ordnance Department of the Army therefore proceeded to a study of the matter, including an examination of the rifles and cartridges used by other nations.

In late September, 1903, when I returned to my post at Monterey, California, after having spent the summer shooting in army competitions and the National Matches as a member of the U.S. Army Infantry Team, my commanding officer handed me a letter he had received from the Chief of Ordnance, asking him to detail me to make an extensive test of a pilot model of a new rifle that had been developed at Springfield Armory. I was also to express an opinion as to its desirability for issue to the Army to replace the current rifle, the Krag. The rifle and a case of ammunition had also arrived.

This rifle was very similar to the 30-06 Springfield military rifle as we now know it. Its breech action, in fact, was identical. It had a 24-inch barrel, a rod bayonet, an open rear sight operated for elevation by a ramp, adjustable to even hundreds of yards only, but with a peep plate pivoted at the back of the open sight which could be raised for use. The breech action was almost identical with that of the Model 1898 Mauser, except for a combined bolt stop and magazine cut-off on the left side of the receiver, and a two-piece firing pin arranged so that the striker point, the one part most apt to break, could be economically replaced. The 5-shot magazine could be loaded with five cartridges at once by means of an expendable clip similar to the Mauser's. The rifle was numbered J8½T.

The cartridge had a rimless case, very similar to the 30-06 cartridge as we now know it, but loaded with a 220-grain round nose, jacketed bullet identical to the Krag bullet. The powder charge was Laflin and Rand WA smokeless powder sufficient in quantity to give a muzzle velocity of 2,350 fps.

I fired this rifle twice through the Regular Army Qualification Course-slow fire at 200 to .600 yards, rapid fire at 200 and 300 yards, and a skirmish run — and obtained as good scores as I would have had I shot the Krag rifle that I'd used all summer. The rifle, I thought, was a little more accurate than the Krag, and I would have obtained higher scores were it not for the rear sight that could be adjusted to only even hundreds of yards for elevation. I had to hold off a little for elevation at all distances. The recoil was noticeably heavier than that of the Krag, but not particularly disturbing to me. It was intended that this rifle, with its 24-inch barrel, be issued to both infantry and cavalry. In my report I criticized only the rear sight, and stated that otherwise I thought it entirely suitable for our service. Thus I think I was the first officer and rifleman ever to shoot the Springfield rifle on the rifle range.

This rifle was subsequently adopted for service, to replace the Krag, and issuance to troops of the Regular Army started in 1905. But in the meantime it had been found that the quantity of powder giving a muzzle velocity of 2,350 fps was too erosive for the barrel, affording an accuracy life of only about 800 rounds, and accordingly the powder charge was reduced sufficiently to give a muzzle velocity of 2,200 fps. The rifle was now officially called the "U.S. Rifle, caliber 30, Model 1903," and the cartridge the "Ball Cartridge, caliber 30, Model 1903." Popularly the rifle was termed the "New Springfield," but pretty soon the "New" was omitted. A new rear sight was also adopted for it, rather like the sight that had been on the Krag rifle. This rifle was issued to my regiment, the 30th Infantry, in time for the regular target practice season of 1906. The chief difference we found with it, compared with the Krag we had formerly used, was that much more careful and extended practice was needed to accustom some of the men to its heavier recoil. The bore was also more difficult to clean, particularly to *keep* clean, than the Krag bore had been.

After this early season's shooting with my company I was ordered to Fort Sheridan as a member of the U.S. Army Infantry Team, and then to the National

Matches. Here the shooting was with the Krag, the Springfield not yet having been issued to the National Guard. Upon completion of the National Matches I rejoined my regiment which, meantime, had been ordered to Fort William McKinley in the Philippine Islands. Here I found that the regiment had been issued a slightly different type of Springfield rifle, but still called the Model 1903. It was fitted with a knife bayonet to replace the former rod bayonet, and had a slightly different walnut hand-guard above the barrel. It also used a slightly different cartridge. The story of the conversion is an interesting one.

Prior to about 1901 the German army had been equipped with the Model 1898 Mauser rifle using an 8mm (7.9×57mm) cartridge loaded with a 236-grain round nose bullet to a muzzle velocity of 2,200

fps. Groove diameter of barrel was .318". Then after considerable experimentation they changed the bullet to one weighing 154 grains with a very sharp point, called a "Spitzer" point, and increased the muzzle velocity to 2,800 fps. New barrels to take this cartridge were fitted to their rifles, and the groove diameter was increased to .323". The increased velocity and the pointed bullet gave a much flatter trajectory and a greatly increased danger

First issues of the 1903 Springfield had a full 24" barrel, with ramrod-bayonet underneath. Note also forward band position and unusual front sight.

space, a very considerable military advantage. Our Ordnance Department was not slow to investigate this improvement, and as a consequence our cartridge for our Springfield rifle was changed to take a 150-grain sharp point bullet loaded to a muzzle velocity of 2,700 fps. To convert existing Springfield rifles to take this new cartridge the barrels had to be rethroated. To do this one thread was cut off the breech of the barrel, the barrel set back, decreasing its length from 24 inches to 23.79 inches, and rechambered. The neck of the Model 1903 cartridge case was also slightly shortened, and the new cartridge was called the Model 1906. This is why we now have a Model 1903 rifle taking a Model 1906 cartridge, and why the barrel is 23.79 inches long instead of 24 inches. The new cartridge soon became popularly known as the "30-06."

When my regiment started its target practice shortly after my arrival in the Philippines it at once became apparent to us that the new rifle and the new cartridge were slightly more accurate than the older ones, that the recoil was slightly less, and the allowances that had to be made for wind were considerably smaller, all considerable advantages. But we also noticed another difference which was not so good. After firing for a few days the bore of the rifle, particularly on top of the lands near the muzzle, became coated with a substance that looked something like the lead that we occasionally saw in our older black powder rifles. This was a metal fouling from the cupronickel jackets of the bullets fired at such great velocity. As it accumulated in the bore it gradually interfered with the accuracy of the rifle to a small extent. It was almost impossible to remove this fouling and the only thing we could do, at that time, was to keep it down by cleaning the bore with a brass wire bristle brush. From then on, until we found the solution for this troublesome fouling, I was always distressed with the appearance of the bores of the rifles in my command. I shall refer to this matter of metal fouling later, and show how we gradually solved the trouble.

Meantime an incident occurred which deserves notice. Private Manuel of my company was firing on the range at Fort McKinley when his rifle "blew up." The whole top of the receiver was blown off, and the bolt was blown twenty feet to the rear. Fortunately Manuel received only a few small cuts on the face. There was no question about there *not* having been an obstruction in the bore because he had previously fired two loads from his clip, and those shots had been marked on his target. I was on the firing point only twenty feet away at the time. I immediately took the rifle into the Ordnance office in Manila and we investigated it as carefully as we could there. The only conclusion we could come to was that it had been caused by a defective and very much overloaded cartridge. Of course, as we now know, this was caused by a brittle receiver that occurred in exceedingly rare instances due to the steel used and the method of heat treatment. This trouble was completely cured after World War I by the adoption of a new method of heat treatment, and then by a new steel, and finally all rifles numbered under 800,000 (those having the old steel and old heat treatment) were condemned. The matter is discussed in detail elsewhere.*

In the spring of 1909 I was ordered from the Philippines to the United States as a member of the Army Infantry Rifle Team. Before going to the National Matches we held our initial team practice at Fort Sheridan, Illinois, and two days a week at Camp Logan on the Illinois National Guard range, where we could get experience in shooting in high winds, the Fort Sheridan range being a very sheltered one. This was the first competition season I took part in where the Springfield rifle was used. The rifles shot splendidly with the specially selected ammunition issued to us for the matches. We were still having trouble with metal fouling. Some of us were keeping this at a minimum by rubbing a thin coating of powdered graphite on our bullets before loading them, and others used a light coat of a heavy grease called Mobilubricant, similarly rubbed on the bullets.

Then, through my correspondence with Dr. Walter G. Hudson, I learned that British gunmakers had developed a strong ammonia solution which completely dissolved and removed all traces of metal fouling. Dr. Hudson gave me the formula for it. The bore of the rifle, clean and cold, was plugged at the chamber with a rubber cork, and a short section of rubber tube was slipped over the muzzle. The solution was then poured into the bore until it rose in the tube, let remain in the bore for 30 minutes, then poured out, the bore flushed with water, and dried. Every trace of the fouling was dissolved and the bore was like new. If certain precautions were observed its action was perfect and safe. I tried it on my rifle and it worked perfectly. Then the whole team tried it with similar fine results. After that we cleaned our rifles in this manner each noon and

night. I shot particularly well that year. My average at 600 yards for the entire year's shooting was 49.5 out of a possible 50 points.

That year the Union Metallic Cartridge Company offered special match ammunition. Several of my friends who had tried it said that it was splendidly accurate. It was loaded with a 172-grain bullet having a very sharp pencil or "spire" point. I bought some of it, and used it in

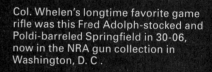

Col. Whelen's longtime favorite game rifle was this Fred Adolph-stocked and Poldi-barreled Springfield in 30-06, now in the NRA gun collection in Washington, D.C.

the Adjutant Generals Match, calling for twenty shots at 1,000 yards, and won that match with it with a score of 99 points, which was said to be the highest score ever fired at 1,000 yards with the service rifle. The following day I also used this ammunition in the Wimbledon Cup Match, also 20 shots at 1,000 yards, and came in second in that match with a score of 97. Thus I ended my competitive military rifle shooting in a burst of glory.

After these competitions I rejoined my regiment, which meantime had been ordered from the Philippines to Fort Jay, New York, and shortly after that I was detailed as Inspector-Instructor with the Connecticut National Guard, and then ordered to Washington to the Division of Militia Affairs. On completion of that detail I again joined my regiment, the 29th Infantry, in the Panama Canal Zone, and served there until the outbreak of World War I when I was promoted to major and assigned as Ordnance Officer of the 79th Division. Later I was placed on the general staff in charge of infantry training in the United States. After the war was over, not having had any battle experience, I thought I would be handicapped in the infantry so I transferred to the Ordnance

Department. My first assignment was to Frankford Arsenal, where all the small arms ammunition for the Army was manufactured. After I had been there ten days the commanding officer fell sick, and I became the commanding officer, and remained there for the next three years.

I at once started out to try to improve the quality and the accuracy of the service ammunition. It was suggested to us that, under the heat and friction generated in the rifle barrel, tin was a good lubricant. Accordingly we made up some of the 150-grain cupronickel jacketed bullets slightly smaller in diameter than normal and

*Hatcher's Notebook by Maj. Gen. Julian S. Hatcher. The Stackpole Company, Harrisburg, Pa., 1947.

tin-plated them with a coating .002-inch thick. It worked. No more metal fouling and much better accuracy. The National Match ammunition for 1921 was loaded with this tin-plated bullet, which the shooters immediately termed "tin can" ammunition, and it shot with splendid accuracy, better than ever before. Then a serious defect developed with its use. The tin alloyed with the steel of the bore, the resultant alloy had a low melting point, and the bore washed out or eroded very quickly — entirely too short an accuracy life. So this experiment failed.

As most of you well know, I have always been an avid experimenter with sporting rifles. The modern ammunition for such rifles employed bullets jacketed with gilding metal — 90% copper, 10% zinc — and apparently these gave no trouble with metal fouling. So next we tried

that an effective range of over 5,000 yards could be obtained with the new projectiles. The most promising bullet tried was one of about 172 grains, sharply pointed, and with a 9-degree boat-tail, but we did not seem to be able to make it shoot with satisfactory accuracy. While we were working with this bullet I was ordered to Camp Perry as Ordnance Officer of the National Matches. While I was there I tried my hand at a little shooting again, this time with the small bore, as I had no time from my duties for 30 caliber shooting. Among other matches I shot in, I was on our International Team in the Dewar Match, but about this time I developed an exceedingly sore boil on my backside. On the day of the Dewar Match I was so sore they had to take me to the firing point in a car and lower me down. Despite so much pain I could hardly move, the sec-

United States. In the meantime, long range barrage fire had gone out of favor in military circles due to great improvement in artillery fire, so we again reverted to our 150-grain flat base, pointed bullet for our standard rifle ammunition, but now jacketing it with gilding metal instead of cupronickel. But that 172-grain boat-tail bullet won't die. It has proved one of the best bullets ever made for 300-meter International Match shooting, and is today again being manufactured at Frankford Arsenal for that use.

Late in 1922 I was relieved from duty at Frankford Arsenal and went to Washington for duty in the office of the Assistant Secretary of War, and after that as Ordnance Member on the Infantry Board, at Fort Benning, Georgia. Then as Executive Officer of the Manufacturing Service in the office of the Chief of Ordnance,

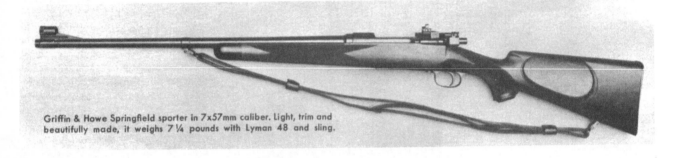

Griffin & Howe Springfield sporter in 7x57mm caliber. Light, trim and beautifully made, it weighs 7 ¼ pounds with Lyman 48 and sling.

a 170-grain pointed bullet jacketed with gilding metal. There was no longer any metal fouling and the accuracy was very good indeed, better than anything tried before except the "tin can" ammunition.

In World War I combat long-range barrage firing with machine guns had been employed very considerably at ranges up to 4,000 and 5,000 yards. We used in our machine guns the normal rifle cartridge loaded with 150-grain bullet. Its extreme range was only about 3,800 yards, and we were completely outranged by the machine guns of most of the other powers, including the enemy. Their machine gun ammunition employed much heavier bullets, that is, bullets with greater sectional density and a much longer controlled range. After the war we started experiments in an effort to increase the effective range of our rifle ammunition. We started making bullets weighing 170 to 180 grains, and with "boat-tails" and sharper points. These were fired experimentally at Daytona Beach, Florida, by Majors Hatcher and Wilhelm of the Ordnance Department, and it was apparent

ond highest score of the match was mine, being beaten only by Virgil Richards.

When I returned to Frankford Arsenal from these matches I went straight to bed to get over that damned boil. Soon Mr. Matthews, the foreman of the bullet shop, came over to see me. He was very much excited. He showed me group after group he had fired at 600 yards with this 172-grain boat-tail bullet, all within 6 inches. He shouted "I've got it, I've got it." He told me he had managed to make this bullet shoot with such fine accuracy by making the core very hard, and then employing as a final die what he called a "rectifying die," one made very perfectly indeed and changed about every 20,000 bullets, or when it began to show the slightest wear. This was the last die used, and the bullet was driven into it with a heavy blow thus making its form most perfect and hard. This became, eventually, the famous 1925 National Match bullet, the most accurate bullet ever used in the Springfield. The only trouble was it had an awfully long range — 5,500 yds. — and it was unsafe to use on many of our rifle ranges in the

and when that duty was over I went to Springfield Armory as officer in charge of research and development. It was exceedingly interesting here to change from the manufacture of the ammunition to the manufacture of the rifle. Springfield had been manufacturing rifles, the best rifles in the world, for over a hundred years. There was nothing that I, of course, a greenhorn at that art, could tell them, but it was most interesting to watch the meticulous care that was used at every step in the manufacture. I was particularly interested in the bedding of the rifles in their stocks, for I'd never realized how much depended on it. One in every ten service rifles, and every National Match, sporting, and target rifle was finally tested for accuracy by firing from a Wood-worth cradle rest at 200 meters. If it did not come up to the standard prescribed for that type of rifle it was sent back to the manufacturing department for correction and almost invariably the trouble would be in the bedding of the rifle in its stock. So far as I was able to determine by questioning the older employees at the Armory, the technique of this bedding was developed, practically as we now do it,* by Freeman R. Bull, who was Master Armorer at Springfield during the 1880–1890 period. In this 200-meter testing service rifles were tested with service ammunition, and averaged about 3½ inches for five-shot groups. National Match and sporting rifles were fired with National Match ammunition, and averaged about 2¾-inch groups, while the heavy barrel target rifles were tested with Palma Match ammunition, and averaged close to 2-inch 5-shot groups.

Besides the regular issue to the services, Springfield rifles were sold to members of the National Rifle Association. In the course of accuracy testing at 200 meters, every once in a while a rifle would deliver an extremely small five-shot group, almost all shots in one hole. We called these "Bumblebee groups." The group fired was attached to all rifles except the service type. When a man bought one of these rifles, accompanied by one of these Bumblebee groups, he was naturally elated. However, while I was on duty at the Armory I had every rifle that made one of these very small groups retested, and invariably it shot a group of about average accuracy, as above.

At Frankford Arsenal all routine and special testing of ammunition for accuracy was done in heavy Mann barrels held in the Mann V-rest, and these barrels were all star gauged ones having a groove diameter of from .3080" to .3082". At the time I left Frankford Arsenal they were making their 172-grain boat-tail bullets also with a diameter of .308". However, when I arrived at Springfield in 1929 I noticed that all these bullets measured .3085". We had frequent conferences with the technical men at Frankford, and one time I asked Mr. Linwood Lewis, the leading ballistic engineer there, why they were now making their bullets so large. He told me that they had determined conclusively that boat-tail bullets of this diameter gave decidedly better accuracy in bores of .308" groove diameter or larger.

I have mentioned "star gauged" barrels above. All National Match, sporting, and target barrels were selected by this method. The star gauge is an instrument that measures the bore and groove diameter of a barrel at every inch of its length from chamber to muzzle. To pass the star gauge test a barrel had to have a groove diameter

of .308" to not larger than .3085", and at no spot could it vary from that range of diameters by more than .0002". As a matter of fact, during the period from 1929 to 1933 when I was on duty there, three-fourths of the barrel production would pass this star gauge test. Note that in Krag rifles of about 1900, also made at Springfield Armory, the barrels varied in groove diameter from .3075" to .311" and larger. The closer tolerances, of course, were due to the great improvement in machine tools and manufacturing techniques which took place in the United States over the intervening period.

The superb record that the Springfield rifle has made in our service for dependability and durability is well-known, as is its remarkable record for accuracy at the National Matches and other competitions where it was used. At the National Matches in the last two years the MI (Garand) rifles, also manufactured at Springfield Armory, are said to have shot as accurately and scored as high as the Springfield 1903 rifle ever did. Our Army has won two World Wars with Springfield rifles.

## Hunting

About 1910 Louis Wundhammer, a Los Angeles gunsmith, remodeled four Springfield 1903 service rifles into sporting type, two of these for Mr. Stewart Edward White and Captain Edward Crossman, the others for gentlemen named Rogers and Colby. He fitted these rifles with excellent, light sporting stocks with pistol grip and shotgun type buttplate, and fitted early style Lyman 48 sights to them, removing the military rear sight (though leaving the sight base intact on these first

rifles), and poüshing and blueing the barrels. These were the first commercial Springfield sporters ever made (though Theodore Roosevelt had had Springfield Armory remodel a 1903 rifle earlier), and no more attractive bolt action sporting rifles have ever been built.† Captain Crossman used his rifle (and also later Wundhammer Spring-fields) very extensively for hunting the deer of California and wrote many articles for the sporting press of those days on it. Mr. White used his on three long extended trips into Africa and killed all the game of that country successfully with it except elephant and rhino, I think. He relates its fine performance in detail many times in his several books. He also had a 405 Winchester Model 1895 rifle with him. He tried many different bullets and loads in the Springfield, and in his last book he stated that if he could have the 220-grain Western boat-tail bullet with tip of lead exposed, loaded to a muzzle velocity of 2,300 fps, he would leave his 405 rifle at home, for that bullet in the Springfield killed better, shot more accurately, and was pleasanter to shoot.

My old friend, the late Ralph G. Packard, used a Springfield 30 caliber rifle on two long trips in Africa. He took a great many buffalo with it, an animal acknowledged to be one of the most difficult to kill. For buffalo, he told me, he used the Remington cartridge loaded with their 220-grain "Delayed Mushroom" bullet.

I imagine that there are no two men who, between them, have killed so many Alaskan brown bear as Jay Williams and Hosea Sarber, both now gone to the "happy hunting grounds." After about

Military target shooting near the turn of the century.

---

*The Ultimate in Rifle Precision, 1958. The Stackpole Co., Harrisburg, Pa.

†Book of the Springfield, by E.C. Crossman (Georgetown, S.C., 1951).

1911 Jay used a 30-06 sporting Springfield exclusively for these bear. His rifle was another of those remodeled by Louis Wundhammer. He used the 220-grain soft point bullet almost exclusively for bear, preferring the same Western bullet that White had found superior in Africa. In 1931 while I was at Springfield Armory I rebarreled this old rifle for Jay. He had completely worn out the original barrel. In correspondence with Hosea Sarber shortly before his death he told me that for all game he used the 170-grain open point bullet, made by the Western Tool and Copper Works, practically exclusively in his rifle. Jay Williams relates his experiences in detail in his book *Alaskan Adventure*,* and also described some of Sarber's bear shooting, as he and Sarber were close companions.

For many years Harold Lokken, an old Alaskan sourdough, used to supply all the poor families along the upper Yukon River with meat. Ralph Packard, who had three long hunts with him, told me that he thought it was conservative to say that Lokken had killed a thousand head of Alaskan big game. Lokken told me, when I met him at Packard's home, that in recent years he had hunted with only two rifles, a 270 Winchester and a 30-06 Springfield; and that while the 270 was an excellent rifle for all Alaskan game he rather preferred the Springfield because once he had to shoot five times at a grizzly to kill it with the 270, something that had never happened to him with the Springfield.

I think that each of these six men took more big game all over the world, with smokeless powder high velocity loads, than any men who have ever lived.

When Crossman had Wundhammer remodel those first Springfield rifles for himself and White he wrote me about them, and I had an eastern gunsmith remodel one for me. I did not particularly like it, and I then had another gunsmith do one over. I shot both these rifles very extensively on the rifle range, with excellent results with the latter. Then Fred Adolph, a German gun-maker who had started to work in this country, sent me a German 30 caliber barrel made of Poldi "Anti-Corro" steel, a non-rusting type. It was 26 inches long, and had a raised matted rib, and its groove diameter was .309" with a 10-inch twist. I sent this barrel to Springfield Armory and had them fit it to a Springfield action and chamber it for the 30-06 cartridge. Then Adolph stocked it with a handsome sporting pistol grip stock for me, and I had Lyman fit a windgauge rear sight to the cocking piece and a gold bead front sight. This was in 1912. Modern Guns, a catalog, by Fred Adolph (Genoa, N.Y., no date) shows this rifle. I thereafter used this rifle for many years for hunting North American game. It replaced the 30–40 Winchester single shot rifle that I had previously used. I shot more big game with this particular rifle than with any other rifle that I have used. In almost every case it killed the animal with one shot. I can remember firing three shots at a moose with it, but the last two were really not necessary. I was simply firing as long as it stood on its feet.

My longest and most successful hunt with this rifle was in the Smoky River country in Alberta north of Jasper Park in 1922. In those days that was a glorious wilderness and full of game. I shot grizzly bear, moose, caribou, sheep, and goat with it, and it never failed to kill on the first shot. On that trip I was using a new 30-06 cartridge that the Western Cartridge Company had recently produced, loaded with their 180-grain open point, boat-tail bullet to a muzzle velocity of 2,725 fps. (probably 2,775 in my 26-inch barrel). That bullet, unfortunately, is no longer made. I thought it was a rattling good killer, and it was accurate too — good for 2-inch groups any day with iron sights.

I also used this rifle practically exclusively in Panama from 1915 to 1917, when I was hunting, exploring and mapping there. The only big game there consisted of a small subspecies of white-tailed deer, tapir, peccary and crocodile, so my rifle was used mainly on small game for needed meat, with my favorite and time

*The Stackpole Co., Harrisburg, Pa., 1952.

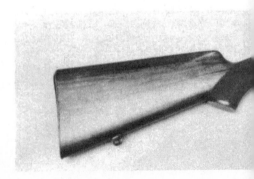

tried small game load, the 150-grain service, pointed, full jacketed bullet and 17 grains of du Pont No. 75 powder (now 18 grains du Pont 4759). Ideal for the purpose, it will shoot through the breast of a grouse and hardly spoil any meat. I had the stem of the Lyman sight plugged so when screwed all the way down it was just right for the full charged cartridge at 200 yards, and when elevated to the first graduation it was just right for this reduced load at 50 yards, a most convenient arrangement. With this reduced load I shot many coati, sloths, agouti, conejo, monkeys, iguana lizards, and many kinds of game birds including creasted guan, which are about the size of wild turkeys. Of all these the best eating by far were the sloths and the iguana lizards. This small game load turns the 30-06 into a real all around rifle for wilderness hunting. I have subsequently shot many grouse, rabbits, and two beavers and one otter with this load. The skins of the last three were not damaged at all. The meat of the beaver, including the fat tail, is the most delicious meat of any wild animal in the United States and Canada. Otters are uneatable.

I also shot four other moose, and quite a large number of mule and white-tailed deer with this old rifle on other hunts. Now, retired after its long and successful shooting history, it rests comfortably in the NRA Museum at Washington.

I think that for all American big game the 30-06 rifle is at its best with one of the 180-grain pointed expanding bullets, choosing the one that shoots most accurately in the individual rifle, and at a muzzle velocity of about 2,700 foot seconds. If the rifle be sighted with a scope mounted 1.5 inches above the bore and zeroed for 200 yards, the bullets will group about 2¼ inches above aim at 100 yards and drop 9½ inches at 300 yards. No one can estimate range exactly, but most hunters with a little experience can tell if the

game is beyond 200 yards, and if it is too far away to be hit with any certainty. Between these two distances it will be somewhere between 250 and 350 yards. Then if the hunter aims for the backbone of the animal above the chest area the bullet will drop enough to penetrate the chest or it will strike the backbone, both absolutely fatal shots on all our big game. If the animal does not drop to the shot immediately it certainly will after a mad rush of 25 to 100 yards.

The recoil of the 30-06/180-grain cartridge in an 8-pound rifle is not too severe for ninety per cent of our sportsmen. They will not hesitate to use it on the range, to become accustomed to it, and to get it zeroed precisely. When this is done a 30-06 rifle is as good as any, and in fact I think better than most any other for American big game.

Roaming around big game country in the West this past year I found my objections to those rifles using ultra high velocity magnum cartridges of heavy recoil (so often selected by modern sportsmen) more and more confirmed. If they shoot accurately they are fine for the expert rifleman, yet anything but suitable for the sportsman who takes his rifle in hand only for a couple of short weeks in the hunting season. The recoil is so unpleasant that our weekend sportsmen never practice with such rifles. They never learn to handle their rifles or their zeroes, they flinch horribly when shooting them, and they cannot hit the proverbial barn with them. They kill no surer than the 30-06 except perhaps for a paunch shot, and every real hunter abhors such a shot — it's cruel and the meat is ruined. In the majority of such cases that I have investigated it is the guide who has shot the trophy, not the sportsman. No, for all American big game the 30-06 Springfield rifle, or a good 30-06 of another brand, is never a mistake.

First commercial Springfield sporter, probably, was this Louis Wundhammer stocked 30-06, made in 1912 and used by Stewart Edward White in Africa. One of four such rifles ordered by Capt. E.C. Crossman (see Crossman's *Book of the Springfield* for another view), the rifle shown carries Rock Island Arsenal serial number 166,436, and barrel date of February, 1910.

# The Rifles of James Paris Lee

Part One. A thoroughly researched and detailed account of Lee's numerous contributions to firearms technology and advancement. New information and a long-lost model are offered here for the first time. ▌Larry S. Sterett

JAMES PARIS LEE was one of the most brilliant of all the inventors who contributed to the art of gunmaking. Born at Harwich, Roxboroughshire, Scotland, on August 9th, 1831, to George and Margaret (Paris) Lee, he migrated with his parents to Shades Mills (Gait), Ontario, Canada, in 1836. His education began at the old Gouinlock School in Gait, but was completed at Dickie's Settlement, Dumfries, under a Mr. William Telfer.

James' father, George Lee, was a skilful watchmaker and jeweler. When James was nearly 17, he entered his father's shop to learn the trade. His interest in firearms began to blossom about the same time, for one of his first experiments was to make a rough stock and fit it to the barrel and lock of an old horse pistol he'd been given. When everything was complete the pistol had to be tested and, in his own words, "I got my brother Jack to touch the gun off with a spunk, the immediate effect of which was to blacken my face with powder and hurl the barrel about 20 yards in an opposite direction."

On October 15, 1847, George Lee recorded in his diary: "Jimmie has shot himself and will go limping through the world during life!" James had been hunting in Dickson's woods near Gat and was returning in the evening, cold and wearied, with his shotgun over his shoulder when it fell to the ground and discharged. The charge passed completely through the heel of his right foot from the left side, taking with it a piece of his leather boot and searing the flesh to the degree that profuse bleeding did not occur. Dragging himself on his hands and knees through nearly 200 yards of brush to reach a road, he was found by a passing farmer and taken home. After nine months in bed, James Lee was again up and about, but it was nearly a year and a half before he was able to move about freely.

Above – James Paris Lee as he looked in 1899 at age 68. A rare photograph of one of the world's foremost but least known firearms inventors.

Having finished his work with his father, James traveled to Toronto to learn the practical side of the trade. After spending 6 months with a manufacturing jeweler named Jackson, on King Street, he decided to go into business for himself, and to open a shop in Chatham.

Boarding the Gait-London-Chatham stage one day in 1850, James Paris Lee set out on a journey that was to affect his life in more ways than one. Hardly had he settled in Chatham and put out his sign, when he met 16-year-old Caroline Chrysler, the second daughter of one of Chatham's most respected families. It was apparently love at first sight for both, but the marriage was delayed for two and one-half years because of her age. Said to have resembled Empress Eugenie, the famous French beauty of the period, Mrs. Lee was an amiable woman who accompanied her husband on nearly all his later journeys to Europe and in America, until her sudden death in London, England, in 1888, due to heart failure. The union produced two

was being left to rot. Its transportation was so costly that bulk shipments of the bark were unprofitable. Lee conceived the idea of extracting the tannic acid from the bark and shipping it out of the woods in condensed liquid form. In a letter dated July 27, 1898, to a friend, the Honorable James Young, Lee described this ill-fated experience.

"... It looks rather queer to sell tan-bark at $40 per barrel. That experiment took me into the hemlock forests in their original beauty. Great hunting here! I wondered at the great wealth of hemlock bark, and why it could not be transferred to market in a more profitable form. Result was I got a small portable engine through a blazed way (there were no roads at that time), stationed it on the banks of a beautiful lake, erected a mill to grind the bark, and a long copper pan 4 feet wide and 50 feet long, to evaporate the leechings into a thick syrup, getting the tanning strength of eight cords into a 40-gallon cask. The first test of it succeeded in burning up the

ber of magazines, the cartridges in which were placed one above the other. After firing, and ejection of the empty case, a rod pushed a loaded cartridge into the chamber, and at the same time transferred a cartridge from one magazine to another nearest the chamber. Unfortunately metal cartridge cases were not readily available at this time and the mechanism would not operate properly with those available. As a result this rifle never was commercially manufactured, and whether one survives today is not known to the author. It did, however, embody a principle that was to appear later in the rifles of many nations.

While the 40-shot repeater was hanging fire (perhaps literally), Lee developed a successful method of converting the Springfield muzzle-loading rifle into a breechloader, followed by a single-shot cavalry carbine. On July 22, 1862, U.S. Patent No. 35,941, was issued to him for an "Improvement in Breech-Loading Fire Arms." While the patent drawing is for a pistol — only one model of which is

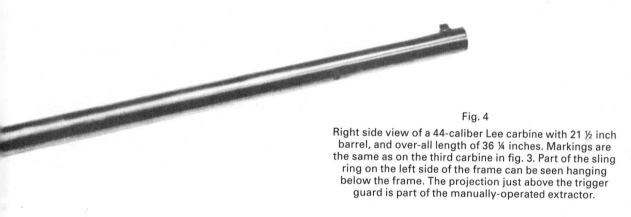

**Fig. 4**
Right side view of a 44-caliber Lee carbine with 21 ½ inch barrel, and over-all length of 36 ¼ inches. Markings are the same as on the third carbine in fig. 3. Part of the sling ring on the left side of the frame can be seen hanging below the frame. The projection just above the trigger guard is part of the manually-operated extractor.

sons, both of whom later assisted their father in his work.

Remaining in Chatham for nearly 5 years, the Lees moved to Owen Sound for a brief period and then on to Janesville, Wisconsin. Shortly before the Civil War, James Lee was induced to move from Janesville to Stevens Point, Wisconsin, on the Wisconsin River, and to set up as a watchmaker and jeweler. (The 1860 Federal Census lists Lee as a resident of this town of 1533 inhabitants, his occupation, watchmaker.)

### Early Venture

The Stevens Point newspaper, The Wisconsin Lumberman, credits Lee with being the "inventor and pioneer in the manufacture of...extract of hemlock." In the area the valuable bark of the hemlock

leather. They didn't dilute enough."

In any case, the end result was to seal the fate of the enterprise, proving unfortunate for everyone concerned.

The extensive lumbering operations indicated a very successful future for the area, but James Lee admitted that the abundance of game and the grandeur of the forests helped to attract him. Deer, bear and wolves were to be found around Stevens Point, and nearly all of his spare time was devoted to hunting or to the production of a repeating rifle to replace the old muzzle-loading models. Not content with three or four shots, Lee wanted to produce a 40-shot repeater and, after numerous attempts, he was successful. The well-made model, which showed much promise, consisted of a rifle with a hollow sheet metal buttstock containing a num-

known to exist today — mention is made in the specifications of "... a rifle or piece with a long barrel," and this was the type later manufactured by the Lee's Fire Arms Co. of Milwaukee, Wis.

### Lee's First Contract

In March of 1863, Lee submitted one of his breech-loading alterations of the Springfield rifle to the U.S. Ordnance Department for trial. The rifle was not satisfactory, and in November a second type was submitted. This second model, and a later third model, were acceptable, but a contract for their manufacture was not forthcoming. However, a request for a breech-loading carbine for testing was made, and by April, 1864, Lee had produced one, based on his 1862 patent. This carbine was also acceptable, but some ex-

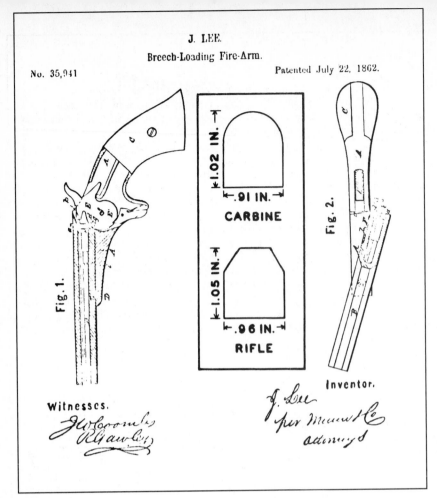

J. LEE.
Breech-Loading Fire-Arm.

No. 35,941.

Patented July 22, 1862.

CARBINE

1.02 IN.

.91 IN.

1.05 IN.

.96 IN.

RIFLE

Fig. 1.

Fig. 2.

Witnesses.

Inventor.

**Figs. 1 & 2**
The patent drawing on which the Wisconsin-made tee arms were based. Standing-breech profiles (inset) of the single shot Lee carbine and rifle made in Milwaukee, Wis.

November 2, 1864.

The Articles stated the objectives of the new firm to be "manufacturing in the City of Milwaukee Fire Arms of the pattern and form specified in Letters Patent and the Schedule accompanying the same, issued by the Government of the United States to James Lee, and also of other patterns if deemed advisable." Incorporation was approved on March 8, 1865. Capitol stock was valued at $100,000, in shares of $100 each. Of this amount only $10,000 was actually paid in. The firm was to be managed by 7 directors, elected on the first Monday of each year. The original 7 included:[2]Charles F. Ilsley, James Kneeland, James Lee, Thomas L. Ogden, Lester Sexton, Solomon Taintor and Daniel Wells Jr. Kneeland was elected president of the Board, with H.F. Pelton, Secretary. James P. Lee was appointed Superintendent of the Works. The Honorable W.D. McIndoe was not listed as being on the Board, possibly because a conflict of interest charge might be leveled in connection with a military contract.

The armory was established at 454 Canal Street in October, 1864, and the job of procuring materials and equipment began. (Canal Street is now Commerce Street in Milwaukee, and the 454 area is a part of the Joseph Schlitz Brewery complex.) A number of parts were presumably bought elsewhere in the finished stage, ready for assembly. These included sling bars and rings, buttplates, and front and rear sights, which appear identical to those made by the Burnside Rifle Co. of Rhode Island, and which are referred to as "Burn-sides" by Col. McAllister in one report.

Barrels were supplied by E. Remington & Sons of Ilion, New York. A total of 1136 barrels were shipped to Milwaukee for rifling and chambering, and to be fitted with sights and extractors. This arrangement was ideal since the Remington firm was equipped to produce barrels, and government inspection and proof was taken care of by the Ordnance Department inspectors before the barrels were shipped to Milwaukee.

## Contract Troubles

In April, 1865, the official order for the delivery of the carbines was issued by the Ordnance Department as follows below.[3] Note that caliber 44 is shown in this letter; caliber was not given in the letter of May 7th, 1864:

traction difficulties were experienced. No doubt expecting a contract, Lee offered to provide 1000 of the carbine model for testing, with delivery to be within 6 months of the date of the order. The offer was approved, as indicated by the following communication:

James Lee Esq.
Washington D. C.
Ordnance Office
May 7th 1864
Sir,

Your letter of April 19th to the Secretary of War offering to furnish 1000 of your breechloading carbines at $18 has been referred to this office with authority to enter into such contract with you. Should you therefore present to this Department a carbine free from the defects mentioned in Captain Benton's report the contract will then be given you. The defect was "The cartridge case ejector frequently failed to start the case, the projection next to the case (on the ejector) appears to be too short to take a firm hold on the rim of the case." The carbine must be presented this or next month.

Respectfully
Your obt Svt
George D. Ramsay
Brig. Gen. Chf of Ord

Lee improved the extractor design without difficulty, and his request for permission to manufacture the gun frames of malleable cast iron instead of wrought iron was accepted. But he had no facilities for manufacturing the carbines in quantity, and his request for an increase in the contract price was rejected.

As for Lee's original plans for manufacturing the carbines, it is a matter for conjecture. He may have intended to have the carbines made elsewhere, under his name, or he may have intended to subcontract the parts and to assemble the carbines himself, with workmen hired for his purpose. In any event, since the letter from Gen. Ramsay did not specify a time of delivery, Lee decided to form a company and make the carbines.

The Honorable W.D. McIndoe, a Congressman and a friend of Lee, apparently saw some potential in the carbine. He helped Lee gain financial backing for the new firm, which was organized in Milwaukee on October 13, 1864[1]. Various sources list this firm as Lee Arms Company, Lee Fire Arms Company, Lee Firearms Company, Lee's Firearms Company and Lee's Fire Arms Company. However, the last form is the one appearing on the Articles of Association filed with the Secretary of State in Madison, Wisconsin, on

**Fig. 3**

Breech details of three tee carbines, showing rear sight locations, trigger guard variations and markings. The crudely-marked top carbine is considered the first specimen made (No. 1). The middle carbine is unmarked, while the third carbine has the standard markings found on commercial production pieces. The two frame holes in the lower carbine are for attaching the sling bar. Note the higher standing-breech on the first two carbines, compared to that of the third. (No. 2183).

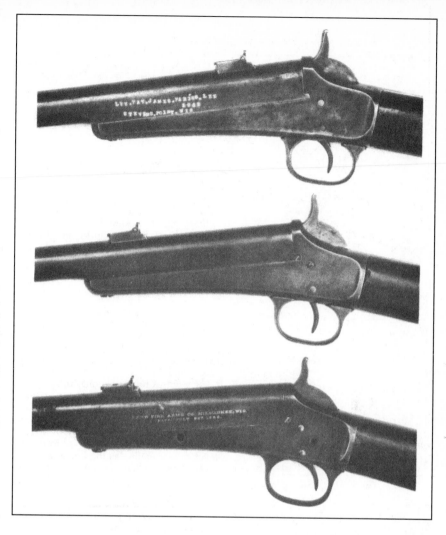

Mr. James Lee
Milwaukee, Wis
Ordnance Office
April 18, 1865
Sir,

　　You will please deliver to the Inspector of Small Arms, the one thousand breech loading carbines Cal. 44 and appendages the order to furnish which was given to you on the 7th day of May, 1864 for which eighteen dollars ($18) will be paid for each carbine including appendages that is approved by the Inspector. Please forward to this office as soon as possible two (2) carbines to be used as standards in the inspection and reception of the above. These one thousand carbines will be packed in suitable boxes, for which a fair price, to be fixed by the Inspector will be paid.

　　Respectfully
　　Your obt Svt
　　A. B. Dyer
　　Brig Gen. Chf of Ord

Although the order called for two carbines to be used as standards, a single carbine was shipped to Ordnance for inspection on August 31, 1865. It was rejected. In so doing the following reasons were advanced by the inspector, Gen. W. A. Thornton:

*The barrel, indicates rough rifling and to remedy which it has been leaded to such an extent that the edges of the lands are quite round. It is badly ringbored at the muzzle and the breech-chamber is roughly reamed. Front sight ... can be readily pushed out by the fingers. The hammer has a corner broken from the middle notch. Notches roughly filed ... The mainspring is apparently too weak ... The breech piece is ... very doubtful in strength through screw holes at points of junction to the barrel and in tang joining it to the stock. The stock is very roughly cut in bedding the main spring and too deeply cut for the tang of the breech piece ... It is therefore liable to be easily broken. The butt plate has a seam in the material ... The sear spring is broken ...*

In January, 1866, the two models originally called for in the order of April,

1865, as inspection standards, were finally furnished. After inspection they were reported on as follows:

*Office of Inspector of Contract Arms*
*No 240 Broadway*
*New York, January 26, 1866*
*Maj. Gen 'l A.B. Dyer*
*Chief of Ordnance*
*General,*

　*I have the honor to inform you, that I have inspected two model Carbines, furnished by James Lee Esq. of Milwaukee and respecting which I have to report that I find,*

*Carbine No. 1.*
*Frame — of Malleable Cast Iron and thin at front end where the screw connects it to the barrel.*
*Stock — Split at top butt screw hole.*
*Barrel — Chamber torn in rifling.*
*Connection Screw — Thread torn.*
*Butt Plate — Seams in material out side.*
*— Top Screw hole countersunk too deep.*

*Carbine No. 2.*
*Frame — of Malleable Cast Iron.*
*Barrel — Torn in rifling.*
*Mainspring — Crooked at Set Screw.*
*In all other conditions I consider these*

*arms are well gotten up, and I respectfully recommend their acceptance as Models with the understanding that like Carbines furnished to the United States shall be equally as good in workmanship and free from defects.*

　*Respectfully, I am sir,*
　*Your obedient servant*
　*W. A. Thornton*

Even with the recommendation the Ordnance Department refused to accept the two carbines as inspection standards on the grounds of incorrect caliber. According to a letter to Gen. Thornton "... they (the carbines) gauge only .42 calibre while my order of April 13th 1865 calls for .44 calibre. Please see if the carbines will take the cartridge for Spencer carbine cal. .44; if so these may be returned for stamp as model carbines for the inspection."

Thornton apparently informed Lee that the carbines were unacceptable, due to an error in caliber, although Thornton had informed the Chief of Ordnance "... I did not verify them as to the size of their bore when I made their inspection." Lee immediately went to Washington to try and clarify the matter, but was unsuccess-

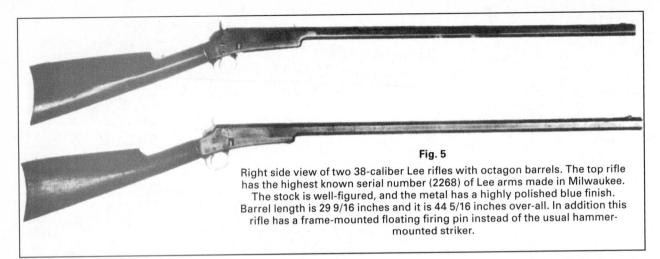

**Fig. 5**

Right side view of two 38-caliber Lee rifles with octagon barrels. The top rifle has the highest known serial number (2268) of Lee arms made in Milwaukee. The stock is well-figured, and the metal has a highly polished blue finish. Barrel length is 29 9/16 inches and it is 44 5/16 inches over-all. In addition this rifle has a frame-mounted floating firing pin instead of the usual hammer-mounted striker.

ful. By mid-spring the two carbines had been returned to Milwaukee.

By this time Lee may have been convinced that the military were not going to accept his carbine, for one reason or another. It should also be remembered that the Civil War was now over, and the arms were not needed; the caliber may have been only an excuse to hedge on a contract. To recover some of the losses, Lee began to explore the civilian market. Unfortunately surplus arms were flooding the market, and could be bought at a fraction of the cost of the new Lee carbines.

Possibly in an attempt to help a local industry the *Milwaukee Daily Sentinal* published an article entitled: "HOW BREECH LOADING GUNS ARE MADE — A Visit To Lee's Arms Manufactory" on page 1 of the March 23, 1866, edition. (Note that the name of the firm shows still another form attributed to the Milwaukee enterprise.) The article appeared as follows:

We recently paid a visit to Lee's Arms Manufactory, situated on the Canal, in the sixth ward of the city, and were conducted through the various departments by the gentlemanly President, James Kneeland, esq. and the Superintendant and inventor of the arms, James Lee, esq.

Comparatively few of our readers are acquainted with the manner of making guns, and we venture to give a brief account of our tour of observation.

The barrels of the gun are purchased in the rough state and brought to the manufactory here. They are made of the best decarbonized steel. The first process is to mill the barrel down to its proper size and form. During this process it has to pass through 19 different operations. It is then taken to the rifling machine. In order to insure greater accuracy in firing the gun, the barrel has to be grooved or rifled, so as to give the ball, on issuing from the gun, a rotary motion, which like the motion of a top, keeps it unerringly on its course. It has been found by experiment that the shorter the twist in the bar-

rel, the longer the range and the accuracy obtained. The twist in the Whitworth gun, which is acknowledged the best now to be known, has one turn in 20 inches. The twist of Lee's gun is one turn in 23 inches. The rifling machine, at each revolution, takes a cut of but one eighty-thousandth part of an inch. This apparently incredibly small cut is necessary from the fact that a larger one would be liable to tear the barrel and such an accident would render it useless. The shavings from the machine are as fine as the finest of wool. After rifling, the barrel is taken to the polishing room and a fine finish put upon it. It is then taken to the blueing furnace and beautifully colored. It is now ready for use. The barrel passes through 43 different operations from the forging to the blueing process.

The breech is then taken in hand. It is made from the best de-carbonized iron, requiring to be kept at a red heat for 16 days. It is first put through a milling machine, then filed, drilled, polished, and blued, passing through no less than 60 different processes from the forging to the blueing.

The lock is perhaps the simplest part of the gun, having only four pieces — a hammer, trigger, mainspring and trigger-spring. It is so simple that the most inexperienced could take it apart or put it together. Yet the hammer passes through 20 different and separate processes, the trigger through ten, the mainspring through six.

The stocks are made from Wisconsin black walnut, which from its hardness has been found to be the best material for the purpose. As the lock is situated in the breech of the gun, there is comparatively little work about the stock. It is made wholly by machinery; first grooved for the mountings, then formed into the proper shape, then sweated and polished, and lastly mounted.

Every portion of this gun is made by machinery and each part of every gun is the same. The advantage of this is in the fact that when a part of the gun is either lost or broken it can be replaced by another from the manufactory at but little cost. Every gun is subjected to a rigid test, and

any imperfection, no matter how small, condemns it. All the machinery and tools used have been made expressly for the manufacture of the arm, and the company have been at an enormous outlay for the requisite machinery. The manufactory is now in excellent working order, and will soon be able to turn out a large number of guns daily, and will furnish employment to quite a number of men. None but the best of mechanisms are employed, however, as the variation of even so much as a thousandth part of an inch in any of the parts of the gun would spoil it for use.

The arm deserves a minute description, but with our imperfect knowledge of its mechanism, we cannot hope to do it justice. It has many advantages over the ordinary rifle. There are only 8 pieces in the whole gun — less than half the number in either Burnside, Henry or Spencer rifles — and they are so simple that anyone can put them together with ease. It can be loaded and fired 20 times a minute by an expert sportsman, and can be used with one hand when occasion requires; it being light and almost self-working. Its penetration is truly wonderful. With but 23 grains of powder a ball was driven through an inch board, 6 inches of cotton, tightly compressed, and a body of water 6 feet in extent. The force required to accomplish this fact connoisseurs will appreciate. The arm is very light — the heaviest now manufactured being only eight pounds and six ounces. The effective range of the gun is about three-quarters of a mile and its accuracy at that distance is as great as that of any other arm in the United States.

The company is now manufacturing four different sizes of guns, an army carbine, weighing 5 pounds, 6 ounces, a light sporting rifle, weighing 6½ pounds, a heavy sporting rifle, weighing 8 pounds, 5 ounces, and one an ounce heavier.

The manufactory is now busy on a government contract for carbines. The demand for sporting rifles is greater than the supply, and the manufactory will have to be enlarged to enable it to furnish enough for the trade.

This arm has been commended highly by the chief of ordnance bureau and

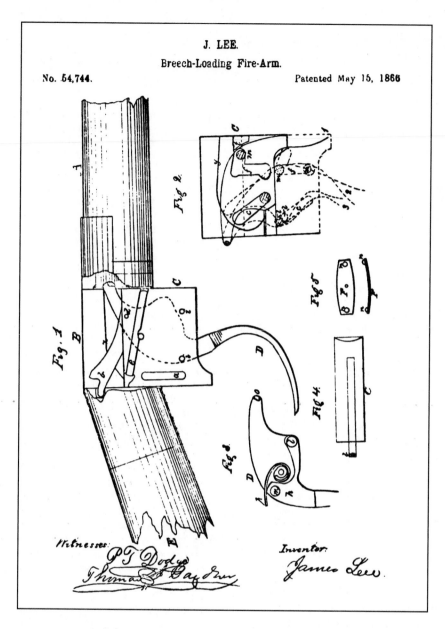

J. LEE.
Breech-Loading Fire-Arm.

No. 54,744.

Patented May 15, 1866

Witnesses:

Inventor:
James Lee

or from 10 to 12 times per minute with one hand. It has a greater Accuracy, Force and Penetration, with the same quantity of powder, than any other breech-loading rifle, and more than double the force and penetration of any muzzle-loading gun ever made. With 23 grains of powder (only about one-quarter the quantity the Berdan gun requires), it will throw a half-ounce ball of 44–100 of an inch calibre through 10 inches of green, or 12 inches of seasoned pine timber.

In November, 1866, one Lt. Col. J. McAllister visited the "… armory of Mr. Lee …" in order to "… examine into the progress that has been made, the expenditures incurred and the materials on hand for filling the contract, and report the same with such remarks and recommendations respecting a settlement of the case …" On December 20, 1866, after completing the visit, Col. McAllister filed his report.

## Lee's Claim Settled

In January, 1867, James Lee wrote to the Secretary of War, E.M. Stanton, requesting compensation for the expenses incurred while attempting to fulfill the contract for the carbines. In due course the request found its way to the then Chief of Ordnance, Bvt. Major General A.B. Dyer. In his reply to Stanton, dated February 18, 1867, Gen. Dyer stated that Mr. Lee had acted in good faith, and should be compensated. But instead of requesting that the contract be fulfilled for 1000 carbines at $18 each, he recommended a compromise. Assuming that Lee's total expenses at the date of McAllister's report were $20,350. 15, the tools and equipment were worth $6,000, and that rifles and parts on hand could be sold for $6,175, the net loss would only be $8,175.15, which the government should be willing to share to the extent of $4,087.57. This method of settlement, according to Dyer, would thus save the government a minimum of at least $6,000.

A year later, the matter still not settled, Lee wrote to Washington protesting the unfairness of the suggested settlement. In turn Dyer stated that Lee had no claim other than the "one of damage which … could only be … properly acted on by legislative authority." This was in accordance with the Congressional act of March 3, 1863, and in December, 1868, "General Jurisdiction Case No. 3263: James Lee vs. the United States" was decided.

by many prominent sportsment and soldiers. As a sporting rifle it possesses great advantages over others and is fast superseding all rivals. Wisconsin inventors have introduced many useful improvements in every department of science, but none is more important than the invention of this breech-loading arm. Mr. Lee has made the construction of firearms a life study, and has succeeded in bringing perfection in this gun. We feel a pride in the success of the invention as should every resident of Wisconsin.

After reading this article, one begins to wonder whether it was written by a reporter for the newspaper or by an advertising agency. The facts do not bear out some of the statements made in the article.

Under the heading "Fire Arms and Ammunition" the same issue carried an advertisement that appeared periodically into November, 1866. It read:

Lee's Fire Arms Company on the Canal water power, Milwaukee, are manufacturing Lee's Patent Breech-Loading Rifle which the company now offer to the public.

The company own the patent and are the exclusive manufacturers of the Arm in the United States.

In offering to the public this Gun the company claim that it is more complete and perfect in every particular, and cheaper than any other arm in use. The superiority of **LEE'S PATENT BREECH-LOADING RIFLE**, consists in its simplicity of mechanism — it having only about one-half the number of pieces that other breech-loading guns have. Its Superior workmanship, the Barrels of the finest Decarbonized Cast Steel. Rifled in the most approved manner in 6 grooves of equal width to the lands, sharp Whitworth twist, once round in 23 inches — its rapidity in firing over all others. It can be fired 20 times per minute,

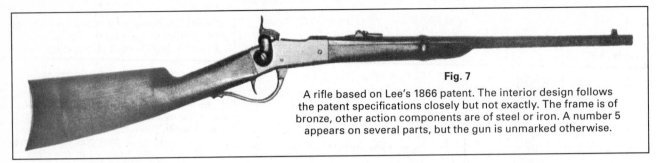

**Fig. 7**
A rifle based on Lee's 1866 patent. The interior design follows the patent specifications closely but not exactly. The frame is of bronze, other action components are of steel or iron. A number 5 appears on several parts, but the gun is unmarked otherwise.

The verdict depended on whether the carbine was to have been 42 caliber or 44 caliber, which in turn depended on when the contract originated. Lee maintained that the letter of May 7, 1864, accepting the carbine evaluated the month before, constituted the contract, and the carbines submitted later followed this accepted pattern. The Government maintained the order dated April 18, 1865, calling for "… one thousand breech-loading carbines Cal. 44 …" was the actual contract.

Lee had asked $12,000 for expenses and $3,000 for damages. The Court awarded him $6,175 for damages only, since he "… still maintains his machinery and a large amount of material …" Interestingly, the Court held the letter of May 7, 1864, to be the valid contract and advanced the opinion, "When the carbines were needed the calibre was not a matter of serious importance; when they were not needed,5 the calibre became the controlling element"

It is almost certain that by this time Lee's Fire Arms Company was no longer in business. The attempt to sell the civilian market had failed and only 102 carbines had been sold by December of 1866, and these at a loss of $4.50 each. The rifles and carbines were not advertised after November, 1866, and the firm is not listed in the Milwaukee city directories after 1867.

There are many unanswered questions connected with James Paris Lee and his activities, not the least of which are the dates of his residence in various cities. When the Lee family left Stevens Point for Milwaukee is not exactly known. James Lee is not listed in the Milwaukee city directory until 1866, nor in Stevens Point after the autumn of 1864. It is probable, therefore, that the move took place at about the same time of the formation of Lee's Fire Arms Company. Lee doubtless had been in Milwaukee numerous times previously and would have made several contacts. The Lee residence is listed as 130 Prospect in the 1866 to 1873/74 city directories, although Lee is listed with Lee's Fire Arms Company only in 1866 and 1867. In 1900 a boyhood friend of Lee wrote that

Lee had gone to Ilion, N.Y., to work at the Remington factory following the failure of the Milwaukee business. Lee had become acquainted with the Remingtons previously, having used their barrels for his Milwaukee-made carbines and rifles, and it was a tradition of the Remington firm at this time to invite inventors to use the facilities at the Remington Armory. Thus the Lee family apparently stayed in Milwaukee while James Lee worked in Ilion, at least until after May, 1874, when the *Milwaukee Daily Sentinal* noted that Lee had gone east to renew tests of his gun at Springfield (Armory).

The type of arm made at the Milwaukee factory was based on U.S. Patent No. 35, 941. As previously mentioned, the patent model was for a single shot pistol having a spur trigger and a barrel which pivoted horizontally to the left. A tongue on the barrel breech prevented vertical play. The centrally positioned outside hammer was designed so that when it was in the half-cock position the barrel could be swung out for loading. But when the hammer was fully cocked the barrel could not be moved. Extraction of the fired case was done by a manual movement of an extractor sliding in a groove on the right side of the barrel. The rim of the case was acted upon in much the same manner as in double barrel shotguns.

The frame provided for a separate steel breech plate, indicating the frame was to be produced from a softer metal, and at least one brass frame pistol of this same basic design is known to exist. It is said to have a single 6 stamped on the breech of the 44-caliber barrel, which is 8⅝ inches long. Over-all length is reported to be 13 inches.

## The Pilot Rifle

Of the long arms based on this patent — 32 are reported to exist — none have spur triggers and the barrels all pivot to the right instead of to the left. Two different standing breech shapes exist, as shown in fig. 1. with the rifles having one shape and the carbines another; carbine breeches also vary slightly in height. The arms were apparently available chambered for

three different rimfire calibers, although only two — 44 and 38 — were advertised, but for exactly which cartridges is a matter for debate. Herbert Uphoff has said that the 44 Henry and 44 Ballard Long cartridges will chamber in some of the 44 caliber arms, but the possibilities of others cannot be overlooked.

The 38 caliber cartridge may have been the 38 Extra Long, but the first mention of a 38 caliber appears in the 1866 advertisments, or about when the 44-caliber carbine was rejected for military use. Yet a recent Norm Flayderman catalog listed a Lee rifle with 1864 markings chambered for a 38 rimfire cartridge.

Several arms were no doubt made prior to the formation of Lee's Fire Arms Company, but only one specimen — a carbine — is known to exist today, unless the just-mentioned 38 caliber rifle is one, which is doubtful. Crudely made, this early carbine resembles the later models but has a differently shaped stock and front sight, and a slightly longer barrel, plus other minor differences. The barrel is very unevenly stamped, on the left side, near the breech, in three lines. The double S in "Pariss" is so stamped:

**LEE. PAT. JAMES. PARISS. LEE**
**1862**
**STEVENS. POINT. WIS**

The greatest difference between this carbine, stamped with a number 1 under the barrel, and the later models is the degree to which the barrel may be swung aside for loading — about 170 degrees to the right, compared to some 8 degrees for the later models based on the same patent. The patent provided for a barrel stop, but this particular carbine does not have one.

Uphoff thinks this carbine is possibly the sample submitted for testing as a standard in June, 1864, since it has the improved extractor on the bottom of the barrel, instead of the side-mounted type mentioned in the patent.

The sights on the carbines are of Burn-side type — dovetailed front blade, and an L-shaped rear, secured to the barrel by a single screw, and having notches for 100 and 500 yards, with a notched aperture for 300 yards. The rifle has a dovetailed front sight, similar to those on the carbines, and an L-shaped rear sight, with a reversible slide having different notches, dovetailed into the barrel.

The carbines made in the Milwaukee factory, if marked, are neatly stamped in about the same barrel position as on the Stevens Point carbine, but in two lines, as follows:

**LEE'S FIRE ARMS CO. MILWAUKEE, WIS  PAT- JULY 22- 1862.**

Rifles were stamped the same way, but in a single line on the top of the barrel.

Carbines and rifle barrel lengths vary from those advertised, apparently because of very liberal manufacturing tolerances. Reported barrel lengths of known carbines range from 21 to 21½ inches, except for No. 1, which has a barrel of 21 15/16 inches long and all barrels are 44 caliber. Rifle barrels vary from 25¼ to 30¾ inches; the average 44-caliber barrel runs 29 inches, the 38-caliber barrels averaging 28¾ inches. This would tend to indicate that the two extremes may not have been standard rifles, but possibly special orders. The barrels were rifled as noted in the advertisement, except for the original sample, which has been reported to have five grooves and a gain twist.

Many of the carbines have sling bars and rings on the left side of the frame. Apparently all of the contract models were so intended, but only two of the known rifle specimens have sling swivels. Of these two rifles only No. 1659 is considered authentic; the front swivel is mounted on a base dovetailed into the barrel about 18 inches ahead of the breech, while the rear swivel is on a plate inletted into the stock 7 inches from the toe.

Here are many unanswered questions concerning the Milwaukee firm and the Lee carbines and rifles based on the 1862 patent. Why are no low number models known? The lowest number located — after the Stevens Point model — is 1247, a rifle. What happened to the rest of the 255 finished carbines, of which 102 had been sold, as reported on December 20, 1866? Were they numbered consecutively? Were the parts for the rest of the contract carbines destroyed, or were they used to produce civilian carbines and rifles to order? This suggests the reason for the apparent random numbering arrangement of the known rifles and carbines. Whatever the answers, Lee carbines and rifles do exist, but obviously Lee's Fire Arms Company of Milwaukee did not fare well.

## Rare Lee Design

James Lee continued to work on a better rifle design, even while attempting to sell the 1862 design and attending to his work on Canal Street. On May 15, 1866, shortly after work had been suspended on the military carbines, U.S. Patent No. 54,744 was issued to "James Lee, of Milwaukee, Wisconsin." The specifications list the patent as an "Improvement in Breech-Loading Fire-Arms," but the drawing is for a "Breech-Loading Fire-Arm." The action of this arm comprised a rectangular breechblock of "iron," moving vertically in the receiver well, and operated by an under lever with an extractor at its forward end. The front of the breechblock was beveled on the upper edge to help force the cartridge into the chamber. A small metal bar was recessed into the top of the breechblock in such a way that when lever was operated to lower the block "… the rear end of (the bar) is held up, while

its front end is carried down with the block, thereby forming an inclined way extending from the lower side of the bore up to the top of the frame … up which the cartridge-shell slides when thrown out by the ejector." The whole affair resembled a merging of the Peabody design of 1862 and the Sharps design of 1848.*

Lee had mentioned to his friend James Young that while at the Remington plant

---

*The only specimen of this Lee patent design to appear so far is owned by John T. Amber, editor of the Gun Digest. A Short rifle or carbine, it has a military style barrel of about 52 caliber, rifled with three broad grooves. The "small metal bar" mentioned above is pivoted in the top of the breechblock, near the middle. Its rear end is hooked to catch on the top rear of the receiver mortise, which is not as it appears in the patent drawing. Besides acting as an inclined plane for the ejection of fired cases, the slender steel bar also served as a loading tray or platform. The receiver is of brass, but all other action components are of iron or steel. As the illustrations show, there is a locking arrangement for the lever. The number 5 appears on several action parts, but the gun is unmarked otherwise. The exact cartridge called for is not certain, but one of the Spencer bottleneck types appears likely.

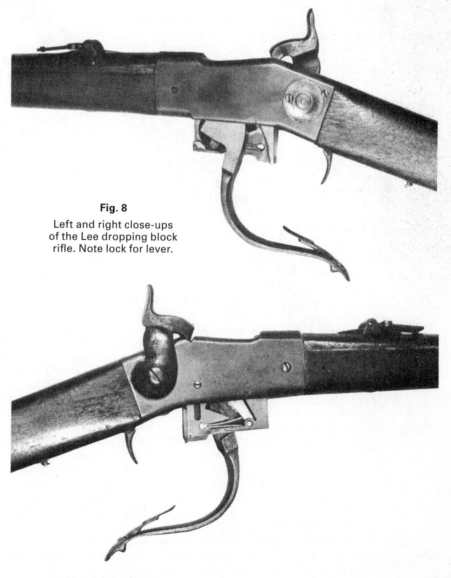

**Fig. 8**

Left and right close-ups of the Lee dropping block rifle. Note lock for lever.

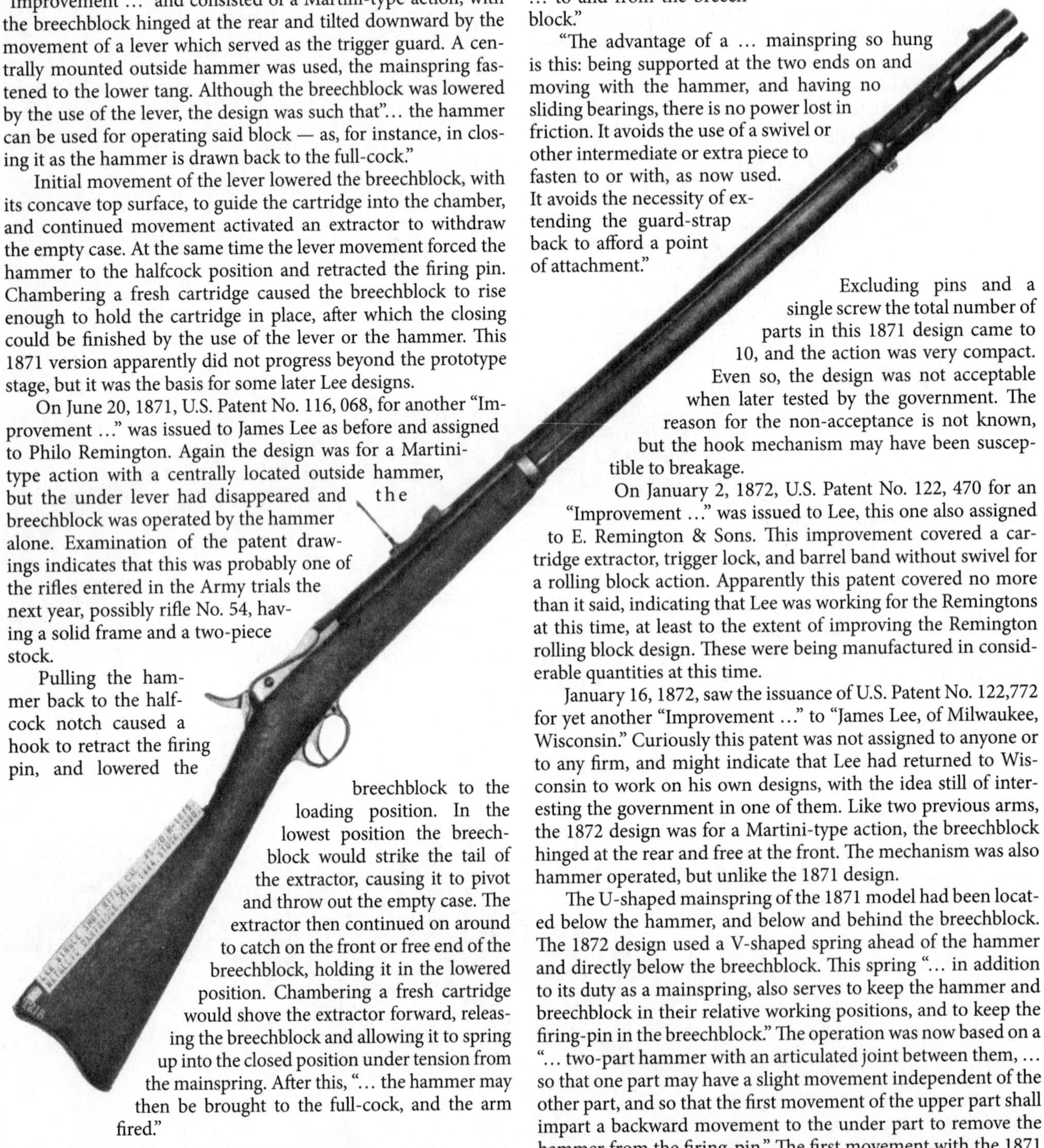

he tried not only all kinds of experiments, but that his thoughts, both day and night, became so absorbed with them that sleep often became impossible. Sleep may have been impossible, but ideas were not, for the 1870s were the most productive of Lee's inventive years.

On May 16, 1871, U.S. Patent No. 114, 951 was issued to "James Lee, of Milwaukee, Wisconsin, Assignor to Philo Remington, of Ilion, New York." This patent was also listed as an "Improvement ..." and consisted of a Martini-type action, with the breechblock hinged at the rear and tilted downward by the movement of a lever which served as the trigger guard. A centrally mounted outside hammer was used, the mainspring fastened to the lower tang. Although the breechblock was lowered by the use of the lever, the design was such that"... the hammer can be used for operating said block — as, for instance, in closing it as the hammer is drawn back to the full-cock."

Initial movement of the lever lowered the breechblock, with its concave top surface, to guide the cartridge into the chamber, and continued movement activated an extractor to withdraw the empty case. At the same time the lever movement forced the hammer to the halfcock position and retracted the firing pin. Chambering a fresh cartridge caused the breechblock to rise enough to hold the cartridge in place, after which the closing could be finished by the use of the lever or the hammer. This 1871 version apparently did not progress beyond the prototype stage, but it was the basis for some later Lee designs.

On June 20, 1871, U.S. Patent No. 116, 068, for another "Improvement ..." was issued to James Lee as before and assigned to Philo Remington. Again the design was for a Martini-type action with a centrally located outside hammer, but the under lever had disappeared and the breechblock was operated by the hammer alone. Examination of the patent drawings indicates that this was probably one of the rifles entered in the Army trials the next year, possibly rifle No. 54, having a solid frame and a two-piece stock.

Pulling the hammer back to the half-cock notch caused a hook to retract the firing pin, and lowered the breechblock to the loading position. In the lowest position the breechblock would strike the tail of the extractor, causing it to pivot and throw out the empty case. The extractor then continued on around to catch on the front or free end of the breechblock, holding it in the lowered position. Chambering a fresh cartridge would shove the extractor forward, releasing the breechblock and allowing it to spring up into the closed position under tension from the mainspring. After this, "... the hammer may then be brought to the full-cock, and the arm fired."

## Unique Mainspring

This June, 1871, design used a unique U-shaped mainspring, the only other spring in the arm being a short, flat, trigger spring.

The mainspring "... is attached to and moves with the hammer, and has no fixed position ... yet performs all the duties of an expansile and contractile spring ... to raise the breechblock and to attach and detach a hook ... to and from the breech-block."

"The advantage of a ... mainspring so hung is this: being supported at the two ends on and moving with the hammer, and having no sliding bearings, there is no power lost in friction. It avoids the use of a swivel or other intermediate or extra piece to fasten to or with, as now used. It avoids the necessity of extending the guard-strap back to afford a point of attachment."

Excluding pins and a single screw the total number of parts in this 1871 design came to 10, and the action was very compact. Even so, the design was not acceptable when later tested by the government. The reason for the non-acceptance is not known, but the hook mechanism may have been susceptible to breakage.

On January 2, 1872, U.S. Patent No. 122, 470 for an "Improvement ..." was issued to Lee, this one also assigned to E. Remington & Sons. This improvement covered a cartridge extractor, trigger lock, and barrel band without swivel for a rolling block action. Apparently this patent covered no more than it said, indicating that Lee was working for the Remingtons at this time, at least to the extent of improving the Remington rolling block design. These were being manufactured in considerable quantities at this time.

January 16, 1872, saw the issuance of U.S. Patent No. 122,772 for yet another "Improvement ..." to "James Lee, of Milwaukee, Wisconsin." Curiously this patent was not assigned to anyone or to any firm, and might indicate that Lee had returned to Wisconsin to work on his own designs, with the idea still of interesting the government in one of them. Like two previous arms, the 1872 design was for a Martini-type action, the breechblock hinged at the rear and free at the front. The mechanism was also hammer operated, but unlike the 1871 design.

The U-shaped mainspring of the 1871 model had been located below the hammer, and below and behind the breechblock. The 1872 design used a V-shaped spring ahead of the hammer and directly below the breechblock. This spring "... in addition to its duty as a mainspring, also serves to keep the hammer and breechblock in their relative working positions, and to keep the firing-pin in the breechblock." The operation was now based on a "... two-part hammer with an articulated joint between them, ... so that one part may have a slight movement independent of the other part, and so that the first movement of the upper part shall impart a backward movement to the under part to remove the hammer from the firing-pin." The first movement with the 1871 design had been to pull the hammer back to the halfcock position to lower the breechblock; with the 1872 design the first step was to press the thumb-piece of the hammer forward to relieve

**Fig. 9**

The M1875 Lee-Springfield rifle. Caliber 45-70, 32½-inch barrel, 49¼ inches over-all. Markings on tang of receiver are: U.S. PAT. MARCH 16, 1875. The tang of the buttplate is marked U.S. All three swivels are missing — the rear one found at the front of the trigger guard, and the two at the front band; one was for stacking.

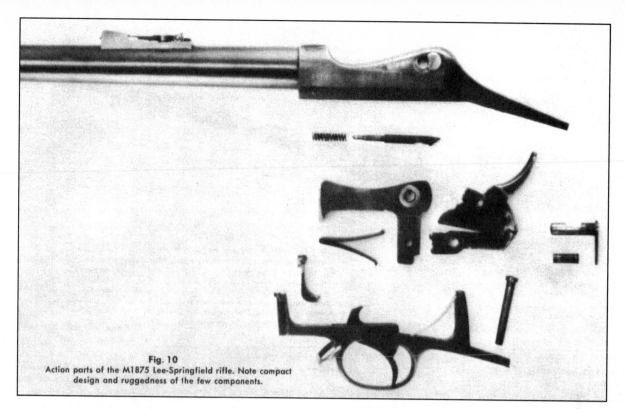

**Fig. 10**
Action parts of the M1875 Lee-Springfield rifle. Note compact
design and ruggedness of the few components.

the pressure on the firing pin, with continued pressure lowering the breechblock. After a fresh cartridge was chambered, the breechblock was raised by pulling back on the thumb-piece "... as in the act of cocking, which will first raise the breech to a closed position, and by continuing that motion will cock the arm."

One other noteworthy feature of the 1872 design was its take-down. "The breechblock, hammer, and mainspring can all be removed together without disturbing their relative positions by taking out the pin that the breechblock swings on, which, for cleaning or repairs, is quite important."

The 1872 design, coupled with the extractor of the 1871 design, was tested during the government trials of 1872 as entry No. 61. Like the previous 1871 design, it used a solid receiver and a two-piece stock; the buttstock was secured by a throughbolt screwing into the base of the frame, in the same manner as the Peabody-Martini.

On June 6, 1872, Congress approved the appointment by the Secretary of War of a "Board for the Selecting of a Breech-System for Muskets and Carbines" to consist of one general officer, one ordnance officer, and one line officer each from the cavalry, infantry, and artillery. $150,000 were appropriated for manufacturing the arm selected.

## 1872 Trials

The Board met on September 3, 1872, and continued in session until May 5,

1873. During this time a total of 95 arms or models were examined and/or tested, including 9 arms of foreign manufacture and three designs by James Paris Lee.* The Lee arms were entries No. 53, 54, and 61, and all were listed as "Muskets, calibre .50." The Board stated that "... the service .50 calibre musket-cartridge was employed whenever possible ..."

Firing tests were conducted at Springfield Armory and, after nearly 25,000 rounds had been fired, the tests were concluded. A total of 21 arms were then selected for more severe tests. Of Lee's designs, only No. 61 was among the semi-finalists; it was not selected when this group was later narrowed to the 6 arms that ultimately resulted in the selection of the Springfield "trapdoor" design — later to become the famous Model 1873.

The author has been unable to locate either the arm or the patent relating to entry No. 53 in the 1872 trials. This gun apparently used a sliding bolt in somewhat the same manner as the straight-pull design of 1895. However, a cam-lever at the upper rear of the bolt was used to lock and unlock the bolt by camming a lug on the underside of the bolt down into and up out of a recess in the receiver. This arm also had a one-piece stock and ejection of the empty cartridge cases was upward.

While the Springfield conversion design had been adopted by the Army, the search for a better one went on, and apparently the 1872 Lee model (No. 61 above) had made an impression, for in 1874 Congress approved the expenditure

of $10,000 for further development of the Lee design.

On March 16, 1875, James Lee was issued U.S. Patent No. 160,919 for another "Improvement ..." The application had been filed on May 9, 1874, the last time Lee is mentioned in the Milwaukee papers as being in Milwaukee, he having gone east to renew tests of his gun at Springfield.6

The 1875 model used a one-piece stock following the contours of the 1873 Springfield stock, with the barrel, bands, band springs, swivels, sights, buttplate and ramrod also following the 1873 pattern. It was only logical to use the Springfield parts, since the Lee and Springfield models were both being manufactured at the Armory, with the Lee rifle on a trial basis for testing.

The V-shaped mainspring of the 1872 model was retained in the 1875 model, and pushing forward on the thumbpiece of the hammer lowered the breechblock, causing its bottom edge to strike the extractor, thus ejecting the empty case and locking the breechblock in the loading position. (According to the patent specifications the mainspring, not the breechblock, struck the extractor to eject the case, but in the manufactured rifle it is the breechblock.) Shoving a fresh cartridge into the chamber moved the extractor out

---

*Based on Lee patents and descriptions given in the Ordnance Board reports, entry No. 54 was constructed on Lee's patent No. 116,068 of June 20, 1871, and entry No. 61 is covered by Lee's patent No. 122,722 of Jan. 16, 1872

**Fig. 12**
The 1879 Lee rifle, as adopted by the U.S. Navy. Note the plain, ungrooved magazine and the straight bolt handle projecting ahead of the receiver bridge. Many writers have called all Lee turnbolt rifles the M1879, but that's like saying every Ford car is a Model T. The M1879 was only the first of several Lee turnbolt models. This particular rifle is marked on the receiver as noted in the text, while the barrel, just ahead of the receiver, is marked: "P." over "W.M.F." with an anchor below.

of the way, unlocking the breechblock and allowing it to rise automatically, via the compressed mainspring. The gun could then be cocked and fired as usual. The entire loading and ejecting process could be done so rapidly that Lee said: "... I have fired 30 cartridges in about three-fourths of a minute, taking each cartridge by hand separately from the cartridge-box."

If the Lee was not to be fired immediately after loading the hammer could be moved back until a "click" was heard, which indicated that the breechblock was fully locked and the firing pin had been retracted. The rifle was "safe" in this position. When the rifle was to be fired immediately after loading the final locking of the breechblock was accomplished during the cocking of the hammer, not as a separate movement.

With a barrel length of 32½ inches and a length over-all of 49¼ inches, the M1875 Lee was still more than 2½ inches shorter than the issue Springfield with the same barrel length. This was due to its compact receiver, which also permitted it to be in-letted into the stock with a simple mortise.

Another feature of this Lee design was its unique take-down. A lip on the front edge of the trigger guard assembly, with attached trigger and trigger spring, slipped into a notch in the lower part of the receiver ring below the barrel, and a single bolt through the rear tang held everything together — simplicity itself.

Only 143 of the M1875 Lee-Springfield rifles were manufactured, according to the Ordnance Report for June 30, 1875, the appropriation having been expended. The design failed to dislodge the Springfield as the issue rifle of the Army; in fact the single-shot Springfield reigned supreme as the choice (?) of the U.S. Army until 1892, many years after other nations

had adopted breech-loading magazine rifles. Stored at Rock Island Arsenal after their trial, the M1875 Lee rifles were finally sold at one of the government auctions for $36 each.

## 1875 Design Fails

The March, 1896, issue of the now long-defunct English Arms & Explosives magazine reported that in 1875 Mr. James Lee had offered the British authorities a Martini-Henry rifle with the block operated by the hammer, instead of by the lever, and in various trials it had given some wonderful results in the rapidity of firing. Spare cartridges were carried in a single column type magazine, but not fixed to the rifle, which was a single shot. Instead, the magazine, which would hold 30 rounds, was hung from the left shoulder. Upward of 28 shots per minute were fired with the rifle, but it still did not satisfy the requirements of the British for a new rifle. The model offered the British was no doubt the solid-frame Martini-type based on the 1872 patent, rather than the model which was produced at the Springfield Armory about this time.

A vertical (Martini-type) action Remington-Lee rifle, which resembles the Springfield model but which would not chamber a 45-70 cartridge, was listed in Flayderman's catalog No. 70. It had a two-piece stock with full military fore-end and two bands. The barrel length was given as 32½ inches, with Remington markings on top. Minor manufacturing differences, such as frame contours, top of the breech-block, etc., indicate that this may have been an 1872 model of the type offered to the British.

On April 27, 1875, U.S. Patent No. 162, 481 was issued to Lee for a magazine box, but the specifications have not been located. It is therefore not known wheth-

er this is the magazine referred to in the British trials above.

Following his failure to interest the British in a rifle, Lee apparently returned to the U.S. to work for the Winchester Repeating Arms Co., for whom he is reported to have developed a refinement of their lever action Model 73. This was in 1877, and he was still attempting to perfect a rifle the U.S. government would accept.

On August 7, 1877, U.S. Patent No. 193, 831 was issued to Lee, "of Milwaukee ..." also covering an "Improvement ..." The application was dated October 9, 1876. (Lee is not listed as being in Milwaukee after 1874, but three years later this address still appears on patent papers.)

The 1877 design was also based on a hammer-operated Martini action. The breechblock was lowered by shoving forward on the thumbpiece of the hammer, but the hammer was a one-piece type instead of the two-piece as previously. The new hammer was a rebounding model, only in contact with the firing pin during the firing cycle. The V-shaped mainspring, with spurs added, was the only spring in the entire action, performing all necessary acts required of a spring. Other improvements were in the shape of the firing pin, the pivot pin for the breechblock, and the sear, plus a slightly reshaped receiver and trigger guard assembly. Altogether there were only 15 parts in the 1877 design, including 7 pins. The design was simple, easy to operate, and apparently reliable, but the fact remained that it was a single shot at a time when repeaters were becoming the vogue.

In accordance with an act of Congress dated November 21, 1877, another Ordnance Board was convened for the purpose of selecting a magazine rifle. This time a total of 29 arms were examined, and No. 25 was one entered by James Lee

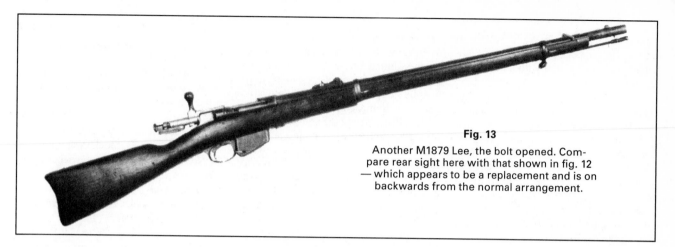

**Fig. 13**
Another M1879 Lee, the bolt opened. Compare rear sight here with that shown in fig. 12 — which appears to be a replacement and is on backwards from the normal arrangement.

of Hartford, Conn. (As noted above, the 1877 patent was issued to Lee at Milwaukee, but the rifle entered in the trials a few months later places Lee in Hartford, Conn. Later patents will include Ilion, N.Y., and again Hartford.) Which Lee model this was is not known to the author, but it is assumed that it is the 1877 design, possibly with the magazine mentioned previously. This opinion is based on Lee's statement that the 1877 design "... can be loaded and fired at the rate of 37 times per minute, ..." Regardless, it was beaten out when the Board selected the Winchester-manufactured Hotchkiss, and recommended that $20,000 be spent toward obtaining a trial lot for field testing.

### 1879 Bolt Action

Returning to the Remington Armory in Ilion, Lee was provided a workshop by Philo Remington, and such assistance as he needed. His perseverance at last paid off, for in 1878 the Lee bolt action rifle, capable of firing 30 rounds a minute, became a reality. On September 6, 1878, application was filed for a patent, and on November 4, 1879, U.S. Patent No. 221, 328 was granted to "James Lee, of Ilion, New York," for a design that was to become the most famous of all Lee rifles.

Alden Hatch in his book *Remington Arms in American History* relates a curious tale about Lee. During 1878 and 1879, while Lee was working on his bolt action rifle, he was living in a room at the Osgood Hotel in Ilion. He frequently took his drawings and models back to his room to work on them at night. The room directly above his was rented by an enterprising German, who also worked for Remington. It has been said that the German bored a hole in the floor of his room and lay on his stomach for hours, his eye glued to the hole to watch what went on below. The name of the German? Franz Mauser, a brother of the inventors of the Mauser repeating rifle — Peter Paul and

Wilhelm Mauser. Whether the watching was profitable or not is debatable, as the Mauser rifles were not equipped with box magazines until 1886. However, the fact remains that Lee later sued the Mauser brothers for patent infringement.

Lee apparently wanted to manufacture his rifle on his own, so the Lee Arms Company of Bridgeport, Conn. was formed sometime in 1879 in order to do so.[7] The address of the firm, at the foot of Clinton Avenue, next to the New Haven Railroad, was the same as that of the Sharps Rifle Company, which was listed in the Bridgeport city directories until 1886. Apparently Lee's financial backers were also of the same group, for E.G. Westcott, president of the Sharps Rifle Company in 1879, was later listed as treasurer of the Lee Arms Company. Previous to 1878, Westcott was listed as president and treasurer of the Sharps firm, but in a rare Sharps folder dated 1878, and apparently intended for British trade, Westcott is listed as vice-president and treasurer, and A.W. Winchester is president. In 1881-82, after the Sharps firm had ceased operations, Winchester is listed as the Sharps treasurer. The backers apparently lost interest in the rifle manufacturing business shortly after the new Lee firm was formed. The last Sharps catalog consisted of an 1879 edition with a blue 1880 price list attached, and operations were suspended in October, 1880, after only a few of the Lee rifles had been manufactured.[8]

The Lee patents were taken over by Remington, a natural move since the rifle had been developed at the Remington Armory, and the manufacture transferred to Ilion under license. The rifles were produced by Remington for the Lee Arms Company, which continued to act as the selling agent, commercially advertising the rifle in the Army & Navy Journal from April 13 to November 27, 1880.

The 1879 patent was very simple and direct. It provided for a "... bolt-gun hav-

ing an opening through the bottom of its shoe or receiver, a detachable magazine ... with rear and of different lengths ... to allow the cartridges to lie therein in an inclined position, and with their flanges (rims) overlapping one another ..." It also provided for two other magazine modifications, including one that circled the gun stock, a firing pin with a knob on the end to allow the pin to be drawn back by hand or to the halfcock position, an extractor and a ".... curved sliding plate (cut-off) ... to allow the rifle ... to be used as a single-loader ..." The actual arm followed the patent specifications closely.

The first rifles were marked on the upper left side of the receiver:

**The Lee Arms Co. Bridgeport Conn.
U.S.A.
Patented Nov. 4th 1879**

This was followed by a serial number and an inspector's initials, such as W.W.K., W.M.F., and P. Rifles purchased by the U.S. Navy were also stamped with U.S. above an anchor.

The straight bolt handle projected to the right, just forward of the receiver bridge. The one-piece bolt cocked on closing. There were two locking lugs, consisting of the root of the bolt handle with its integral guide rib, and a small lug directly opposite which locked into the left side of the receiver. The cocking piece knob was small, flat, and smooth. The rotating extractor slipped into the front of the bolt and was retained by a hooked piece which fitted into the guide rib. The degree of rotation of the extractor was established by a groove in the bolt body just ahead of the guide rib.

The barrels, 29½ inches long, were rifled with 5 wide grooves. Over-all length was 48½ inches, weight about 8½ pounds.

A gas escape port was located in the left side of the receiver ring ¾-inch back of the forward edge, in the event of case

The firing pin could be drawn back to the halfcock position to serve as a safety when carrying it with a live round in the chamber.

The M1879 stock extended to within three inches of the muzzle and had a nose cap. Two bands were used, both retained with conventional leaf springs. The upper band held a sling swivel; the lower swivel was retained by a front trigger-guard screw. A cleaning rod fitted into a groove in the bottom of the fore-end and extended to the muzzle. There was no upper hand-guard and the grip of the stock was straight. The buttplate was of steel, curved, in the same basic shape as on the Springfield M1873.

Two different rear sights have been observed on the M1879. The more common one is a folding tangent, graduated on the notched elevation slide to 500 yards, and on the leaf to 1200 yards. It is adjustable for windage by sliding the crossbar, which has "buckhorn" side elements.

The M1879 was chambered for the 43 Spanish, 44-77 (bottleneck), 45-70 Gov't. and 45-90 Winchester cartridges. The magazine held 5 cartridges and was plain, without grooves or corrugations.

Both sporting and military versions of the M1879 were apparently produced. However, the bulk of the production was the military model.

In 1876 the Navy Bureau of Ordnance had recommended that "... we should adopt a magazine gun, which for naval purposes is in every respect preferable." By 1879 a total of 2500 of the 45-caliber Hotchkiss rifles had been bought for testing. A year later, in the Annual Report of the Secretary of the Navy, mention was made that the Hotchkiss guns, along with 250 each of the Remington Keene and Lee guns — chambered for the 45–70 Gov't, cartridge — were enough to arm the 75 ships then in commission with repeating rifles, and to test the relative value of the three systems — magazine in butt, beneath the barrel, and detachable.

In 1881 it was reported that the "... 300 Lee breech-loading rifles are being manufactured at the Remington Armory." By 1882 the 300 "Lee Arms Co." rifles had been delivered and introduced into the service.

Other countries buying the Model 1879 included Spain, Argentina, and China. The Chinese purchase was the basis for a humorous comment attributed to the inventor some years later. The Chinese were well pleased with the Model 1879, and had used the rifles to defeat some French troops. Afterward an eminent Chinese gentleman named Yung Wing brought several young Chinamen to the United States to complete their education at eastern colleges. Being in the area he stopped by Hartford to see James Lee at his home, and to compliment him on his rifles. During the conversation Lee jokingly commented that he was never quite sure whether the Chinese Government had selected his rifle on its merits, or because they believed its inventor to be a Chinaman, his name being Jim Lee.

**References**

1. "Lee Firearms Company in Milwaukee," Harry Wandrus. Hobbies — The Magazine for Collectors, December, 1949.

2. H.L. Uphoff lists 6 of the same individuals as shareholders. The exception is an Alexander Mitchell, instead of Thomas L. Ogden. He also lists the president of the Board as Charles F. Ilsley, with James Kneeland, Daniel Wells, Jr., Lester Sexton, and James Lee as directors.

3. This was the only Ordnance Department contract granted to a mid-western arms company.

4. Col. McAllister reported that Lee had on hand 202 carbines in various stages of completion, and that 255 had been finished, 102 of these last sold at $22.50. A full list of the parts Lee had on hand was furnished, their cost, etc., and Col. McAllister noted that Lee stood to lose some $6500 if he finished his contract. A compromise settlement was suggested by Col. McAllister.

5. The Civil War was over.

6. Mention has been made in one source that James Lee enjoyed the distinction among private inventors of being moved by the government from his home at Stevens Point, Wis., to Springfield Armory in Massachusetts to supervise the manufacturing of his rifle. This is doubtful, since only the 1862 patent carried the Stevens Point address, and succeeding patents up to this time carried the Milwaukee address, plus the fact that Lee is listed as residing at 130 Prospect Street in the Milwaukee city directories during the 1866-1874 period. Possibly the government agreed to move his family from Milwaukee to Springfield so that they could be with him.

7. During this period another Lee Arms Co. came into being. Whether it was connected with James Paris Lee is moot. Gluckman and Gardner both list the Lee Arms Co. of Wilkes-Barre, Pa., as makers of "Red Jacket" rimfire revolvers around 1877-80, and Gardner indicates "... possibly before and after" this date, and tacked on "James Paris Lee." Sharpe says that Lee moved to Wilkes-Barre after he had sold his rifle rights to Remington, and there formed a new Lee Arms Co. to make a variety of rimfire revolvers. Only Sharpe and Gardner mention James Paris Lee as connected with the Wilkes-Barre firm, and only Sharpe actually states Lee formed the company. Apparently very little is known about this firm and its organization, but if James Paris Lee was connected with it, it represents his sole departure into the handgun field — other than his 1862 patent for a single shot handgun. This time factor is about correct, as many Lee designs originated during the 1870s. The author's opinion is that James Paris Lee was not connected with the "Red Jacket" revolvers; the main flaw is the apparent term of existence for the firm — 1877-80. Gardner says Roland L. Brewer of Pittston, Pa., (1878–84) was granted U.S. Patent No. 239,914 on April 5, 1881, for a revolving firearm, the patent assigned to J.F. Lee, of Wilkes-Barre. The last name and the location are right for the Lee Arms Co. making revolvers. The same Brewer was later issued three firearms patents — assigned to the Colt. This would seem to indicate the maker of "Red Jacket" revolvers was J.F. Lee, not J.P. Lee. Possibly some reader has better information.

8. What may have been one of the first M1879 Lee rifles apparently produced at the Sharps factory used parts identical to those on the M1879 Sharps-Borchardt military rifle. The rear sight is the same as the Borchardt, the two bands are Borchardt-type (secured with wood screws through the bottom instead of with springs as on the later production) and the buttplate is of flat checkered steel — Borchardt design. The 43 caliber barrel, 32½ inches long is rifled with 6 grooves. Total length is 51⅜ inches. No markings appear on the wood or metal. The magazine holds 5 cartridges. The bolt is one-piece but the handle is behind the bridge instead of in front as on the standard 1879 rifles. Only one such rifle is known.

## Bibliography

*The Fuller Collection of American Firearms*, Harold L. Peterson, Eastern National Park & Monument Association, 1967.

*Digest of U.S. Patents Relating to Breech Loading and Magazine Small Arms 1836–1873*, by V.D. Stockbridge. Reprint by Norm Flayderman, Greenwich, Conn., 1963.

*Small Arms Makers*, Col. Robert Gardner, Bonanza Books, New York, 1963.

*The Breech-Loader In The Service 1816–1917*, Claude E. Fuller, N. Flayderman & Co. New Milford, Conn., 1965.

*Guns Through the Ages*, Geoffrey Booth-royd, Bonanza Books, New York, 1961. "Lee's Firearms Co.," Herbert L. Uphoff, *The Gun Report*, June and July, 1967.

*The Lee-Enfield Rifle*, Major E.G.B. Reynolds, Herbert Jenkins, London, 1960.

*Suicide Specials*, Donald B. Webster, Jr., The Stackpole Company, Harrisburg, Pa., 1958.

*The Book of Rifles*, W.H.B. Smith and Jos. E. Smith, The Stackpole Company, Harrisburg, Pa., 1963.

"Model 1875 Lee-Springfield," Gordon F. Baxter, Jr., *The Gun Report*, November, 1960.

"Remington-Lee Rifle," Ludwig Olson, *The American Rifleman*, April, 1966.

"The Rifles of James Paris Lee," Robt. H. Rankin, *Guns & Ammo*, March, 1964.

*Remington Arms in American History*, Alden Hatch, Rinehart & Co., New York, 1956.

*American Gun Makers*, A. Gluckman and L.D. Satterlee, The Stackpole Company, Harrisburg, Pa., 1953.

*The Rifle in America*, Philip B. Sharpe, Funk & Wagnalls, New York, 1947.

*The Gun and its Development*, 9th ed., W.W. Greener, Reprint by Bonanza Books, New York, 1967.

"James Paris Lee," James Young, *The Saturday Globe*, Toronto, Can., June 9, 1900.

*The United States Navy Rifle, Calibre 6 Millimeters, Model 1895, Description and Nomenclature*, P.R. Alger and N.C. Twining, Lockwood & Brainard, Hartford, Conn., 1896.

"The Lee Straight-Pull Magazine Rifle," E.G. Parkhurst, *American Machinist*, November 22, 1900.

*Winchester, The Gun That Won The West*, H.F. Williamson, The Sportsman's Press, 1952.

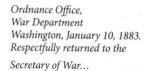

# The Rifles of James Paris Lee

Part Two. Born in Scotland in 1831, Lee was brought to Canada in 1836, moving eventually to Stevens Point, Wisconsin, sometime before 1860. His first military contract, made in 1864, was hardly successful. A rare dropping block design based on Lee's 1866 patent is pictured and described, as are Lee's M1875 rifle, the various trials of his rifle designs, and his 1879 system — the first one of his great magazine design, and the rifle which would prove to be the forerunner of the British S.M.L.E.

■ Larry S. Sterett

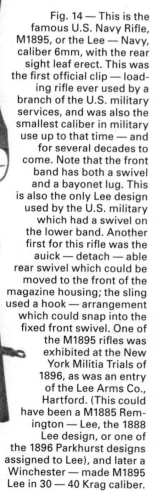

Fig. 14 — This is the famous U.S. Navy Rifle, M1895, or the Lee — Navy, caliber 6mm, with the rear sight leaf erect. This was the first official clip — loading rifle ever used by a branch of the U.S. military services, and was also the smallest caliber in military use up to that time — and for several decades to come. Note that the front band has both a swivel and a bayonet lug. This is also the only Lee design used by the U.S. military which had a swivel on the lower band. Another first for this rifle was the auick — detach — able rear swivel which could be moved to the front of the magazine housing; the sling used a hook — arrangement which could snap into the fixed front swivel. One of the M1895 rifles was exhibited at the New York Militia Trials of 1896, as was an entry of the Lee Arms Co., Hartford. (This could have been a M1885 Remington — Lee, the 1888 Lee design, or one of the 1896 Parkhurst designs assigned to Lee), and later a Winchester — made M1895 Lee in 30 — 40 Krag caliber.

REALIZING THE NEED and, possibly sensing the handwriting on the wall, the Ordnance Department convened the Board of 1882 to pick a suitable magazine rifle. By late September 1882 the Board had tested and examined a total of 53 rifles submitted by 20 inventors, including the M1879 and M1882 versions of the Lee rifle in 45–70 Gov't, caliber. Rifle No. 10 was a M1879 entry of the Lee Arms Co., and No. 36 was a Remington — Lee M1882 with an improved bolt. Rifles No. 24, 31, and 35, were Spencer — Lee rifles entered by J. W. Frazier of New York City.[9] The early trials narrowed the field to three basic designs — the M1882 Lee, the Hotchkiss, the Chaffee — Reece — and additional testing was recommended.

Ordnance Office,
War Department
Washington, October 9, 1882

*Respectfully returned to the Secretary of War:
A careful examination of the report … convinces me that … while the Lee gun is entitled to the first place, the comparative merits of the three guns put them nearly on a par in point of excellence.
… I respectfully recommend that the $50,000 available … be expended in providing the Lee, the Chaffee — Reece, and the Hotchkiss magazine guns for trial in the hands of troops.*
  *S. V. Benet,
  Brigadier — General,
  Chief of Ordnance.*

The recommendation was approved by Robert T. Lincoln, Secretary of War and Benet was asked to learn the prices of each type of gun:

Ordnance Office,
War Department
Washington, January 10, 1883.
*Respectfully returned to the*

*Secretary of War…*

*The Remingtons make the Lee gun, and will supply them at $16.66 each in about three months. The prices given for the Lee and Hotch — kiss are fair. I respectfully recommend that 750 guns each of Lee and Hotchkiss may be procured by contract …
In this connection I have to state that as the Lee and Hotchkiss are patented articles and can only be procured from parties owning the patents, the question arises whether or not contracts can be made with them without previous advertisement. If not contrary to law I respectfully recommended it.*
  *S. V. Benet,
  Brigadier — General,
  Chief of Ordnance.*

*Respectfully returned to the Chief of Ordnance.*

*…the making of a contract with the proprietors of the Lee and Hotchkiss guns without advertisement is authorized for the reason that such advertisement would be a useless expense, as… definite articles are wanted, for which there can be no competition.*

*John Tweedale
Chief Clerk
War Department, January 10, 1883.*

Ordnance Office,
War Department
Washington, D.C.,
December 15, 1885.

Fig. 15 — Right side of the Lee M1895 action. What appears to be a small number 7, near the rear of the breech opening, is supposed to be the number 1. Fig. 16 — Left side view of the Lee M1895 action, showing the bolt stop, bolt release and firing-pin lock. The inscription on the receiver reads, in two lines: MANUFACTURED BY THE WINCHESTER RE-PEATING ARMS CO./NEW HAVEN, CONN. U. S. A. PAT OCT 10, 93, JAN 30, 94, OCT 5, 95.

*The Secretary of War.*

*Sir: I have the honor to transmit herewith a tabular statement of the results reached in the trial of a number of each of the magazine rifles issued to the troops. (Author's note: 713 rifles each of the Lee, Hotchkiss, and Chaffee — Reece [designs] were issued to the troops, and Springfield Armory had produced 3,937 spare magazines for the Lee.) These guns were recommended for trial, in the order named, by a board of officers convened in 1881, under authority of law ...*

*The reports from 149 companies have been received ... as follows:*

*Comparing the three magazine guns with each other the reports are:*

*For the Lee, 55; Chaffee — Reece, 14; Hotchkiss, 26.*

*As magazine guns, therefore, the reports are largely in favor of the Lee.*

*Comparing the magazine guns with each other and with the Springfield service rifle as single loaders, the preference is for the Springfield, as follows: For the Lee, 5; Chaffee — Reece, 0; Hotchkiss, 1; Springfield, 21.*

*Comparing the magazine guns and the Springfield for all uses, the preference is for the Lee, 10; Chaffee — Reece, 3; Hotchkiss, 4; and the Springfield, 46; being largely in favor of the Springfield.*

*...I am satisfied that neither of these magazine guns should be adopted and substituted for the Springfield rifle as the arm for the Service.*

*...The Springfield rifle gives such general satisfaction to the Army that we can safely wait a reasonable time for further developments of magazine systems.*

Fig. 17 — Essential parts of the Lee MI 895. Parts common to all small arms are omitted in this Figure and in Fig. 20. The parts in both Figures are numbered the same, so that they may be compared. No. 1, receiver; 2, bolt; 3, firing pin; 4, mainspring; 5, firing-pin collar; 6, cam lever; 7, trigger guard and magazine; 8, cartridge elevator; 9A, bolt-stop thumb -piece; 9B, bolt-stop; 10, extractor; 11, extractor spring; 12, sear; 13, sear fly; 14, trigger; 15A, trigger spring; 15B, fly spring; 16, elevator spring; 17, elevator-spring shaft; 18, lock pin; 19, firing-pin lock; 20, bolt release; 21, trigger-spring stop-pin; 22, trigger-spring screw.

*Very respectfully,*
*your obedient servant,*
*S. V. Benet,*
*Brigadier — General,*
*Chief of Ordnance.*

Thus, the Springfield single shot rifle was to remain the mainstay of the U. S. Army for another 7 years.

The original arrangement between Lee and Remington called for Remington to manufacture the rifles for the Lee Arms Co. This arrangement did not work out and, in 1884, Lee had entered into an agreement with Remington to manufacture and sell the rifle on a royalty basis. As a result, rifles manufactured after this time were marked:

**E. REMINGTON & SONS, ILION, N.Y. U.S.A. SOLE MANUFACTURERS AND AGENTS**

On March 25, 1884, "James P. Lee and Louis P. Diss, of Ilion, New York Assignors to E. Remington & Sons, of Same Place" were issued U. S. Patent No. 295,-563 for a "Magazine for Fire-Arms." The basic design was for an improvement of the 1879 model and consisted of a very light sheet-iron magazine with "... spring or detent which holds the cartridges in the box when not attached to the arm, and in corrugating the body of the box (magazine) ..." This same Diss was issued 8 other firearms patents between 1884 and 1888, with most assigned to E. Remington & Sons.

## Sales to the Navy

The 1884 Annual Report of the Secretary of the Navy stated that 700 Lee magazine guns had been purchased on advantageous terms for armament on new cruisers. The model is unknown to the author: that "advantageous" might refer to a closing out of the 1879 model, but this is only an opinion.

In 1885 an improved Lee rifle appeared. This is sometimes called the 1884/85 Lee, but it is usually listed as the Model 1885 Remington-Lee. The rear locking system, with cocking on closing, was retained, but a separate bolt head was used. The extractor was attached to the bolt head, and both were held in place by a hooked piece that fitted into the guide rib and slid rearward to lock. The cocking piece was changed slightly, the flange almost doubled in size.

The barrel was 32'/2 inches long, and rifled the same as the 1882 model. Over-all length of the 1885 model was 52 inches, and the weight was about 8½ pounds.

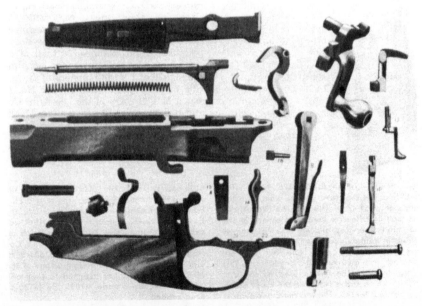

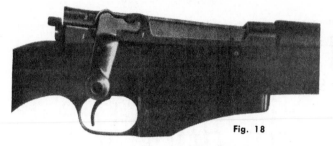

Fig. 18          Fig. 19

Fig. 18 — Right side view of the Lee M1899. The knurled piece at the rear of the receiver is the safety. Forward of the trigger guard is the magazine cut-off, which the M1895 did not have. Fig. 19 — Left side view of the Lee M1899, showing the bolt-stop and safety lock.

There was no upper handguard, but the two bands, the nose cap, the two sling swivels and their location, the sights, and the 5-round magazine with two vertical grooves were the same as on the Model 1882.

The Model 1885 was Remington marked, per the 1884 agreement, except that after 1888 E. Remington & Sons became the Remington Arms Company. These markings were on the upper left side of the receiver, and the serial number usually followed the second line of the marking. Rifles bought by the U. S. Navy were marked on top of the receiver ring with U.S.N. over an anchor: these markings sometimes had two lines below them consisting of an identification number and an inspector's initials, making a total of 4 lines on the receiver ring.

E. Remington & Sons went into receivership in 1886. (Lee recovered the rights to his designs in accordance with his contract with Remington, and apparently left for England to try to interest the British Government in his magazine rifle.) Of the Remington brothers, Sam was the businessman, so when he died in 1882 the firm started to slip slowly toward bankruptcy. Philo and Eliphalet III tried to keep the huge Armory in operation, and if a sizeable foreign or U. S. order for the Lee rifle had been obtained they might have been able to do so. Turning out a quality product for which the demand is limited is expensive. For two years the receivers finished the work in process and took what small orders were obtained. Then in March, 1888, Marcellus Hartley, founder of the Union Metallic Cartridge Company, and Thomas G. Bennett, son-in-law of Governor Oliver Winchester (Remington's main competitor), bought E. Remington & Sons, with all of its physical properties and its reputation, for two million dollars. The name was changed to the Remington Arms Company, but the quality products for which the firm was known remained the same.

On May 22, 1888, U. S. Patent 383,363 for a "Magazine Fire-Arm" was issued to "James P. Lee, of New York, N. Y." In the patent introduction Lee lists himself as an engineer and a resident of New York (City), although he is not so-listed in any of the other patents with which the author is familiar.

The patent relates to the 1879 patent and was "... chiefly designed to improve the construction and increase the efficiency of such fire-arms." The arm had been previously patented in England on August 18,1887, and examination of the drawings indicates that this is the basic design for the famous Lee-Enfield rifle used throughout the British Empire for over 60 years.

The wide cup extending below the receiver breech for the attachment of the separate buttstock, so familiar a sight on later Lee-Enfield rifles, is illustrated for the first time. The removable bolt head, which could also be used as a tool for unscrewing the firing pin from the cocking piece, is covered in this 1888 patent, as is the entire striker assembly so much a part of the Lee-Enfield rifles.

Two magazine modifications, which make use of U-shaped follower springs instead of the common zig-zag type, are covered by the patent. Surprisingly, the cartridges illustrated in the magazine are rimless instead of the rimmed or flanged type then in use. The magazine catch is a transverse type, such as became popular later on autoloading pistols, instead of the previous lever type in the upper part of the trigger guard directly ahead of the trigger.

The Annual Report of the Secretary of the Navy for 1888 mentioned that 1500 Lee rifles "... of the latest construction ..." had been bought from the Lee Arms Co. for immediate use on ships nearing completion. These would have been the M1885 design, and were no doubt manufactured by the newly formed Remington Arms Company, probably under license from Lee. So far as the author can learn the Lee Arms Company did not have manufacturing facilities, although it apparently continued to exist as a sales agency. Mention was further made by the Secretary that arms being purchased were "... as few as we can pending caliber reductions ...," and that Lee had been selected as the builder of reduced-caliber Navy weapon(s), and a contract signed. Apparently the Navy, regardless of what the Army was doing, was planning to reduce the caliber from .45-inch to something much smaller, in keeping with the trend in Europe and England at this time.

In the 1889 Report the Secretary of the Navy mentioned that the 1500 stand of Lee magazine rifles mentioned in the previous report had been completed by the Lee Arms Co. and the work on them very favorably spoken of by the inspector.

## Trials of 1891

The U. S. Army was still without a magazine rifle. On November 24,1890, the Adjutant General's office issued a general order for a board of officers to select a magazine gun to replace the single-shot Springfield. The Board convened at New York on December 16,1890, and remained in session until July 1, 1892. A total of 53 guns were examined and tests were made at Governors Island, New York, during July, 1891. Four of the rifles entered in these trials were connected directly or indirectly with

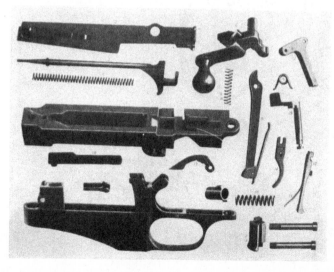

Fig. 20 — Essential parts of the Lee M1899. No. 1, receiver; 2, bolt; 3, firing pin; 4, mainspring; 5, firing-pin collar; 6, cam lever; 7, trigger guard and magazine; 8, cartridge elevator; 9A, bolt-stop; 9B, bolt-stop spring; 10, extractor; 11, extractor spring; 12, sear; 13, bolt retainer (new); 14, trigger; 15, trigger spring; 16, elevator spring; 17, elevator-spring sleeve; 18, extractor-spring stop (new); 19, safety lock (new).

# J. P. LEE.
## MAGAZINE BOLT GUN.

No. 547,583.                          Patented Oct. 8, 1895.

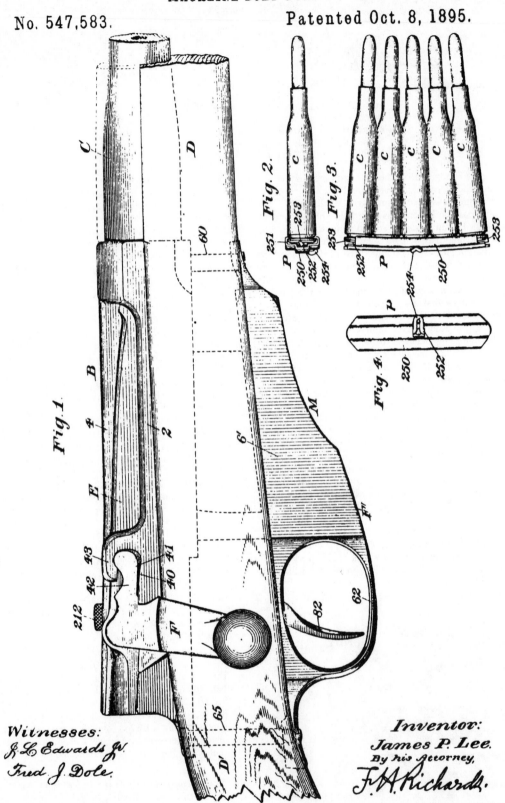

Witnesses:
J. L. Edwards Jr.
Fred. J. Dole.

Inventor:
James P. Lee.
By his Attorney,
F. H. Richards.

Lee's 1895 U.S. Patent, No. 547,583, covered his design for a
straight pull bolt action rifle. This became the Lee Navy 6mm.

James Paris Lee, as follows:

Rifle No. 1, entered by the U. S. Army Chief of Ordnance, Washington, D. C, was apparently the Lee-Metford or Magazine Rifle Mark I, adopted by England on December 22, 1888. The first models were sometimes referred to as the Lee-Speed. This was not the official name, but Greener and several other authors of this period did not always differentiate between the Lee-Speed, Lee-Metford and Lee-Enfield. The Lee-Speed rifle shown in *The Gun…*[*] is identical to the Lee-Metford and resembles the drawing in Lee's 1888 patent closely. Speed was the name of an employee at the Royal Small Arms Factory at Enfield Lock, possibly that of the Superintendent.

Rifle No. 39, entered by the Lee Arms Co., South Windham, Conn, was probably the M1885. This address in Connecticut is not that of the 1879 firm, but the author has no other information relating to it. By whom rifles No. 25 and 26 were entered is not known to the author, but perhaps these were Remington Arms Company entries.

Again the Lee lost out, this time to the Krag-Jorgensen (No. 5) entered by a Capt. Ole Krag from Norway. The U. S. Army never adopted a Lee design as an official arm, but the U. S. Navy used Lee rifles for nearly 20 years.

Lee had apparently been busy on the new rifle the Navy had requested, for the Secretary of the Navy reported in 1892 that specifications had been given to Lee for a 236 caliber arm. In 1893 it was further reported that while the Army Krag and several European designs had been examined and compared, work was continuing with Lee on the 236.

The year 1893 was a big one for Lee. Beginning on August 19, 1892, Lee had filed patent applications for a series of " … new and useful Improvements in Magazine-Guns …," and on October 10, 1893, the U. S. Patent Office granted patents to "James P. Lee, of Ilion, New York" in profusion. Patent Nos. 506,319; 506,320; 506,321; 506,322 and 506,323 were issued for a "Straight-Pull Bolt-Gun" (first three patents), a "Magazine-Gun" and a "Fire-Arm Magazine Case" respectively. On the same date U. S. Patent No. 506,339 was issued to "Francis H. Richards, of Hartford, Conn., Assignor to James Paris Lee, of same place." Richards' patent was for a "Straight-Pull Bolt-Gun" and the application had been filed on September 26,1892, the same date on which Lee had filed the application that became Patent No. 506,321. (Note that patents issued the same day list Lee as at Ilion, N. Y. and Hartford, Conn.) Francis H. Richards is listed on the patent drawings as being Lee's attorney, but on the specifications as a witness; the second witness on the drawings does not appear on the specifications of the first three patents. On the patent for the "Magazine-Gun" a W. G. Richards is listed on both the drawings and the specifications, and again on the specifications for the Richards patent as a witness; Francis H. Richards is listed as the inventor on this last patent (No. 506,339.) The witness whose name appears on

*W. W. Greener, London, var. eds., 1881 — 1910.

| | Magazine Capacity | Weight | Caliber |
|---|---|---|---|
| No. 1 Lee Speed, England | 8 rds. | 9 3/8 lbs. | 303 |
| No. 25 Lee No. 1, American | 10 rds. | 8 1/4 lbs. | 303 |
| No. 26 Lee No. 2, American | 5 rds. | 8 1/4 | 300 |
| No. 39 Lee No. 3, American | 10 rds. | 8 1/4 lbs. | 300 |

the drawings of all the patents listed above appears to be H. Mallner.

## Lee Straight Pull Rifles

The patents all relate to the straight-pull rifle that the U. S. Navy would later adopt as the M1895. The arms are designed for use with detachable 10-round magazines (staggered column) with their release in the trigger guard. The cartridges shown are rimmed, and about 30 caliber-very similar to the 30–40 Krag. Provision was made for loading the magazine with 15-round clips while the magazine was still attached to the rifle. The receiver walls are solid on this design and the ejection is upward, instead of to the right. Other than the firing-pin spring and magazine spring the only spring in this particular design was a U-shaped type that served as sear and trigger spring. There was no safety. The Lee Patent No. 506,321 and the Richards patent are for a model not quite the same as on the other patents, and many of these particular two patent drawings appear to be the same. Basic operation of the rifles covered in the 1893 patents is much the same, as will be covered later in connection with the M1895 Lee-Navy rifle.

The 1894 annual Navy report mentioned that the Navy had designed the barrel, stock, and cartridge, and tested all. Apparently the reference is to the 236-caliber Lee rifle and cartridge, on which work had been underway to some degree for nearly 6 years.

On October 2,1894, at the United States Torpedo Station, Newport, Rhode Island, the Navy tested 12 rifles, including the Lee straight-pull model. Two of the rifles tested were straight-pull designs, including the Lee, one was a slide-action, and the rest were turn-bolt designs, 5 of these last entered by Remington. On November 19, 1894, another trial was held with three additional rifles, including a Luger 6mm rimless caliber design. One of the tests involved penetration (pine?) as related to caliber; the 236 Navy penetrated 23 inches as opposed to 10 inches for the 45–70 Gov't. cartridge, and 18 inches for the 8mm Austrian Mannlicher cartridge.

In May, 1895, a Navy Board, convened at Newport, officially adopted the Lee Straight-Pull, with the shape of the stock, fittings, sling strap, and bayonet determined by the Board. The 1895 report of the Secretary of the Navy mentioned that the 1894 Board had adopted the Lee Straight-Pull, although it may have been unofficial at that time. Bids for 10,000 rifles of the Lee design were requested, and Winchester got the contract. (Lee had sold the rights to manufacture the rifle to the Winchester firm.) However, Williamson in *Winchester …* says that the contract was for 15,000 of these Lee patent rifles, while factory records indicate 20,000 were made, of which 1,700 were sporting models. The factory records show that all

Fig. 21 — The M1882 Remington-Lee rifle as used by the U.S. Navy. Note the position and type of bolt handle; the head of the cocking piece, and the two vertical grooves in the magazine. The upper band still has two swivels. This model is often mistakenly called the M1879; it definitely is not, but it's a much better design than the original. This particular rifle is marked as indicated in the text, and the left side of the receiver has PATENTED NOV. 4th, 1879. One MI 882 rifle is the Royal Military College Museum of Canada is marked on the receiver: E. REMINGTON & SONS, ILION, N. Y., U. S. A./SOLE MANUFACTURER AND AGENTS/PATENTED NOV. 4th, 1879. The rifle is chambered for the 45–70 Gov't, cartridge, and has the 5-round magazine with two vertical grooves. The bolt handle, cocking piece, and guide rib are polished bright and the rear sight lies immediately in front of the receiver ring; the rear sight is of the type shown in Fig. 12 (See Part One of this article, pp. 48–60, 26th ed. GUN DIGEST.) except it is reversed and in the correct position. Another M1882 rifle in the same collection is completely nickel-plated, except for the highly polished blued magazine, which is without grooves. The stock on this particular rifle is checkered on the fore-end and grip, and the rifle is unmarked. This rifle was in the collection of Porfirio Diaz, once President of Mexico.

Fig. 22 — The M1885 Remington-Lee, caliber 45–70 Gov't. The only noticeable differences from the M1882 are the size of the cocking-piece head, the method of fitting the extractor to the bolt, and the smaller cut-out of the receiver ring on the right side. Markings on this rifle are as indicated in the text. Note there are still two swivels on the upper band. Barrel length of this rifle is 32⅝ inches, giving an overall length of 52 inches. Serial number is 53142.

of them were manufactured in the three years of 1896–1898, as follows:

There were no receivers numbered from 11,719 to 12,002, 13,701 to 13,733 or 14,980 to 15,000, which cuts the 20,000 total by nearly 400 rifles.

| Serial Numbers | Year |
|---|---|
| 1 – 1917 | 1896 |
| 1,918 – 10,512 | 1897 |
| 10,513 – 20,000 | 1898 |

## First Official Clip Loader

The 1897 Navy Report mentions that 10,000 Lee (236 caliber) rifles had been delivered and issued to vessels in commission. Thus the Lee-Navy design became the first clip-loading rifle ever officially used by armed forces of the United States, and the smallest official caliber-disregarding the 22 rimfire-until the introduction of the 5.56mm (223) over 60 years later.

The straight-pull design was not new by any means. Austria had used at least 7 different models of straight-pull rifles by the time the U. S. Navy adopted the Lee. Switzerland had also been using a straight-pull rifle. Most of these designs had used a system of revolving or rotating locking lugs. Lee's design, patented in 1893, used a wedge-type locking lug integral with the bottom of the bolt. Although correct-ed in later models, once the bolt was locked down in the M1895 it could not be unlocked without pulling the trigger or pushing down on the "dead-lock actuator" on the left side of the receiver.

On October 8, 1895, U. S. Patent No. 547,583 was granted to "James P. Lee, of Hartford, Conn.," for a "Magazine Bolt-Gun." The 16 pages of drawings show clearly that this is the rifle manufactured for the U. S. Navy, even to the extent of illustrating the 6mm rimless cartridge in the 5-round clip.

The M1895 Lee-Navy uses a wedge-type locking lug integral with the bottom of the bolt. By slamming the bolt handle forward the wedge is cammed down into contact with a recoil shoulder in the receiver. Since the wedge is below the line of recoil, discharge tends to lock the breech mechanism securely. After firing a straight-back pull on the bolt handle cams the wedge up out of its recess; a continuation of the movement draws the bolt to the rear until it is stopped by the bolt-stop, which also controls the ejection.

The extractor on the 1895 design is a peculiar floating type-entirely different from that employed in the turnbolt system-on the left side of the bolt. It has three functions-extraction, ejection, and as a stop for retaining the cartridges in the magazine. The extractor remains stationary until the bolt has moved rearward about 1¾ inches. A lug on the bolt then strikes a lug on the extractor, imparting a violent jerk to the cartridge, pulling it from the chamber and literally throwing it out to the right. An unusual method to say the least.

The 1895 design had no safety, as such, but it did have a "firing-pin locker." This device located on the left side of the receiver wall at the breech, moved in a vertical plane only: when pushed upward it retracted and locked the firing-pin out of engagement with the sear arm. When the rifle was to be fired the "locker" could easily be pushed down out of engagement, allowing the firing pin to re-engage the sear. Two other devices appeared that were not often seen on other designs; The movable bolt stop and the "dead-lock actuator" for the sliding bolt. Located on the left side of the receiver, they locked the bolt closed, but permitted it to be unlocked to remove the chambered cartridge, and the bolt to be removed from the rifle entirely when necessary. Pressing the lock actuator downward would unlock the bolt, causing the rear portion to spring upward, after which it could be drawn back to extract the cartridge.

The 1895 design was essentially a repeating rifle. When a clip of 5 cartridges, with a confining hook at each end of the clip, was inserted into the magazine, either end up, a fixed cam released all the cartridges for feeding. There was no magazine cut-off on this model.

Williamson says that in November, 1897, after the Navy contract had been completed, Winchester introduced a sporting version of the M1895 Lee-Navy to list at $32. It was described thus:

*"This gun is known as the Lee Straight-Pull Rifle, and has been adopted as the small arm for use in the United States Navy. The caliber of the gun is .236 in. (6mm) and it shoots a smokeless powder cartridge with a hardened lead bullet, having a copper jacket plated with tin, and giving an initial velocity of 2,550 feet (777.24 meters) per second. The magazine holds 5 cartridges, which may be inserted separately or at one time, in which latter case they are placed in the magazine in a pack, held together by a steel clip. The superiority of this rifle over all other types of bolt guns lies in the fact that the operation of opening and closing is by a 'straight pull' instead of the customary 'up turn' and 'pull back.'"*

The sporter, sometimes known as the Winchester-Lee model, was available in 6mm caliber only, with a 24-inch nickel-steel barrel. It weighed 7.5 pounds with the sporting halfstock. The quality was good, but the price was high, and sportsmen were just not ready for a bolt action arm that cost more than the popular lever action so The Lee Straight-Pull sporter hardly got off the ground, although it was listed in Winchester catalogs until 1902.

The 1895 patent mentions a previous patent,-No. 513,647, issued January 30, 1894, to James Lee for a "Bolt-Gun." While this patent incorporates some of the features later used in the M1895 rifle it is mainly for a straight-pull design with a 10-round cartridge packet with an outside-mounted cartridge lifter. (Patent No. 547,-582 was for a 5-round "cartridge

Fig. 23-Top: This is one of the improved Lee rifles with Bethel Burton magazine, of the type entered in the British trials of 1882-87. Note that barrel, fore-end, and bands are identical to those on the older Martini-Henry rifles, indicating that this may be one of the first of the Lee-Burton models. The later Lee-Burton types, which were tested extensively, had a very slim fore-end and only one band, not two • Middle: A Norwegian 6.5x55 Krag-Jorgensen, which served as the basis for our own M1892 Krag rifle • Bottom: M1896 U.S. Krag, caliber 30–40.

packet" as used in the 1895 rifle, and was issued to Lee on the same day as the rifle patent.) The right hand side of the action, as illustrated in this patent, is numbered so that the
lifter arm indicates the number of cartridges in
the magazine. The basic idea was good, and 16
pages of drawings are devoted mainly to the
packet and the cartridge lifter, but apparently
it did not reach commercial production.

## Last Lee Patent

The 1895 patent was apparently the last
one issued to James Paris Lee, although several
later ones were assigned to the Lee Arms Company. In 1896, because of his own poor health,
Lee had sent one of his two sons-George-to
England with the M1895 Straight-Pull Rifle to
effect its sale to the British. After examining
the rifle the Commander-in-Chief, the Duke
of Cambridge, is reported to have asked young
Lee: "Why did you not show us this rifle before?"

On March 16, 1897, U. S. Patent No.
579,096, was issued to "William P. Lara-way,
of Hartford, Conn. Assignor to the Lee Arms
Company, of Connecticut." The application
had been filed on April 20, 1896, and the patent was for a "Combined Bolt-Stop and Car-
tridge-Ejector for Bolt-Guns" to be embodied
on a gun similar to that shown on an application of the same date made by one Edward
G. Parkhurst. However, the Parkhurst patent
was not issued until almost a year later. The
Lara-way patent, and the later Parkhurst patents, had previously been patented in England,
France, Belgium, Italy, and Austria.

The Laraway invention was a very simple
leaf arrangement which slid into a groove on
the left side of the receiver to act as a bolt stop
and to eject the extracted case out the right
side of the receiver. Provision was made for the
bolt stop to be depressed to allow removal of
the breech-bolt.

The M1895 Straight-Pull Rifle had proved
to be easily operated, quick to load and accurate, but a few years of usage revealed some
weaknesses not so apparent on adoption. The
extractor (not attached to the bolt) had a rather
brief life; the bolt-stop was not self-closing; the
sear-fly was slightly dangerous and the loading
clips were of uneven tension.

To eliminate these weaknesses some new
parts were added and a few were done away
with completely, the result being a net reduction of 10 parts. This new rifle, the M1899
Straight-Pull, retained the best features of the
M1895 and was, according to all reports, safe,
sure, and reliable. However, U. S. Navy records
show that the only Lee Straight-Pull rifle tested
by them ended with the adoption of the M1895
design. No trials were ever held for any later
models.

## The 1899 Straight Pull

The M1899 Straight-Pull Rifle is covered
in U. S. Patent No. 599,287, issued on February
15, 1898, to "Edward G. Parkhurst, of Hartford, Connecticut, Assignor to the Lee Arms
Company, of Connecticut." The patent was for
a "Magazine Bolt-Gun," but it is basically for

Fig. 24 — This particular rifle — listed as the South American Model and available only in 43
Spanish caliber — apparently falls somewhere between the M1882 and M1885. The front band
has only one swivel; the receiver ring resembles that of the M1885; the head of the cocking
piece is too large for the M1882 and too small for the M1885. The rear sight is immediately in
front of the receiver ring, and is identical to the sights on the two M1882 rifles in the Royal Military College Museum (Canada). Barrel length, over — all length and weight are about the same
as for the M1885. The reproduction is from the J 903-04 *Price List of Military Arms, Equipments
and Ordnance Stores*, published by M. Hartley Co., of New York, listed as "Agents: Remington
Arms Co." This is the same Hartley who bought E. Remington & Sons in 1888, and formed the
Remington Arms Company. Hartley also owned at least three other firms, including the Union
Metallic Cartridge Company, and operated all of them separately. Note that this South American Model, with 4 magazines and a bayonet, sold for only $18.

Fig. 25 — An advertisement for the Model 1899 Remington — Lee rifle from the 1903 — 04
Hartley Price List. Note that only 3 calibers are listed as being available — two rimless and
one rimmed. Bolt construction, locking lug recesses, and sear details are plainly visible in the
cutaway view.

improvements on certain features of Lee's patent No. 547,583. Details in the patent follow
the M1899 rifle closely, and it is worth noting
that the cartridges shown in the Parkhurst patent appear to be of about 7mm caliber, rimless and bottlenecked. It had apparently been
Lee's intention to make the caliber of his rifles
7mm, since this caliber had been adopted and
found effective by several foreign powers. Just
how effective was proved to us a few years later
in Cuba, when we ran into the 7mm Spanish
Mausers. However, this was the era of high-
velocity and small calibers-the Army even
experimented with a new rimmed 22 caliber
centerfire cartridge-and the Navy apparently
decided a 6mm cartridge would not only provide a flatter trajectory and deeper penetration
but lighter ammunition.

The M1899 had a magazine cut-off, allow-

ing its use as a single-shot with 5 cartridges in
reserve. A bolt retainer (13)-see Straight-Pull
Fig. 20-performed the same job as the sear
fly (13) in the M1895 and did away with this
delicate part and its spring. The bolt release
or dead-lock actuator (20) of the M1895 was
done away with, allowing the bolt to be unlocked by simply pulling rearward on the bolt
handle. The safety lock (19) did away with the
firing-pin locker (19) and performed the functions of locking down the bolt to the receiver
and camming back the firing-pin, positively
securing both. It performed the same function
as the safeties of the Krag, Mauser, and later
Springfield.

The extractor spring stop (18) of the
M1899 provided a stop for the extractor and
its spring during the forward movement of
the bolt. This lengthened the life of the spring,

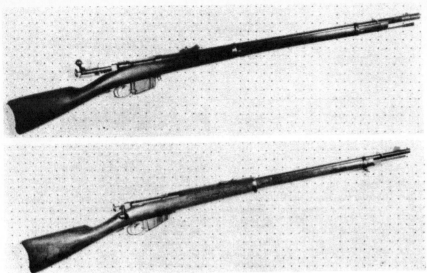

Fig. 26 — M1885 Remington-Lee rifle with the bolt in retracted position. Markings are as on the previous M1885, except top of the receiver ring is marked, in 4 lines: U.S.N.//N°.../A.CD. (There is no number above the dots.) Serial number is 53222, and the barrel length, other details, etc., are the same as on the previous MI885. The upper band on this rifle does not have swivels or provisions for them; it may be a misplaced lower band. From the Remington Arms Company collection.

Fig. 27 — The M1899 Remington-Lee rifle, caliber 30–40 Krag. The rifle is cocked, as indicated by the position of the cocking-piece. Note that this model has a hand-guard, while the M1879, M1882, M1885 and the South American Model do not. Note also that swivels are on the upper band and at the forward trigger guard screw. From the Remington Arms Company collection.

since it was no longer forced out of a niche (twice as deep as it was thick) when under its greatest tension.

To remove the bolt from the M1895 the bolt stop was pressed down, where it remained after the bolt was replaced, unless it was pushed back up. If the shooter forgot to push the bolt back into place, the next rearward movement of the bolt would remove it completely from the receiver, along with the extractor and its spring: the latter two items usually fell to the ground. The M1899 Straight-Pull design had a spiral spring which automatically forced the bolt stop back into position after it was depressed.

In the M1899 design the extractor and spring were held together with a rivet, the flanged head of which slid into a cut in the bolt. This eliminated the annoyance created by these parts in the M1895, where they could easily become lost when the bolt was removed from the receiver.

The clip for the M1899 was redesigned to facilitate loading, provide uniform tension, and retain the cartridges in place when the magazine cut-off was in use. In both the M1895 and M1899 Straight-Pull rifles the clip remained in the magazine, even though the cartridges had been released, falling out the bottom of the magazine after the first or second shot.

The M1895 had a 28-inch barrel, was 47 inches over-all and weighed 8.5 pounds with sling and bayonet. The barrel length of the M1899 was also 28 inches, with an over-all length of 47.6 inches. Other data on this model is indefinite, and just how many of the M1899 rifles were made is not known. Since the Navy was apparently not interested, perhaps only one or two experimental specimens were produced. The rear sight on both models was graduated to 2000 yards in 100-yard increments from 800 yards on the leaf. The battle sight was set for 300 yards and could be moved to 600 yards before raising the leaf. These settings were for the regular service ammunition having a velocity at 60 feet of 2460 fps. No adjustment for windage was provided, as the drift at battle settings was considered negligible.

Before leaving the M1895 Straight-Pull series one note of historical interest should be mentioned. When the U.S.S. Maine was sunk in the harbor at Havana, Cuba, during the Spanish-American troubles, the rifles aboard were M1895 Lee-Navies. These rifles were later recovered by divers and sold at Government auction to Francis Bannerman Sons of New York City. A list of their serial numbers appeared in the Bannerman catalog, which could identify rifles recovered from the *Maine*.

On May 31, 1898, U. S. Patent 604,904, was issued, as before, to "Edward G. Parkhurst ... for a "Magazine Bolt-Gun." But this time the patent was not for a straight-pull design. Instead this patent covered a "turn-bolt" gun, and "... its general object being to provide certain improvements whereby these weapons may be rendered more durable and efficient in service and whereby their constructive features are simplified and improved, reducing the cost of manufacture ..." One unusual feature of this design for a Lee firearm was the Mauser-type extractor, which extended two-thirds the length of the bolt. The bolt head was removable and instead of rear locking lugs there were now two front locking lugs on the bolt head. The bolt rotated 90° to unlock, and cocking was still on closing.

The firing pin was inserted into the hollow bolt body from the front, as in the previous models, and a large flange was provided to prevent the gas from a pierced primer escaping rearward. The rear of the firing pin had interrupted threads so the cocking piece could be slipped on longitudinally and locked in place with a one-eighth turn. The cocking piece now had a knurled section for easier manual cocking.

## New Turn-Bolt Rifle

A main feature of this design was a clip for loading the non-detachable magazine. The magazine, an integral part of the trigger guard, assembly, projected slightly below the stock line. It held 5 rounds in a single column, and the cartridges illustrated in the patent drawings were rimmed, of about 6mm caliber. Located on the left side of the magazine was a vertically-sliding cut-off, which allowed the rifle to be used as a single shot while keeping a full magazine in reserve. The magazine lips could be contracted or expanded slightly by means of a cam operated by a vertical-sliding mechanism on the right side of the magazine. With the lips apart the magazine could be loaded by stripping the cartridges down out of the clip. Releasing the lips prevented the cartridges from moving upward, except when being chambered in the normal manner.

The trigger and sear of this design were almost identical to the corresponding parts of the previous Lee turnbolt rifles. However, a coil sear spring was used in place of the U-shaped leaf spring of the Lee designs. Whether any rifles based on this design were actually produced is not known to the author.

The last Lee turnbolt design was the Model 1899, for smokeless cartridges. The bolt head had dual-opposed locking lugs, in addition to the rear locking lug and guide rib, and was exceptionally strong. Offered in both sporting and military versions, the receiver was marked on the upper left side:

Remington Arms Co. Ilion, NY.

and on the left side:

Patented Aug. 26th 1884.
March 17th 1885. Jan. 18th 1887.

In the military version the caliber was stamped on top of the barrel, ahead of the middle band. Several calibers were available, including the 236 Lee, 6mm Navy, 7mm Mauser, 30–40 Krag (30 U.S. Gov't.) and 303 British. The Michigan State Militia adopted and bought 2000 of this model, chambered for the 30–40 Krag cartridge, in 1900. Cuba is reported to have bought 30,000 of them chambered for the 7mm Mauser cartridge.

The military Model 1899 weighed about 8% pounds, the barrel was 29 inches long and over — all length was 49½ inches. Unlike previous models the M1899 had an upper hand-guard extending to the middle band. A short, straight, tangent rear sight, located about three inches behind the middle band, was graduated to 700 yards: the leaf was graduated to 1900 yards, but there was no provision for windage adjustment. The front sight was a detachable blade, its rear face angled some 45 degrees.

The stock of the military Model 1899 was much the same as that on previous models, except for the nose cap, which was designed to support the handle of a knife bayonet. As

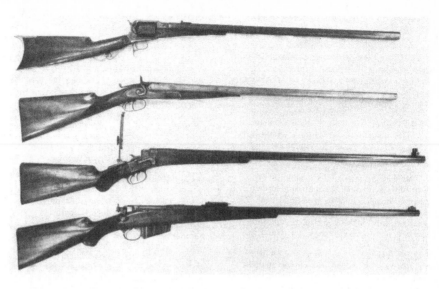

Fig. 28 — Top to bottom: The Remington-Beals revolving rifle. M1858; double-barrel Remington- Whittmore shotgun; Remington No. 3 Improved Creedmoor Hepburn Rifle; and the M1899 Remington-Lee Sporting Rifle, a design which is still modern nearly 75 years later.

previously, the sling swivels were on the upper band and the front of the trigger guard, and a cleaning rod was held in the fore-end beneath the barrel.

One distinguishing aspect of the Model 1899 was the extremely large knurled head on the cocking piece. This, coupled with the upper handguard and a 5-round magazine with three grooves instead of two, makes the M1899 easy to identify.

The 1899 extractor, a small leaf with a hook on the end slides into a recess on the side of the detachable bolt head; it resembles some of the latest modern designsWith the extractor in place the bolt head, which has a hole bored vertically crosswise near the rear end, is inserted into the bolt body until it lines up with a matching hole in the guide rib of the body. A locking bar, with pin to fit these two holes, is then positioned at approximately 90° to the bolt body, and rotated to line up with the guide rib, of which it will become a part; just before line-up occurs the rear end is lifted slightly to provide clearance for a positioning lug and then let down to engage a matching slot in the guide rib.

The Model 1899 cocked on closing the bolt, as did the previous models. When locked the front lugs were in a vertical plane, and the rear lug and guide rib in a horizontal plane; the left lug was slotted for-and-aft for an ejector in the left receiver wall.

The military M1899 rifle reportedly sold for $30 in 1905, with 4 extra magazines; the knife bayonet, with scabbard, was available for $5 more.

Phil Sharpe mentions that a carbine model with 20-inch barrel, weight some 7 pounds, was available in the same calibers as the rifle. It was not equipped for a bayonet, as the fore-end ended about three inches in front of the middle band. Over-all length was 39½ inches. The author has never seen one of these carbines, which reportedly listed for $28 in 1905.

## Model 1899 Sporters

The sporting 10 version of the M1899 was offered in the same calibers as the military model, and a number of other available calibers have been reported by various sources. These last included the 30–30 Winchester, 32 Winchester Special, 32 Remington (rimless), 32–40 Winchester, 35 Winchester, 35 Remington (rimless), 38–55 Winchester, 38–72 Winchester, 405 Winchester, 43 Mauser, 44–77 Sharps, 45–70 Gov't. and 45–90 Winchester.

The walnut stock had a shotgun-type butt with a hard-rubber plate and a pistol grip, with cap. The grip area and the slim fore-end were well checkered, the latter with a small black hard-rubber cap. Sling swivels were not standard, but could be had on special order.

Barrels were round, lengths of 24-or 26 inches were standard. A heavier 28-inch barrel could be had on special order, as could Lyman sights and stock variations. Standard sights consisted of a rear sight adjustable for windage and elevation, and a front bead mounted on a heavier base dovetailed into the barrel.

These sporters varied from 8½ to 9 pounds, and were priced at $25 in 1905. Discontinued in 1906, they no doubt remained in stock for several years.

A limited number of "special" deluxe sporting rifles were also available. These had select English walnut stocks with full pistol grips and fancy grip caps. The butt was finished English-style with separate heel and toe plates. Checkering on the grip and fore-end was of the finest, and special attention was given to the finish on all metal parts.

Barrel length of the "Special" was 26 inches-half-octagon and half-round. Sling swivels were standard, the front unit attached to the underside of the barrel midway between the muzzle and the fore-end tip, the rear swivel attached to the underside of the buttstock.

The sights comprised a Lyman bead front, and a Lyman folding leaf rear on the barrel. In addition, there was a Lyman "wind-gauge" cocking-piece sight designed especially for the M1899 action.

The low-volume "special" sporter sold for $60 in 1905.

Although James Paris Lee's old heel wound began to trouble him shortly after the U. S. Navy had adopted the Lee Straight-Pull rifle, it was not until 1897-98 that his general health forced his confinement to bed for many months at his home in Hartford. The extent of his illness can be glimpsed from the remarks Lee made in a letter to his friend, James Young, dated July 1, 1898.

"... I am simply a wreck in human form. This disease is surely gaining on whatever intellect I possessed. Little as it was, it is less today. I sit for hours without uttering a word, and I cannot even walk, as my old shot heel bothers me. I had to give up all business two years ago ... I live entirely in the past ... In the mornings (lie abed till noon) I think of Galt ... and would like to end my days there ..."

In April, 1899, on the advice of a Vermont doctor-a brother-in-law of his son George-Lee traveled to the Post Graduate Hospital in New York City. His troubled heel was cut open and a small portion of the bone removed. In it were found 5 lead pellets embedded there for nearly 52 years. The operation was a success. Lee's health began to improve at once and, although slightly lame, he was able to visit Galt in August of that year. He also was apparently able to return to business, at least to some extent, as indicated by the Improved Lee Model 1901 (straight-pull). However, it is also possible that his two sons were actively engaged in the business at this time.

Described as being above average height, strongly built, with dark hair and dark gray eyes, Lee's warm-hearted, easygoing manner gained him many friends. His inventions reportedly brought him several fortunes, and if he had been as successful in managing his patents and finances as he was in inventing, he might have been a millionaire. However, the expenses of his kind of an inventor were necessarily large, and the last few years were not highly productive; the 1899 models were probably the last ones to reach the manufacturing stage. Even so, Lee continued to work on his designs until his death on February 24, 1904, at South Beach, Conn.

No account of the Lee firearms would be complete without including the British portion of the Lee history. For it was in England that the Lee designs became famous, so much so that the name Lee became almost a household word.

## English Beginnings

In England a Small Arms Committee was formed in 1879 to deal with several small arms problems, including the Martini-Henry rifle and the "... the desirability or otherwise of introducing a magazine rifle for naval or military use, or both." Over the next few years a number of American and European designs were examined and tested. The trials were carried out at the Proof Butts at Woolwich Arsenal by a sergeant and three picked marksmen of the Royal Welch Fusiliers. The tests performed included:

(1) Rapidity of fire without aiming.

(2) Rapidity of fire with aiming, at both stationary and moving targets.

(3) Exposure to the weather for three days without cleaning after firing; exposure to a sand blast and firing without cleaning; rough usage; safety tests.

Following the tests all weapons were forwarded to the Royal Small Arms Factory for examination.

Included in the trials held during May and June of 1880, were the arms of Hotch-kiss, Kropatschek, Lee (rifle and carbine), Winchester M1876, Gardner, Green, and Vetterli rifles. The Lee arms were based on his patent of November 4, 1879, in which the mainspring was compressed as the bolt was closed. This was considered a disadvantage, as it prevented the feel of the cartridge being chambered. It was thus thought possible that a cartridge could stick or jam, yet be driven on into the chamber, causing a premature explosion with an unlocked bolt.

The extraction was not considered satisfactory, but the chamber was partly at fault; The rifle and carbine barrels, of the 45-caliber Martini-Henry pattern, were made at the Royal Small Arms Factory, Enfield Lock; these were chambered to take solid-drawn brass-case Gatling service ammunition loaded with 85 grains of black powder behind a 480-gr. bullet. The extractor appeared to have sufficient camming action to start case withdrawal, but its form was considered poor. The guns were returned to Enfield Lock for investigation and repair.

The magazine position was well liked, since it did not alter the balance of the rifle when full or empty, and it was easily loaded. In general the Lee rifle made a good impression, and it was deemed easy to manufacture.

Specifications of the two Lee rifles tested at this time follow:

**LEE RIFLE:**

Caliber ....................................45

**Grooves:**

    Number........................................... 7

    Form ........................... Henry Rifling

    Depth ....................................... 0075″

    Rate of twist ................. 1 turn in 22″

**Mechanism:**

    Closing ................................... By bolt

    Opening .. Spiral spring and firing pin

**Length Over — all**........................... 53″

**Weight** ............................... 9 lbs. 5 ozs.

**Magazine Cap**......................... 5 rounds

**Sights**........................... To 1,400 yards

The Lee Carbine weight was 6½ lbs. and over all length was 43.5 inches. Sights on the Carbine were graduated to 800 yards.

A month after the trials were over the Lee rifle was returned from Enfield with an improved extractor. It was then used to fire 45 rounds of the Gatling cartridges, which were easily extracted, with an average rate of fire of 20 rounds in 52 seconds. Things were looking up for the Lee design.

The Royal Navy wanted a magazine rifle, but two years later nothing had been decided. The best rifles from the previous trials were to be tested again, plus any other new designs that might be authorized; all were to be capable of firing the Gatling cartridge, the machine gun cartridge then in use.

## Further English Trials

In November, 1882, the following rifles were submitted for trial: Schulhof (3), Improved Lee, Spencer-Lee, Chaftee-Reece, Gardner, and Mannlicher. On 3rd May, 1883, the Committee reported that all rifles submitted had been tried and compared to the Martini-Henry, but that all had failed on some point, and were now being altered or repaired. A new Small Arms Committee had been formed, and this time the inventors or their agents were allowed to demonstrate and fire the rifles on the range. More than half of the rifles were quickly rejected, and the inventors of several others were told that their rifles would be rejected unless they could be altered to take the Gatling cartridge. With all rifles taking the same cartridge, the trials continued until 31st October, 1883. At this time it was reported that two Lee designs — the Improved Lee modified at Enfield Lock and the Lee with the Bethel Burton magazine made at Enfield Lock — were promising, but three rifles — a new magazine rifle designed by Owen Jones, employed at Enfield Lock, the Spencer-Lee, and the Mannlicher — were still to be tested.

While waiting for the Spencer-Lee and the Mannlicher rifles to arrive, 6 additional rifles were received for testing, including a Remington-Lee model. Of the 6 new rifles submitted, only the Remington-Lee warranted much interest, but it was not chambered for the Gatling cartridge and was therefore not tested. The other 5 rifles were either too heavy, too complicated, or not chambered for the Gatling cartridge.

By August, 1885, the Small Arms Committee had examined or tried nearly 50 magazine rifles and quick-loading systems. Of these all but three had broken down during testing, or had been rejected for other reasons. The three left were the Improved Lee Magazine Rifle, the Improved Lee with Bethel Burton magazine, and the Owen Jones Magazine Rifle. All three had been improved or manufactured at the Royal Small Arms Factory at Enfield Lock, and the Lee Magazine Rifle was the only survivor of the original testing started 5 years before.

These three rifles had fore-ends of like shape, with a single barrel band a few inches behind the muzzle. A front sling swivel was attached to this band, another to the underside of the buttstock. All had a short upper handguard extending from the receiver ring to the rear sight. From this approximate location the fore-end was reduced in depth. All three rifles carried cleaning rods in a groove in the bottom of the fore-end. The Lee rifle had a one-piece stock, the others separate butt-stocks. All had straight grip stocks; the two Lee models had conventional combs, while the Owen Jones was similar to the latter Enfield models with-

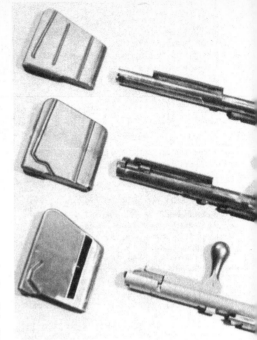

Fig. 29 — Row 1: Breech-bolt of the MI 889 Remington-Lee with the 3-groove magazine • Row 2: Breech-bolt of the MI 885 Remington-Lee with the 2-groove magazine • Row 3: Breech-bolt of the M1879 Lee with the M1879 magazine. The wide slot in the magazine was apparently added later by an owner to show the number of rounds remaining in the magazine; it is not considered to be an original feature. Fig. 30 — Top to bottom: Breech-bolts of the Models 1879, 1885 and 1899 Lee and Remington-Lee rifles, with the bolt heads removed to show the methods of attaching the extractors.

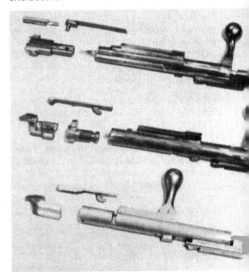

out a pronounced comb.

The Lee-Burton receiver had a very long upper tang, extending almost to the comb; the rear tang of the trigger guard was as long. Both were fastened together by two bolts passing through the grip of the stock from the underside. The Burton magazine fastened to the right side of the action; in use it projected upward above the barrel about 1½ inches. When not in

Fig. 31 — The small rimfire revolver which may or may not have been a product of James Paris Lee. The octagon barrel is 2¼ inches long and the top flat is marked: RED JACKET No. 3. The 5 — shot cylinder is 1 3/16 inches long and 5 chambered for the 32 rimfire cartridge. Weighing 10 ozs., over — all length is about 6 inches. It is nickel — plated and the grips are natural pearl. The revolver functions single action only, and the spur trigger has a terrible pull; the hammer does have a half — cock notch. The topstrap is marked: THE LEE ARMS CO./WILKESBARRE, PA. in two lines, with a narrow groove passing between the two lines to serve as a sighting groove. The front sight is a narrow brass blade. Over — all construction and finish are fair, but the steel appears to be rather soft.

use it could be lowered alongside the receiver. It could be loaded with up to 5 cartridges while in the firing position, a point in its favor.

The Improved Lee trigger guard and receiver had short tangs; the guard was attached to the receiver by two bolts from below, one at the rear and one at the front, ahead of the magazine well. The magazine — a plain, ungrooved model — was readily detachable, but it could not be loaded while attached to the rifle (in this early model) and this was felt to be a disadvantage. The cocking piece differed from those on the U. S. Lee rifles.

## Setback and Success

The Owen Jones rifle operated by a slide under the buttstock, and was extremely rapid but it was not as cheap to manufacture as the Lee. Still, the Committee apparently thought it superior to the two Lee models and recommended it for trial by the Army and Navy.

While the Committee had been testing magazine rifles the Enfield factory had been developing a barrel of smaller caliber for the single shot Martini-Henry rifle; they'd decided on a 402 caliber with 7-groove Metford segmental rifling, developed over two decades before. These consisted of shallow grooves shaped to the segment of a circle. It was felt that the Owen Jones and the two Lee designs should be tested with the new 402 caliber Metford barrels before a final decision was made. Steps were taken to fit the new barrels, when suddenly the Owen Jones rifle was dropped from further tests because of manufacturing difficulties. The bottom magazine was considered to be the better position, so the Improved Lee Magazine Rifle emerged the victor.

Still smaller calibers were being developed in Europe. After some study 303 caliber barrels with Metford rifling were fitted to the Improved Lee actions and about 350 of the resulting Lee-Metford rifles were issued to the British Army for trials. The results were satisfactory and, on December 22,1888, the Magazine Rifle, Mark I, was approved for manufacture.

British Army Orders, dated 1st December, 1889, contained the following description of the new rifle:

### MAGAZINE RIFLE, MARK I

**Weight**...................................... 9 lb. 8 oz.
**Weight of Magazine** (empty) ...... 4¾ oz.
**Weight of Magazine** (filled ............13 oz.
**Length** .......................................... 49 in.
**Barrel and Rifling:**
**Length**.................................... 30.2 in.
**Calibre**...................................... 303 in.
**Rifling** ................. Metford segmental
**Grooves** ..................................... Seven
**Grooves,** depth ....................... 004 in.
**Lands,** width............................ 023 in.
**Spiral,** left — handed .......... 1 turn in
10 in., or 33 calibres

The rifle embodies the Lee bolt action, with rear locking. The cocking-piece is so arranged that the action can be set at half — cock, in which position the rifle can be carried in safety. Covers are fitted to the bolt and the bolt-head to protect the action in sand and mud. A safety-catch is fitted on the left side of the body, the pulling back of which, when the rifle is at full-cock, prevents any effect being caused by pressing the trigger. When springs are "eased," and the cocking-piece is in the forward position, it locks the action and prevents the bolt from becoming accidently opened.

The magazine consists of a sheet-steel box, inserted in the body through an opening underneath, and directly in front of the trigger guard. It is held in position by a spring in the body engaging in a notch on the magazine. It holds 8 cartridges and can be filled when in position on the rifle, or when detached ... they are fed into the chamber by the forward movement of the bolt. A cut-off is fitted to the right side of the body which, when pressed inwards, stops the supply of cartridges from the magazine, thus enabling the weapon to be used as a single-loader. When the cut-off is pulled out, the lower edge of the face of the bolt-head, on the bolt being driven forwards, engages the top edge of the uppermost cartridge in the magazine and forces it into the chamber. The magazine can be removed from the rifle by pressing a small lever inside the trigger-guard. One magazine is attached, by means of a chain link, to each rifle: a spare magazine is also issued with each arm.

The stock, like that of the Martini-Henry rifle, is in two pieces, the fore-end and the butt. ...

The butt is secured to the body of the rifle by a stock bolt. The buttplate ... is fitted with a trap ... to house an oil bottle and a jag ...

The nose-cap is fitted with a bar on top for the attachment of the sword bayonet, which is positioned underneath the barrel ...

A wooden hand-guard is fixed over the breech end of the barrel to protect the hand when the barrel becomes hot. It is held place by two steel springs, which clip round the barrel.

The rifle is provided with two sets of sights. The foresight and the backsight are fixed in the usual positions on the barrel.

The foresight is a square block, with a vertical cut through it .... The lowest, or "fixed" sight, is that for 300 yards .... The highest graduation is for 1,900 yards. The rifle is also fitted with extreme range sights. The front sight, which is called the dial sight, is graduated from 1,800 yards up to 3,500 yards. It consists of a bead fixed to a revolving index hand. The index is set to the correct distance, which is marked on the edge of the dial plate, and aim is taken by aligning the bead on the object aimed at through a circular hole in the aperture sight ... Both these sights are on the left side of the rifle ...".

## Changes, Changes

On August 8, 1891, the name was changed to the Lee-Metford Magazine Rifle, Mark I, and 5 months later on January 19, 1892, it became the Lee-Metford Magazine Rifle Mark I*, through some sight modifications.

Eleven days later, acting on recommendations to increase the magazine capacity from 8 rounds to 10, to lighten the barrel, modify the bolt head, and some dozen other minor modifications, the War Office officially approved the Lee-Metford Magazine Rifle, Mark II. The new rifle weighed 9 lbs. 4 oz., four ounces lighter than the Mark I.

Three years later a safety catch was added to replace the one which had been omitted since the Mark I*, and the rifle became the Lee-Metford Magazine Rifle. Mark II*. Other minor modifications necessary to the operation of the safety were also made at this time.

On September 29, 1895, in answer to demands from the British Cavalry, the Lee-Metford Magazine Carbine, Mark I, was approved for manufacture. Magazine capacity was 6 rounds, the barrel was 20¾ inches long, overall length 39 15/16 inches, weight 7 lb. 7 oz. Other modifications to the sights, stock, handguard, bands, nose-cap, etc., were made at this time.

In an attempt to overcome the destructive effect of Cordite powder erosion on the shallow Metford rifling, new barrels with Enfield rifling, as developed at the Royal Small Arms Factory, were fitted.† The Lee-Metford rifles with the new barrels became the Lee-Enfield Magazine Rifle, Mark I, on November 11, 1895, the Start of a long line of Lee-Enfield Rifles. On August 17, 1896, modification of the Cavalry carbine to include the new Enfield rifling was approved, with other necessary changes, and the Lee-Enfield Magazine Carbine, Mark I, came into being.

On 19th May, 1899, the clearing rod and clearing rod hole, etc., in the fore-end of the rifle and carbine were omitted, and the designation became Mark I*. The omission of the clearing rod was extended to all 303 caliber arms then in service, including the various Martini patterns.

The next L-E to be introduced was another carbine. It appeared on August 1, 1900, and was intended for the British Land Services. It had a special barrel, fore-end and handguard, weighed 7½ pounds, and was 40% inches long.

In January, 1900, the Small Arms Committee was completely re-organized to include representatives concerned with manufacture, inspection, requirements, and experience with service arms and ammunition. A representative of the National Rifle Association also became a member of the Committee. The Boer War was in progress and in June of 1900 the Small Arms Committee recommended that the Lee-Enfield

---

† Henry Metford had, in fact, patented the so-called Enfield rifling in 1860, even prior to his segmental rifling.

rifle be replaced with a new one. To strengthen their position they listed 7 defects of the Lee-Enfield, and questioned whether an automatic rifle might not be desirable. They went so far as to test an Italian model.

## The S.M.L.E.

In late 1900, the Superintendent of the Royal Small Arms Factory let the Small Arms Committee know that he had been able to alter the Lee-Enfield to overcome the defects they had mentioned, and could manufacture the new rifle at once at little or no increase in price. In the memorandum the Superintendent listed 12 alterations which would be made.

The altered rifle was tested at Hythe in December, 1900, and on January 12, 1901, the Secretary of State approved the manufacture of 1,000 Shortened Modified Enfield Rifles in lots of 500 each of Pattern A and B, for troop trials.

The 1,000 rifles were tested by units of the Royal Navy, Royal Marines, Cavalry and Infantry, following a program of 8 parts. The rifle was well received and, on November 10, 1902, the Committee recommended it for adoption with some modifications in the sights and magazine. On December 15, 1902, the R.S.A.F. Superintendent submitted a Short Rifle with 12 minor modifications. The rifle was approved by the Committee and introduced on December 23, 1902, as the Short Magazine Lee-Enfield Rifle, Mark I, for the Infantry and Cavalry. It weighed 20 ounces less than the Enfield it replaced. The first of the S.M.L.E. rifles was a reality.

The new rifle was 41 9/16 inches long, its barrel 25 3/16 in. The bolt cover was omitted, the cocking-piece was shorter, the magazine

was ⅛-inch deeper, and the Navy version was equipped with a cut-off. Buttstocks were issued in three lengths, a safety was located on the left side of the receiver, and changes were made in the fore-end, hand-guard, bands, nose-cap, swivels, and several other components. A few months later some additional changes were made and the rifle was re-introduced on 14th September, 1903.

On January 13, 1902, Lee-Metford Carbines fitted with Enfield barrels and extended nose-cap wings were re-named Lee-Enfield Mark I Carbines. Later, on September 6, 1902, Lee-Metford Mark II* rifles fitted with Enfield barrels became Lee-Enfield Mark I Rifles, if they had the old fore-end nose-cap; if they had the newer, more solid fore-end and nose-cap they became Lee-Enfield Mark I* Rifles.

The year 1903 was to be a busy one. The Lee-Enfield Mark I and I*, and the Lee-Metford Mark II and II* rifles were given new barrels, sights, and other minor modifications and re-introduced on January 16, 1903, as the Short Magazine Lee-Enfield (Converted) Mark II. On August 12, a new cut-off for the S.M.L.E. Mark I was approved for British Naval Service only. November 2nd, the Lee-Metford Mark I* became the Short Magazine Lee-Enfield (Converted) Mark I, a conversion which was declared "obsolete" before it was ever manufactured.

During March, April and May, 1905, as a result of a questionnaire to the British Forces in India, trials were held at Hythe between the Long and Short rifles to compare velocity, accuracy, systems of sighting and speed of loading. The trials indicated that the Long rifles were more accurate, but the Short rifles were handier and better adapted to snapshooting. A

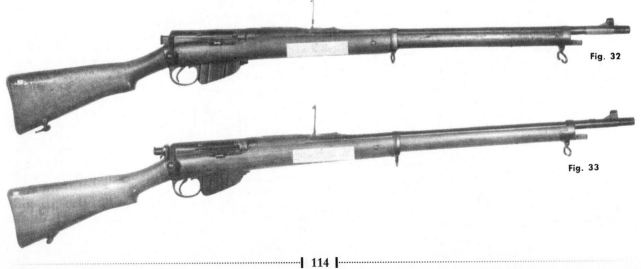

**Fig. 32**—The Lee-Metford Mark II. Adopted on January 30, 1892, the new rifle weighed 9 lb. 4 oz and had a magazine capacity of 10 rounds instead of the previous 8. Note the short handguard, extending only from the receiver ring to the rear sight; the rear sight leaf is erect.

**Fig. 33**—The Lee-Enfield Mark I*, advanced from the Mark I by omission of the clearing rod. This rifle is very similar to the previous Lee-Metford Mark II*, except for the new barrel. Note the safety catch on the cocking piece.

Fig. 32

Fig. 33

new pattern was sealed and, on 2nd July, 1906, the Short Magazine Lee-Enfield Rifle, Mark I*, was introduced. It weighed 4½ ounces more than the Mark I, and differed slightly in the magazine, buttstock and plate, swivels and screws, striker, sights, and hand-guards. On the same day a new conversion was also introduced. The Long Lee-Enfield rifles, Mark I and I*, and the Lee-Metford rifles, Mark II and II*, were converted to become the Short Magazine Lee-Enfield Rifle Converted, Mark II*, which differed from the Converted Mark II, but slightly, in the butt-stock, magazine, and swivel and keeper screws. Six weeks later, on 17th August, 1906, a coin-slotted striker keeper-screw was approved for all Marks of the S.M.L.E., and on 25th October, the cut-off was returned and fitted to all S.M.L.E. rifles in the British Army — the Royal Navy already had them.

## Hythe and Enfield Tests

Trials were held at Hythe and Enfield periodically in an attempt to improve the S.M.L.E. A reliable charger-loading feature was in particular demand by the troops, and several other modifications had been recommended. On 31st October, 1906, 6 rifles, which had been sent to Aldershot for testing, were reported as satisfactory. On 26th January, 1906, the modifications were completed and the Short Magazine Lee-Enfield Rifle, Mark III, was approved. The new rifle weighed 8 lb. 10½ oz., and differed from the Mark I and I* slightly in the sights, fore-end, hand-guards, cut-off, bands, buttplate, nose-cap, locking-bolt and bolt-head, and the receiver body had a bridge charger-guide.

On June 17, 1907, a number of conversions

were approved to bring the Lee-Enfield Mark I and I* and Lee-Metford Mark II and II* rifles in line with the new Mark III. The converted rifles weighed 8 lb. 14 ½ oz., and were listed as the Short Magazine Lee-Enfield Converted Mark IV.

On July 1, 1907, another lot of Mark I and I* Lee-Enfield, and Lee-Metford Mark II and II* rifles were converted by adding a bridge-type charger-guide, new magazine, and modified sighting system. The new conversions became the Charger-Loading Lee-Enfield , Mark I*, and Charger-Loading Lee-Metford, Mark II. Each weighed about 9 lb. 5 oz.

On January 4, 1908, a number fo the British Navy's S.M.L.E. Mark I rifles were converted to the S.M.L.E., Mark I** models. Later the same year the S.M.L.E. Converted Mark II rifles became the S.M.L.E., Mark II**, and the S.M.L.E. Converted, Mark II* became the S.M.L.E, Mark II***, with the conversions being made at the Royal Naval Ordnance Depots at Chatham, Portsmouth, and Plymouth. Most of the changes were convered with the trigger guard, magazine, and installation of a charger-guide, with minor changes in the receiver and bolt, stocks, and various screws.

On 1st February, 1909, the Mark II Lee-Metford Charger-Loading conversions were discontinued and the already converted rifles became the Charger-Loading Lee-Enfield Rifles, Mark I*. On November 3, 1910, a new service cartridge—303 S.A. Ball Cartridge Mark VII—was introduced, necessitating an alteration in the sights of all the rifles then in service, plus some minor alterations to the magazines of certain Marks.

As war in Europe approached haste was

made to see that as many rifles as possible were available to handle the Mark VII cartridge. On 22nd April, 1914, the S.M.L.E. Mark I* became the S.M.L.E. Mark I***, and later the same year two other conversions were made, without any apparent change in pattern, other than a C.L. (Charger-Loading) on the sights. On 18th August, 1915, Mark I** rifles in the Royal Navy which had not been altered for charger-loading were so altered to handle the Mark VII cartridge and re-named S.M.L.E. Mark I***.

On January 2, 1916, six minor modifications were made to the Mark III, including the removal of the long range dial and aperture sight, and the rifle became the Short Magazine Lee-Enfield, Mark III*.

Prior to World War I some consideration was given to adopting an entirely new design with forward locking lugs and of smaller caliber. A Mauser-type rifle for a 276 caliber rimless cartridge was made in prototype form and became the Pattern 1913. When the war started it was decided to retain the 303 caliber and the new rifle was modified to handle it, thus becoming the Pattern 1914. The rifle was a limited standard and was not widely used, except in sniping versions.

## Advent of the Rifle No. 1

Following the war the search to find an improved bolt action went on. In 1922 a modified pattern was sealed for the Short Magazine Lee-Enfield Rifle, Mark V, which differed from the Mark III in 10 features. The Mark V was tested, but not officially adopted; it was eventually abandoned for a new design which became the Mark VI. The Mark VI was recommended on December 14, 1923, by the Rifle Subcommittee and it was to retain the best features of

(continued on page 118)

Fig. 34—The Short Magazine Lee-Enfield Mark I. Introduced on December 23, 1902, it weighed 1¼ lbs. less than the Lee-Enfield it replaced, and became the first of the long line of S.M.L.E. rifles.

Fig. 35—The old official stand-by—the S.M.L.E. Mark III*—for over two decades, and still serving in some areas after half a century. It looks rugged, too.

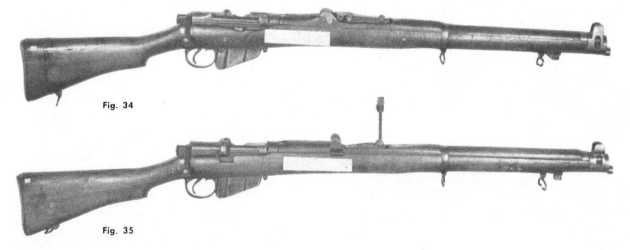

Fig. 34

Fig. 35

# Lee-Enfield Rifle No. 4, Mark I*

## Historical Notes

The No. 4, Mark 1 Lee-Enfield marks the last of an illustrious line of British Lee rifles that began in 1888 and passed through a bewildering maze of Marks and Numbers, models and revisions. After World War I, British ordnance began looking for ways to improve the old and famous Mk. III series and by 1931 developed the prototype S.M.L.E. (Short Magazine Lee-Enfield) Mk. VI. When the British revised their nomenclature system, this rifle became the Rifle No. 4, Mk I. The major improvements were an aperture rear sight, a simplified bolt-retaining system and bolt release, and a socket type spike bayonet. As is the custom in the British service, the new rifle was harshly criticized, especially the spike bayonet. (It is interesting to note that British ordnance defended the bayonet as being specifically designed to penetrate German overcoats). In 1939, the rifle was redesigned for mass production, but the early World War II years were fought with the Mark III*.

The No. 4, Mk. I* was the North American version. Almost one million were made at Long Branch Arsenal in Canada,

and over a million by Savage Arms Corporation. The Savage made rifles are curiously stamped "U.S. Property," even though they were never intended for our use; perhaps this was prompted by political subterfuge. The major difference between the Mk. I and Mk. I* is the bolt release (see illus.).

As a military rifle, the Lee-Enfields are excellent, but they are not in the same design class as Mausers and Mannlichers. They do not lend themselves to sporterizing. British ordnance does not consider the bolts to be interchangeable. These rifles fire one type of cartridge, the 303 Enfield (British). The 303 Savage cartridge is **not** the same.

## Disassembly

Raise the rear sight (3). See illustration on opposite page. Rifle Mk. I: depress bolt release and withdraw bolt all the way to the rear; release bolt release and raise bolt head (28) Rifle Mk. I*: withdraw bolt until bolt head (28) aligns with cutout on guide groove, which allows the bolt head to be pushed up and out of its channel. With bolt head raised in line with the bolt rib, the entire bolt may be withdrawn. Press magazine catch (21) and remove magazine (18). Unscrew band screws (43 & 44) up over the stock. Unscrew guard screws (15 & 16) and remove the trigger guard (14) with trigger (12). Work forestock (35) down and off. Buttstock (32) can be removed by unscrewing the stock bolt (33). The stock bolt is frequently packed with felt and this should be removed first. (If the buttstock is sound and tight, its removal is not recommended.) Unscrew safety screw (8) and extract safety assembly. (Reassembly can be tricky. Be sure the safety bolt and catch are in position shown in illustration before reseating). Sear (9) and magazine catch (21) can be removed by driving out their respective pins (11 & 22).

To disassemble the bolt, first unscrew the bolt head (28), then the firing pin screw (27). The firing pin (25) can be unscrewed only from the front of the bolt. This requires a special wrench. Do not try it with ordinary tools. The firing pin (25) and firing-pin spring (26) will come out the front of the bolt.

Unscrew extractor screw (31), insert end of screwdriver behind lip of extractor (29) and force extractor forward, then out of front of bolt head. Insert a small screwdriver between top of extractor spring (30) and upper wall of bolt head until nipple on spring clears its receptacle. From rear, push spring forward and out.

Remove magazine follower (19) by depressing the rear, allowing the front of the follower to clear the two protruding lips on front of magazine.

## Parts List

1. Barrel
2. Receiver
3. Rear Sight
4. Ejector Screw
5. Safety Bolt
6. Safety Catch
7. Safety Bolt Spring
8. Safety Bolt Spring Screw
9. Sear
10. Sear Spring
11. Sear Pin
12. Trigger
13. Trigger Pin
14. Trigger Guard
15. Rear Guard Screw
16. Front Guard Screw
17. Front Guard Screw Bearing
18. Magazine
19. Magazine Follower
20. Magazine-Follower Spring
21. Magazine Catch
22. Magazine-Catch Pin
23. Bolt
24. Cocking Piece
25. Firing Pin
26. Firing-Pin Spring
27. Firing-Pin Screw
28. Bolt Head
29. Extractor
30. Extractor Spring
31. Extractor Screw
32. Buttstock
33. Stock Bolt
34. Stock-Bolt Lock Washer
35. Forestock
36. Rear Hand Guard
37. Front Hand Guard
38. Buttplate
39. Rear Sling Swivel
40. Rear Stock Band
41. Middle Stock Band
42. Front Sling Swivel
43. Sling Swivel Screw
44. Front Stock Band
45. Stacking Swivel
46. Stacing Swivel Screw
47. Front Sight Guard
48. Oiler (in buttstock)

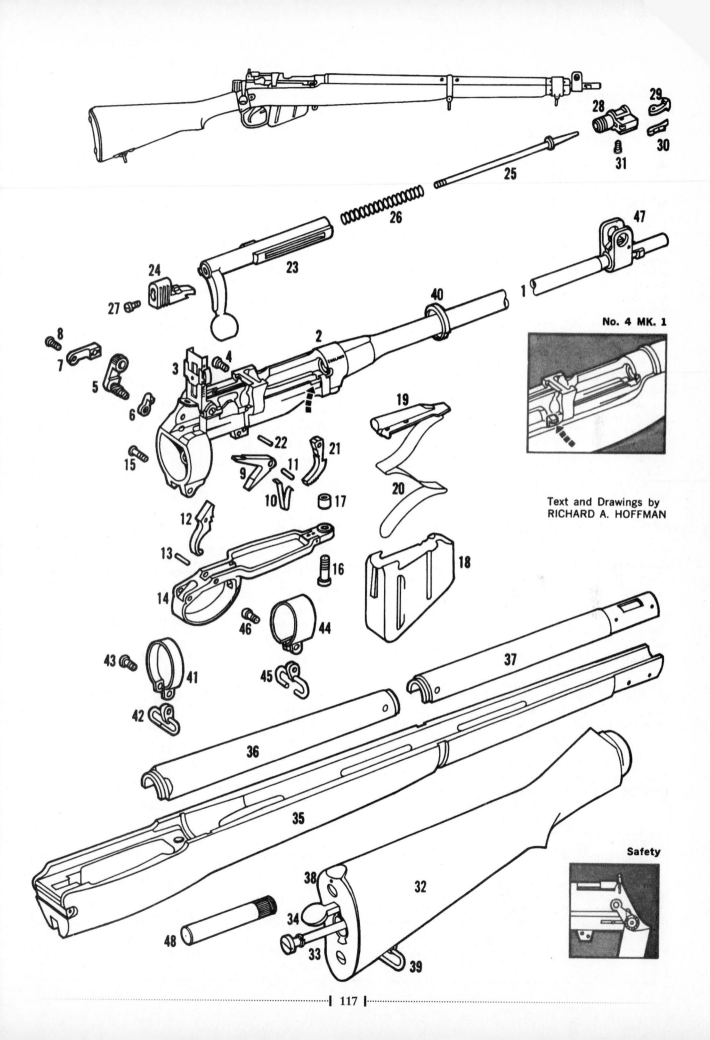

No. 4 MK. 1

Text and Drawings by
RICHARD A. HOFFMAN

Safety

(continued from page 115)

the Mark III. By 1924 the Mark VI was being modified for trial. By early 1926 six prototypes of the Mark VI had been manufactured for trial, and over the next 13 years the design was modified and re-modifed to emerge officially on November 15, 1939, as the No. 4 Rifle, Mark I†. The Lee-Enfield name was no more, for in May 1926, a new system of nomenclature had been introduced. Under the new system the S.M.L.E. Rifle Mark III—the old standby—became the Rifle No. 1, Mark III. Basic design was the same, only the name had changed. The British had used Lee-Metford and Lee-Enfield rifles for 38 years, and would continue to do so for another 38 or more years under a different designation.

Some other famous rifles which also used the Lee centrally-located box magazine include the Swiss Schmidt-Rubin 1889, 1893, 1911 and 1931; Italian Vetterli-Vitali 1887; Dutch Beaumont-Vitali 71/88 and 1888; French Berthier 1890, 07/15, 1916 and 194; Czech ZH29; Russian Mouzin (Mosin) 1891, 1910, 1891/30, 1930, 1938 and 1944; Canadian Ross 1910 Mark III; Remington Model 8, German Mauser 1888; and Austrian 1886, 1888, 1888/90, 1890 and 1895. Several of the rifles listed use the Mannlicher clip in a fixed single-column magazine. Lee and Mannlicher were contemporaries and the Mannlicher version may or may not have been influenced by the Lee design. The 1895 Lee and 1898 Parkhurst designs (assigned to Lee) employ clip-loaded magazines very similar to those employed by Mannlicher. Who influenced whom? Both inventors may have developed by the same designs independently.

Today, 90-odd years after Lee's original 1879 invention, the basic Lee magazine design is used on almost all military auto-loading rifles, such as our M16, M14, and AR-18, the Soviet AK-47, the German G-3, and the British FN L1A1. Machine rifles, such as the BAR, and various submachine guns have used the design, plus most auto-loading pistols, and even a few shotguns. A number of commercial sporting rifles use the Lee-type magazine and untold numbers of rimfire rifles with detachable box magazines have been manufactured. The original Lee patent of November 4, 1879, was a dwarf in material size—two pages of drawings and three pages of text—but a giant in scope. James Paris Lee would have been proud.

†The Short Magazine Lee-Enfield, Mark II, and Mark III rifles were manufactured in Australia, and the later No. 4 Rifle, Mark I* was manufactured in Canada and the United States, but these were not considered to be part of the Lee-Enfield history.

## References

9. On March 6, 1883 Hugo Borchardt obtained U.S. Patent No. 273,448 for a detachable magazine for magazine guns, which he assigned to Joseph W. Frazier of New York City. (Borchardt had designed the M1878 Sharps-Borchardt rifle for the Sharps Rifle Co., to which he had assigned Patents No. 185,721 and 206,217, on December 26, 1876, and July 23, 1878, respectively. This would place him in Bridgeport at about the same time as James Lee.) Frazier had filed his patent application on January 4, 1883, and on December 18, 1883, U.S. Patent No. 290,636 for a "Magazine Fire-Arm" was granted to "Joseph W. Frazier, of New York, N.Y., Assignor, by Mesne Assignments to the Spencer Arms Company, of Same Place." This patent covered the adapting of the Lee detachable box magazine—patented by Lee on November 4, 1879—to the slide action rifle patented by Christopher M. Spencer and Sylvester H. Roper on April 4, 1882, in U.S. Patent No. 255,894. The Frazier design consisted of the Spencer-type slide action rifle, with its breechblock pivoted at the rear and free at the front to swing above and in line with the chamber of the barrel. The box magazine was attached to the breechlock and moved up and down with it in normal operation, but was still readily detachable for replacement with a loaded magazine. The chambering and ejection of the cartridges were covered by the Spencer-Roper patent. This then became the basis for the Spencer-Lee rifles entered in the U.S. and British rifles trials of the 1880s.

10. Alden Hatch relates an incident involving a Remington-Lee Sporting Rifle that shook Bridgeport almost to its very foundations. A local lad, returning home empty-handed from a deer hunt, decided to take a short cut through a field loosely fenced with barbed wire. On the field were a number of half-sunken stone structures resembling beehives. Deciding that one of these would provide a safe backstop for some rifle practice, he fastened a piece of paper onto the wooden door of one and paced of a hundred yards. Adjusting his sights, he took careful aim with his Remington-Lee and pulled the trigger. With a blinding flash of light the sky vanished and the earth split open with a thunderous roar. Three days later, when the lad came to in a hospital, he learned his "safe" backstop had been on e of the U.M.C. powder-storage magazines. Bridgeport had shivered and windows had been broken as far away as Long Island. That the lad had survived was a wonder. Shortly thereafter the present Powder Park—now a part of the Remington Arms Company complex—was obtained. The new Park is tightly fenced, closely guarded, and the powder magazines are bullet-proof.

## Photo Credits

Figs. 16, 19, 22, 23, 24, 26. U.S. Army Rock Island Arsenal.

Fig 36. National Park Service.

Fig. 37. British Crown Copyright. By Permission of the Controller, HMSO.

Fig. 17. Remington Arms Collection.

Fig. 21. Globe & Mail, Toronto.

Patent Drawing—E. I. Dupont de Nemours & Co., Inc.

The author realizes that many questions concerning the activities of James Paris Lee may still be unanswered. There may even be other Lee designs which have not been covered, and such information would be most welcome. In particular the author would welcome data and photographs on the experimental and limited productions designs, even on the variations of the known commercial models.

The author is indebted to the following individuals for their help, and to each goes a special thanks: John T. Amber, Gordon F. Baxter, Jr., Thomas E. Hall, Daniel R. Kuehn, Judith Topaz, Herbert L. Uphoff, James S. Watson, and Eldon G. Wolff.

For those interested in exploring the history of the Lee-Enfield rifle in greater detail, the author highly recommends The Lee-Enfield Rifle, by Major E. G. B. Reynolds (New York, 1968).

**Gun Digest**

29th Anniversary
1975 Deluxe
Edition

Edited by John T. Amber

# The 1903 Springfield

An interesting and detailed account of the most famous military rifle in United States history — including the numerous variations made since its birth. ▮ Al Miller

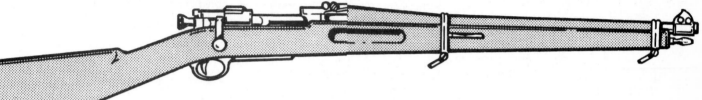

WHETHER OR NOT the Springfield 03 was the best military rifle of its time is still open to argument; Mausers, Lee-Enfields — each has its protagonists. Regardless of their respective virtues though, there can be little doubt that the 03 was the best prepared and finished. No service arm, before or since, ever enjoyed so much painstaking care during its manufacture.

Stocks were made out of good, solid walnut, superior to many found on commercial sporters today. Although machine-inletted, the marriage of wood to metal was unbelievably close, especially on those rifles fashioned between the wars when quality, not time, was the watchword. Metal fittings, all machined from forgings, were carefully polished before bluing. Bolt heads were knurled, triggers serrated. For a while, even buttplates were machine-checkered. Tool marks were rare. Each rifle was a "finished" product when it left the armory.

They were accurate, too. National Match Springfields ruled the target ranges both here and abroad for many years and the service model was no slouch in that department, either.

Every 03 in my racks, including the World War II versions, will keep five shots inside 2½" at 100 yards. This, of course, from a rest and using match ammo, but with issue sights. Perhaps I've been lucky but I've never owned or fired an inaccurate Springfield; nor one which could be described as "just so-so."

The oft-repeated charge that the 03 made a better sporter than a military arm may have some justification. Many of its design features — the excellent finish, the close tolerances — hint of a conception by riflemen, target shots and hunters, rather than by soldiers.

The inherent sporting qualities of the Springfield were noticed shortly after its birth. Teddy Roosevelt had one armory-altered in late 1903, a special stock fitted (serial number 0009), which he took to Africa in 1909. He characterized it as "the lightest and handiest of all my rifles," and he managed to kill an impressive number of animals with it, including both hippo and rhino, using the original 150-gr., full-patch bullet at 2700 fps.

Stewart Edward White, the sportsman-novelist, was another of the early Springfield users. He collected upwards of 400 African trophies using one or another of his 03 sporters, among others, and judged the new rifle-cartridge combination ideal medicine for lions.

White's first Springfield sporter was made up by Louis Wundhammer about 1910, this first rifle one of four that had been ordered by Capt. E. C. Crossman.* Later, Owen, Griffin & Howe, Hoffman, Linden and several others made them.

*The first Stewart. Edward White rifle, serial number 166,346, has a Hock Island arsenal barrel dated February, 1910. Made by Louis Wundhammer of Los Angeles, it is one of four such Springfield 1903 sporters ordered by Capt. E. C. (Ned) Crossman. One was for Capt. Cross-man, the other two for Robert C Rogers and John Colbv. See Grossman's *Book of the Springfield* (Georgetown, S. C, 19511 or the *Gun Digest*, l5th edition.

These were handsome rifles, a bit heavy by modern standards but each a thing of beauty: choice wood, tasteful engraving and checkering — and if they were not too well used, still capable today of formidable accuracy. Until the middle 'thirties, when Winchester brought out their Model 70, Springfield sporters set the standards by which other hunting and target rifles were judged.

For years, the 03 was this nation's official service rifle. It lost that title to the Garand in 1935, but with the advent of World War II the 03 and its descendants, the A3 and A4, saw active duty as late as the 1950s. The Springfield's battle honors include campaigns in the Phillipines, Central America, the Caribbean, Mexico, the Western Front during World War I, every theater in World War II and, finally, Korea.

Turned out to pasture, the Springfield's career is far from over. During the past two decades, thousands have found their way into the hands and gunracks of American sportsmen. The NRA offered them, via the Director of Civilian Marksmanship, to its members at bargain rates over the years; surplus stores sold them; every sporting goods store of any stature at all tallied some in its inventory. Today these veterans, most civilianized by fancy stocks, scopes and professional blue jobs, can be seen by the score each fall when the redcoated hordes invade mountain and forest. The 03 isn't dead yet.

But they're getting scarce, at least, the "as issued" specimens are — and the gun collecting fraternity is becoming aware of it. During the past year, Springfield prices have soared. If a man has any ambition to collect them, the time to start is now.

## The Early Models

"Sired by Mauser, out of Krag" is the way one wag described the Springfield. Its official birthday was June 18, 1903 when the Chief of Ordnance accepted it, the official designation: *U.S. Magazine Rifle, Model of 1903, Caliber .30*. It came with a 24" barrel, rod bayonet, ramp type rear sight and an odd looking blade with two large holes drilled through it for a front sight. The bolt handle was curved but wasn't swept back. The forward barrel band was located right at the nose of the stock.

The 1903 cartridge, which came into being at the same time, was slightly longer than the current '06 round and fired a 220-gr., full-jacketed round nose bullet at 2200 fps.

In 1905, the rod bayonet was shunted aside in favor of the knife type and, about the same time, an improved leaf rear sight, resembling that used on the Krag, was mounted in place of the unsatisfactory ramp.

Meanwhile, the ever-busy Germans had opened their bag of tricks again, surprising the shooting world by introducing a radical pointed bullet they called spitzges-choss. This new pointed shape enabled them to send the 154-gr. bullet from their 8mm service round at the then astonishing speed of 2800 fps. Quick to see the advantages of the new design, our ordnance people got busy in their ballistics labs and whipped up the now famous 30-06 cartridge.

Pushing a 150-gr. pointed bullet out of the muzzle at 2700 fps, the 06 case was reduced to 2.49" long, necessitated by the 03 case having been too long for the new spitzer bullet by .070". Several thousand 1903 rifles had been produced by this time but, rather than re-barrel them, it was decided, in the interests of economy, to shorten and re-chamber the existing barrels. Two-tenths inch (.200") was shaved off the breech, the chambers altered for the new cartridge, and the threads cut two turns deeper. This operation left the barrels 23.79" long (chamber and bore) and all Springfield 03 barrels made since then have measured the same. Over-all barrel length became 24.006".

The next major change took place in 1918 when the steel used to make receivers and bolts was strengthened. Those critical parts were double heat treated, a process which made the surface metal extremely hard while allowing the core steel to remain relatively soft. Actions fabricated in this manner have weathered test rounds developing pressures of 125,000 psi without a whimper. The tough surface not only wears well but with a little use, cams and runways smooth to a mirror-like glaze, making those particular actions the slickest Springfield ever built.

Despite the time, effort and expense which must have been spent creating the new process, nobody bothered to record the exact point when the change was instituted. Authorities agree it took place somewhere around receiver No. 800,000, but nobody's really sure. Nevertheless, 800,000 is the magic number, it being generally accepted that actions made subsequently are the stronger. Although "low numbered" Springfields, that is, those with serial numbers under 800,000, are regarded as weaker and less desirable, it should be remembered that each was subjected to 70,000 pound test loads, and that these were the same rifles which created the Springfield's reputation in the wars and on the game fields. Nevertheless, it is true that the shattering of several of the earlier case-hardened actions brought on the change in heat treatment in early 1918.

Rock Island 03s received the improved double heat treatment starting with receiver No. 285,507. From No. 319,921 on some R.I. receivers were made of a nickel steel similar to that used later in producing the wartime A3s and A4s. Springfield Armory didn't adopt nickel steel until 1928 but again, no one there in Massachusetts noticed the exact time of the changeover. In all probability rifles produced after No. 1,290,266 boasted nickel steel actions.

Variations in the quality of steel are primarily of interest only to purists. It goes without saying that any high-numbered 03 — always assuming good condition — will accomodate modern loads with perfect safety.

## The Pedersen Device

To back up slightly: Shortly after the U.S. declared war on Germany in 1917, a well known arms designer of the day, one J. D. Pedersen, approached the War Department with an intriguing invention. The Pedersen Device, as historians call it, was essentially an automatic pistol mechanism with a stubby, integral barrel which could be slipped into the 03's receiver in place of the regular bolt. Once locked in place — this was accomplished by a flip of the magazine cutoff to "Off" — a long box magazine containing 40 cartridges resembling the 32 ACP was inserted into the right side of the bolt and presto! The Springfield was converted into an instant semiautomatic rifle!

Only three alterations to the rifle were necessary: an ejection port had to be cut into the left side of the receiver; the magazine cutoff had two grooves milled in it, and a small "kicker" was added to the sear. None of these modifications prevented the rifle from using the regular service round when the original bolt was in place.

Although the pistol-sized cartridge fired an 80-gr. bullet at a mere 1300 fps, General Pershing recognized its lethal potential and ordered 100,000 Pedersen units. Some 65,000 had been completed when Armistice Day arrived but none were ever issued to troops. A few years after the war, most of the devices were destroyed. A few, as usual, managed to escape the crushers and are now eagerly sought after by collectors.

It's easy to recognize the 03s modified for the Pedersen unit. There is a small, lozenge-shaped ejection port on the left side of the receiver, and to quell any further doubts the legend, *U.S Springfield Armory Model 1903 Mark I* is inscribed on the receiver. Records concerning this variation are sketchy but it's believed that one rifle, appropriately modified, was produced for each of the Pedersen devices manufactured.

When World War I ended, the Battle Reports and recommendations concerning the various weapons used were reviewed. The 03 came through with flying colors. Complaints were few and suggested changes even fewer. One, that was accepted, concerned the bolt handle. It was angled backwards slightly to bring it more in line with the trigger.

The Marine Corps, always marksmanship oriented, altered the sights of their rifles: the width of the front blade was increased to .10" and undercut, while the diameter of the rear peep was doubled. In addition, the triangular-shaped open sight in the rear leaf was dispensed with. 03s with Marine Corps sights are very much in demand by collectors.

## Type C Stocks

After a considerable amount of experimentation, a new service stock, the Type C was chosen in 1928. The original Type S stock had been criticized for its abrupt drop at the heel and because many felt it was too short. The new stock was straighter, its buttstock contour reminis-

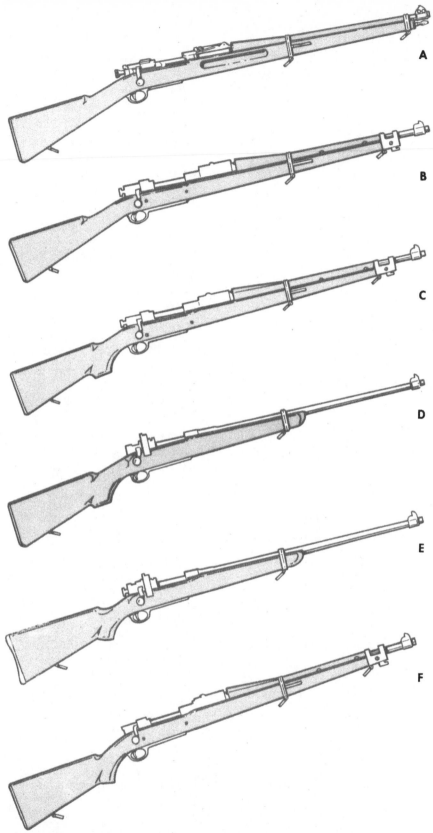

**A** — Original Model 1903. When it was accepted by the Army in 1903, the Springfield was equipped with a ramp-type rear sight and a rod bayonet. Note that the bolt handle turns straight down. **B** — The Type S stock was supplied with the service model 03 until it was supplanted by the Type C in 1929. **C** — The Model 1922 MI stock was supplied on National Match 03s issued to Service Teams. **D** — The Model 1922 MI issue stock (caliber 22). Note how this oversized pistol grip stock differs from NRA stock on the same action-barrel. **E** — The Model 1922 MI stock (caliber 30). This was commonly called the NRA or Sporter slock. **F** — The Type C stock was adopted in 1929. Rifles so equipped were designated Model 1903A1.

cent of those found on good shotguns. A hand-filling integral pistol grip had been added and the finger grooves, so pronounced on the old S stock, were deleted. Rifles with the new stock were designated Model 1903Als.

Although the semi-automatic Ml was chosen to succeed the 03 in 1935, almost a year passed before the last bolt action rolled off the production line at Springfield Armory. A few more were assembled in 1937 and another handful, the last, were produced in 1939. With receiver No. 1,532,878, the 03 became just another obsolete military rifle — or so everyone believed at the time.

Just before production ceased, a second gas escape port was drilled through the forward receiver ring. Up to this point, only one port, about ⅛" diameter, had pierced the ring on the right. Why an additional hole was put on the left is anyone's guess. I've only noticed a handful of 03s so made, all with serial numbers above 1,500,000. When the wartime A3s and A4s appeared, only one port was evident, this time on the left side.

Late in 1941, sensing the hot breath of war and unable to supply our rapidly expanding military forces sufficiently with the new Ml, the War Department issued a contract to the Remington Arms Company to begin production of the 03. Except for the name Remington and the serial numbers, which started with No. 3,000,000, this version of the 03 was a faithful replica of the Armory model in every respect.

With an eye toward increasing production, Remington's engineers took a critical look at the old design. After a few months of fiddling with slide rules and handmade prototypes, they came up with the *U.S. Rifle. Caliber .30. Model of 1903A3.*

Why not A2? Because a Model A2 had already been approved and was in service. Not really a rifle, it was simply a modified barreled action, altered to fit inside the breech of a tank cannon and used for practice to reduce training expenses.

Old-timers howled in anguish when the first A3 appeared. Barrel bands, floorplate and trigger guard were made of stamped metal. To add insult to injury, the barrels, most still bearing lathe scars, had only two grooves instead of the traditional four. Critics admitted that the rear-mounted receiver sight might offer some advantages but most insisted that the rifle would never stand up under battle conditions.

Despite the outraged cries and dire

predictions, the A3 performed creditably throughout World War II, seeing service in every theater and adding new luster to the name Springfield. It was sturdy, as dependable as its famed forefather, and just about as accurate.

This last surprised everyone. The ability of a 4-grooved barrel to group better than a two-groover, if any, must be slight. From a rest, my 03s and A3s deliver the same accuracy: 2" to 2½" at 100 yards with match ammo. The life of a 2-grooved tube is reputedly shorter than the four if AP ammunition is used, but evidently the Army felt the difference in longevity was more than offset by lower manufacturing costs and greater production.

### Two Million A3s

Remington turned out most of the two million A3s but Smith-Corona also added another 200,000 or so to the total. A number of the latter will be found with 4-groove and, occasionally, 6-groove barrels which were supplied by High Standard, Savage and several other subcontractors.

The A4, the sniper's model, made its bow in 1943. It was simply an A3 equipped with a Weaver 330C telescopic sight (the Army called it the M73B1 carried in a Redfield Jr. mount. The bolt handle was altered to clear the scope and no iron sights were fitted.

To the best of my knowledge, Remington took no special pains with bedding or action but the A4 sniper standing in my rack is blessed with what must surely be one of the smoothest actions ever made. Its condition indicated that it had never been issued yet the trigger is crisp and light — almost too light — and the rifle will consistently group all shots within 1¼".

The number of A4s produced was very small, something on the order of 28,000 all told. Few were issued before 1944 but many were still in action as late as the early 1950s. The Marines used them in Korea, mounting 8- and 12-power target scopes on them.

There's no way of knowing how many survived but the number must be small. The rarest of all have serial numbers beginning with a "Z" prefix; fewer than 2900 were made.

Of all the Springfields produced, the cream were the target and sporter rifles which trickled out of the Armory during

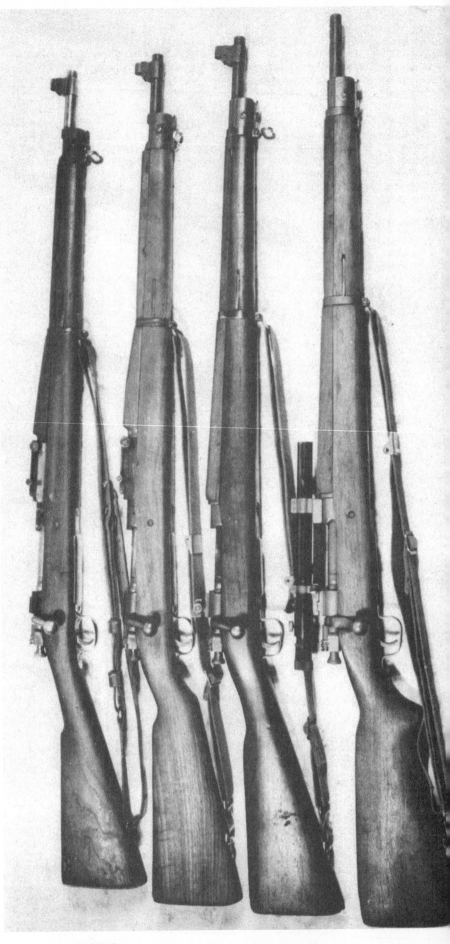

1903 Service. Left to right: 1903 with S stock; 1903A1 with WW II semi-pistol-grip stock; 1903A3; 1903A4, the sniper's model with a modified Type C stock.

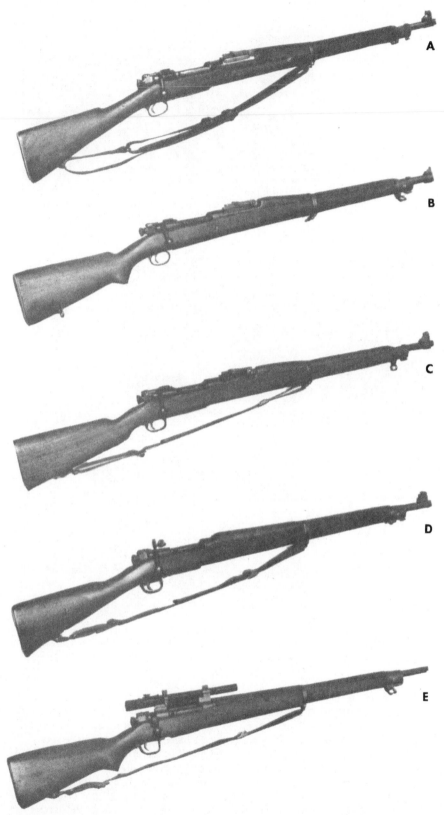

the quiet years between wars. Less than 2,000 ever saw the light of day in any given year but each was a handcrafted marvel.

Assembled from carefully selected parts, with cocking cams, bolts, sight leaves, extractors and runways polished, stocks fashioned from first-class, straight-grained black walnut, equipped with star gauged barrels and target sights, the National Match Springfields, NRA Sporters and the other limited edition models represented the Armory's finest achievements. Little wonder they dominated the target ranges for so many years.

When I was a boy, the word "star gauged" had a magic ring. This interesting device was a feeler gauge used at the Armory to measure the uniformity of a barrel's bore. If land and groove measurements were within one ten-thousandths of an inch (.0001") from chamber to muzzle the barrel was judged match grade, and a small "star mark" was stamped on the lower edge of the muzzle crown. In U.S. shooting circles a star gauged barrel was regarded as the ultimate.

## Target-Sporter Models

More than a dozen different match, target and sporting models were created by Springfield Armory between 1921 and 1940. (Some 1,000 or fewer National Match versions of the A3 rifle, purportedly equipped with Redfield micrometer rear sights, were produced from about 1953 through 1956, but I haven't been able to find a photograph of one of these or a specimen.) Some were designed exclusively for service teams; most were made available to NRA members. In addition, a series of full-fledged 30-caliber target rifles was issued. They were characterized by long, heavy barrels, micrometer sights on the receiver, globe sights at the muzzle, mounting blocks for telescopic sights — some were even decorated with adjustable buttplates and other match-rifle equipment. These remarkable rifles, weighing from 12 to 13 pounds, were just about unbeatable on the range.

During one period, the Armory even made up a few "free rifles" for the International Teams. These had longer, heavier barrels, set triggers, long hook buttplates and palm rests. They were about as good as anything Europe had to offer, and they tipped the scales at a hefty 14 pounds.

Some of those old rifles are still floating around, most of them pretty worn now. I'd never pay extra money for one myself unless it is accompanied by the original Ordnance Dept. bill of sale and its star gauging record.

A — The 1903 Springfield in early standard-issue forms. It has the original S stock with grasping grooves and greater drop, at heel. B — The 1903A1 was simply the standard 03 mounted in a Type C stock. C — 1903A1 in a wartime C stock. Notice the blunted pistol grip, the general absence of clean stock lines. D — The 1903A3. The World War II version of the 03 has a receiver peep sight and is characterized by the use of stamped parts and a two-groove barrel. E — The 1903A4. The sniper's model is equipped with a Weaver 2y2X scope in Redfield Jr. mounts and the Type C stock. No iron sights were fitted.

Needless to say, a clever gunsmith can counterfeit a National Match model without too much trouble. A bit of judicious polishing, a close fitting stock, a homemade star mark on the muzzle, the rifle's serial number engraved on the bolt — as always, it pays to be prudent when purchasing a used firearm.

Chances are, if you do run across one of those old specials, it will be an NRA Sporter. Several thousand were made and quite a few, relatively speaking, seem to have survived.

The Sporter, like the other specials, was put together from near-perfect parts and given the same care as a National Match rifle during production. The barrel — star gauged, of course — was slightly tapered; a Lyman 48 receiver sight was mounted on the bridge but the standard service blade was retained up forward; the stock contour was distinctly different from the service style, resembling those on commercial rifles.

While on the subject, it should be noted that the Armory developed several different stocks. The S and C stocks, which have already been mentioned, were relegated to the service rifles, including the N.M. models, but there were various other supplied for the specials.

The Model 1922 or NRA Model as it was popularly known, featured a shotgun-style butt, a well-turned pistol grip and short, sport-er style fore-end. This was used on the 22 rimfire Springfields and on the 30-06 Sporters when these (and other later versions) were sold for civilian use through the DCM.

This same M1922 NRA stock — except for having finger grooves — was used on the 1922 "Match Springfield," a 30-cal. rifle introduced that year. This rifle was a fore-runner of the "Style T" Match 03 rifle first offered in late 1929 and made in limited numbers for a few years.

The M1922 Ml stock, in its NRA form, differed little from the M1922 stock, but the "issue only" version was considerably different — while a half- or sporter stock, the fore-end had finger grooves, the pistol grip profile showed a flatter angle, and the rear of the buttstock looked like the service rifle or S stock in drops, dimension and form.*

---

*There were numerous other stock styles over the years, some experimental, others of limited production. For full and complete information on all of these, and for the finest account of Springfield rifles extant, see *The '03 Springfield*, by Clark S. Campbell, published by Ray Riling Arms Books Co., 6844 Gorsten St., Philadelphia, Pa. 19119.

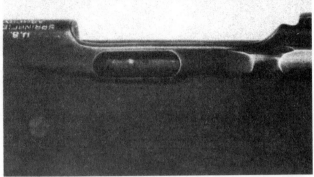

An ejection port on the Mark I Springfield allowed the small Pedersen-designed cartridge cases to escape the semi-automatic bolt. Note the slight stock cutaway beneath the port.

Those Mark I 03s modified to accept the Pedersen device were plainly marked as such on the receiver ring.

Mark I parts. Top, sear and cutoff from a standard 03; bottom, sear and cutoff from a Mark I Springfield modified to accept the Pedersen device.

## The Springfield Sporter

To get back to the Sporters: They're heavy by today's standards, scaling pretty close to 9 pounds. Weighty though they may be, those I've fired were very accurate with actions as smooth as silk.

A great number served as the basis for some of the classics turned out by such people as Niedner, Shelhamer, Griffin & Howe and Stoeger during the 1920s and the early '30s.

The first 22 practice rifle based on the 03 action was a single shot. It was fitted with a 24-inch barrel bored off-center at the breech so that the regular firing pin would hit the rim of the small case. The cartridge, by the way, was a special 22 Long Rifle featuring a Pope-designed bullet. It was manufactured by Peters for a limited time and called the "22 Stevens-Pope Armory." Only a few of these arms were produced. Except for the bores, their appearance was indistinguishable from the service rifle.

Another chip off the old block was the Gallery Practice Rifle, Model 1903. Except for chamber and barrel, it too was a duplicate of the issue rifle. Although some

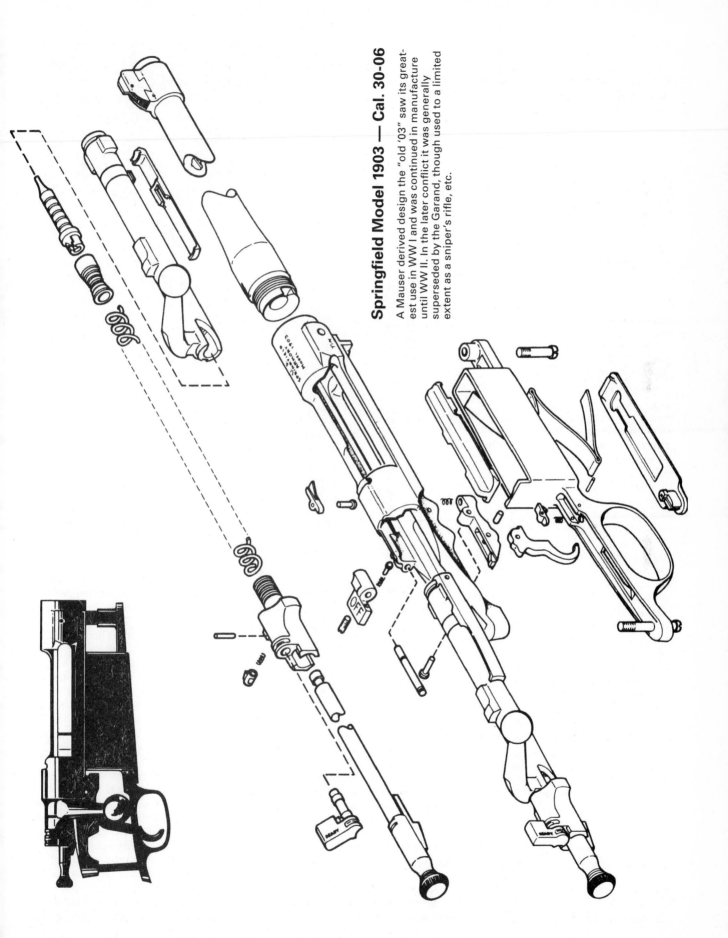

## Springfield Model 1903 — Cal. 30-06

A Mauser derived design the "old '03" saw its greatest use in WW I and was continued in manufacture until WW II. In the later conflict it was generally superseded by the Garand, though used to a limited extent as a sniper's rifle, etc.

The NRA Sporter. Assembled from carefully selected parts, fitted with star-gauged barrels and stocked with dense-grained walnut, these rifles sold for $41.50 forty years ago. They were heavy but superbly accurate.

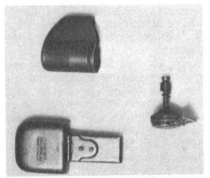

Curiosa. Relics of the days when the 03 ruled the target range. Top, front sight protector; lower left, rear sight protector; right, rear sight micrometer adjuster.

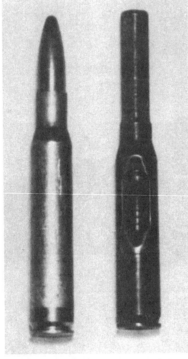

22 Short cartridge adaptor (right), used in the Gallery Practice Rifle of 1907. A 30-06 Military round is shown for comparison.

Micrometer sight adjustor. One of the accessories offered the serious competitor of the early 1920s when the 03 dominated the ranges. These tools permitted accurately controlled small changes in elevation.

of its design features smacked of genius, its accuracy left much to be desired.

Rather than fashion a new bolt or firing pin assembly, Springfield engineers (Majors J. E. Hoffer and J. T. Thompson) created an adaptor cartridge. Made entirely of steel, they were deliberately made shorter than the standard 06 round to prevent one of the latter from being chambered by mistake. Each adaptor contained an integral firing pin and a tiny slot in the side which permitted a 22 Short cartridge to be inserted. The devices could be loaded into the magazine, worked through the action and extracted exactly like the service cartridge. From a training standpoint, the approach was ideal, especially for those ROTC and National Guard units located far from regular outdoor ranges. It meant that the troops could train with a rifle of standard size and weight, shoot from all positions and even practice rapid-fire on indoor ranges.

Clever as the idea was, the adaptors proved impractical. When fired, the bullet enjoyed about half an inch of free travel before it struck the rifling. After a few rounds, lead and grease built up at this point. Accuracy suffered accordingly. In addition, the adaptors tended to rust

in short order, requiring an exasperating amount of maintenance to keep them in operating condition. Most aggravating of all — as far as the shooters were concerned — was the fact that unloading the spent 22 cases was a miserable and frustrating chore.

Despite these shortcomings, it wasn't until 1919 that plans for a new 22 trainer were started. More like the target rifles we know today, its bolt was two-piece and a 5-shot magazine jutted below the floorplate. It still looked in 1920 like the issue rifle except for a Lyman 48 micrometer sight mounted on the receiver. Chambered for the regular 22 Long Rifle cartridge, these prototype versions were the first really accurate 22s that Ordnance had ever developed.

## The Model 1922

Two years later (in June of 1922) a refined version, called the *U.S. Rifle. Caliber .22. Model 1922*, was issued. It was the first Springfield to have the half-stock style that was soon to become famous as the "Sporter" stock. By mid-1924 some 2000 M1922 rifles had been made, their price just over $39.

The improved-mechanism Model 1922 Ml which followed also had in its "as issued" form, a half-stock with an oversize flat-angle pistol grip. These had an excessive amount of drop at the heel. The NRA version had the graceful Sporter stock, as before. Bolt travel was still as long as that of the standard 03, a full 3.3 inches, but chamber dimensions were better, the 5-shot magazine was now flush, and the Lyman 48 C receiver sight had ½-minute clicks.

The 1922 M2s, introduced in late 1932, wore a new stock. While a half-stock, it was not the Sporter NRA style used earlier; instead, it had finger-grooves in the fore-end and a buttstock profile about like the N.M. stock. These M2s had a short bolt throw, speed lock ignition and provision for headspace adjustment. That last was incorporated in the locking lug assembly on the final production models.

M2s can still be found hard at work on small bore ranges around the country. Many carry the letters "A" or "B" after

A "long-slide" Lyman 48 micrometer sight, here seen on a Sedgeley sporter.

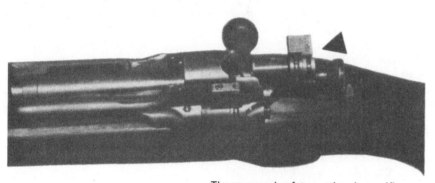

The reversed safety on the above rifle (arrow) must have been taken from a match rifle, for the serial number on the bolt doesn't match that on the receiver. It pays to be cautious when shopping for collectors items.

This 1903A4 Sniper rifle has a 2½X Weaver telescopic sight in a Redfield Jr. mount, and saw active duty as late as the Korean conflict. Note the altered bolt handle.

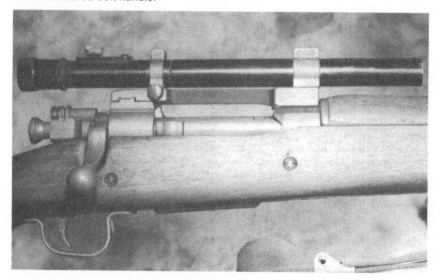

their serial numbers. Those markings signify that the rifles were originally issued as M1922s or M1922s M1s and later arsenal modified to M2 specifications.

"Star Gaging Record" card used to indicate bore and groove dimensions of selected 03 barrels.

Sighting tube. A small number of "sighting tubes" made at Springfield Armory and issued to service rifle teams. The minimum sight setting was 600 yards.

The International Match Rifle, Caliber 30, Model 1924, carried a checkered pistol grip stock, a hooked buttplate, a ball-type palm rest, a Lyman 48 receiver sight and a heavy 30" barrel. These also had double-set triggers of one type or another (see Campbell's book). An identical rifle was made in 22 Long Rifle, using the Model 1922 Ml action, for our successful U.S. International teams, but with the action considerably re-designed. Twelve of the 1924 match Springfields in 22 caliber were made in 15 days, the result of a last-minute order for them!

The old 03 wasn't perfect. Its sights were too delicate for battle conditions; the two-piece firing pin, which failed on occasion, affected lock time adversely; the high bridge made for an overly tall sighting plane and the Springfield action could never cope with escaping gas as well as the Mauser. Nonetheless, it was the best rifle that ever came out of the Armory — and it could shoot. The average 03 was more accurate than any of its contemporaries. Regardless of its shortcomings it looms high on the list of the world's great rifles.

The 03 helped make a lot of history

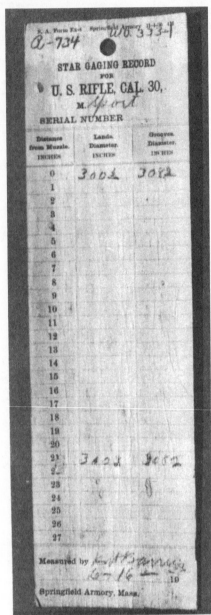

| Distance from Muzzle. INCHES | Lands. Diameter. INCHES | Grooves. Diameter. INCHES |
|---|---|---|
| 0 | 3002 | 3082 |
| 1 | | |
| 2 | | |
| 3 | | |
| 4 | | |
| 5 | | |
| 6 | | |
| 7 | | |
| 8 | | |
| 9 | | |
| 10 | | |
| 11 | | |
| 12 | | |
| 13 | | |
| 14 | | |
| 15 | | |
| 16 | | |
| 17 | | |
| 18 | | |
| 19 | | |
| 20 | | |
| 21 | 3402 | 3082 |
| 22 | | |
| 23 | | |
| 24 | | |
| 25 | | |
| 26 | | |
| 27 | | |

Measured by _____

Springfield Armory, Mass.

during the first half of this century; on target ranges, battle ground and game fields. More than four million were produced but age, wear and tear, combat, lend-lease and sporterizing have taken their toll. The 03, in military dress, is rapidly disappearing from the scene.

But not entirely. A handful are still on active duty. While watching General Eisenhower's funeral, I noticed the familiar silhouettes when the Presidential color guard hove into view. Sure enough, they were armed with the old bolt actions. Some months ago I saw the Army Drill Team in action. They too were equipped with 03s. I've no idea why they carried them but it was a nostalgic sight to a guy who learned to shoot and run through the Manual of Arms with one.

I remember crossing the English Channel one gray day in June of '44. The ship rolled sluggishly as the helmsman threw the wheel hard over to avoid a floating mine. Several of the troopers broke out their M1s and emptied them at the shiny, dark globe without result. A lanky, tobacco-chewing sergeant muttered an apology as he elbowed up to the rail, cradling a weather-beaten 03 tenderly in his arms. Balancing easily against the ship's gentle heave, he slid into the leather sling and sighted carefully for what seemed to be an eternity. The Springfield's bark was lost in the dull boom of the exploding mine and, as the echoes lost themselves over the tortured water, the marksman cast a scornful glance at the M1s. "Firepower, hell! I'll stick to my 03!"

If the 03 ever needs an epitaph, that should do as well as any.

# The Action that Served Two Armies

■ Wilfrid W. Ward

The 1917 Enfield (a cutaway) action. (Photo courtesy the Smithsonian Institution, Washington)

**B**RITAIN OFTEN HAS been inadequately prepared for her wars, but not always. This article tells how her preparations to build a new super rifle prior to World War I served not only her own purposes, but later those of her ally, the United States. Ironically, the preparations flowed from British troubles during the Boer War, where the Boers, using Mausers, had usually outshot the British. The press called for a Mauser-actioned service rifle. More realistically, Lord Roberts advocated better rifle training.

Plans for a new rifle began in 1910. On August 26th, the Small Arms Committee was requested by the Director of Artillery to "consider a new mechanism for a new magazine rifle, also any other points, *exclusive of ballistics*, which you may think necessary." This Committee was a typical British institution, which

had been founded some years earlier to advise in such matters. It was not universally admired; indeed, the February, 1905, issue of *Arms and Explosives* was acid in its criticism of the Committee to which it referred as "nothing more than a chance assembly of officeholders." This was overly harsh, and Skennerton is probably right in saying that the Committee's advice was a "good cross section of professional opinion and experience."[1]

The Committee met on September 2nd and advised a rifle which was to be used by cavalry and infantry, of approximately the same size as the existing 303 rifle, but with a one-piece stock. It should retain the butt trap, as well as the principles for attaching the bayonet and supporting the barrel, but the nosecap would be lightened in as far as this was compatible with the proper support of the bayonet. The handguard would run the

## Wilfrid W. Ward 1931-1992

A massive heart attack took Wilfrid Ward in December, 1992. He died on stand at a pheasant shoot not too far from his home in Hampshire, in England.

Trained in the law, his abiding passion was firearms. He himself was a pistol shot, shooting on U.K. teams in the '50s and as recently as 1992 in our own Masters shoot. He at one time amassed a considerable collection of duelling pistols and he was, of course, a two-time winner of our own John T. Amber Award for excellence in gun writing.

He leaves a wife, a daughter, a son, and a host of friends and readers. As his Editor and his friend I can say there are not enough writers and not enough gentlemen like him. He will be missed on both counts.

Ken Warner

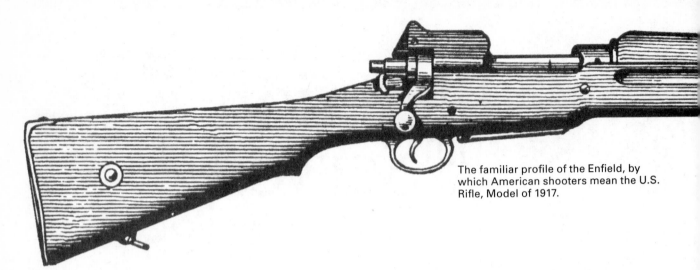

The familiar profile of the Enfield, by which American shooters mean the U.S. Rifle, Model of 1917.

full length of the barrel, and a barrel of 2 pounds 14 ounces was advised.

Furthermore, the recoil was to be about the same as that of the existing rifle. The magazine, which was not to have a cut-off, would carry ten rounds and be charger-loaded with a rimless cartridge. The action, which was one of the fundamental alterations to be incorporated, was to be a Mauser type, giving strength, reliability and symmetry. Forward locking lugs would be used together with a secondary safety shoulder to the bolt. The bolt head should be either detachable or solid with the bolt. A rotary bolt movement would produce primary extraction, and the extractor would not rotate with the bolt. The trigger was to be connect-

ed to the body of the action and not the trigger guard. The safety catch could be locked in both cocked and fired positions. Finally, the striker would be controlled by the cocking piece.

The sights — which eventually turned out to be one of the most advanced and praised aspects of the whole development — were, if possible, to incorporate an aperture backsight calibrated up to 1600 yards and a battle sight (also aperture) for use up to 700 yards. The long-range sight from the Lee-Enfield was to be retained for greater distances.

Further reflection on September 12th led to the recommendations being confirmed, save that the bolt head was to be revolving and detachable. The action

would cock on opening by the rotation of the bolt, the handle of which was to be as near the trigger as possible. By November 3rd the Royal Small Arms Factory at Enfield Lock was instructed to produce a design for such a rifle, and also a rifle for experimental purposes. The design for the rifle and the aperture sight (from Hythe) was ready by December 13th, when the assistant superinten-dant attended upon the Small Arms committee, and by April 3rd he again came bringing an experimental 276-caliber rifle. It was suggested that a different nosecap be fitted and that a bead fore-sight be provided for use with the aperture sight. In addition, a battle sight (not so far included) would be added. The stock in front of the

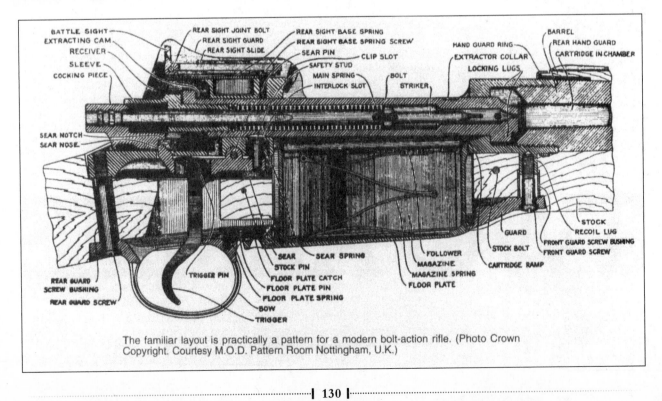

The familiar layout is practically a pattern for a modern bolt-action rifle. (Photo Crown Copyright. Courtesy M.O.D. Pattern Room Nottingham, U.K.)

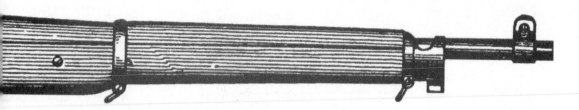

body was also considered too thick. The rifle then underwent rapid-fire trials leading to various minor alterations. Troubles were encountered with the ejection and the sight.

At this stage, the caliber of the new weapon had not yet been decided. The choice was between .276-inch and .256-inch. A series of trials were held in which the 276 caliber was very much more successful, resulting in a report, Minute 1197A, that considered the 276 caliber to have achieved a result which was "very fair for an experimental rifle with experimental ammunition."

The smaller caliber was abandoned quite soon thereafter.

We need not pursue the detailed history of the new rifle through its experimental stages, save to say that the chief source of its difficulties was enabling it to cope with the 276-caliber cartridge. This extremely powerful round generated high pressures, which in turn caused excess heat, extraction difficulties and bulged barrels, even in the two specially designed experimental rifles produced at Enfield for the purpose of the trials. Designated the Experimental Pattern Rifles 1911 Models A and B, they were followed in 1912 by two further models: the Experimental Pattern Rifle 1912, Models 1 and 2. More tests took place in June, 1912, and December 1912, at Hythe, the latter sighting trials. It was also at this stage that the difficulties encountered with the ten-shot magazine led the next experimental rifles to be fitted with five-round magazines; a modification of design which was not only incorporated into the Pattern 1913, but its successor the Pattern 1914. The use was licensed by Mauser and, almost incredibly, full royalty payments were made after the end of hostilities on the whole production. By this stage, the experiments on the design were finished, and a trial order for a nominal 1,000 weapons was put in hand at the Enfield manufactory. The new weapon was designated the "Rifle, Magazine, Enfield, .276-inch" and was officially so described by the War Office on March 15, 1913. These arms were distributed to troops in the British Isles, Egypt and South Africa, in order that they

might undergo the most thorough tests.

A variety of advantages were claimed over the 303. Greater power in the cartridge gave flatter trajectory and higher muzzle velocity, while greater strength (which was needed for this cartridge) was provided. Yet this was achieved with simplification and reduction of components. In particular, the front-locking bolt gave the hoped-for advantage of greater rigidity to both body and bolt. The action and bolt could be stripped without tools. The one-piece stocking allowed a lighter nosecap to be used. This improved the balance, and was not only cheaper to produce, but less likely to break. The aperture backsight was particularly successful, giving the rifle an increased sightbase. In addition, there was a fixed aperture battle sight. Other advantages were the heavier barrel, made possible by other weight savings. The magazine, being entirely within the stock, was less susceptible to accidental damage; moreover it remained open when empty. Overall, it was claimed the rifle showed a general improvement in ease of handling.

While these qualities were justifiably claimed for the rifle itself, the combination with the new cartridge was far less successful. Had it not been for the outbreak of war, the problems (largely oc-

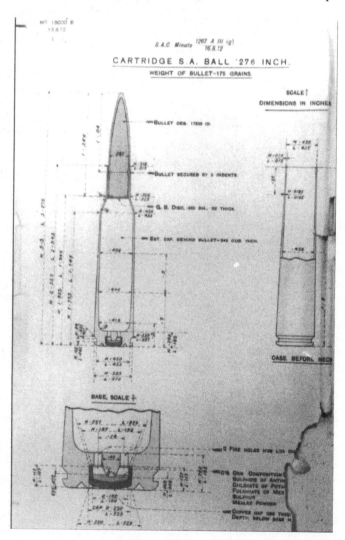

Small Arms Committee Minute setting out detail of 276 cartridge for P13 rifle. (Photo Crown Copyright. Courtesy of M.O.D. Pattern Room Nottingham, U.K.)

(above) Camouflaged sniper using P14. Though the picture is clearly posed, it was almost only in this way that the rifle saw active service. It was very successful. (Photo courtesy Imperial War Museum)

(right) Home Guard Corporal Batchelor's expression of happy anticipation seemed too good to miss. He was a veteran and probably had experience bayonet fighting during the 1914 war. (Photo courtesy Imperial War Museum)

casioned by the power of the 276 round) would probably have been overcome. The problem was being considered during the summer of 1914. Eventually, the authorities decided to use the new rifle, but with the well-tried, though less powerful, 303 cartridge.

This was not quite the end of the P13, because in late 1915 some of the original thousand P13s, by then returned to store, were converted to 470 caliber for use against snipers' plates — armored firing port covers — and at least one was tried in France. Similar use had been made of heavy-caliber big game rifles, and the latter turned out to be more efficient. These were superseded by the introduction of armor-piercing 303 rifle ammunition. The P13 again was retired, and re-emerged only briefly as an idea in similar context in the 1930s (see below). Its positively final appearance was during the 1939-45 war, when a number were rebuilt and re-issued as sniper rifles. (I am indebted to Mr. David Penn for calling my attention to these.)

The specifications for the substitute rifle, designated "Rifle, Magazine, .303-inch, Pattern 1914," were approved in

October, 1914, and six examples made from the improved version of the 1913 trials rifle were ready in April, 1915. The new pattern was simpler to make than the Lee-Enfield, nonetheless production did not go smoothly, or indeed at all, in Britain. B.S.A., one of Britain's principal arms manufacturers, declined the contract. An order was placed with Vickers for 200,000 rifles to be delivered at a rate of 2000 per week from July 31, 1915, and rise to 3000 a week from November 27. For a variety of reasons, the Vickers rifles were at first delayed, and later the project was abandoned with only a few prototypes to show for it.

In the United States, the arms industry was more accommodating, and contracts were entered into by Winchester

smooth, and a renegotiation of the contracts was deemed necessary. This was completed on December 31, 1916. The new grand total for rifles was 1,811,764. Difficulties had also arisen over the actual cost of the work done. These were sorted out by the British representatives. Britain had agreed to pay all expenses and to buy the plant on completion of the orders.

Before this could happen, however, the United States entered the war as Britain's ally. By the spring of 1917, it was apparent the Enfield S.M.L.E. 303 rifle had served satisfactorily in the trenches, and the 303 Pattern 14 was needed only in a specialized role for snipers and reserve troops. (This policy continued after the 1939–1945 war, and can be vouched for by the author, aged 13, who met his first

(403,126) came out at $28.38 each. Soon after this, the whole enterprise was sold by Britain to the American government at a price of $9,000,000. This was a big loss, but by this stage it was clear that Britain's needs would be covered by 303 Lee-Enfields. The expanding U.S. Army, on the other hand, was shorter of weapons than it had been at any time since the earlier part of the Civil War. The solution was a statesmanlike one, and a success.

Pausing to ask oneself how great a success the new rifle had been up to this point, the answer is only a limited one. Blame must go in many different directions, and a high proportion be laid to bad luck. Nonetheless, there were those who behaved irresponsibly. Perhaps this was occasioned by the fact that the companies concerned were being offered contracts of almost undreamed of size, and as good businessmen they felt compelled to accept first and work out later. Also, in fairness to those involved, one must remember that in the end American industry did find a way. The combination of unpreparedness, tight inspection procedures, lack of enough expert labor (particularly toolmakers) and pressure for fast production was just too much for success. Had the British government insisted on its contractual rights, the likely outcome would have been the ruin of two if not all of the contracting manufacturers. As it was, a substantial sum was saved from the ruins ($9,000,000) by the sale of the whole plant and apparatus to the United States. The balance of the British contract arms were to be completed whilst at the same time work began on the new U.S. rifles. This way Britain's new ally was armed with a first-class rifle (now accepted as the best used in

Strengthened M17 with grenade throwing device used by British Home Guard. (Photo courtesy Imperial War Museum)

Repeating Arms Company of New Haven, Connecticut; Remington Arms Company of Delaware; and Remington Arms Company of Ilion, New York, to make 2,000, 6,000, and 3,000, rifles a day to a total of 3,400,000 in all, for a staggering total of $102,500,000. Tools and gauges were dispatched from Britain, and a British military inspectorate was established in the United States. Again, progress was not

P14, aged about 30, in 1945 in his school cadet force.) Accordingly, production was brought to an end, with an approximate total of 1,233,000, Pattern 14s being produced. The 604,901 rifles made at Eddystone by Remington Arms Company were the most expensive, and together with bayonet and scabbard cost $43.75 each; those from Winchester (225,008) $36.82; while those from Remington Arms UMC

the 1914-1918 war), her small military arms industry preserved, and an acceptable compromise reached.

This was not quite the end of the P13/P14 concept in the British service. Apart from the use of the existing 303 rifles for sniping and in lesser theatres, and the later use by the Home Guard of Model 1917s (see below), there was one final flirtation with the action in 1936. That year,

This is the 276 experimental rifle made in 1912. (Photo Crown Copyright. Courtesy M.O.D. Pattern Room Nottingham, U.K.)

Finally, the 276 Pattern 1913 Rifle looked like this. (Photo Crown Copyright. Courtesy M.O.D. Pattern Room Nottingham, U.K.)

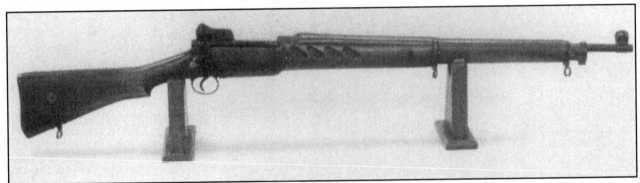

This is the sealed Pattern 1914 Sniper rifle with offset telescopic sight. Mounting the sight directly over the line of the bore obstructed charger loading. (Photo Crown Copyright. Courtesy M.O.D. Pattern Room Nottingham, U.K.)

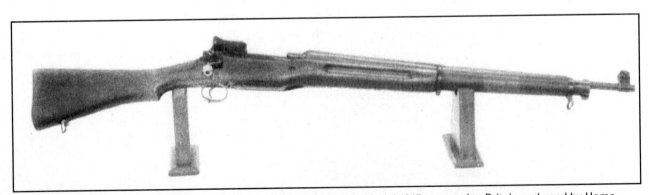

Here is a Winchester-made Model 1917 exported to Britain and used by Home Guard. Note painted band distinguishing from 303 P14.

the Small Arms Committee decided that a rifle with armor-piercing capability was desirable. The result was the "Rifle, Magazine, Experimental, .276 High Velocity." It fired a rimless magnum 276 round and was shaped in the style of a sporting rifle. There were also mounts for a telescopic sight. In 1939, B.S.A. made two prototypes with Mauser-type bolt systems and a built-in five-round magazine. History, however, repeated itself and the same problems of overheating and bullet stripping were encountered, as with the P13. Eventually the war led to a final repetition — the scheme was scrapped. The rifle was called after Captain J.R. Ainley who led the design team.[2]

After the sale by Britain, the first necessity was a complete evaluation of the rifle from an American viewpoint. This led to the abandonment of the 303 caliber in favor of the 30-06 rimless round. Next, and in some ways even more important, inter-changeability of parts was introduced. These decisions, like the British one to replace the experimental 276 with the well-tried 303, turned out well for America both militarily and commercially. Inter-changeability of parts cut production times greatly, and whilst the P14 had only been turned out at about fifty a day, in one day a record 250 Model 1917s were produced. Setting the caliber at 30-06 was clearly a wise decision. As well as the obvious convenience of keeping to one caliber, the performance of the rimmed cartridge had left a lot to be desired, particularly in terms of feeding from the magazine. When the new model arrived in American military hands, *Arms and Explosives* (Sept. 1,1917) tells us that the new rifle received a sympathetic welcome, a reaction not always accorded to new weapons by soldiers. Though doubts had been expressed in advance, the action showed itself quite strong enough to cope with the Springfield round, which had a chamber pressure of some 10,000 pounds more than the 303.

By the time the United States troops got to France, the pattern of trench warfare was well established. That most warlike of Americans, Captain Herbert W. McBride (author of *A Rifleman Went to War* and one of the most famous snipers of the era) had missed the South African War because he was not British. Not to be caught a second time by such a technicality, in 1914 he enlisted in the Canadian forces and was in France from 1915 to 1917. He did his sniping with the Canadian Ross rifle, but formed a favorable im-

Model 1917 closeup of backsight. The aperture battle sight, horizontal when the main sight is raised, can be seen at the base of the backsight. (Photo Crown Copyright. Courtesy M.O.D. Pattern Room Nottingham, U.K.)

pression of the Model 1917 when he had returned to the U.S. as an instructor. (The rifle is also said by the Editor and Wiley Clapp to have been used by Sergeant York in his famous exploit. Doubts are cast on this by Dr. Ezell and an anonymous 1969 *American Rifleman* writer, who both attribute a Springfield to him. The latter article includes York holding a Springfield pictured with his son. In light of such a conflict of authorities, one can only say that if he had had one, it would probably have done him very well! Silencing 35 machine guns, killing 25 and capturing 132 Germans, all with a rifle and a Government 45, doesn't just depend on the make of the rifle.)

There is no doubt that the American version of the Enfield rifle was a great improvement upon its 303 relation. It was simplified, incorporating most of the good points of the P14 and the Springfield. At the same time, there is no reason to doubt that, had the original development at Enfield not been interrupted by war, a first-class rifle would have emerged.

The post-sale development was on strictly American lines. Thus, when one examines the ultra-rare trench-firing device (which I illustrate by courtesy of the Springfield Armory Museum and the Museums and Parks Service), one finds the designer has departed from the British system of raising the whole rifle in a frame containing a separate trigger mechanism, and has hinged the butt, thus permitting the rifle's own trigger and optical sight to be used. The development of the equally rare Pedersen Device, which converted the 1917 — only a few made — into a semi-automatic rifle, was brought to an end with the arrival of peace. In 1934, though not acting for the U.S. government, Remington produced a "Model 1934" as an export to Honduras. Argentina, too, is reputed to have received rifles.

Rumors of the new version of the Enfield had crossed the Atlantic to *Arms and Explosives* by April, 1917, together with justifiable comment on the superiority of the British aperture sight. Final details of the various changes were not published

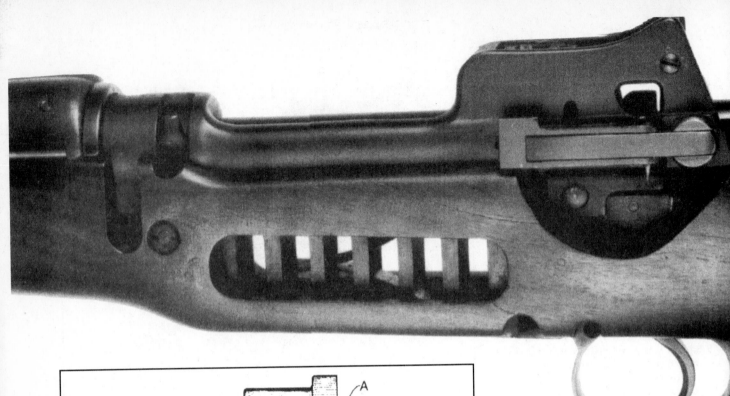

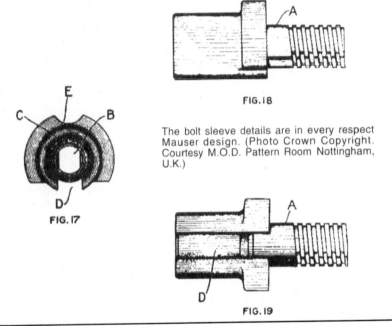

FIG. 18

FIG. 17

FIG. 19

The bolt sleeve details are in every respect Mauser design. (Photo Crown Copyright. Courtesy M.O.D. Pattern Room Nottingham, U.K.)

Cutaway Model 1917, close-up of action, right side. (Photo courtesy the Smithsonian Institution Washington)

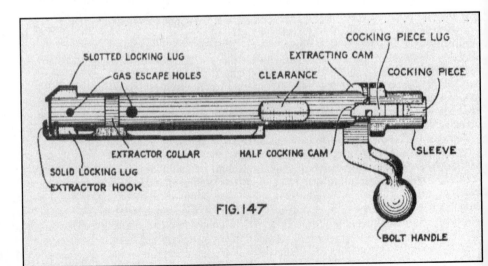

SLOTTED LOCKING LUG
GAS ESCAPE HOLES
COCKING PIECE LUG
EXTRACTING CAM
CLEARANCE
COCKING PIECE
EXTRACTOR COLLAR
HALF COCKING CAM
SLEEVE
SOLID LOCKING LUG
EXTRACTOR HOOK
BOLT HANDLE

FIG. 147

Seen from below, the 1917 bolt is clearly a Mauser layout. (Photo Crown Copyright. Courtesy M.O.D. Pattern Room Nottingham, U.K.)

until August, 1917. In the September 1st issue, despite the very strict British censorship, the same paper reported more. The U.S. press, forgetting that the action had been originally designed for the powerful 276 round, expressed fears that the 52,000 pounds of pressure generated by the 30-06 cartridge would prove too much for an action which had only handled the 42,000 pounds of the 303 round. In fact, the 30-06 and the original 276 produced roughly the same pressures. The reaction of the American users was almost universally favorable, although this must have been hard in some instances, bearing in mind that a great deal of the design was still foreign, and that it largely displaced a popular American rifle. The American decision had been to embody chosen changes, but only if they would not occasion delay in production of the new weapon.

*Arms and the Man* welcomed the new arrival, praising the heavy barrel and the rimless cartridge. (In fairness we must not lose sight of the fact that the P13 was designed for such a cartridge.) The writer, however, hit on the greatest merit, namely the aperture backsight. This, he considered, would make the rifle "stand apart from all others." It was a true prophecy. His other comment that the new naming of the rifle the "U.S. Rifle Model 1917" was "an extraordinary fate for a weapon designed by the British Small Arms Committee" had a ring of jingoism about it, which might have seemed more appropriate from Enfield rather than Washington D.C. Even the proudest Briton could not but agree with one comment that its most striking feature was its "entire lack of beauty."[3]

It would have been too much to hope for that everyone would get it right, though they probably tried harder then in matters of weapons than they do today. The *New York Sun* attacked the change with the headline "Why Our Forces in France Must Use Inferior Rifle," and continued to say that the U.S. Expeditionary Force was to use British Lee-Enfield rifles, rechambered to use the U.S. Springfield cartridge. To make matters worse, the illustration was of the 1895 Lee-Enfield rifle. Furthermore, the writer had gone on to deduce that such a combination would produce an inaccurate weapon, in which he was almost certainly right. To cap it all, he lamented the lack of a telescopic sight for shooting at extremely long ranges.

Such errors at such a time could not go uncorrected, and the NRA's former president, General George W. Wingate, joined Captain Mattice, the officer in charge of the U.S. Enfield project, to correct the record in Arms and the Man. Mr. Skerrett (the author) was said to have shown that he had done considerable research, but "that he was not a practical rifleman." The General's conclusion was that "to enable the soldier to shoot with greatest accuracy and rapidity, the modified Enfield is to my mind superior to the Springfield as the latter is now sighted."

One could continue to quote contemporary sources, but suffice it to say that the near-unanimous view on both sides of the Atlantic was that the "Modified Enfield" was the finest rifle yet developed. Like every other manufacturing process, it had its problems. The Model 1917's were the difficulties encountered in heat-treating the rifle, both at Eddystone and Springfield. It was not absolutely without fault, but it was infinitely ahead of its competitors on both sides of the conflict.

By 1939, the U.S. was re-equipping itself with the semi-automatic Garand, thus the Model 1917 no longer occupied as high a place as it had at the end of hostilities in 1918. Though downgraded to "limited standard" in 1943, it was by no means finished, and appropriately many thousands were exported to Britain under the Lend-Lease agreement. At the beginning of the 1939 war in Britain, home defense was in the hands of the Local Defense Volunteers, who were armed with anything from shotguns, bored out to fire solid ball, to pitchforks. This force was soon reconstituted as the Home Guard. After the regular army had time to reorganize itself and replenish its supplies after the vast losses suffered in the retreat from France in 1940, official attention was turned to the Home Guard. From the status of peasant skirmishers, it became a well-armed, if elderly, force, officered and manned largely by seasoned soldiers who had been service in the 1914 war. In such hands, the Model 1917 was a potent and valued weapon. To distinguish them from the 303 caliber P14, the 3006 Model 1917 rifles were marked with a red band. Though the cartridges of the two rifles were not interchangeable, considerable logistic problems must have arisen from the presence of both rifles in the same units. The P14, too, had not been battle-tested apart from sniping and was restricted to reserve units and a variety of non-standard formations.

Thus, this great and under-used action returned to the country of its origin. By the accidents of timing, it was too late for effective and prolonged service with European users other than for snipers

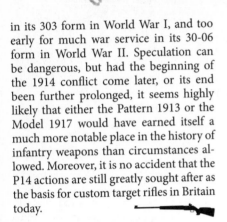

in its 303 form in World War I, and too early for much war service in its 30-06 form in World War II. Speculation can be dangerous, but had the beginning of the 1914 conflict come later, or its end been further prolonged, it seems highly likely that either the Pattern 1913 or the Model 1917 would have earned itself a much more notable place in the history of infantry weapons than circumstances allowed. Moreover, it is no accident that the P14 actions are still greatly sought after as the basis for custom target rifles in Britain today.

The U.S. idea of a trench rifle involved a hinged stock and a periscope, all hand-held. (Photo courtesy Springfield Armory Museum, Museums and Parks Service)

## Acknowledgements

I am particularly indebted to Mr. Herbert Woodend of the M O D Pattern Room, Nottingham; to Mr. David Penn, keeper of firearms at the Imperial War Museum; and its trustees for their help and guidance in the preparation of this article and for the opportunity to photograph their exhibits. In addition, I owe thanks to Dr. Ed Ezell and the Smithsonian Institution for photographs of the cutaway Model 1917, and to The Springfield Armory Museum and the National Parks Service for the opportunity to photograph the trench-firing Model 1917 device. Mr. Pete Dickey of the NRA of America provided me with relevant extracts from *Arms and The Man*, and Dr. DeWitt Bailey and Mr. W.S. Curtis those from *Arms and Explosives*. Finally, I refer those readers who seek further information on this very interesting subject to Mr. Skennerton's invaluable work *The U.S. Enfield*, where once again he has almost certainly produced the metaphorical, if not the actual, last word on the subject.

*Wilfrid Ward*

## Footnotes

[1] Ian Skennerton, *The U.S. Enfield* (Margate, Australia: Ian Skennerton, 1983) p.2.

[2] Herbert Woodend, *British Rifles: A Catalogue of the Enfield Pattern Room* (No HMSO, 1981).

[3] "A Causerie About Rifles," Arms and the Man (Washington DC: NRA, June, 1918).

# Military Small Arms of World War II

■ Charles T. Haven

**W**ITH THE victorious completion of World War II, and the return of millions of GI's from world battle areas, military small arms have become of vital, instead of merely academic, interest to most civilians, for in some cases they will prove as much life and death items to the civilian at home as they were to the soldier in the field.

This is brought about by the tremendous influx of "souvenir" weapons and ammunition into the country. Thus, while the first Military Small Arms article in the 1944 Edition of "The Gun Digest" was written so that its readers might recognize weapons seen in news reels or referred to in the papers, the present purpose is to provide information, and in some cases warning, concerning the weapons themselves as they will be seen and handled.

In general, from a safety point of view, the first thing to do with any weapon is to make sure that ammunition to be used is the *correct* ammunition for that gun. The second rule is to make sure that the weapon is safe to fire even though the ammunition to be used with it is suitable for its general type. This applies to American as well as European arms; an obsolete Damascus barrel shotgun loaded with super-duper, nitro express loads is just as dangerous to its user as a worn out Mauser rifle loaded with 8 mm. Mannlicher cartridges.

There have been plenty of excellent weapons made in Europe in the past and plenty of fine arms have been, and will be, sent over to this country; but owing to slave labor conditions, poor material towards the end of the war and a general abuse of weapons in war, many of these arms are unsafe, even with the ammunition originally intended for them.

It is a very good form of life insurance to take any foreign weapon, and the ammunition you intend to use in it,

to a competent authority on firearms for examination before you put your face or hands next to a potential 50,000 pounds or so of breech pressure and pull the trigger. Even United States military weapons may be unsafe if the wrong ammunition is used in them.

## Cartridge Characteristics

In the first place, it is advisable to steer clear of any ammunition whose bullets are *not* of normal color, which is either copper or nickel. Specially marked bullets indicate special loads which may get the civilian shooter into trouble in one way or another. In general, the United States marking for special loads in both rifle and pistol cartridges has been adopted by most of the European countries and is as follows:

A red tip bullet indicates tracer ammunition which will set fire to dry brush and should never be fired for target or hunting purposes.

A blue tip bullet is incendiary and is even more likely to set fires than tracer ammunition.

A black tip bullet is for armor piercing, apt to be of higher velocity than normal and may give added strain to rifle actions using it.

.45 and .38 caliber pistol ammunition and also shotgun shells were made for government use in tracer loads and will be recognized by a red tipped bullet, or *tracer* marked on the shell.

Standard British bullet markings duplicate United States markings as to black, red and blue, but have two additional color markings. Armor piercing is marked with a *green* bullet tip as well as a black one; then there are two types of tracer ammunition, a tracer Mark II which burns a thousand yards and carries the standard *red* insignia, and a tracer Mark VI which burns for only six hundred yards, designated by a *white* tip on the bullet.

One of the greatest potential sources of trouble through error and misunderstanding, in connection with foreign guns and ammunition, is the German so-called "8 mm. military cartridge." Actually, there are a number of different 8 mm. cartridges and a number of different rifles for them.

The first and most common is the model of 1898 Mauser and the so-called 8 mm. Mauser cartridge, although to be exact, it is 7.92 mm. This is listed in Germany as the "8" or 7.92×57 mm. rimless cartridge. The 57 mm. stands for length of the cartridge case, 7.92 or .315 being the actual diameter of the bullet. This, in its latest loadings, was the standard German military cartridge and was designed to be used in the 1898 Mauser, in its various models and modifications, and the four different versions of a semi-automatic rifle in use by the German army in the latter stages of World War II: the Gewehr '41, Gewehr '41M, Gewehr '41W and Gewehr '43. It was also used in the standard German rifle caliber machine gun for both ground and aircraft mountings. The rifles chambered for it use it from a Mauser type charger, which does not enter the action, and out of which the cartridges are stripped into the magazine. It is a rimless cartridge with a pointed bullet, very similar in appearance, though slightly shorter and stouter, to our .30-'06. The military type loads have the usual variations of standard ball, tracer and armor piercing, indicated by red and black nosed bullets.

A high velocity load and also an explosive load for machine guns are sometimes encountered. This ammunition is extremely dangerous in a rifle and should not be fired under normal range or hunting conditions. The high velocity load is indicated by a green band around the bullet and the explosive bullet, which is composed of a phosphorous pellet and a lead azite exploding charge, with an inertia firing pin, is indicated by a bullet that is black two thirds of the way up from the neck of the cartridge case and either bright copper or bright silver at the point. This ammunition is even dangerous to disassemble as it may explode in handling. In general, it is advisable to keep away from any military rifle caliber ammunition with unusually marked bullets, and here is a very good example of it:

The modern pointed bullet load, while the case is the same as an earlier load, listed as the model 1888, which uses a round nose, 230 grain bullet, is too high powered for weapons designed for the '88 cartridge, such as the model of 1888 military Mauser and some of the earlier sporting Mauser and Haenel-Mannlieher rifles. Military loads should be used only in modern weapons.

The "8 mm." cartridge, as loaded in this country by the ammunition companies, has a round nosed, hunting bullet with pressures suitable for use in any of the following weapons: The 1888 and 1898 Mauser military rifles, the Sauer-Mauser sporting rifle, the Schilling-Mauser sporting rifle Model 1888 and the Haenel-Mannlieher, model of 1888. No cartridge of the 8×57 dimensions should be used in any other repeating rifle except these and no other cartridge should be used in any of them.

Numerous double barreled and over and under combination rifle and shotgun weapons have been made in Germany, chambered for an 8×57 mm. Mauser cartridge, but in this case it is a *rimmed* cartridge, instead of a *rimless*, to aid in extraction from a break open type weapon. The case dimensions of the 8 × 57 rimmed and rimless are identical and 8×57 rimless ammunition will fire successfully in some of the rifles made for the 8×57 rimmed cartridge. Extraction difficulties can be overcome with an alteration of the extractor. It is, however, advisable to check sporting rifles carefully and, if possible, fire them under proof conditions with this ammunition before shooting such weapons from the shoulder, as there may be variations in pressure between American or military loads and the load in the rimmed case for which the rifle was intended. There are also several

other lengths of 8 mm. German sporting cartridges and any sporting weapon, even if it is marked "8 mm.", may be chambered for one of these.

The next most common "8 mm." cartridge found in European weapons imported before World War II, and one that is loaded commercially here, is the 8×56 mm. rimless Mannlicher-Schoenauer, Model of 1903. This uses a round nosed bullet and is a typical rimless bolt action rifle sporting cartridge designed for the Mannlicher-Schoenauer rifle, model of 1903. This should under no circumstances be used in any other weapon as it is shorter in case length than the 8 × 57 mm. Mauser cartridge and will cause headspace trouble and blown cartridges and actions if it gets into a gun chambered for the longer cartridge. Guns chambered for this will, of course, not accept 8 mm. Mauser ammunition without deforming the case and it should never be forced into their chambers.

Another, and entirely different, "8 mm." cartridge is the 8 mm. Austrian-Mannlichcr, designed for the model of 1895 Austrian-Mannlicher military rifle of the straight pull bolt type. This is a rimmed cartridge, very much heavier in the body than other 8 mm. cartridges, which cannot be used in any other weapon except the model of 1895 Austrian military rifle. It uses a round nosed, steel jacketed bullet of 210 grains weight and a muzzle velocity of about 2000 feet per second.

Another "8 mm." European cartridge is the French 8 mm. Lebel cartridge, originally the model of 1886, modified to a pointed, boat tailed bullet at a later period. This in its modern loadings is characterized by a pointed, boat tailed, solid bronze bullet, a rimmed very short, fat case and a muzzle velocity of a little over 2000 feet per second. It is used only in the Lebel military rifle in various models, in three or five shot clips. It was loaded in this country in a sporting load prior to the war, but no standard sporting rifles are made for it. It has become at least semi-obsolete in France by the adoption of the 7.5 mm. rimless cartridge, model 1924-29.

These cartridges are all commonly and loosely called 8 mm. military rifle cartridges, although most of them are available under normal peacetime conditions in sporting type loads. With the exception, under certain conditions, of the 8×57 rimmed and rimless, none of these cartridges are interchangeable and some of them will cause blown weapons if they are wrongly used.

Another cartridge that will be met

with extensively in captured trophy weapons, and one which exists in a number of variations, is the "9 mm." pistol cartridge, or to be more exact, the "9 mm." pistol *cartridges*, as there are several that are very easily mixed up.

Taken in the order of their size and power, the smallest is the 9 mm. Browning short. This is identical to our American .380 automatic Colt pistol cartridge which has been manufactured in this country since about 1908. While we do not consider it of military power, it has been used in Europe for a number of standard military pistols, including the Italian Beretta model of 1934, the Hungarian Model of 1937, Czechoslovakian models of 1924 and 1938 and other pocket type pistols issued for military purposes. It is a good medium power cartridge and pistols chambered for it are usually straight blowback actions of medium size and weight.

The next European cartridge in size is the 9 mm. Browning Long. This is a potential trouble maker and should be watched very carefully as it is interchangeable as far as case size is concerned with a Colt .38 ACP, which is a much more powerful cartridge. There are only three pistols made in Europe which are intended for the 9 mm. Browning Long. These are the F. N. Browning Model 1903, the French Le Francais, Model 1928, and the 9 mm. Webley & Scott automatic pistol, Model of 1913, used by the South African mounted police. But since the 9 mm. Browning Long is not at present manufactured in this country, owners of such pistols may try to use the available .38 ACP. *Leave this one alone* as it might cause unfortunate results. Nothing made here will work in them properly.

The next cartridge in size is the commonest of all European cartridges, known in this country as the 9 mm. Luger and in Germany as the pistol cartridge Model 1908, or 9 mm. Parabellum. This was originally designed for the Luger pistol of that year, called in Europe the Parabellum or Pistole '08. The bulk of the heavier European military pistols in use during World War II were chambered for this load. The list includes the F. N. Browning 9 mm. High Power M1935, the Polish Radom, M1935, the Spanish military Astra, the German Walther HP or Pistole 1938, and the Luger.

The earlier Italian service pistol, the Glisenti M1910, is chambered for the same size case but the Italian loadings are very much less powerful than the German and no ammunition that is not beyond all doubt the standard Italian load should ever be used in the Italian Clisenti pistol.

The 9 mm. Luger was also the popular submachine gun cartridge of most of the European nations; unfortunately for the user of captured material, the submachine gun loadings are much higher pressure than normal pistol loadings and will wreck some of the pistols designed for standard loads.

In general, it may be said that during the war all German pistol loading of 9 mm. Luger ammunition is distinguishable by a narrow black band on the bullet just in front of the mouth of the case. All other war time ammunition of this caliber may be high speed loads and should be treated with care. Common distinguishing features that are known to represent high speed loads are: an entirely black bullet in either a brass or steel case, a copper jacketed bullet in a steel case and a gray bullet in a steel case.

Pre-war European loadings with standard brass cases and nickel or copper type bullets are usually of pistol pressure. Italian ammunition, even for Italian submachine guns, is usually loaded to lower pressure than German. American loadings of the 9 mm. Luger ammunition will work satisfactorily in any European pistol that is otherwise in good shape, except the Gli-senti, which has a relatively weak breech action.

There are three other 9 mm. cartridges, all longer than the Luger, which have been in limited use in Europe. These are the 9 mm. Bayard for the Bergmann-Bayard pistol M1908, the 9 mm. Steyr, for the Austrian-Steyr pistol M1911, and the biggest one of all, the 9 mm. Mauser for Mauser pistols chambered for that size. None of these will chamber in weapons designed for the 9 mm. Luger cartridge and they are all somewhat more powerful than the normal loadings of this cartridge. Guns chambered for them should be used only with their own ammunition, which in most cases is not obtainable in this country. Such guns should be considered as souvenirs unless a little of the proper ammunition turns up.

The other common pistol cartridges in Europe are identical with their American versions, notably the .32 automatic Colt, known in Europe as the 7.65 mm. Browning, and the .25 automatic Colt, known in Europe as the 6.35 mm. Browning. These cartridges and their loadings are interchangeable with their American equivalent and in well made weapons are as safe as cartridges manufactured in the same country as the guns.

There is one peculiar cartridge in limited use in France which is not obtainable here; this is the 7.65 mm. long M1935, used in the French M1935 automatic pistol marked MAS. It is about half again as long as our standard .32 automatic Colt pistol cartridge and uses the same type of straight rimless case. Neither this pistol nor its ammunition have any duplicates in this country.

## U.S. Weapons

United States small arms of rifle caliber, which include several rifles as well as light and medium weight machine guns, use a cartridge which has always been the subject of some misunderstanding even by a great many soldiers. This is the U. S. cartridge ball, caliber .30 Model 1906 in one of several loads. Originally, the Model of 1906 used a flat based, 150 grain bullet at 2650 feet per second with a breech pressure of about 50,000 pounds. This was the cartridge with which the First World War was fought. Since then, it has been modified to the M1 load brought out in the middle 1920s, which used a 172 grain bullet of boat tailed type at about 2700 feet per second. A further modification just prior to World War II was listed as the M2 load, which returned to the original 150 grain flat based bullet, but increased the muzzle velocity to 28-2900 feet per second. This was the standard load used during World War II. The cartridge is commonly called the .30-'06 from its original designation of caliber .30 Model 1906.

Hunting loads for use in military or sporting rifles chambered for this cartridge have varied from a 110 grain bullet at over 3000 feet per second to a 220 grain bullet at about 2500, but the cartridge is always the standard rimless case of our military weapons.

Two cartridges which are frequently confused with the .30-'06 are the .30-30 Winchester, which is a rimmed hunting cartridge designed for lever action hunting rifles in the middle 1890's and never used for military purposes, and the .30 Model of 1892 or .30 Army, which was standard for the Krag rifle used by the United States Army between 1892 and 1903. It is also commonly called the .30-40. This is a rimmed cartridge with a 220 grain bullet, at about 2000 feet per second, which bears little resemblance to our present army cartridge. None of these cartridges will interchange between different weapons.

We have also used during World War II another .30 caliber cartridge, listed as the .30 carbine M1, which is a straight cased cartridge using a .30 caliber round nosed 110 grain bullet at about 2000 feet per second and which has been used in the Carbine M1 and M2. This will not interchange with the standard rifle cartridge.

The standard United States Infantry rifle of World War II has been the United States rifle, caliber .30 M1, popularly known as the Garand, from John C. Garand its inventor. It was adopted as standard by the United States Army in 1936. This is a gas operated semi-automatic rifle, taking its gas from a port near the muzzle. It loads with an eight shot clip which is thrown out when all the cartridges have been fired. It gives to our soldiers nearly three times the fire power of men armed with the bolt action rifle.

Other rifles used by our forces during World War II include the Model 1903 Springfield, which was originally adapted from the basic Mauser turning bolt design of 1898. This is a five shot rifle which has been the standby of the army for many years. It fought through the First World War and proved itself, by the results of many international military rifle matches, to be the most accurate military rifle in the world at the time of its adoption.

Another U. S. Army rifle is the Model 1917, popularly known as the Enfield, as it was a First World War adaptation of the Pattern 1914 British Enfield which was being built for the British government in this country. These were extensively used in World War II as a great many reserve stocks of this rifle were available at the time we entered the war. This is also a turning-bolt Mauser type rifle with a five-shot magazine.

Another semi-automatic of recent development, the Johnson short recoil semi-automatic rifle, with a ten-shot rotary magazine capacity, loading from standard Springfield clips, was used in limited numbers by several United States forces, including the Marine Parachute and Raider Divisions, the Army First Special Service Force and some organizations equipped by the Office of Strategic Services.

As mentioned in the article on "Our Small Arms and Their Makers," a modification of the standard Springfield rifle, Model 1903, streamlined for modern production, was also used by our forces. This was listed as Model 1903A3.

As World War II was essentially a war of movement, emphasis was placed on lightness and mobility, so the light machine gun, exemplified by weapons weighing not much over twenty pounds but giving great fire power to the advanced units, was an important part of Infantry equipment of all nations. Our best known example of this weapon was the BAR, or Browning Automatic rifle, one of the contributions of the great John Browning to United States armament in the First World War. This is a gas-operated, bipod-mounted gun fired from a prone position with a shoulder stock and weighing about twenty pounds.

While the war was in progress an adaptation was made of one of Browning's heavier guns, the light tripod model of the 1917 Browning, to bipod use with a shoulder stock. This was listed as the 1919A6, retained the belt feed and weighed about 35 pounds total.

The Lewis gun of the First World War was also used in limited quantities, especially in the Navy and Coast Guard. This is a gas-operated, air-cooled light machine gun, weighing about 26 pounds and fed from a pan or drum type magazine with a capacity of 47 or 94 rounds placed horizontally on top of the breech.

The Johnson light machine gun, a twelve and a half pound weapon, capable of full and semi-automatic fire, loaded from the left hand side with a 20-shot box magazine and fired either from the shoulder or a light bipod, was also used by some of our Armed Forces, particularly the United States Marine Paratroopers and the Army First Special Service Force.

All these weapons used the standard .30-'06 cartridge in one of its modern loadings; toward the latter part of the war, standard issue was M2 loading in ball, tracer, armor piercing and incendiary varieties, which were designated by the colored tips of the bullets.

A late development of World War I, the submachine gun, which is distinguished from the light machine gun by its use of pistol ammunition rather than rifle ammunition, was also extensively used during World War II. The first weapon of this type to be developed in this country, the Thompson submachine gun, or Tommy gun, was used in a number of models by the Armed Forces of the United States since its first employment by the Marine Corps during the Nicaragua campaign in the 1920's. The Tommy gun weighs about ten pounds and shoots the hard hitting .45 automatic pistol ammunition from several types of magazines, including the earlier 50-shot drum and 20 and 30 shot box magazines. It has been issued in several models, the later ones simplified for more rapid production. The bolt is cocked open and the gun will fire either full or semi-automatic depending on the position of the fire control switch. It provided rapid fire at relatively close range and was especially useful to paratroops, jungle fighters, raiders, commandos, etc.

Another gun using the same ammunition is the Reising submachine gun, manufactured by the Harrington & Richardson Arms Company in several models. This was used by the United States Marines in the early part of the war. It is peculiar among submachine guns in that it fires both full and semi-automatic from a closed bolt, whereas most of these weapons fire from the open bolt position.

Two other submachine guns were developed by the Ordnance Department during the war. These are the M2 and the M3. The M2 is a simplified Thompson gun type weapon, which was never issued in any quantity as before it was in production the M3 was developed. The M3 is an American answer to the cheap live and ten cent store European type submachine gun made extensively from metal stampings. It weighs about nine pounds and can be folded in a bundle less than a foot long by sliding in its extension stock and removing the barrel. It fires only full automatic and is designed to place great fire power in the hands of a great many troops. It was issued extensively to all of our Armed Forces and also considerable quantities were dropped via parachute into occupied areas for use by underground patriot movements, etc.

All United States submachine guns have been chambered for the .45 automatic pistol cartridge except the M3, which was also chambered for the 9 mm. Luger cartridge for dropping into countries where that load is more common than our .45 ACP.

A weapon intermediate between the pistol and the submachine gun is the United States carbine in several models, listed as the Ml and variations, and the M2. This was a cooperative development of the Winchester Repeating Arms Company and the United States Ordnance Department shortly before our entry into World War II. Its original form was a 15-shot semi-automatic weapon, gas-operated, with a bolt similar to that of the Garand rifle but with an intermediate gas piston action which is a basic Winchester development. It used a straight cased .30 caliber cartridge, muzzle velocity of about 2000 feet per second, 110 grain bullet. With a weight of less than five pounds, it was much shorter than the rifle. An M2 model was adopted in September, 1944, that fired either full or semiautomatic and used a 30-shot magazine. The carbine provides accurate fire up to about 300 yards. It was used by many special troops not commonly equipped with rifles, including officers up to the rank of Major, by direction, and was frequently seen in newsreels in the hands of officers of much higher rank.

The standard pistol of our armed forces since 1911 has been, and still is, the famous Colt .45 automatic. This is another invention of John Browning, developed by the Colt Company between 1900 and 1911 and adopted in that year. This is an 8-shot, powerful, compact pistol using a .45 caliber bullet with a striking force of over 300 foot pounds. To augment this pistol during the First World War, Colt and Smith & Wesson revolvers were chambered for the same cartridge, which was held in 3-shot clips for the revolvers. Many of these revolvers were still in use during World War II. They are designated as Model 1917 revolvers.

In addition, both Colt and Smith & Wesson revolvers, chambered for the .38 special cartridge, have been in extensive use during World War II by the Navy and Coast Guard and were standard issue for these branches of the Service. The cartridge supplied to them was a .38 Special revolver cartridge with a metal jacketed bullet which was also supplied in tracer type for signalling purposes. While this might seem to be a reversion to the old .38 caliber which was unsuccessful about the turn of the century, the present .38 caliber cartridge is a far more accurate, more powerful load than the one proved unsatisfactory at that time.

These are the weapons of our fighting forces, normally called Small Arms, which went with the Infantryman as he locked in hand to hand combat with the Japs and the Nazis.

## Weapons of Our Allies

The small arms of the rest of the world follow the same general trends reflected in those used by the United States.

Great Britain employed the famous Short Magazine Lee Enfield rifle, originally developed and adopted about 1890. This is a turning bolt rifle with a 10-shot charger loaded magazine and a very fast, smooth bolt action.

In line with the streamlining of equipment for production, a modification of the Pattern 14 Enfield was manufactured in this country for the British by the Savage Arms Company. It was listed as the rifle No. 4, Mark I. Simplified construction throughout for easy machine manufacture included such features as a simple spike bayonet with no handle as we know it, and two groove rifling instead of the original British five grooves.

In the light machine gun field, the principal British weapon is the famous Bren. This is a gas-operated, bipod mounted light machine gun, weighing about twenty pounds and feeding from an overhead box magazine inserted in the magazine holder in the top of the gun. It was used by the Infantry in the field and also in a light, mechanized vehicle designated as the Bren gun carrier.

The British also used a slightly different gun, listed as the Vickers Berthier, which, in common with the Bren, was developed from the original Czechoslovakian weapon of the middle 1920's. The Lewis machine gun, similar to those used in this country, except that it is chambered for the .303 British cartridge, was also in use in the various British services, both in the radiator fitted model and in the stripped down aircraft type. Multiple Lewis gun mounts, with as many as six or eight firing at once, were used in anti-aircraft work.

All British rifles and light machine guns are chambered for the standard .303 British cartridge which uses a flat based, pointed bullet with a muzzle velocity slightly less than a United States cartridge but otherwise generally similar to it, except that it is a rimmed cartridge instead of rimless and not as convenient for feeding in most types of automatic weapons.

It should be noted, by those who have either British guns or ammunition as souvenirs, that this cartridge bears no resemblance whatever to the .303 Savage cartridge as made in this country. This latter is a sporting cartridge very similar to the Winchester .30–30 and is about as far away from a military type as is the .30–30. It will not interchange with any military cartridge.

The British also, particularly in their commando units, were great users of the submachine gun, employing all models of the U. S. Tommy gun in the original .45 caliber and several British submachine guns designed on the five and ten cent store principal. Most of these guns were designed and manufactured for not much more than ten dollars and look like the results of a collaboration of Rube Goldberg and the late Mr. Woolworth. Commonest among them is the Sten submachine gun in several models or Marks, and also the Lanchester, all chambered for the 9 mm. Luger cartridge in its higher power loadings.

The British have never relied extensively on the pistol, always considering the side arm as very much a secondary weapon. The standard British pistol for many years was the .455 caliber Webley revolver. It used a .45 caliber bullet of 250 grains but of a very low velocity in comparison to American loadings.

A .455 Webley & Scott automatic pistol, issued to the British Navy at the time of the First World War, was a very square, awkward looking weapon, although excellently made. It was chambered for a .455 auto-pistol cartridge which is again weaker in power, although with about the same bullet, as our .45 ACP.

The standard British service pistol of World War II was the .380 pistol No. II Mark I. This was a tip-up hinged frame revolver similar to the Webley but chambered for a .380 or .38 caliber cartridge somewhat less in power than our .38 special, and far below anything we have used as a service cartridge since 1909. This cartridge uses a case exactly the same as our .38 Colt New Police or .38 Smith & Wesson revolver cartridge and different types of bullets, including a 172 and a 200 grain of low velocity. In addition, great quantities of both Colt and Smith & Wesson revolvers chambered for this cartridge were made in this country for sale to the British. Any of these weapons will also take the standard .38 Colt New Police or .38 S & W regular cartridges. They will not chamber a .38 short or long Colt, or .38 S&W Special.

Many American weapons of all types have been supplied to our Allies under lend-lease. After Dunkirk, hundreds of thousands of U. S. rifles Model 1917 and other small arms were sent to Great Britain. Newsreel shots of British soldiers often showed them equipped with these arms.

Among our other Allies, Russia has made great strides in weapons of all types since World War I. A number of models of the original Russian Moisin-Nagant turning bolt rifle, 7.62 mm. caliber, were in use during World War II. These included the original models (some made in the U. S. during World War I) and a number of modifications developed in the 1920s and '30s. In addition, Russia used three semiautomatic rifles. The first was the Simonov Model 1936, a gas operated rifle; some models were capable of full as well as semi-automatic fire from a 15-shot detachable magazine. The later and better semi-automatic rifles were the Tokarev, Models 1938 and 1940, both relatively similar to each other except for details and modifications. These guns tap their gas through ports in the top of the barrel to drive rearward an operating rod, which in turn sends back the bolt cover and unlocks the bolt by camming up its locking surface from engagement with an abutment that crosses the entire receiver. The action, although automatic, is very similar to the old hand operated Lee straight pull rifle and a very positive and excellent design.

The standard Russian light machine gun is the Dektyarov which weighs slightly over twenty pounds. It is a gas-operated weapon, fired from a bipod and shoulder stock and fed by a flat pan magazine of somewhat similar appearance to that of the Lewis gun.

All Russian rifle caliber weapons use the standard rimmed 7.62 Russian cartridge which has been loaded in this country for hunting purposes since unused stocks of Russian type rifles manufactured by American makers were sold in this country after the collapse of the Imperial Russian Government during World War I. The cartridge is an excellent hunting cartridge of a power comparable to our .30-'06.

The Russians used a number of types of submachine guns, including a modified Bergmann, known as the Fedorou, plus adaptations of the Finnish Suomi and captured German models. While the captured weapons and the Finnish gun are chambered for the 9 mm. Luger cartridge, truly Russian submachine guns are unique in that they are chambered for the 7.63 mm. Mauser pistol cartridge, which is most uncommon in submachine guns.

The latest Russian submachine gun, a "5 & 10c store" type, is similar to the U.S. M3 and the Sten. Listed as the Russian model 1942, it has a stock which folds upward over the barrel and a pistol grip and magazine holder which is used for a forward hand support.

The Russian hand gun of the First World War was a peculiar weapon known as the Nagant revolver. It has a cylinder which moves backward and forward to form a gas seal by inserting the cartridge case into the breech of the barrel at the time the gun is fired. It is of relatively small caliber (7.5 mm.) and low stopping power. This gun was also used in World War II to some extent, as were German Luger pistols and particularly the German Model of 1898, 7.63 mm. Mauser, which has been very popular in Russia for a number of years. Russia also used an automatic pistol, the Tokarev, designed by the Russian arms inventor of that name from the basic Browning Model 1911 type action. It had an outside hammer, locked breech, short recoil type, but was unusual in that this, like the standard Russian submachine gun, is chambered for the 7.63 mm. Mauser cartridge, and handles the cartridge very excellently in this strong type of locked breech action. The Tokarev pistol can be used with standard 7.63 mm. Mauser pistol cartridges as manufactured in the U.S.

Among our other Allies, the Dutch used a turning-bolt Mannlicher rifle in the 6.5 mm. caliber and the Danish-Madsen light machine gun. The Dutch also adopted, during World War II, the Johnson semi-automatic rifle and the Johnson light machine gun in U. S 30-'06 caliber, as described under United States weapons, to replace and augment their earlier arms. The standard Dutch side arm is a

Luger pistol, originally manufactured in England and chambered for the standard 9 mm. Luger cartridge.

French Infantry rifles of the earlier models include the 1886 tubular magazine, turning-bolt Lebel rifle and several models in use during the First World War, which were turning-bolt Lebel rifles of very much modified Mannlicher types but resembling a Mannlicher in that they took their cartridges in three or five shot clips which entered and became part of the action. All of these were chambered for the original 8 mm. Lebel cartridge, which has a rimmed case of relatively poor shape. An improvement in French ammunition for later type weapons occurred between 1925 and 1929, culminating in the 7.5 mm. rimless cartridge of modern type. This is used in two French rifles, the MAS and the Lebel Model 1934, and also in the latest French machine gun — the Chatellerault Model 1929, a weapon similar in general type to the Bren but using the unusual feature of two triggers, one for semi- and one for full automatic fire. Some few of the early Chauchat long recoil French automatic rifles of the First World War, chambered for the original 8 mm. Lebel cartridge, were also used in World War II, but this weapon is practically obsolete.

One French submachine gun, the Pistolet Mitrailleuse, Model 1938, was developed as of that date to take the 7.65 mm. long pistol cartridge. This was a simple blowback weapon with no special features of interest.

French pistols and revolvers are also relatively poor according to our standards. The 8 mm. Lebel revolver dates back to the 1890's and uses a metal jacketed bullet with a muzzle energy well below our small .38 caliber pocket revolver. The latest French sidearm is the MAS automatic pistol Model 1935A, chambered for a 7.65 mm. long cartridge. This has no duplicate in this country and is a relatively poor cartridge.

Another French automatic pistol which, although not officially used by the French government, has been manufactured there since 1928 is the Le Francais, chambered for the 9 mm. Browning long cartridge and consequently not useable with any ammunition available in this country. This is a peculiar double action weapon with a straight drive firing pin which is not cocked by the automatic action. The barrel breaks upward to load by releasing a catch at the right side above the trigger guard and it is not necessary to draw the slide back at any time. It is not a weapon that we would consider particularly desirable from American military standards.

Among the small nations, either fighting on our side or overrun by the Germans, the Belgians used a turning-bolt Mauser type rifle of 7.65 mm. caliber and standard Mauser characteristics. Belgium is, however, the seat of the famous Fabrique Nationale d'Armes de Guerre plant, manufacturers of Browning's automatic weapons and particularly automatic pistols. The earliest of the Browning military pistols is the Model 1903, 9 mm. Browning long, a straight blowback weapon, chambered for a cartridge that is not manufactured in this country and not interchangeable with any cartridge made here. It looks like an overgrown model of our .380 Colt, slightly longer but otherwise very similar. The Browning pistols, Model of 1910 and military Model of 1922, which is an enlargement of the 1910 pocket, are chambered for the 7.65 mm. and 9 mm. short or .380 pistol cartridges common in this country. These are straight blowback weapons characterized by a mainspring around the barrel and of hammerless design.

The latest of the Browning military pistols has been particularly popular throughout Europe and was extensively used by the Germans after their capture of the F. N. plant. This is the M1935 Browning pistol, chambered for the 9 mm. Luger cartridge — in appearance somewhat similar to our .45 Model of 1911. It uses, however, a simplified and modernized version of the locked breech action and a double column magazine holding 13 cartridges. It is also sometimes fitted with a shoulder stock.

Another Browning modification is found in the Radom pistol, manufactured at the Government Armory at Radom on the Vistula river in Poland for the Polish Army since 1935. This plant was also overrun by the Germans and the Radom is commonly found as manufactured for them there. It is chambered for the 9 mm. Luger cartridge and is of generally Browning locked breech characteristics somewhat simplified for modern production. It is an excellent weapon in the examples made by the Polish, but some very crude German manufactured models are encountered. The Polish also used a Mauser rifle of the standard German type.

The Czechoslovakians, the originators of the ZB gas-operated light machine gun which was widely copied throughout Europe and listed by the Germans as the Model 1926 gun, also used the Mauser type rifle in the standard German 7.92 mm. caliber, and have made three small military type pistols. The first, the Model of 1924, is a turning barrel, locked breech action chambered for the 9 mm. short or .380 automatic Colt pistol cartridge. The Model 1927 is similar to the Model 1924 except that it is chambered for the .32 cartridge and is a straight blowback. Both of these models have a small outside hammer and are of single action design. A model 1938, the latest of the Czech pistols, is very different from either of the others. It is one of the few pistols that uses a double action system entirely as the hammer follows the slide down and is not cocked by the automatic action. This is chambered for the .380 cartridge, is a straight blowback, but with an exceptionally strong retractor spring. These are all well made weapons in the models made by the Czechs. Rougher copies of them were turned out by the Germans during the latter part of the war.

## Weapons of the Axis

Of the arms of our enemies, those of Germany were, of course. the largest number which we encountered and also the most numerous to return to the United States as souvenirs and relics. Germany's standard Infantry rifle of the past 50 years or so has been the Gewehr '98, invented by Paul Mauser and commonly called the Mauser rifle. This is a turning-bolt, staggered column magazine repeater — the ancestor of most military rifles used in the world since the turn of the century, including our Model 1903 Springfield. The most common Mauser in use during World War II was a carbine model closely approximating the Springfield in general size and shape. Earlier, longer barrel models are also still met occasionally. This, in common with the other German rifle caliber small arms, uses the 7.92 or "8 mm." rifle cartridge described in the first part of this article. A simplified model was made after 1942 that is of very doubtful quality.

The standard Mauser was augmented during the war by four models of semi-automatic rifles which were developed and put into service as the war progressed. These were the Gewehr '41, '41M, '41W and '43. They were all gas operated rifles, three of which used a bolt with folding lugs similar to the Russian Dektyarov light machine gun. Gas was tapped either at the muzzle or, in the latest model, about three quarters of the way up the barrel to drive operating rods positioned on top of the barrel instead of below as in our Garand. These weapons, particularly those made in the latter part of the war, were very cheaply made of castings and stampings; some give evidences of not standing up very well. It is advisable to be careful of these weapons; they are not suitable for conversion to sporting arms as little change in the shape of the stock can be made on account of the gas system. They should not be altered to any other cartridge and should be tested and watched very carefully even with a German load before using them.

The Germans also used a number of special weapons of rifle or carbine size and weight which included the Fallschirmjaeger Gewehr '42, or paratroopers rifle — in effect a light machine gun with the unusual feature of semi-automatic fire with the bolt closed between shots. This was a very poorly constructed weapon weighing only a little over ten pounds-, which is very light for an arm of this type. It probably didn't stand up too well.

The Germans developed a cartridge as an answer to our carbine cartridge — the 7.92 short. It had a lighter bullet of the same diameter as their standard rifle cartridge but in a short, bottle-necked case. This was used in a machine carbine, capable of either full or semi-automatic fire. Manufactured from stamped parts, it was exceptionally well made for an arm of this type. It was listed as the machine pistol '43, or carbine '44. As it is a full or semi-automatic weapon, it falls into the machine pistol class, gas operated by a piston on the top of the barrel which seems to be a very popular arrangement in Germany.

Austrian and Hungarian troops were armed with the straight pull Mannlicher rifle of bolt action repeating type, using a rimmed 8 mm. cartridge and the breech system of Ferdinand Ritter Von Mannlicher, second in popularity only to that of Mauser among military rifles.

The German army was extensively supplied with submachine guns, ranging all the way from the original Bergmann Muskette up through the Neuhausen, Solothurn S1-100, Erma and a number of others, to the latest Schmeisser folding stock paratroopers submachine gun, Model of 1940. These follow the general pattern of submachine guns all over the world — for the most part simple blowback weapons weighing 8 or 10 pounds, cocked with the bolt open and utilizing the 9 mm. Luger pistol ammunition. There was one exception and that was the Steyr-Solothurn Sl-100, which is listed by the Germans as the Austrian Model 34 chambered for the 9 mm. Mauser pistol cartridge, which is much less common than the Luger.

The use of great quantities of storm troopers, secret police, SS Corps members, etc., gave rise to the need of enormous quantities of handguns by the German military establishment. The original German official pistol was the Luger Model 1908, which is a short recoil, locked breech automatic originally designed as the Borchardt by an American who came from Connecticut. German troops have always used, more or less unofficially, the Mauser Model of 1898, chambered for the original Mauser 7.63 pistol cartridge, relatively rarely for the Mauser 9 mm. pistol cartridge and more commonly for the Luger 9 mm. cartridge, as considerable quantities were made chambered in the latter load for the Prussian Army during World War I. Pistols chambered for 9 mm. Luger cartridges can always be identified by a large figure 9 cut into the grip and painted RED. Otherwise they will be smaller caliber, approximately .30, and chambered for the bottlenecked Mauser cartridge. A .35 caliber pistol, not marked 9 is chambered for the 9 mm. Mauser cartridge, which is very hard to obtain; it will not use the 9 mm. Luger cartridge satisfactorily.

Shortly before World War II, in 1938, the German Army adopted the Walther Model 1936 HP, or Heeres Pistole, meaning army pistol. This is designated officially by the Germans as the Pistole 38, and has been a very popular souvenir weapon. It is a well designed short recoil, locked breech action pistol, but has the very dangerous drawback that it can be assembled without its locking yoke in place and will fire that way at least once. It will not, however, do the firer or the pistol any good if it is so fired. This feature should be checked before the pistol is fired. It is chambered for the standard 9 mm. Luger cartridge, but its locking action is such that it is particularly dangerous to use the high velocity submachine gun loads in it — this should never be done.

In addition to these standard weapons, the Germans have used the Austrian pistols of World War I and later improvements, which include the Steyr Model 1911, an outside hammer, short recoil pistol, chambered for the 9 mm. Steyr cartridge (which is NOT the same as any of the other 9 mms.), and the Hungarian Model of 1937, a simple blowback pistol of small size made with an outside hammer and chambered for the 9 mm. Kurz or Colt .380 cartridge. This is an excellent little pistol and usually very well made.

The Czechoslovakian pistols in all three models were commonly found in use by the Germans, as was the Polish Radom after the capture of Poland. Weapons made in captured plants, under German supervision, particularly toward the latter part of the war, are all extremely crude and very roughly machined. Their material may also be questioned in some cases and it is advisable to be pretty careful of them.

In addition to standard military types, nearly all the pocket pistols in use in Europe for the last 30 odd years have been found with official German army marks on them and apparently were issued to all kinds of special troops, police, etc. Nearly all of these are chambered for one of three cartridges which are commonly available for this type of pistol. Those marked 9 mm. Kurz or 9 mm. Corto, are chambered for the .380 ACP cartridge. Those marked 7.65 mm. or 7.65 Browning, are chambered for .32 ACP, and those marked 6.35 mm. or 6.35 mm. Browning, are chambered for the .25 ACP. They range in types from simple blow-back to some curious and complicated locked breech systems. Many of them are good, some of them not so good; it is advisable to have an expert check them.

The universal light machine gun of the German army consists of a series of progressive models of what was originally the Dreyse MG 1913 of the First World War. These are all recoil operated, air-cooled light machine guns, weighing in the neighs borhood of 25 pounds, and normally fired from a bipod mount with a shoulder stock. They can also be attached to an elaborate tripod and fed with a belt for use as a light-heavy machine gun. The first improvement of the Dreyse, listed as the Dreyse-Solo-thurn Model of 1934, is one of the guns supposed to be manufactured in Switzerland but was actually made out of parts which were classed as "baby carriages" and other household items and made in Germany and shipped to Switzerland for assembly. This also uses a round radiator and a crutch-like shoulder stock with a bipod.

The next improved version of the Model 34 is similar in general appearance but different in a number of details, especially in that it uses a turning-bolt head instead of a turning barrel sleeve in its action.

The last version of this gun, the MG42, is made almost entirely of stampings and is notable for its extremely high cyclic rate of fire. The gun fires at a rate of nearly 1500 shots a minute and sounds like a ripping sheet as it goes off. This is higher than any other ground gun — higher than most military authorities consider practical. All these models are chambered for the standard German Infantry rifle cartridge.

Italy used a Mannlicher type, turning-bolt rifle of 6.5 mm. (.25) caliber which has the usual characteristics of these weapons. It is called the Mannlicher-Carcano and uses a rimless .25 caliber cartridge similar in general appearance to the Mannlicher-Schoenauer cartridge as manufactured in this country for sporting rifles, but different in a number of characteristics. As Italian rifles are not particularly well made, it would be extremely unsafe to use in them any ammunition manufactured in this country. They should be used only with Italian ammunition made for them; some of those that have come over here look as though they should not be used with any ammunition at all, as the workmanship is extremely poor and the materials are soft.

The most common Italian light machine gun was the Breda. This was made in several models and is a typical bipod mounted, shoulder stock, light machine gun with, however, some unusual features. It has a box magazine on the right hand side of the gun. The action is a combination of recoil and blowback which requires the use of greased ammunition. Some of these guns were made in the 6.5 caliber and some in a caliber similar to, 30-'06, listed as the 7.35 mm. Italian cartridge. There were some Italian rifles also chambered for this cartridge and they should by no means be used with any such cartridge as our .30-'06 even though the bore appears to be about the same size as they were not intended to stand pressures such as our ammunition develops.

The standard Italian submachinegun was the 9 mm. Beretta Model of 1938, a blowback gun, fed from a box magazine inserted from the bottom. One uncommon feature of this machine gun is the bayonet which is fitted to it for close fighting. It also uses the system of two triggers, one for semi- and one for full automatic fire. This is one of the better made Italian weapons. It uses the Italian 9 mm. Luger type cartridge, but with the Italian loading of lower power.

The Italian handgun of the First World War, the Glisenti, looks somewhat like the Luger but is entirely different from it in action. It is a short recoil action with a breechblock of relatively weak application of what is sometimes called the "prop up" locking system. The Italian variation is so pivoted that it is really only a rotating wedge and the pistol might almost be classed as a straight blowback. While the cartridge is the same case size as the 9 mm. Luger, Italian loadings are at least 25% lighter in power and pressure, so the Glisenti pistol should not be fired with anything except Italian ammunition. In fact, this is another one of the weapons that it is better not to fire at all, although it has an interesting automatic action and is a very desirable relic for design study.

This pistol was augmented in World War II by the Beretta pistol Model of 1934, adopted by the Italian army in that year. This is a pocket size, straight blowback with an outside hammer, chambered for the 9 mm. Corto or .380 pistol cartridge and is excellently designed for this cartridge. Beretta's arms are all much better made than most other Italian weapons; Beretta pistols, made up to the last year or two of the Italian participation in the war, are of excellent workmanship. The last production was relatively poorer in finish but still good in design. This pistol was also chambered for the 7.65 mm. or .32 ACP cartridge and. issued in this caliber for military purposes. Some of them were supplied to the German army by the Italian makers before the surrender of Italy.

Japanese infantry weapons have been publicized as being of very small caliber and, consequently, of extremely low power. The Arisaka rifle, year '38, is to. all intents and purposes a model 1907 Mauser with the exception of a very clever light metal action cover which travels back and forth with the bolt and keeps dirt and sand out of the action when the bolt is closed. The caliber is 6.5 mm. or .25 caliber; actually, the cartridge is on paper only about 10% less effective than our standard .30-'06 ammunition. The weight of the bullet is 139 grains, velocity 2500 feet per second. It is by no means the next thing to a shooting gallery .22, as frequent news accounts implied. It is apparent, however, that the Japanese did not entirely trust the power of a .25 caliber cartridge as they changed in 1939 to a 7.7 cartridge very similar to the British .303; as they were at that time at war with China, such a change in the middle of hostilities indicates serious doubts as to the quality of ammunition then in use. However, they continued to use .25 caliber as well, for our troops ran into rifles and light machine guns chambered for it all during the war.

The Japanese Ordnance must have been a very complicated business and owners of Japanese souvenirs will find themselves in nearly as much trouble as Japanese Ordnance men on account of the bewildering variations in Japanese ammunition. In addition to the rifles, the Japanese used several machine guns of rifle caliber. These were the 1922 hopper fed Nambu, a light bipod mounted gun in .25 caliber, the 1936 Type 96, a top magazine light bipod mounted gun somewhat similar to the Bren, in .25 caliber, and the 7.7 caliber version of it listed as the type 99 or 1939. Japanese rifles are of very poor quality and workmanship — they should be considered as *relics only!*

The Japanese rifle chambered for the 7.7 cartridge is also listed as the model 1939 rifle. To complicate matters further, rifles and machine guns did not take the same type of ammunition in all cases. In the 6.5 there was a full charge load for rifles and the old fashioned heavy machine guns, and a reduced charge load for the Nambu Model 1922 gun and the 1936, Type 96 gun. This could also be used in the rifles but rifle type ammunition would probably jam in the machine guns. In the 7.7 caliber there were three different types of cartridges, rimmed, semi-rimmed and rimless. Rimmed cartridges were used only in aircraft guns, the semi-rimmed in heavy machine guns of the Hotchkiss type and the rimless in Model 1939 rifles and machine guns.

The Japanese also are the only ones who departed from the standard bullet markings for AP, tracer, etc. Their markings are very light lacquered bands at the mouth of the case: pink for ball ammunition, green for tracer and black for AP.

Japan designed no sub-machine guns of her own, but did develop three automatic pistols which are definitely of native design. The first of these, the Model of 1914 Nambu invented by General Kijiru Nambu, looks like the Luger but with a locked breech, short recoil prop-up action more closely resembles the Mauser. It is distinguishable by a recoil spring on the left hand side of the frame only. The next model is a modification listed as the Model 1925 and distinguishable by two recoil springs, one on each side of the bolt. The third pistol is an entirely different one, the Type 94. It uses a slide and spring around the barrel and pivoted inside hammer.

All three pistols are chambered for the 8 mm. Nambu pistol cartridge, a bottlenecked rimless cartridge similar in appearance to 7.65 mm. Luger but by no means the same. *NO* Japanese pistol should be fired with any other cartridge as, particularly in the case of the Model 94, the action is not strong enough to handle cartridges of American or European type for the workmanship is relatively poor.

These are the Infantry weapons with which World War II has been fought by the United States, their Allies and their enemies. The trend has been toward better automatic and semi-automatic weapons and a great many more of them. The firepower of the average Infantry Battalion has increased in the last 25 years by geometric rather than arithmetic progression, and this trend may well be reflected in sporting arms over the next few years. The First World War changed the hunting arms in this country from the lever action to the bolt action, and while the manufacturers are not yet in a position to announce any quantity of new designs, it is probable that some new sporting automatics will appear on the market as the result of World War II.

# MILITARY SMALL ARMS-PISTOLS ¼ ACTUAL SIZE

**COLT PISTOL**
**U. S. M11**
Caliber: 45 A.C.P.
Length: 8½"
Shots: 7
Weight: 39 oz.
Action: Short Recoil — Semi Auto
UNITED STATES — BRITISH EMPIRE

A1

**WEBLEY PISTOL**
**M 1913**
Caliber: 455
Length: 8½"
Shots: 7
Weight: 36 oz.
Action: Short Recoil — Semi Auto
BRITISH NAVY

**TOKAREV PISTOL**
Caliber: 7.62 MM
Length: 7¾"
Shots: 8
Weight: 30 oz.
Action: Short Recoil — Semi Auto
RUSSIA

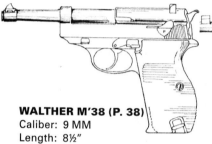

**WALTHER M'38 (P. 38)**
Caliber: 9 MM
Length: 8½"
Shots: 8
Weight: 34 oz.
Action: Short Recoil — Semi Auto
GERMANY

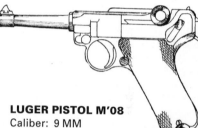

**MAUSER PISTOL M'98**
Caliber: 7.63 MM
Length: 12"
Shots: 10
Weight: 45 oz.
Action: Short Recoil — Semi Auto
GERMANY — RUSSIA, ETC.

**LUGER PISTOL M'08**
Caliber: 9 MM
Length: 8¾"
Shots: 7
Weight: 30 oz.
Action: Short Recoil — Semi Auto
GERMANY, ETC

**F. N. BROWNING**
**M 1935**
Caliber: 9 MM
Length: 7¾"
Shots: 10-15
Weight: 32 oz,
Action: Short Recoil — Semi Auto
BELGIUM — FRANCE
GERMANY

**PISTOL M'35 A**
Caliber: 7.65MM Long
Length: 7½"
Shots: 8
Weight: 26 oz.
Action: Short Recoil — Semi Auto
FRANCE

**STAR PISTOL**
Caliber: 7.65 MM
Length: 7¼"
Shots 7
Weight:
Action: Blowback — Semi Auto
FRANCE

**GLISENTI PISTOL M'10**
Caliber: 9 MM
Length: 8¼"
Shots: 7
Weight: 32 oz,
Action: Short Recoil — Semi Auto
ITALY

**BERETTA PISTOL M'34**
Caliber: 9 MM Corto
Length: 6"
Shots: 7
Weight: 23½ oz.
Action: Blowback — Semi Auto
ITALY

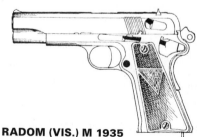

**RADOM (VIS.) M 1935**
Caliber: 9 MM
Length: 8"
Shots: 8
Weight: 36 oz.
Action: Short Recoil — Semi Auto
POLAND — GERMANY

# MILITARY PISTOLS and REVOLVERS ¼ ACTUAL SIZE

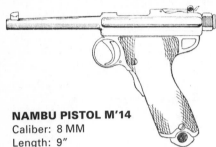

**NAMBU PISTOL M'14**
Caliber: 8 MM
Length: 9"
Shots: 8
Weight: 31 oz.
Action: Short Recoil — Semi Auto
JAPAN

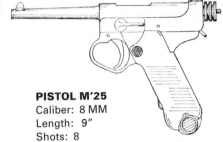

**PISTOL M'25**
Caliber: 8 MM
Length: 9"
Shots: 8
Weight: 32 oz.
Action: Short Recoil — Semi Auto
JAPAN

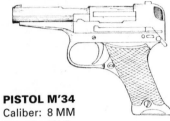

**PISTOL M'34**
Caliber: 8 MM
Length: 6⅝"
Shots: 6
Weight: 27 oz.
Action: Short Recoil — Semi Auto
JAPAN

**ZECH M 1938**
Cal.: 9mmShort(380)
Length: 7⅝"
Shots: 8
Weight: 32 oz.
Action: Blowback — Semi Auto
CZECHOSLOVAKIA — GERMANY

**STEYR PISTOL M'11**
Caliber: 9 MM
Length: 8½"
Shots: 8
Weight: 38½ oz.
Action: Short Recoil — Semi Auto
AUSTRIA

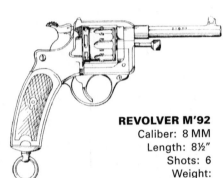

**REVOLVER M'92**
Caliber: 8 MM
Length: 8½"
Shots: 6
Weight:
Action: Double Action Revolver
FRANCE

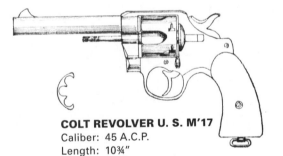

**COLT REVOLVER U. S. M'17**
Caliber: 45 A.C.P.
Length: 10¾"
Shots: 6
Weight: 40 oz.
Action: ouble Action Revolver
UNITED STATES

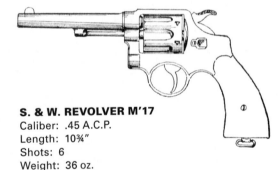

**S. & W. REVOLVER M'17**
Caliber: .45 A.C.P.
Length: 10¾"
Shots: 6
Weight: 36 oz.
Action: Double Action Revolver
UNITED STATES

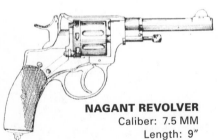

**NAGANT REVOLVER**
Caliber: 7.5 MM
Length: 9"
Shots: 7
Weight: 28 oz,
Action: Double Action Revolver
RUSSIA

**ENFIELD NO. 2 MK 1**
Caliber: 380
Length: 9½"
Shots: 6
Weight: 27½ OZ.
Action: Double Action Revolver
BRITISH EMPIRE

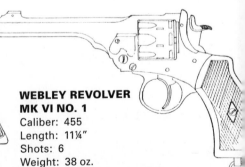

**WEBLEY REVOLVER MK VI NO. 1**
Caliber: 455
Length: 11¼"
Shots: 6
Weight: 38 oz.
Action: Double Action Revolver
BRITISH EMPIRE

# MILITARY SMALL ARMS-RIFLES ⅛ ACTUAL SIZE

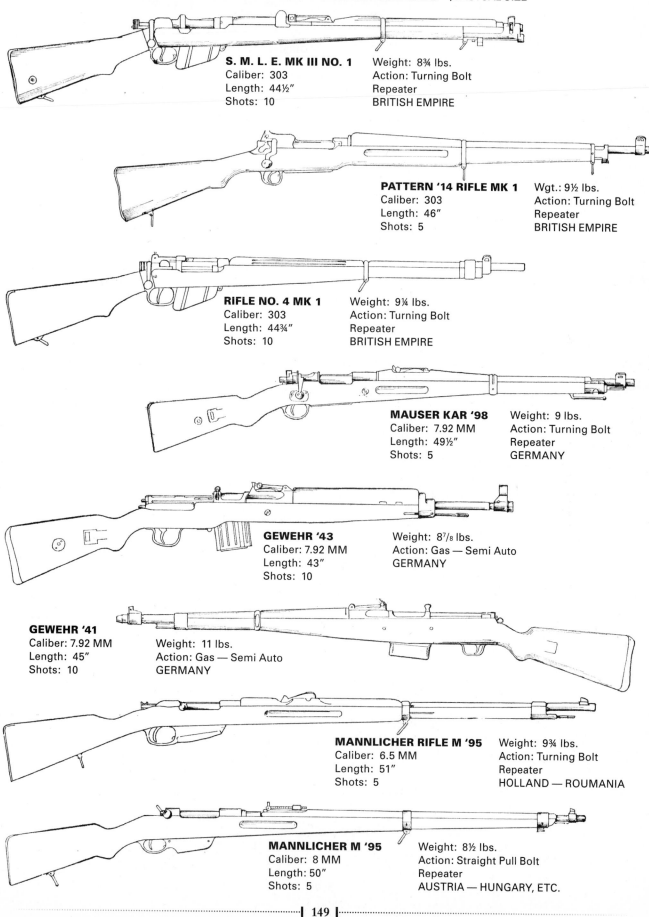

**S. M. L. E. MK III NO. 1**
Caliber: 303
Length: 44½"
Shots: 10

Weight: 8¾ lbs.
Action: Turning Bolt
Repeater
BRITISH EMPIRE

**PATTERN '14 RIFLE MK 1**
Caliber: 303
Length: 46"
Shots: 5

Wgt.: 9½ lbs.
Action: Turning Bolt
Repeater
BRITISH EMPIRE

**RIFLE NO. 4 MK 1**
Caliber: 303
Length: 44¾"
Shots: 10

Weight: 9¼ lbs.
Action: Turning Bolt
Repeater
BRITISH EMPIRE

**MAUSER KAR '98**
Caliber: 7.92 MM
Length: 49½"
Shots: 5

Weight: 9 lbs.
Action: Turning Bolt
Repeater
GERMANY

**GEWEHR '43**
Caliber: 7.92 MM
Length: 43"
Shots: 10

Weight: 8⅞ lbs.
Action: Gas — Semi Auto
GERMANY

**GEWEHR '41**
Caliber: 7.92 MM
Length: 45"
Shots: 10

Weight: 11 lbs.
Action: Gas — Semi Auto
GERMANY

**MANNLICHER RIFLE M '95**
Caliber: 6.5 MM
Length: 51"
Shots: 5

Weight: 9¾ lbs.
Action: Turning Bolt
Repeater
HOLLAND — ROUMANIA

**MANNLICHER M '95**
Caliber: 8 MM
Length: 50"
Shots: 5

Weight: 8½ lbs.
Action: Straight Pull Bolt
Repeater
AUSTRIA — HUNGARY, ETC.

# MILITARY SMALL ARMS-RIFLES ⅛ ACTUAL SIZE

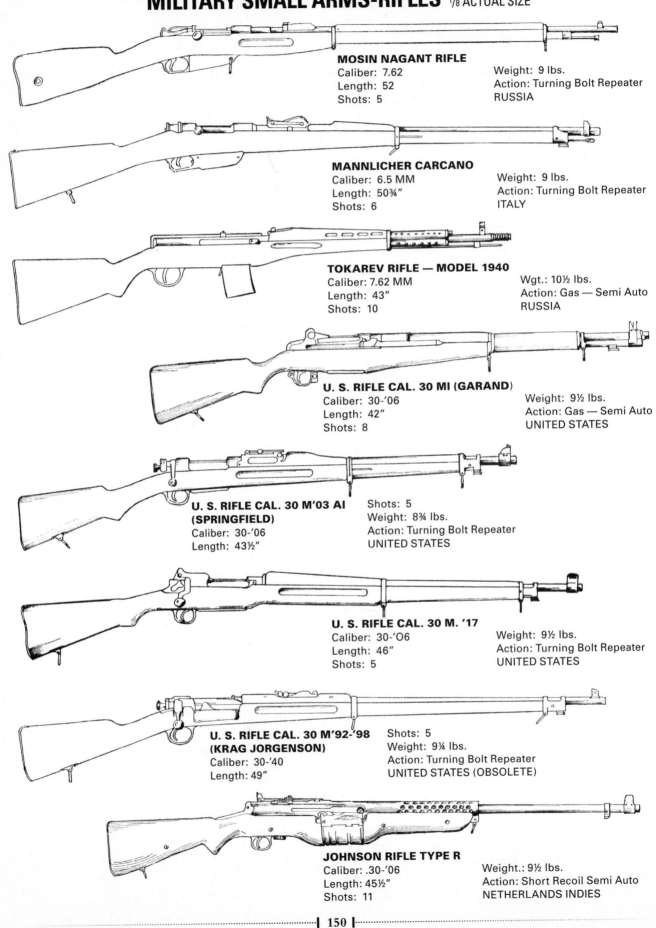

**MOSIN NAGANT RIFLE**
Caliber: 7.62
Length: 52
Shots: 5

Weight: 9 lbs.
Action: Turning Bolt Repeater
RUSSIA

**MANNLICHER CARCANO**
Caliber: 6.5 MM
Length: 50¾"
Shots: 6

Weight: 9 lbs.
Action: Turning Bolt Repeater
ITALY

**TOKAREV RIFLE — MODEL 1940**
Caliber: 7.62 MM
Length: 43"
Shots: 10

Wgt.: 10½ lbs.
Action: Gas — Semi Auto
RUSSIA

**U. S. RIFLE CAL. 30 MI (GARAND)**
Caliber: 30-'06
Length: 42"
Shots: 8

Weight: 9½ lbs.
Action: Gas — Semi Auto
UNITED STATES

**U. S. RIFLE CAL. 30 M'03 AI (SPRINGFIELD)**
Caliber: 30-'06
Length: 43½"

Shots: 5
Weight: 8¾ lbs.
Action: Turning Bolt Repeater
UNITED STATES

**U. S. RIFLE CAL. 30 M. '17**
Caliber: 30-'O6
Length: 46"
Shots: 5

Weight: 9½ lbs.
Action: Turning Bolt Repeater
UNITED STATES

**U. S. RIFLE CAL. 30 M'92-'98 (KRAG JORGENSON)**
Caliber: 30-'40
Length: 49"

Shots: 5
Weight: 9¼ lbs.
Action: Turning Bolt Repeater
UNITED STATES (OBSOLETE)

**JOHNSON RIFLE TYPE R**
Caliber: .30-'06
Length: 45½"
Shots: 11

Weight.: 9½ lbs.
Action: Short Recoil Semi Auto
NETHERLANDS INDIES

# MILITARY RIFLES and CARBINES ⅛ ACTUAL SIZE

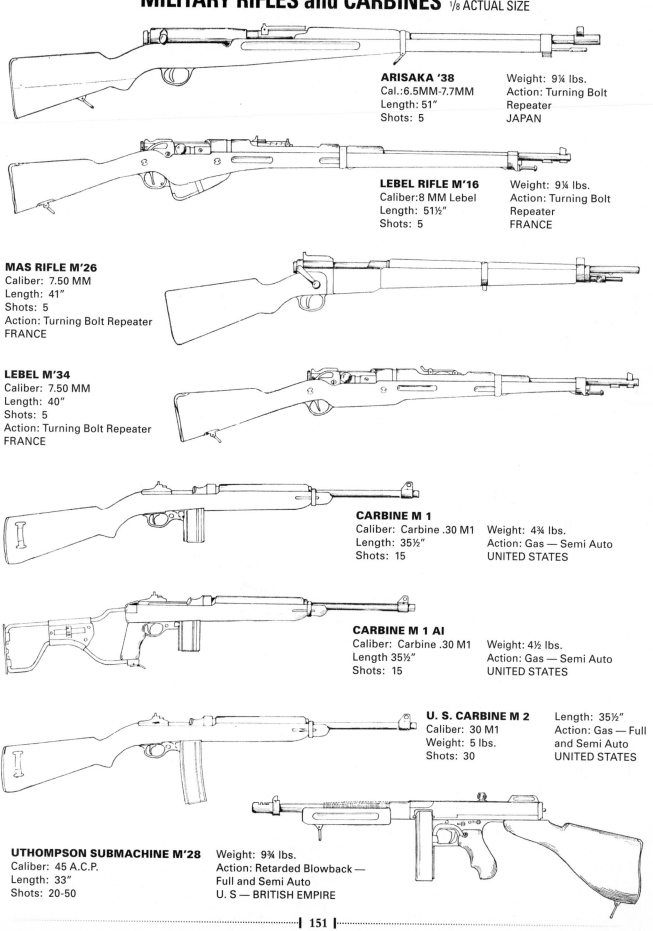

**ARISAKA '38**
Cal.:6.5MM-7.7MM
Length: 51"
Shots: 5

Weight: 9¼ lbs.
Action: Turning Bolt
Repeater
JAPAN

**LEBEL RIFLE M'16**
Caliber:8 MM Lebel
Length: 51½"
Shots: 5

Weight: 9¼ lbs.
Action: Turning Bolt
Repeater
FRANCE

**MAS RIFLE M'26**
Caliber: 7.50 MM
Length: 41"
Shots: 5
Action: Turning Bolt Repeater
FRANCE

**LEBEL M'34**
Caliber: 7.50 MM
Length: 40"
Shots: 5
Action: Turning Bolt Repeater
FRANCE

**CARBINE M 1**
Caliber: Carbine .30 M1
Length: 35½"
Shots: 15

Weight: 4¾ lbs.
Action: Gas — Semi Auto
UNITED STATES

**CARBINE M 1 AI**
Caliber: Carbine .30 M1
Length 35½"
Shots: 15

Weight: 4½ lbs.
Action: Gas — Semi Auto
UNITED STATES

**U. S. CARBINE M 2**
Caliber: 30 M1
Weight: 5 lbs.
Shots: 30

Length: 35½"
Action: Gas — Full
and Semi Auto
UNITED STATES

**UTHOMPSON SUBMACHINE M'28**
Caliber: 45 A.C.P.
Length: 33"
Shots: 20-50

Weight: 9¾ lbs.
Action: Retarded Blowback —
Full and Semi Auto
U. S — BRITISH EMPIRE

# AMERICAN and ENGLISH SUBMACHINE GUNS ⅛ ACTUAL SIZE

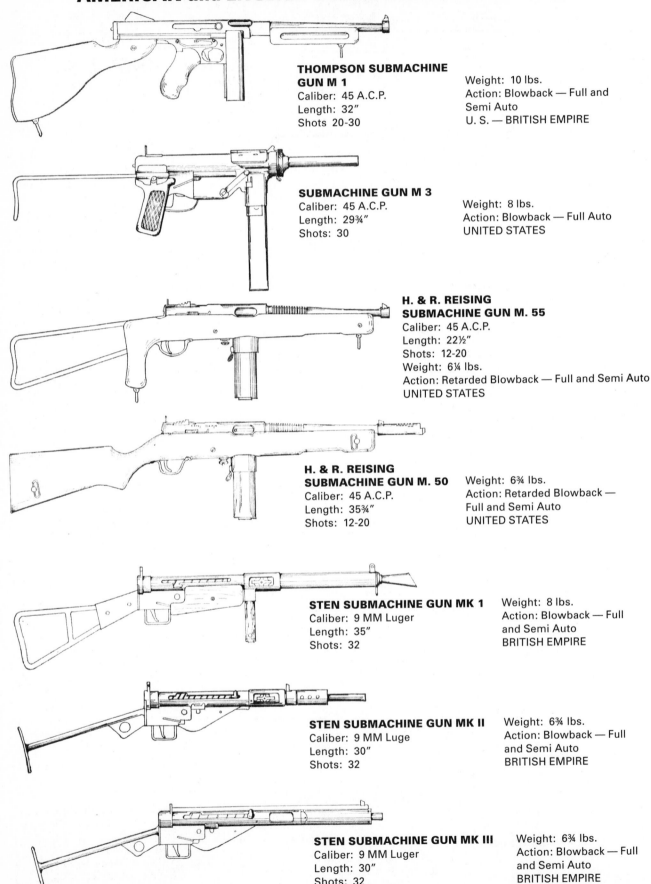

**THOMPSON SUBMACHINE GUN M 1**
Caliber: 45 A.C.P.
Length: 32"
Shots 20-30

Weight: 10 lbs.
Action: Blowback — Full and Semi Auto
U. S. — BRITISH EMPIRE

**SUBMACHINE GUN M 3**
Caliber: 45 A.C.P.
Length: 29¾"
Shots: 30

Weight: 8 lbs.
Action: Blowback — Full Auto
UNITED STATES

**H. & R. REISING SUBMACHINE GUN M. 55**
Caliber: 45 A.C.P.
Length: 22½"
Shots: 12-20
Weight: 6¼ lbs.
Action: Retarded Blowback — Full and Semi Auto
UNITED STATES

**H. & R. REISING SUBMACHINE GUN M. 50**
Caliber: 45 A.C.P.
Length: 35¾"
Shots: 12-20

Weight: 6¾ lbs.
Action: Retarded Blowback — Full and Semi Auto
UNITED STATES

**STEN SUBMACHINE GUN MK 1**
Caliber: 9 MM Luger
Length: 35"
Shots: 32

Weight: 8 lbs.
Action: Blowback — Full and Semi Auto
BRITISH EMPIRE

**STEN SUBMACHINE GUN MK II**
Caliber: 9 MM Luge
Length: 30"
Shots: 32

Weight: 6¾ lbs.
Action: Blowback — Full and Semi Auto
BRITISH EMPIRE

**STEN SUBMACHINE GUN MK III**
Caliber: 9 MM Luger
Length: 30"
Shots: 32

Weight: 6¾ lbs.
Action: Blowback — Full and Semi Auto
BRITISH EMPIRE

# GERMAN SUBMACHINE GUNS ⅛ ACTUAL SIZE

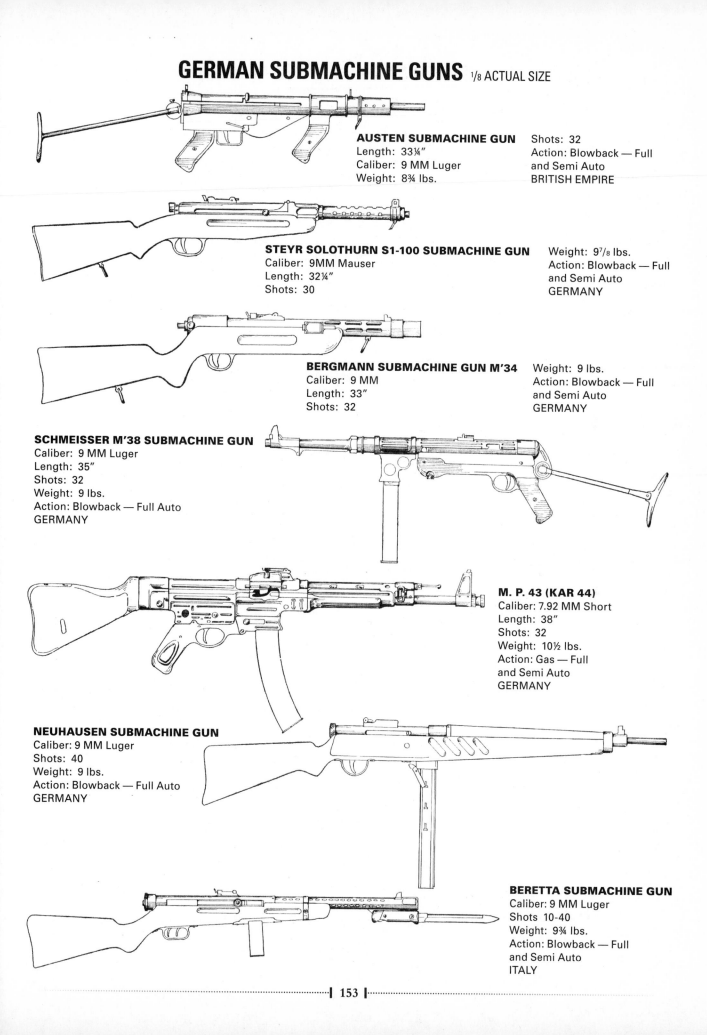

**AUSTEN SUBMACHINE GUN**
Length: 33¼"
Caliber: 9 MM Luger
Weight: 8¾ lbs.
Shots: 32
Action: Blowback — Full
and Semi Auto
BRITISH EMPIRE

**STEYR SOLOTHURN S1-100 SUBMACHINE GUN**
Caliber: 9MM Mauser
Length: 32¼"
Shots: 30
Weight: 9⅞ lbs.
Action: Blowback — Full
and Semi Auto
GERMANY

**BERGMANN SUBMACHINE GUN M'34**
Caliber: 9 MM
Length: 33"
Shots: 32
Weight: 9 lbs.
Action: Blowback — Full
and Semi Auto
GERMANY

**SCHMEISSER M'38 SUBMACHINE GUN**
Caliber: 9 MM Luger
Length: 35"
Shots: 32
Weight: 9 lbs.
Action: Blowback — Full Auto
GERMANY

**M. P. 43 (KAR 44)**
Caliber: 7.92 MM Short
Length: 38"
Shots: 32
Weight: 10½ lbs.
Action: Gas — Full
and Semi Auto
GERMANY

**NEUHAUSEN SUBMACHINE GUN**
Caliber: 9 MM Luger
Shots: 40
Weight: 9 lbs.
Action: Blowback — Full Auto
GERMANY

**BERETTA SUBMACHINE GUN**
Caliber: 9 MM Luger
Shots 10-40
Weight: 9¾ lbs.
Action: Blowback — Full
and Semi Auto
ITALY

# LIGHT MACHINE GUNS  1/8 ACTUAL SIZE

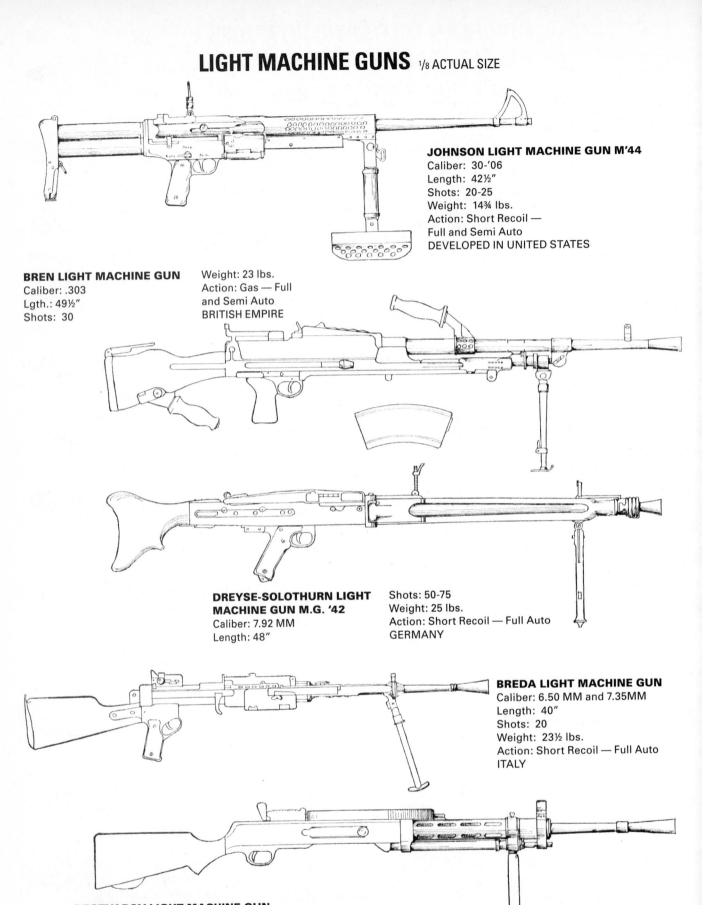

**JOHNSON LIGHT MACHINE GUN M'44**
Caliber: 30-'06
Length: 42½"
Shots: 20-25
Weight: 14¾ lbs.
Action: Short Recoil —
Full and Semi Auto
DEVELOPED IN UNITED STATES

**BREN LIGHT MACHINE GUN**
Caliber: .303
Lgth.: 49½"
Shots: 30

Weight: 23 lbs.
Action: Gas — Full
and Semi Auto
BRITISH EMPIRE

**DREYSE-SOLOTHURN LIGHT
MACHINE GUN M.G. '42**
Caliber: 7.92 MM
Length: 48"

Shots: 50-75
Weight: 25 lbs.
Action: Short Recoil — Full Auto
GERMANY

**BREDA LIGHT MACHINE GUN**
Caliber: 6.50 MM and 7.35MM
Length: 40"
Shots: 20
Weight: 23½ lbs.
Action: Short Recoil — Full Auto
ITALY

**DEGTYAROV LIGHT MACHINE GUN**
Caliber: 7.62 MM
Length: 50"
Shots: 47

Weight: 18½ lbs.
Action: Gas — Full Auto
RUSSIA

# EUROPEAN MILITARY CARTRIDGES ACTUAL SIZE

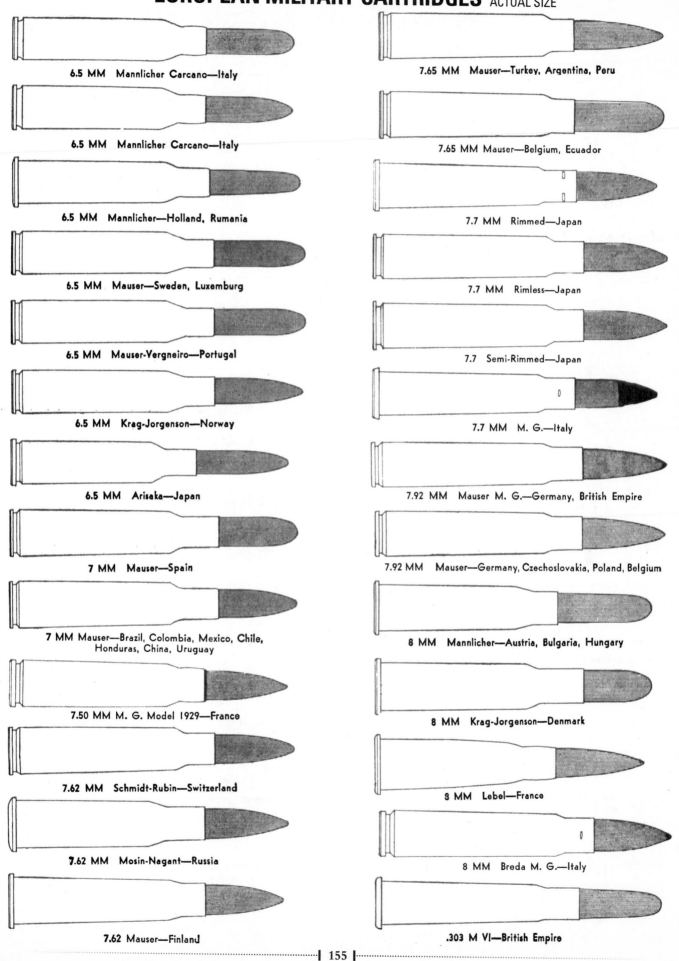

6.5 MM   Mannlicher Carcano—Italy

6.5 MM   Mannlicher Carcano—Italy

6.5 MM   Mannlicher—Holland, Rumania

6.5 MM   Mauser—Sweden, Luxemburg

6.5 MM   Mauser-Vergneiro—Portugal

6.5 MM   Krag-Jorgenson—Norway

6.5 MM   Arisaka—Japan

7 MM   Mauser—Spain

7 MM Mauser—Brazil, Colombia, Mexico, Chile,
Honduras, China, Uruguay

7.50 MM M. G. Model 1929—France

7.62 MM   Schmidt-Rubin—Switzerland

7.62 MM   Mosin-Nagant—Russia

7.62 Mauser—Finland

7.65 MM   Mauser—Turkey, Argentina, Peru

7.65 MM Mauser—Belgium, Ecuador

7.7 MM   Rimmed—Japan

7.7 MM   Rimless—Japan

7.7   Semi-Rimmed—Japan

7.7 MM   M. G.—Italy

7.92 MM   Mauser M. G.—Germany, British Empire

7.92 MM   Mauser—Germany, Czechoslovakia, Poland, Belgium

8 MM   Mannlicher—Austria, Bulgaria, Hungary

8 MM   Krag-Jorgenson—Denmark

8 MM   Lebel—France

8 MM   Breda M. G.—Italy

.303 M VI—British Empire

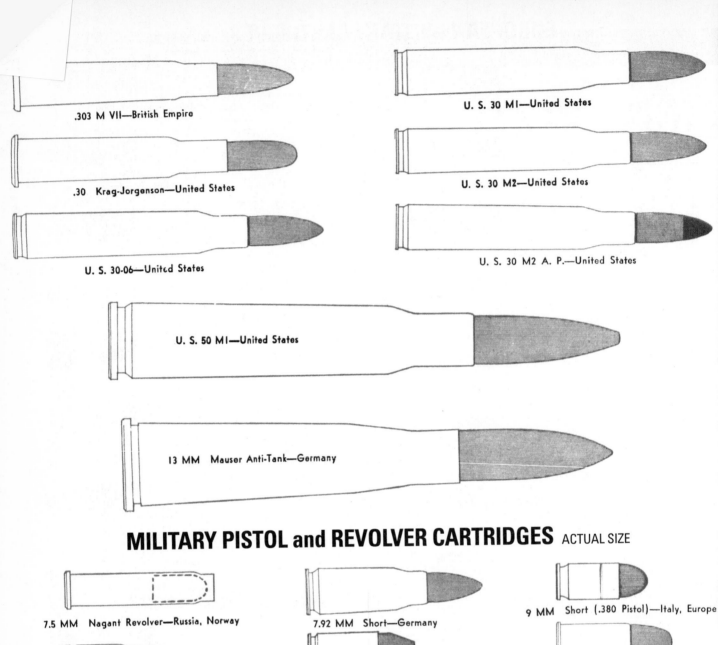

.303 M VII—British Empire

.30 Krag-Jorgenson—United States

U. S. 30-06—United States

U. S. 30 MI—United States

U. S. 30 M2—United States

U. S. 30 M2 A. P.—United States

U. S. 50 MI—United States

13 MM   Mauser Anti-Tank—Germany

# MILITARY PISTOL and REVOLVER CARTRIDGES ACTUAL SIZE

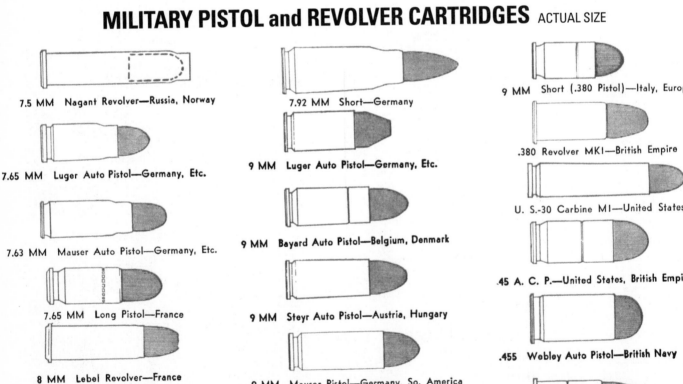

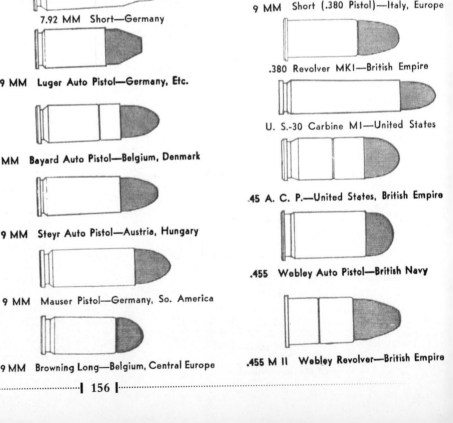

7.5 MM   Nagant Revolver—Russia, Norway

7.65 MM   Luger Auto Pistol—Germany, Etc.

7.63 MM   Mauser Auto Pistol—Germany, Etc.

7.65 MM   Long Pistol—France

8 MM   Lebel Revolver—France

8 MM   Nambu Auto Pistol—Japan

7.92 MM   Short—Germany

9 MM   Luger Auto Pistol—Germany, Etc.

9 MM   Bayard Auto Pistol—Belgium, Denmark

9 MM   Steyr Auto Pistol—Austria, Hungary

9 MM   Mauser Pistol—Germany, So. America

9 MM   Browning Long—Belgium, Central Europe

9 MM   Short (.380 Pistol)—Italy, Europe

.380   Revolver MKI—British Empire

U. S.-30 Carbine MI—United States

.45 A. C. P.—United States, British Empire

.455   Webley Auto Pistol—British Navy

.455 M II   Webley Revolver—British Empire

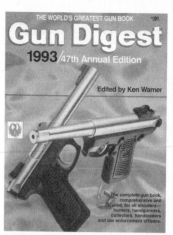

# The 30 Carbine

...smaller than some, but big enough most... ∎ David L. Ward

THE 30 M-1 Carbine has been around now for some fifty years. During that time, it has been called any number of nasty things from worthless to impotent. Other diatribes are simply unprintable here. But if the carbine was so utterly useless and totally disliked, why were so many made (in excess of six million — more than any other weapon in WWII) and why has it seen so much use in combat? And most of all, why is it still so popular even in this day of the more sophisticated and more powerful assault rifle?

The answers to those questions lie in plain view for those who wish to look. The M-l Carbine performs very well indeed within the parameters for which it was designed. That's the key. It was designed as a light shoulder weapon to replace the 45 ACP and the submachine gun. At distances inside one hundred yards, it handles that task admirably. It is more powerful and more accurate than the 45. Now before you choke on that, look at the energy figures. From an 18-inch barrel, the 30 Carbine musters more than 1950 fps and 900 foot pounds of energy; the 45 manages a little more than 500 fpe, even if you give it 1000 fps from the Thompson SMG.

There's no contest in the accuracy department, either. My IBM Carbine, manufactured in September of 1943, keeps Military Specifications Ball in six to eight inches at 100 yards with iron sights. Try and match that with your issue 45 pistol or Tommy gun.

It is important to keep the M-1 Carbine in perspective. If you wish to compare it to the M-1 Garand or any semiautomatic rifle, assault or otherwise, it fails miserably. It's underpowered and relatively inaccurate, shooting too light a bullet. And that, I suspect, is most of the problem with the carbine for those who used (or maybe never used) it. It started out on the wrong foot, or they did.

Could it be possible that the U.S. Ordnance

Author and target shot at 50 yards with 1943 IBM Carbine and 110-grain Hornady SP in front of 14.8 grains of IMR 4227. Rifle was capable of respectable accuracy with the right loads.

Department did not provide an adequate explanation of the exact purpose of the carbine for the grunt in the field? I know an inadequate explanation of any topic by our government is hard to fathom, but it could be true. In which case, we begin to see the reason no one could understand why he was issued such a puny toy instead of a Garand. The carbine was never intended to shoot targets at two hundred or three hundred yards, a distance at which many were used, especially in Korea. However, in the up-close-and-personal arena, it offered a lot of controllable firepower and performed as well or better than anything else. Men who fought with them in such a manner generally agree with that statement.

The whole concept that finally emerged as the 30 M-1 Carbine for the U.S. military began after WWI. In the 1920s, both the United States and Germany concluded independently that their main battle cartridges were overly powerful for most combat conditions. The majority of infantry fire-fights occurred at less than two hundred yards, usually much less. A smaller, less powerful round would offer numerous advantages in weight, cost, and accuracy during rapid-fire and still give adequate killing power in most military situations.

Two possible avenues for development were considered at the time: Increase the power of the submachine gun round to lengthen its useful range or shorten the main battle cartridge and chamber it in a smaller automatic rifle. The Germans opted for the latter and by 1934 had a prototype cartridge based on their full-sized 8mm, but with a case only 33mm long. It delivered a 125-grain bullet at 2247 fps from a 16-inch barrel. Called the 7.92 Kurz, it and the rifle that chambered it were the forerunners of all modern assault weapons. The U.S., meanwhile, opted to do nothing because of the logistics and cost of replacing its whole inventory of shoulder weapons. "Use up what we got" — that's what I always say. Progressive thinking.

By 1940, the idea was resurrected in the U.S. However, the Ordnance Department decided to take a step in the direction of a more powerful pistol cartridge to fit into a lightweight carbine rather than drop the recently developed M-1 Garand. What they got is better than the issue pistol and SMG, while smaller and easier to shoot than the full-sized rifle. Looking at how things developed, this probably was the wrong choice, but not necessarily a *bad* choice. The Germans' work on their 7.92 Kurz was kept secret, especially from

(Right) Loads for the 30 Carbine: Left to right—Mil. Spec. Ball, Speer 100-grain Plinker, Hornady 110-grain SP, Speer 110-grain HP and Sierra 110-grain HP.

(Left) Standard U.S. WWI small arms cartridges and those that were conceived later. Left to right: 30-06, 45 ACP, 30 Carbine, 7.62 NATO and 5.56 NATO.

those who signed the Treaty of Versailles, so the U.S. Ordnance Department was pretty much on its own in the development stages.

Designs were submitted by a number of companies, but the short piston, locked-bolt prototype from Winchester won out and became the Caliber 30 M-1 Carbine as we know it. Winchester based the new cartridge on the obsolete 32 Self-Loading, a nearly worthless semi-rimmed round that sent a 165-grain slug out the barrel at a modest 1450 fps. The bullet was lightened to 100 grains, the pressure bumped, and the velocity consequently increased to 1970 fps from the new rimless case in an 18-inch barrel, a substantial boost in horsepower. The 30 Carbine case measures 32.77mm in length, almost the same as the Kurz, but the smaller diameter and smaller powder capacity force it to give up 300 fps to the German cartridge.

When I asked veterans from WWII or Korea about the performance of the M-1 Carbine in combat, their answers were both interesting and quite similar. Inevitably, the first words out were something like "not worth much" or "didn't kill very well" or, for Korea, "it jammed a lot." But the more they talked, the more they mentioned that for close-in work or night patrols or repelling mass infantry charges it worked pretty well — lots of firepower when you needed it. And at shorter rang-

es, the little bullet knocked 'em down quite regularly, multiple hits being somewhat easier to accomplish with the 30 Carbine than with the 45 ACP for the average GI. As for jamming, everything jams when it's frozen or dirty, or both.

Today, the 30 M-1 Carbine is long since retired, at least from the U.S. military, though I expect it is still getting used as a combat arm in a few out-of-the-way places. You could look at the 30 Carbine as a kind of dead end in the evolution of military small arms, much like the woolly mammoth of the Ice Age. It was a good idea at the time, but something better came along and displaced it.

Today, most of the applications for the 30 Carbine are recreational and, as you'll see, for home or self-defense. Currently, AM AC (formerly Iver Johnson) is the only company manufacturing new 30 Carbines for the commercial market. They bought out the Universal people in the mid-1980s and have all of their equipment and materials. AMAC turns out four to five hundred new carbines a month along with one hundred or so improved and revamped Enforcers, a 10.5-inch barreled semi-automatic pistol formerly produced by Universal. They hope to get a stainless steel carbine with a synthetic stock on the market soon. Great for boats and airplanes.

On the used market, there are a pleth-

Hollowpoints available for 30 Carbine: Speer 110-grain (left), and Sierra 110-grain. Speer offers lots of exposed lead and gaping hollow area, great for home defense or close-in varmints, while the Sierra is ideal for longer-range varmints.

The 45 ACP at left and 30 Carbine, with 41 and 44 magnums to the right. From an 18-inch barrel, the Carbine round is easily more powerful than the 45 and is very close to the revolver magnums when they are fired in a 6-inch barrel.

ora of carbines, often at very good prices. Buyer beware, however, as some have seen rough duty in the past forty or so years. Others have been refurbished at the factory (or armory, which one I have no idea) and might make pretty nice shooters.

Also, there are carbines in very fine shape selling at a collector's price. Some folks are willing to pay a premium price for a particular manufacturer, often for one with the Winchester headstamp. But Rock-Ola made the fewest carbines at 228,500; followed by Standard Products with 247,155; IBM with 346,500; Quality Hardware with 359,662; National Postal Meter 413,017; Underwood Elliot Fisher 545,616; Saginaw 739,136; Winchester up there with 828,059; and Inland Division of General Motors topping out with 2,625,000 carbines of all types. Prices will vary according to condition, obviously.

Prices also will vary according to the model or variation. The M-1A had the paratrooper folding wire stock. An original in fine condition will set you back a substantial amount. M-2s, designed for select-fire, are around but are subject to federal registration and taxation. For a select-fire weapon, however, they aren't overly expensive, but they do confuse the collector values. Also, there is an M-3 variation that was an M-2 with a receiver grooved for an infra-red sniper scope. I've never run across one, but for the right amount of cash, I'm sure they're available.

Of all the makes and models out there, the one thing they have in common is they are all shooters in the most basic sense. That is probably the reason the car-

bine is so popular today: It's fun to shoot and doesn't cost you an arm and a leg to do so. Military Specifications Ball is relatively cheap, as long as you don't burn up several hundred rounds per session.

When I was young, my dad would take my brother and me down to the

Light recoil of the 30 Carbine lets everyone enjoy shooting it. Here, author's wife draws a bead on an unsuspecting tin can.

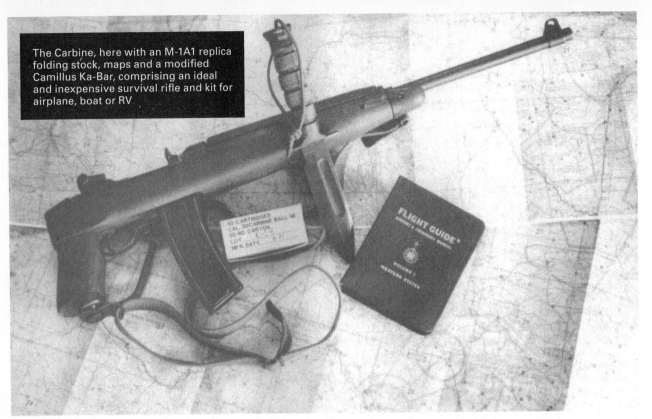

The Carbine, here with an M-1A1 replica folding stock, maps and a modified Camillus Ka-Bar, comprising an ideal and inexpensive survival rifle and kit for airplane, boat or RV

Missouri River outside Kansas City every so often to do some shooting. We'd bang away with the 22s, having lots of fun but always keeping an eye on the stubby bundle wrapped in an oily, old bedsheet. Finally, Dad would take out the carbine (brought back from Guadalcanal, or was it New Britain?) which seemed to us like the most powerful rifle in the world. We got to touch off a few rounds, but ammo was limited then, and we never got to shoot it enough. I decided then that I would have one someday. Finally, after waiting too long, I bought the IBM and have enjoyed it ever since.

These days, nearly every major manufacturer of ammo offers a soft-point load in 30 Carbine. That tells you something about this puny round. A lot of folks use it for a lot of hunting. For shooting small game and varmints, there's no question it is very effective out to around one hundred fifty yards — assuming you have mounted the appropriate sights to allow accurate shooting out that far. And I expect quite a few use it for medium game hunting like deer and black bear-sometimes legal, sometimes not. I understand a number of carbines get toted into the swamps in southern states, looking for bear, alligators, and the like.

And why not? Look at the numbers again. The carbine makes 1900+ fps and 900 + fpe of energy with an expanding bullet. A 44 Magnum in a six-inch barrel is similarly potent, and no one hesitates to hunt deer or bear with a 44 Magnum handgun, do they? So what's the matter with the 30 Carbine? As long as it's legal

for hunting big game where you are, *not one thing*. Just remember to treat it like a long, two-handed pistol and keep your shots less than one hundred yards, preferably less than seventy-five yards. Hunting in the woods or swamp makes that fairly easy.

Legality brings up two points. First, each state has its own set of rules on minimums for big-game hunting with firearms. Here in Colorado, things are divided into two categories for modern arms: rifles and handguns. Within the rifle category, the poor 30 Carbine is eliminated by a requirement of 1000 fps residual energy at one hundred yards. No way. It does, however, meet all other requirements. For handguns, though, if you stuff a 120-grain soft-point into it, then it meets the minimums, since there is no downrange energy requirement. Ironic, eh? In all fairness to the Division of Wildlife, all handgun hunters must qualify at a range under state supervision before they may get a big-game license. Still, they would seem to have things backwards.

The second point concerning legality is the assault rifle classification. A straightforward look at the old carbine would seem to place it right in that category. But that is not always the case. Again in Colorado, and Denver in particular, a law was recently passed banning assault-type rifles. It targets weapons designed for magazines of greater than 20-round capacity. AK-15s, AKs, and Uzis, etc. are out. Mini-14s, Auto-Ordnance Thompson semi-automatics, and carbines are ok. Well, almost. For some reason known

only to the Denver City Council, Plainfield Carbines are not legal. All others are. But the 30-round magazines aren't. Unless you're in the suburbs. Or merely passing through the Denver city limits — with it in a case. Anyway, you had best check with your local police department about the whole thing.

Back to ammunition. If you handload, there is considerable flexibility in the 30 Carbine. Besides the full metal jackets and the softpoints, three other very useful bullets out there will add to the carbine's versatility. The Speer 100-grain Plinker is a round-nose, half-jacket bullet designed for moderate velocities. It can be loaded down to near rimfire speeds and still work the action. Great for rabbits, although so is the Military Specifications full metal jacket stuff. Speer also offers its 110-grain Varminter, which has a round-nose style with lots of lead exposed and a huge hollowpoint. If it feeds in your rifle, it would make an outstanding home-defense bullet in front of 14 or 15 grains of WW 296 or IMR 4227. The third bullet is a 110-grain pointed hollowpoint, ideal for varmints of any persuasion. This last bullet is longer than the round-noses and requires deeper seating, thereby cutting back some on the available powder space. I lost about .5-grain and seated it right on top of the powder. Velocity loss is not bad. This bullet is well worth working up a load or two. It shoots well and definitely damages prairie dogs.

Handloading is pretty straightforward for the 30 Carbine. It headspaces on the case mouth, so there's no crimping allowed. Otherwise, load it just like any straight-walled pistol case. Trim no shorter than 1.286 inches, again because of the headspace. Speaking of trimming, brass is everywhere, some commercial and hordes of G.I. The commercial is a bit lighter with my batch of W-W averaging 69.3 grains and G.I. weighing in at an average of 71.1 grains. It will affect your loads some, so keep an eye on it and don't mix 'em. Also, stick with small-rifle primers; the 30 Carbine pressures are too high for pistol primers.

A number of the faster burning powders work fine for the little 30. The highest velocities come from H110, IMR 4227,296, and 680.I worked with all but the latter and got good results. I don't see any great need to work up a dozen or so loads for your carbine; I ended up with three, all of which shoot about two inches at 50 yards. If you're interested, they are here.

Loaded with expanding bullets, the 30 Carbine will make an excellent home-defense weapon. With a 15- or 30-round magazine, the question of adequate firepower becomes moot. Almost any member of the family can be taught to shoot it well, unlike a handgun of similar power. And unlike a magnum handgun, the light, expanding bullet in a 30 Carbine will lose its momentum more rapidly than a heavy, large-caliber bullet, meaning less penetration should you miss your target — perish the thought! As for the big bullet vs. little bullet controversy, if you don't hit a vital spot, the size or weight of the bullet makes little difference, and the carbine is easier to shoot well than a 44 or 45 ACP.

While on the topic of reloading the 30 Carbine, I should mention that some twenty-five years ago there was considerable interest in wildcatting the little case. Remember, this was before the true assault weapons became so popular or even widely available. Everyone liked the carbine but often found the cartridge disappointing.

Enter Melvin Johnson and son Ed. Melvin developed and marketed the 5.7 MMJ Spitfire, a carbine chambered for a 30 Carbine case necked to 22. It advertised 3000 fps with a 40-grain full-jacketed bullet, which is not too far from M-16 ballistics. The whole thing could be had in

a package with two barrels, one in 30 and one in 22, and at a modest price. Unfortunately, Melvin died as things were getting moving. And according to rumor, his son Ed was killed later in an automobile accident. Either way, the company is out of business, bought out by Plain-field which was bought out by Iver Johnson which was bought out by AM AC. The AM AC people say they could build carbines in 22 or 25 if there was enough demand. On the other hand, how do you know what the demand will be without a rifle to shoot? It's too bad, the rig would have been a dandy. RCBS still offers dies for the 5.7 MMJ, however.

Many others also experimented with necking down the 30 Carbine case. Harold Tucker, of St. Louis, worked with both 22 and 25 calibers. He's out of the business now and was somewhat surprised to have me call and inquire about his work. Apparently, everyone else experimenting with the carbine also has dropped it, since no one I spoke with knew of anyone really working with it. Guy Neil at Hornady has been interested in the 22 version and a 25 version, possibly for silhouette work, but hasn't gotten very far. For everything else, though, modern assault rifles seem to have taken over. Some are about as light and handy, and some are considerably more accurate. Yet the old carbine still has a lot of appeal, and mine is plenty potent and accurate enough for my demands.

Recently, I added a replica of the M-1A1 folding stock to my collection of add-on goodies for the carbine. Although not the answer to a perfect folder, it is well-made (careful, some are not) and makes the carbine even more easily stowable in a car, boat, airplane, or RV. It also just plain looks good. Ram-Line in Wheat Ridge, Colorado, is considering bringing out a synthetic folder for the carbine. If you think that's a good idea, then call 'em and bug 'em about it. While on the topic of stocks, the original on my carbine was quite thick in the area of the grip, just behind the trigger housing. Some judicious wood removal and contouring makes the weapon considerably more comfortable to shoot.

One other use for the old carbine: It may be one of the best outdoor survival rifles around. It's light; the ammo is light;

M-1A folding stock turns the 30 Carbine into a compact rifle for boat, trail or RV, or just for a walk around the place.

and it's adequately powerful with softpoints for harvesting food up to the deer class, should you need to. With the folding stock, it is quite compact — measuring about 26 inches folded. Such modest weight and dimensions take up little space in an RV boat, or airplane.

So it seems that there are a number of uses today for a rifle and cartridge designed fifty years ago. Just remem ber to look at the 30 M-l Carbine as a powerful pistol, not as a wimpy rifle. You'll be much happier with it.

### HANDLOADING YOUR M-1 CARBINE

| Use | Bullet | | Powder | | MV |
| | Gr. Wgt. | Type | Type | Grains | (fps) |
| --- | --- | --- | --- | --- | --- |
| Small Game | 100 | Speer Plinker | 4227 | 13.8 | 1756 |
| Varmints | 100 | Sierra Hollowpoint | H110 | 13.5 | 1842 |
| Home Defense | 100 | Hornady Softpoint | 4227 | 14.8 | 1923 |

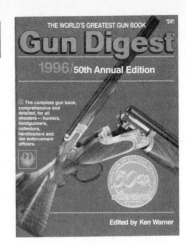

# World War II's Snipers and Sniper Rifles

■ Konrad F. Schreier, Jr.

THERE ARE MANY stories about the various exploits of U.S. Army and Marine Corps snipers of World War II. A surprising number of them are true.

This is remarkable since there were relatively few of these precision combat riflemen. The U.S. armed forces' attitude toward the special skill was that, while unquestionably a useful combat skill, sniping was nowhere near as important as others ranging from leadership to the ability to carry out orders quickly and effectively.

In World War II, the basic requirement of the Army and Marine Corps was for as many "average" riflemen as they could train, and there was little time available for the extensive marksmanship training required by snipers. Adequate sniper rifles were provided, however, and the riflemen who used them were usually those who had shown superior marksmanship skills during regular training. This situation had been true as long as there had been soldiers and Marines. In the Revolutionary War, skilled American riflemen took their toll of the enemy. In the Civil War, Col. Hiram Berdan organized a U.S. Volunteer Regiment, the "Corps of Rifle Sharpshooters," whose marksmanship was feared and respected by the enemy.

In the 1898 Spanish-American War, U.S. Army sharpshooters did some very effective sniping. They did it with the Army-issue 30-caliber Krag rifle or, in a

A sniper with an M1903A4 drawn by *American Rifleman* staff artist Jim Berryman for editor-war correspondent Bill Shadel's April, 1944, story "Snipers in Italy."

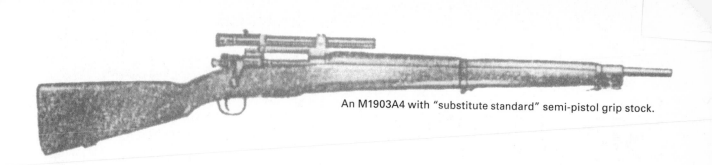

An M1903A4 with "substitute standard" semi-pistol grip stock.

few cases, with civilian target rifles firing the standard Krag ammunition. By this time, Army rifle marksmanship training had been much improved, but there was no such thing as special sniper training.

When the Army adopted the caliber 30 Rifle Model of 1903, the 30-06 Springfield, it proved to be very accurate, and the "Telescopic Musket Sight Model of 1908" was developed for "sharpshooting" with it. Although this sight was later improved and then re-issued as the Model of 1913, it was a primitive periscopic rifle design. It did, however, improve the ability of sharpshooters to hit targets at longer ranges than with the rifle's regular iron sights.

U.S. Army General Orders 23 of 1909 authorized the issue of two Model of 1903 rifles with telescopic musket sights per infantry company, and this order remained in effect through World War II! These rifles were to be issued to soldiers who made the highest scores in training exercises, but no special training regulations for their use were ever published. Unit commanders could decline the issue of these scoped rifles if they felt their unit's assignment would not require them, and this also held true through World War II!

Records indicate that by the end of World War I, at least 1550 Model of 1908 and 5041 Model of 1913 Telescopic Musket sights had been procured. They saw service with U.S. Army units in France in World War I. Unfortunately, their vulnerability to the dirt and moisture conditions of World War I trench warfare severely limited their combat use.

The Army adopted the term "sniping" from the British in World War I, and it was a very important element of the trench warfare tactics of that war. However, in actual World War I combat, most sniping was done by the units' most proficient riflemen using standard-issue iron-sighted rifles. The ranges were short, less than a dozen yards to no more than a couple hundred yards. A sniper had to be an expert marksman who could make the best use of camouflage, cover and con-

cealment. Although they were used, telescopic sights were not required for that.

During World War I, the Army found the two-man sniper team was the most effective. While one man did the shooting, the other was the observer who located targets. Both had to be proficient marksmen since they traded roles. Sniper teams were also expected to observe enemy activities. This was the beginning of the scout-sniper teams much used in World War II and since.

During World War I, troop dissatisfaction with the old Model of 1908 and Model of 1913 scope sights caused the Army to procure some 5000 commercial Winchester A5 scopes to replace them. These were also 6x and mounted on '03 Springfields with standard commercial mounts. The Winchester A5 remained in the inventory until early World War II, but it never satisfactorily met the military requirement for resistance to moisture and dirt.

In the early 1920s, Army Ordnance did some experimenting with sniper sights. While none was adopted, the work led the way to the development of much improved commercial telescopic sights.

Improved commercial scopes led to long-range target shooting with military-caliber rifles. All through the 1920s and 1930s, long-range matches were popular among both civilian and military riflemen, and they were a major event at the Camp Perry National Matches and at many other rifle events.

Although the armed forces had no standard sniper rifle at the time, the following training regulations for snipers were published in 1940:

*19. Snipers a.* Purpose and use. Snipers are expert riflemen stationed in the forward areas of a defensive position for the purpose of firing on enemy soldiers who expose themselves. Specifically, their duties are: (1) to fire on enemy scouts or patrols who attempt to approach or observe the positions; (2) to protect observers and sentinels by firing at hostile snipers who are firing at them; (3) in case of attack by the

enemy; (a) to fire on the leaders of the attack, thus compelling deployment at long range and possibly delaying it; (b) to fire on individuals who are especially active in filtering to the front, and also upon machine gunners. In the attack, when the platoon halts for any purpose, as for example to reorganize following a successful assault, snipers are placed in favorable locations to the front and flanks in order to prevent hostile reconnaissance and delay counterattacks. When a force withdraws from a battle front snipers are usually left in position in order to keep back hostile scouts or patrols. Snipers operate in pairs when sufficient men are available, and scouts are habitually employed and trained for this duty.

*b.* The sniper's post; location; concealment. (1) Sniper's posts or nests are generally located in the same terrain as advanced observation points. In fact sniping and observation posts are sometimes combined, and snipers always observe and report what they see. Usually, the observation posts proper occupy the highest ground favorable for observation, while the sniper's posts are on somewhat lower ground, more favorable for fire. Sniper's posts are, in general, similar to small observation posts.

(2) Temporary posts may be located in trees (preferably trees with plenty of foliage), behind rocks, stumps, hedges or bushes, or in shell holes. More permanent posts are dug into the ground, camouflaged, and provided with overhead cover.

(3) When a sniper's post is manned by a single individual, he performs the duties of both observer and sniper. When there are two men, one acts as observer and the other as sniper.

*c.* Organizing the sector. As soon as the post is occupied the scouts proceed to organize their sector.

*d.* Duties of the rifleman. The scout acting as sniper must be able to fire quickly and accurately on moving or still targets. As the sniper fires, the observer watches the effect. Long-range sniping may be carried on with rifles equipped with telescopic sights.

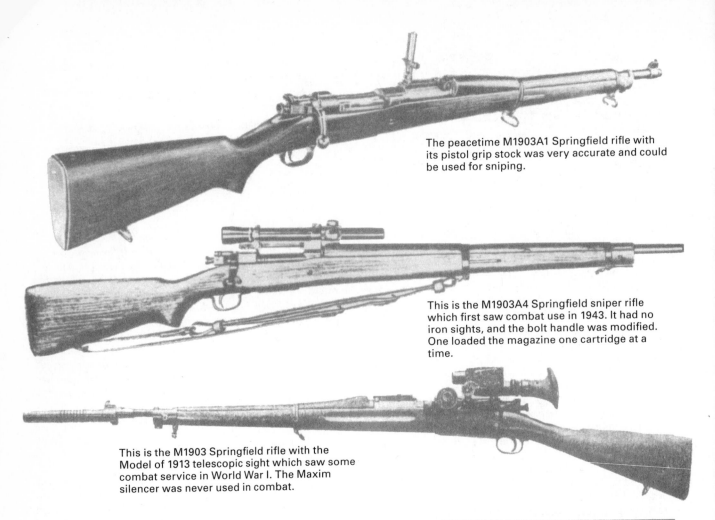

The peacetime M1903A1 Springfield rifle with its pistol grip stock was very accurate and could be used for sniping.

This is the M1903A4 Springfield sniper rifle which first saw combat use in 1943. It had no iron sights, and the bolt handle was modified. One loaded the magazine one cartridge at a time.

This is the M1903 Springfield rifle with the Model of 1913 telescopic sight which saw some combat service in World War I. The Maxim silencer was never used in combat.

**20. Platoon Scouts.** *Each rifle squad includes two men designated as scouts. These men should be good rifle shots, especially trained in the use of cover and concealment, in movements, and in the methods taught in this chapter. At least one, and preferably both, should be equipped with compasses. Both are equipped with tracer ammunition for designating targets.*

While this training regulation mentions the use of rifles with telescopic sights, it was basically intended for sniping with standard iron-sighted guns. However, at the time, the Army often issued the most accurate available issue rifle to riflemen designated as scout-snipers. These could be peacetime '03 Springfields in the "National Match target grade" or the beautifully made M1903A1 Springfield which had a special pistol grip stock and alloy steel action. These were standard issue with iron sights, but capable of superior accuracy.

World War II regulations recognized that the maximum range at which any rifleman could expect to hit a man-size target with any '03 Springfield rifle was about 600 yards. They also recognized that the longer the range, the harder it was to find a man-size target, let alone hit it. In

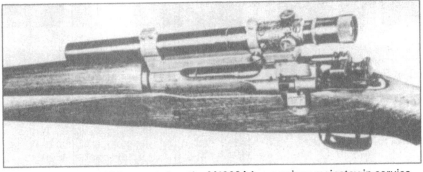

This is the Weaver 330C mounted on the M1903A4 — a sniper mainstay in service.

combat, it was found the longest range at which a rifleman could find and hit man-size targets regularly was 300 to 400 yards. This would become a principal reason the U.S. armed forces adopted scoped sniper rifles in World War II.

Another problem that combat riflemen had was estimating the range to a man-sized target so they could set their iron sights for maximum accuracy at ranges past a couple of hundred yards. Training targets were shot at known ranges, but combat riflemen had to estimate the distance by eye, with no instruments or range-finders to help them.

World War II riflemen received train-

ing in range estimation by eye. The scout-snipers had to be experts at this task, and some received considerable training.

There was no standard-issue telescopic-sighted sniper rifle in the U.S. armed forces when we entered World War II. During the 1930s, practically every Army and Marine Corps regular, reserve or National Guard unit had a rifle team. These teams regularly had scope-sighted '03 Spring-fields privately purchased for use in matches, and these often went into combat with the units and riflemen who had them.

The most popular of these were match-grade '03s with commercial 6X to

Pre-World War II rifle marksmanship training included this prone sandbag rest position recommended for sniping and/or long-range accurate firing.

This 1943 ad shows a Winchester Model 70 target rifle with a high-power telescopic sight. Many such became sniper rifles used in combat.

This Weaver ad featuring their telescopic sight for the M1903A4 Springfield sniper rifle appeared in 1943 magazines.

8X sights in commercial mounts. These found limited combat use throughout World War II, though they were never officially adopted.

Another popular prewar rifle, particularly in the U.S. Marine Corps, was the Winchester Model 70 30-06 target rifle. Most such had sights in the 6X to 8X range, though some had 10x or even more powerful. This was a superb outfit for long ranges. It wasn't officially adopted until after World War II, and a number of them were purchased and remained in use until the Vietnam War!

As soon as the U.S. forces were committed to ground combat in World War II, urgent requests for scoped sniper rifles were submitted from the field. Ordnance immediately tested '03 Springfields with commercial 2.5X sights. The reason the 2.5X types were selected for testing is they seemed best for the sniping ranges up to 600 or so yards, which tactically proved best in combat.

By the fall of 1942, Ordnance selected peacetime Springfield '03s or '03Als with a 2.2X Weaver sight in Redfield Junior mounts. The rifle had its regular iron sights removed and the bolt handle bent to clear the scope. While a few of these were assembled and issued, it was impossible to locate enough selected '03s to build enough sniper rifles to meet the ever-increasing requirement.

Ordnance turned to Remington, who was manufacturing the '03A3 Springfield, and had them equip it with the same Weaver 330 telescopic sight in Redfield

Junior mounts, with the bolt handle bent to clear the scope. The Springfield's regular iron sights were omitted, and either a full-or semi-pistol grip stock was used. The Army adopted this as the Cal. 30 Rifle M1903A4 (Sniper's); the scope was designated the Telescopic Rifle Sight M73 in December, 1942, and it was immediately put in production. The model was first issued to troops in early 1943.

Some 30,000 '03A4 Springfield sniper rifles were built during World War II. They have been frequently criticized by many people. The rough wartime finish and stamped metal parts did not satisfy many riflemen who expected a sniper rifle to have the precision finish and look of a commercial long-range target rifle, but the gun's performance in combat was satisfactory.

U.S. Army records show that the '03A4 Springfield performed as well or better than any other World War II military-issue sniper rifle. An "as issued" '03A4 with its telescopic sight properly zeroed was deadly accurate at ranges out to at least 400 yards. When given a gunsmith-style, target-shooter's fine-tuning, it could shoot very well out to 600 yards and farther, and many gunsmiths who had joined the Army Ordnance Department worked them over. There are records of '03A4 sniper Springfields making effective shots at ranges as long as 1000 yards. This, however, required perfect light and weather conditions.

The '03A4 Springfield remained sniper standard in the U.S. armed forces until the change to 7.62mm NATO-caliber rifles in the late 1950s. They remained in "war reserve" until some were used in the Vietnam War, and there may still be some stored.

At the time the '03A4 sniper Springfield was being developed, the Army Ground Forces Command issued a request for a study of a sniper rifle based on the M-1 Garand. A series of experimental prototypes were built and tested in 1943, but the availability and combat performance of the '03A4 Springfield made this a low-priority project for Ordnance.

This testing did establish several characteristics an M-1 sniper rifle would need to have. One was that the telescopic sight would have to be offset to the left so the Garand's regular iron sights could be used, and so it could be clip-loaded in the usual manner. To do this, a buttstock cheekrest would be required.

The Army adopted two M-1 Garand sniper rifles in mid-1944. The experimental M-1E7 version was adopted as the

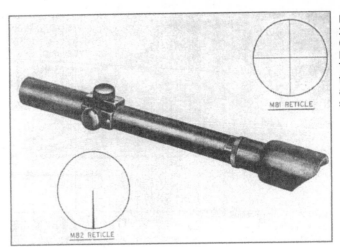

M81 and M82 2.2x sights for the Garand M-1C and M-1D sniper rifles. The M84 with a different reticle was adopted too late to see combat.

M81 RETICLE

M82 RETICLE

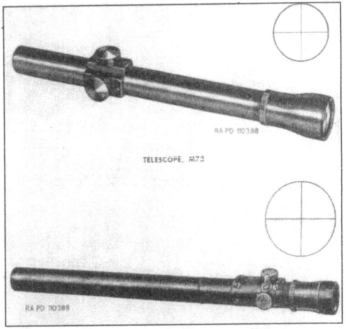

RA PD 110388

TELESCOPE, M73

RA PD 110389

At top is the Lyman Alaskan 2.2X designated the M73; the bottom is the Weaver 330C 2.2X designated the M73B1. The Weaver was the model most commonly issued with the M1903A4 Springfield sniper rifle.

Cal. 30 Rifle M-1C (Sniper's) and went into production at Springfield Armory. It used a Griffin & Howe commercial scope mount on the left side of the rifle's receiver, which would suit any of the several models of standard 2.5X scopes then available.

The M-1C Sniper Garand was the model which first reached troops in World War II. They were some of the best M-1 Garands that Springfield Armory produced and were carefully selected for the modification. Unfortunately, they lacked the accuracy beyond 500 yards that snipers wanted. Garand accuracy was adversely affected by its muzzle-mounted gas cylinder and its multi-piece stock. Some 8,000

M-1C Garand sniper rifles had been built by the end of World War II.

The second sniper M-1 was designed by Springfield Armory to eliminate the need for the threaded holes in the left side of the receiver required by the M-1C model. Designated the Cal. 30 Rifle M-1D (Sniper's), its scope mount attached to the left side of the breech end of the rifle's barrel. A number of M-1D Garand sniper rifles were issued to troops and used in combat in the last months of World War II.

By the end of the war, the U.S. Army had adopted five sniper rifle scopes which could be used interchangeably on any sniper rifle. The M73 was the original

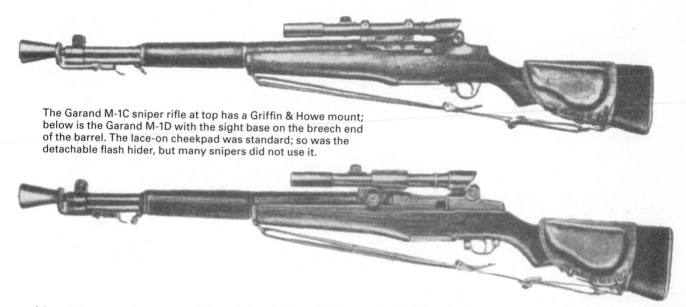

The Garand M-1C sniper rifle at top has a Griffin & Howe mount; below is the Garand M-1D with the sight base on the breech end of the barrel. The lace-on cheekpad was standard; so was the detachable flash hider, but many snipers did not use it.

model, and it was used on most of the '03A4 Springfields. The M73B1, a commercial 2.2x Lyman Alaskan, was adopted as an alternate standard for the M73, but it saw little combat use.

The M81, M82 and M84 scopes were all special models designed to have better resistance to dirt and moisture. The Army described them as 2.5X scopes, but they were all actually 2.2X. During World War II, these sights were mostly assembled on the M-1C and M-1D Garand sniper rifles, and they, along with the M73 and M73B1 scopes, remained in use long after the end of the war.

No matter what kind of sniper rifle a World War II GI or Marine had, he always had problems finding accurate ammunition for it. Many trained with the superbly accurate match target ammunition the Army Ordnance Department had been providing since 1908. However, under wartime or combat conditions, there was no way the Service of Supply could distribute this special ammunition to combat troops with any assurance it would reach the snipers who could use it. The quanities of 30-caliber rifle ammunition in the supply lines were just too vast. Even so, some units departing for combat from the United States did manage to take supplies of this special target-grade ammunition along for their snipers.

Another way World War II Army and Marine Corps snipers found the accurate ammunition they wanted sounds impractical, but it was done. The huge amount of ammo was made in batches known as "lots," some of which had superior accuracy to others. In fact, some of the match target ammunition the Ordnance Department provided was simply the result

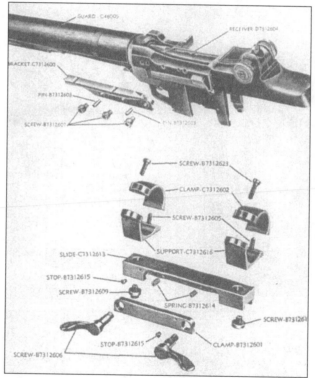

The Griffin & Howe side mount for the M-1C was pretty complex.

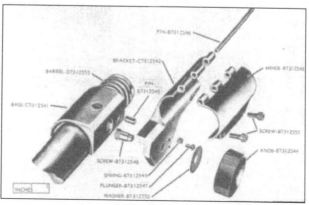

Springfield Armory's mount for the M-1D was hardly simpler.

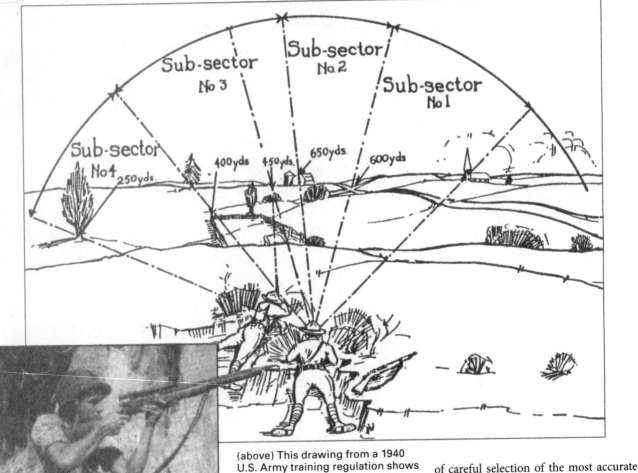

(above) This drawing from a 1940 U.S. Army training regulation shows how a scout-sniper team should organize their sector and select its probable targets.

(left) A Marine Corps sniper in the Pacific with an M1903A4 Springfield. (U.S. Marine Corps photo)

of careful selection of the most accurate production lots.

Snipers could, and did, testfire ammunition from the many lots available in their supplies to find the one which had the best accuracy. Then they would draw a supply of that lot to meet their needs. This was another unauthorized but effective procedure.

After World War II, the effectiveness of Army and Marine Corps snipers was well recognized, but ignored. An unsigned article in the February-March issue of *Army Ordnance* magazine was titled: "Sniping — A Neglected Art." Snipers were among the most resourceful, determined soldiers in the U.S. armed forces, but they seldom received recognition. However, they did get the rifles they needed.

This drawing from a pre-World War II training regulation shows how to set up a training range for eye range estimation. Their use declined when replacement training had to be accelerated, but they always existed at World War II training facilities.

# Guns of Vietnam

For Vietnam use, even the bayonet has been changed.

A lot of years have passed since Korea and WW II — and many more since the Big War. So many that veterans of those bloody affairs would have a hard time recognizing the weapons now serving in Vietnam. Here's a look at most of them. ∎ Col. Jim Crossman

T HE WHITE-HAIRED old gentleman sank into the chair and unbuttoned the choker collar of his worn tunic with a sigh of relief. As he leaned down to unwrap his roll leggings, he said ruefully, "This uniform doesn't seem as comfortable as it was back in the Big War. Something has changed! Which is why I'm here — I had special arrangements made so I could come down here and watch you fellows train and see if there has been any change in the weapons since I was fighting. I brought my young friend here along to see what he could learn."

The "young friend" patted his bulging "Ike jacket." "Don't stand in front of me," he said, "I seem to have put on a little weight recently and I'm afraid one of these buttons will pop off and hurt you! Now I don't expect to see anything new, because

it really wasn't so very long ago when I was in World War Two — less than 25 years ago when I was drafted."

The young man in the green beret nodded respectfully. "Fine, gentlemen, we're glad to have you here and to show you our weapons. I'll try to relate them to the things you knew, but I may miss, because I wasn't born when you were fighting World War II, and my folks hadn't been born when you, sir, were fighting your Big War in 1917! We won't have time to get into all the weapons this afternoon, so we'll skip the artillery and tanks and start right out with something I think you'll recognize."

As he laid the 45 pistol on the table in front of him, delighted smiles of recognition broke out on the faces of the two veterans. John Browning's design has been with us since about 1911. Not

that we couldn't make something lighter than that 2½-lb. beauty, and not that we couldn't go to a more modern cartridge than the 45 Auto, with its 220-gr. bullet at 830 feet per second. In fact, we had agreed with the British and Canadians that we would change to the 9mm cartridge if we changed pistols. But the cost of replacing existing guns with something better seemed to be much greater than the benefit to be gained. The pistol is considered a badge of authority and an emergency weapon, not really a basic combat weapon, so it looks as if Mr. Browning's 45 will be with us for a long time — until something remarkably better comes along.

Another gun the old timers will recognize is also a John Browning design — the 50-cal. M2 machine gun. Although not developed until after WW I, the mechanism follows the same scheme as the 30 cal. M1917, of which we made over 40,000 in 1918. In addition to the M1917A1 — water-cooled — we used the Browning M1919A4 and M1919A6 30-cal. guns in WW II, both air-cooled versions of the older gun. The M1919 gun was most recently used in tanks, although with the change to the 7.62mm cartridge they're probably pretty well gone. But the 50-cal. still goes merrily along as secondary armament — primarily anti-aircraft — on tanks, armored personnel carriers and other vehicles. The 50 cartridge looks like a big '06, and feels like a real big one, with the 660-gr. bullet at a velocity of 2900 fps. The gun is proportionately big, weighing around 82 lbs. without mount.

These are about the only two old-timers left. You'll recall that even between WW I and the end of WW II we had a lot of guns replaced or new weapons introduced — including the M1 rifle, the Thompson submachine gun, the M3 "grease gun," the 2.3" bazooka, the 57mm and 75mm recoilless rifles, the tubular rifle grenade, the 60mm mortar, 37mm, 57mm and other anti-tank guns and many others.

While there was a major change between the two "Big Wars," there has been even more change in the past 20 years and

The 4.2" mortar, unusual in that it has a rifled barrel, started life as a chemical mortar, with HE shells became a popular Infantry support weapon during WW II, still serves in that role.

our ground troops in Viet Nam are using many new weapons — their first use in anger. Unless you have been following these developments carefully, you may well be surprised at the assortment of new weapons.

## The New Weapons

Now that we have gotten the venerable Browning guns out of the way, we can move on to some of the interesting new things. A good way to start is by trying to sort out the rather confusing rifle picture. The fine M14 rifle was developed after WW II, as a result of combat experience. It is patterned after the basic and successful M1 rifle mechanism, but with a better gas system and other improvements for more reliability. It weighs about a pound less than the M1, has a 20-round detachable box magazine, selective semi- or full-automatic fire, and represents a considerable net gain over the M1. It is chambered for the 7.62mm (30-cal.) cartridge, which is shorter and lighter than the 30-06 cartridge, although having the same power — 150-gr. bullet at 2800 fps. This was adopted by many nations as the 7.62mm NATO cartridge.

In the original plan, another rifle, the M15, was to move into the spot which had been held by the Browning Automatic Rifle — the respected old BAR of WW I and II. The M15 was merely the M14 action with a heavy barrel and other minor changes to make it a good, bipod-mounted, sustained-fire rifle. Weighing more than the M14, it still hefted many pounds less than the BAR, and was to serve as the squad base of fire. Unfortunately, it was killed before it ever got in production. It came as no surprise to some of us when, a few years later, it was found that the light M14 couldn't handle the sustained-fire role. The M14E2 has now been devised to handle this job, and some 8000 have recently been made. Essentially it is the M14 action and barrel with a straight line stock, muzzle stabilizer, modified bipod, long sling and a few other changes. Weight has gone up to nearly 13 lbs., but the M14E2 is much more effective in the sustained fire role.

The Air Force was concerned with a defensive weapon for protecting air fields. They didn't need the power of the M14 but were not too happy with the 30-cal. M1 carbine. Finally they settled on the commercial AR15 rifle, which was developed by Armalite and is being made by Colt. Some AR15s were used experimentally in Viet Nam, and suddenly caught the popular fancy partly through their recognized virtues, but mostly because of some grossly exaggerated and inaccurate reporting. After a series of tests, the Army adopted the rifle for certain units

where weight was a major factor. While the Air Force bought the rifle pretty much off-the-shelf, the Army requested some changes to meet their tougher requirements, thus the Army version is known as the XM16E1, while the Air Force model is the M16.

Both, of course, shoot the 5.56mm cartridge. In civilian clothes this is known as the 223 Remington, a slightly larger edition of the 222 Remington. With a 50- or 55-gr. bullet at 3200–3300 fps, the 222 (and the 222 Remington Mag.) is well-known by varmint hunters and bench rest shooters. The 5.56mm cartridge is much smaller and lighter than the 7.62mm, so more of them can be carried in a given weight. Since the muzzle energy is about 50% of the 7.62, the rifle can be made lighter and is easier to handle in full automatic fire. Additional rifles have been ordered for use in Vietnam, so it is apparently proving popular, as would be expected, since it is short, light, compact and easy to shoot. The more powerful M14 is also making a good name for itself and is being used by the Marines and some Army units.

The ground machine gun role is being adequately filled by the M60 air-cooled gun, which was developed as part of the 7.62mm family. With a weight of 23 pounds, a quick-change barrel and the good cut-off gas expansion system, it apparently is doing very well. Using a metallic-link belt, it fires from the open bolt position, and will handle the ball, tracer and all the other 7.62mm cartridges, a rate of fire of around 600 rounds per minute. With the sights and some other unnecessary parts removed, the M60C becomes helicopter armament, about which more later.

The M73 and M85 machine guns were the first we've had specially designed for tank use. Both (the M73 in 7.62mm, and the M85 in 50-cal.) have short receivers and are easier to use inside the tank. Both use push-through type metallic-link belts

The 45 ACP — still used by U.S. fighting men.

The Davy Crockett, a big recoilless rocket designed to give the Infantry nuclear capability. So far it has been used with high explosive shells.

and shoot the usual variety of cartridges. They're usually used only in tanks.

The WWII 30-cal. carbine was designed to largely replace the pistol for personal protection. Unfortunately it looked like a rifle and was used as a rifle — but it just didn't have the stuff. It acquired a bad reputation in some circles and was replaced by the M14 in the changeover. The 45 caliber submachine gun — originally the Thompson but later replaced by the M3 "grease gun" — was also mostly replaced by the M14, with its full-auto fire capability.

## Sniper Rifles

We're in the same position right now as we were at the start of each World War as far as a sniper rifle is concerned — we don't have one. We used the Warner and Swasey low-magnification prismatic scope on the WWI Springfield, a low-power hunting scope on the WWII Springfield (which became the M1903A4), and finally a low-power scope on the M1 rifle — the M1C or M1D. These have all been dropped, in line with the usual Army custom of paying little attention to sniping. But according to the reports, the Marines brought over a batch of Winchester 30-06 M70 target rifles and target scopes, set up a sniper school and then proceeded to show they could make hits at long range. They've decided to go to the Remington 40X in 7.62mm with one of the good variable-power varmint type scopes mounted on it. This oughta teach the VC to keep out of sight!

When the Swiss inventor Mohaupt presented the U.S. with the shaped charge in 1940, this was a real revolution in armor piercing ammunition. This development was based on the Neumann-Monroe principle of "focusing" an explo-

sive charge to give great penetration in steel. While this was an old principle, no one really knew what to do with it until Mohaupt came along. Prior to that time, armor penetration was based on a big projectile at high velocity — the bigger and faster the better. But with the shaped charge, it was merely necessary to put the charge against the plate anyway you could and velocity did not matter. It had one disadvantage — penetration was greatly reduced if the projectile was rotated. We used the 2.36" rocket launcher with a shaped charge in WWII, but swapped it for the 3.5" launcher during the Korea shooting. The Army has now dropped this, but the Marines are using it effectively. In addition to having something like 12 inches of armor penetration, it is a good antipersonnel and anti-materiel weapon. The 12-lb. shoulder-fired launcher shoots a 7½-lb. rocket at a velocity near 500 fps, to a range of about 1300 yards.

The Army is using the M72 LAW — Light Anti-tank Weapon — for anti-tank use, not that there has been much urgent need for this in Vietnam. The LAW is a rocket weapon, with the projectile being fired from its collapsible carrying case, which is a throw-away. In the collapsed position, this 66mm launcher is short and compact, and the assembly weighs only 4½ lbs. When the tube is extended, it provides a guide for the rocket and protection for the shooter. Sights and firing mechanism come into use in the extended position.

One of the remarkable developments of WWII was the recoilless rifle. First used in the shoulder-fired 57mm and followed by the bigger and heavier 75mm, the recoilless principle went back to the crude Davis gun of WW I. By letting gas

blast out of ports in the back end of the rifle, heavy projectiles could be fired at fair velocity with no recoil. Rockets had the same virtue, but at that time were very inaccurate. As rocket accuracy increases, they may well take over the role of the recoilless rifle, since the rocket launcher can be made considerably lighter.

The 57mm and 75mm recoilless rifles, and a later 105mm size, have been dropped, leaving two in use. The 90mm M67 rifle fires a fin-stabilized HEAT (High Explosive Anti-Tank) round at a velocity of 700 fps. The 35-lb. weight of the rifle makes it a bit on the heavy side, but like all recoilless rifles, it puts rifle accuracy and cannon power on a man's shoulder.

The other recoilless rifle being used in Vietnam is the 106mm M40 type, a very powerful weapon designed for anti-tank use but formidable against any target. Normally mounted on a jeep, the 106 can be man-carried for short distances, although its 288 lbs. get tiresome pretty quickly. It fires a HEAT round capable of penetrating a foot-and-a-half of armor, at the respectable velocity of over 1600 fps. It carries a coaxially mounted 50-cal. semiauto rifle, which fires a cartridge with a moderate velocity bullet whose trajectory closely matches that of the big projectile. The gunner ranges and determines lead on moving targets with the 50 cal. spotting rifle and promptly switches to the big gun for a first round hit — the very best kind of hit!

A light, fast, tracked vehicle was designed to carry 6 of these rifles and to be a very mobile and very dangerous anti-tank weapon. The Marines adopted and are using this "Ontos," but the Army hasn't so far.

## New/Old Mortars

While the veteran of 1917 might have trouble believing the recoilless rifles, he wouldn't have a bit of trouble with the 81mm mortar. Some improvements in metallurgy, in ballistics and in operating details are about the only changes. The present M29 mortar weighs less than 100 pounds with the new lightweight, corrugated tube, the new bipod and the light metal baseplate. Accuracy has improved and range has been increased to around 4000 yards, with the 9-lb. shell, which gets a velocity of nearly 800 fps.

Where we started out adopting the 3", 4" and 6" Stokes mortars from the British and the 240mm (10") job from the French, the only other big mortar we have now is the 4.2" M30. This started life as a chemical mortar, but during WW II there was much need for high explosive rounds and little need for chemicals, so the 4.2" shifted its main responsibility. With a 25-lb. shell holding nearly 8 lbs.

(continued on page 174)

(top left) The M14 rifle handles the efficient 7.62mm NATO cartridge. Note how the soldier has taped two magazines together so a full one can be inserted fast.

(top right) M67 90mm recoilless rifle, operated by a two man crew, fires a fin-stabilized explosive anti-tank round — puts rifle accuracy and cannon power on a man's shoulder.

(left) M79 40mm grenade launcher is deadly against VC personnel to almost quarter-mile ranges.

(bottom left) Sustained fire capability is provided by M60 air-cooled machine gun, caliber 7.62mm. With sights and other parts removed, it becomes helicopter armament.

(bottom right) M70 Winchester 30-06 target rifle topped by Unertl scope serves this sniper well. Also in use now is the Remington 40X in 7.62mm with a variable power scope.

(above) The Entac tank-destroying missile is guided after launching by the gunner's directions, transmitted from his joy-stick control through connecting wires.

(upper right) Though dropped by the Army, the 60mm mortar is used by Marines, who like its light weight.

(right) Scoped M1 sniper rifle still sees some use.

(below) The 5.56mm rifle is popular with some troops in Viet (continued on page 174)nam because of its light weight, though it's not as effective as numerous inaccurate and exaggerated newspaper reports have claimed.

(lower right) Slide action 12-ga. riot-type shotgun is a favorite jungle weapon. Bandoliers of ammo are for 7.62mm machine gun.

Claymore anti-personnel mine; it can be fired by remote control.

(continued from page 171)

of HE, shooting to 6,000 yards, this is a flexible and powerful weapon. Weighing around 700 lbs., it is mobile to a degree but not exactly a one-man weapon. Unlike its smaller smoothbore brother, the 4.2" mortar is rifled. The shell has an expanding plate on the bottom which sets up under the powder gas pressure and engages the rifling. Where the fin-stabilized 81mm mortar can be used at any high angle, the spin-stabilized 4." is limited to about 65 degrees, since at higher angles the shell will not turn over.

During various reorganizations, the Army dropped the little 60mm company mortar, but the Marines have always had an affection for it. They are using it in Vietnam, where its 45-lb. weight and 2,000-yard range with a 3-lb. shell work out just right.

Even such a simple and unglamorous weapon as the grenade has changed in recent years. We originally adopted the British "Mills" type (circa WWI), with its serrated cast iron body filled with HE. Somewhere along the way, we changed the HE filling to EC Blank Fire Powder. This very fast burning powder burst the grenade along the serrations quite neatly. While the few big fragments didn't give very good area coverage, they were still dangerous at a considerable distance, but we went back to HE, which increased the effectiveness. This old Mk II type has been passed by progress and the new M26 is being used. This is about the same size and shape, but has a smooth exterior. It has the same old pull ring and safety lever, but there the similarity stops. The body of the M26 is made of square, notched wire, wound into shape, and covered with a thin metal shell. The 6 ounces of Composition B filler breaks it up into a thousand or more fragments, at velocities over 4000 fps.

Although the time delay fuze has been standard for many years, it has some disadvantages — like bounding merrily back in your lap when you throw it so as to accidently hit a tree! Although the present time fuze is noiseless and smokeless in operation, the 4–5 second delay often afforded the other guy a little chance to duck. The latest fuze, now going into production, has an additional impact element so that the grenade will usually go off when it hits something solid. If it doesn't, the time fuze will still fire it. To avoid unpleasantness too close to home the impact element has a delayed-arming feature, which will keep it from going off at your feet if you drop it, and will get it through the nearby brush before the impact element is armed.

A related, but unglamorous, weapon is the new "Claymore" mine. This in effect consists of a block of HE, about 9" long, 3" wide, and an inch thick, slightly curved around the long side. On the outside of the curve, steel balls are imbedded in the HE. The mine is provided with built-in tripod legs and a sight, and can be fired by remote control. When fired, the steel balls are blasted out and cover the area in front like a shotgun pattern.

The rifle grenade is not in fashion in the Army right now, although the Marines are finding it useful. We started with a grenade which had a long rod extending down in the barrel, shifted to the French V-B type with the cup discharger as well as the grenade with the hole down the middle to let the bullet through, then ended up in WW II with the tubular launcher. Designed by Mohaupt for use with the shaped charge antitank grenade, the grenade body was fastened to a hollow tube, which fitted over a tubular extension on the barrel. The grenade tube had stabilizing fins on the outside, thus with the special blank cartridge and an additional booster cartridge, a 1¼-lb. grenade could be thrown over 350 yards. In addition to anti-tank grenades, a wide variety of pyrotechnic signals, smokes, and anti-personnel grenades was developed.

In the Army, hand-held rocket-propelled pyrotechnics have taken over the signaling function from the grenade, while the LAW and 90mm recoilless have taken over the close-range anti-tank work. The fine M79 new 40mm grenade launcher has taken over the anti-personnel role.

The 40mm grenade cartridge looks like a very short, stubby, conventional cartridge. The business end contains a fuze, a streamlined cover and the grenade itself. The grenade is a small ball, about 1½" in diameter, made of flat serrated wire, much like the M26 grenade. It holds a few ounces of the very powerful explosive RDX. The grenade body breaks up into several hundred fragments, at velocities over 4000 fps. The fuze is armed by a combination of spin and setback when the cartridge is fired, and it has a delayed arming feature. Small as the grenade may seem, it is very potent.

The M79 grenade launcher looks much like a short and chubby single-barrel break-open shotgun. The aluminum barrel is rifled. The launcher weighs about 6 lbs. and with the 6-oz. grenade fired at a velocity of 250 feet per second, it is not too unpleasant to shoot — certainly far more comfortable than that abusive rifle grenade. The cartridge uses the high-low principle, where a small charge of powder is burned in a small chamber at high pressure, but is metered out into large chamber where it works against the projectile at low pressure. The powder burns at a pressure of around 35,000 psi, but works against the projectile at only about 3,500 psi. The M79 is one of the really new weapons in Vietnam and has been making a name for itself. With good accuracy, good effectiveness and a range of nearly 400 yards, it is a comforting thing to have in the rifle squad.

## Airborne Ground Weapons

Some 20 years ago I was involved in testing the helicopter for Infantry use, and a year or two later I did a lot of flying for an article on fox hunting from the chopper. However, we were all so interested in them as a means of transportation that we didn't think about arming

105mm howitzer — proved in WW II and Korea — continues its outstanding performance in Viet Nam.

them. Now one of the real surprises of the Vietnam affair has been the effectiveness of the armed helicopter and the rather surprising toughness of the chopper in withstanding enemy fire. Although this article is about ground weapons, much of the armament used on the chopper has been adapted from ground weapons, and since the chopper is used right with the ground troops, we'll sneak in a word or two about it.

Just about everything you can think of has been hung on the helicopter and used experimentally, but the VC have been getting the worst end of four major standardized weapons systems. Two M6OC 7.62mm machine guns have been mounted on outriggers on each side of the aircraft. With power elevation and traverse slaved to the gunner's sight, this is a very effective system, with a rate of fire of 2,000 shots a minute.

The M5 weapons system is based on the 40mm grenade launcher M75. This is a motor-driven automatic launcher, with a rate of fire of 250 shots a minute. The 40mm grenade is descended from the foot soldier's 40mm, but is heavier, holds more HE and has higher velocity and therefore more range. The same high-low principle is used, but the change is from 35,000 to 12,000 psi, giving the heavier grenade a velocity of nearly 800 fps. The launcher is carried in a nose-mounted turret, giving considerable flexibility in elevation and deflection. The turret is slaved to the gunner's sight, much as the machine guns are. The 40mm grenade cartridges are connected by links and feed from the storage area through flexible chuting into the turret.

The ground pounders have been using the SS-10 or "Entac" wire-guided missile as a flexible, effective antitank weapon. This is a rocket which is launched at moderate velocity and which has a long-burning sustainer motor to maintain or slightly increase the speed. The gunner, with a small joy-stick control, actually flies the missile from the launching site. Commands are passed to the missile over two fine wires which pay out of its back end, while a brilliant flare in the tail of the missile helps the gunner keep it in sight.

The chopper people have adopted a four-missile mount, along with sights and other controls, for use on the Bell HU-1 "Huey" series. The SS-11 used on this has a usable range of 500 to 3500 yards, and with 3½ lbs. of HE, is something to be feared.

The fourth standardized weapon system is based on the 2.75" Navy rocket. This rocket is 4 feet long, weighs 18 lbs., carries 1½ lbs. of HE and has a burn-out velocity of 2300 fps. A Huey can carry a couple of 24-tube rocket launchers, which gives considerable firepower. While these are the main systems, there have been many other combinations tried, such as a couple of 7-tube rocket launchers with the machine guns, etc. Although not listed formally in the standard books, one of the very useful systems consists of two eager soldiers "riding shotgun" — standing in the open doorway clutching a light machine gun!

Even the big "Vulcan," the 20mm Gatling gun, has been used experimentally in the chopper. Developed by Army Ordnance, this gun is standard armament on some Air Force planes. The Vulcan is the motor-driven, 6-barreled gun, with the barrels rotating together and never stopping during firing. Each barrel has a rate of fire — depending on how fast you want to drive the gun — of better than 1000 shots a minute, so the combination can get up to 7,000 or better. This is a mighty big gun for the chopper and a more likely version seems to be the "Minigun." This, another Gatling like the big gun, was developed by General Electric, but the Minigun is in 7.62mm caliber.

At the other end of the scale, the tank has had some rather tough going in Vietnam. Between jungle and marsh, this really isn't the best tank country. But on occasions tanks have been used with good results. We have one battalion of M48's in the country, plus smaller units of M60's. Both run about 50 tons and use 7.62mm coaxial M73 machine guns and 50-cal. M85 machine guns in the cupola. Main armament of the M48 is the 90mm gun, while the M60 tank carries the big 105mm gun.

The artillery has been kept busy, starting with the workhorse of WWII — the 105mm towed howitzer. Other old and new artillery weapons have been used, including some of the later self-propelled weapons. Among these are the 105mm and 155mm howitzers, the 8" howitzer and the big long-range 175mm gun, which is seeing its first combat. With a firing range of around 20 miles, plus good mobility on its tracks, this gun can cover a lot of area.

There are many other weapons which have been used to a greater or lesser extent, and some of those noted as having passed out of the picture may have found limited use. Take the shotgun, for example — it is not on the equipment list of a rifle outfit, but it has been used considerably in the jungle, where its short range is no major handicap. The M3 45-cal. "grease gun" is being used by the Marines in some cases, and even the much-castigated M1 carbine probably has seen some use.

The armament on Air Force, Navy and Marine aircraft has been used very extensively and effectively — but that is another story.

As the Green Beret finished, the two veterans struggled back into their uniforms and, after many thanks, headed for their car. The World War I vet was heard to say to his companion, "These kids just don't know what a real war is like! With all these fancy weapons — say, if we'd had weapons like this, we'd have licked the Kaiser in a few weeks!"

Marines like this Ontos, a light tracked carrier, because of the fire power its six 106mm recoilless rifles provide.

# The M14 Rifle
## ... HAIL AND FAREWELL

■ John Lachuk

THE MUCH MALIGNED M14 is being quietly phased out of production. It has apparently been abandoned by the Pentagon brass, though not yet openly repudiated. A search is in progress to find a worthy replacement for the rifle which proved to be modern in name only and has had, the way things look, the shortest life in history from production to obsolescence.

The Army hopes to leapfrog adoption of another conventional shoulder rifle by a crash program to develop exotic weapons such as the SPIW (Special Purpose Individual Weapon), a superposed barreled weapon, firing both grenades and high velocity dart-like bullets; or the Gyrojet, which fires small self-contained plastic rocket projectiles from cheaply cast smoothbore guns. Slanted orifices, in the tail, spin the rockets to impart stability. Even Laser "ray guns" are receiving serious considerations as future weapons.

Despite this feverish activity, it appears likely that such Buck Rogers weapons will be on the drawing board for some time yet. A more familiar but *modern* arm is certainly needed to fill the gap, and possibly to back up eventual use of the far-out types contemplated.

Your editor suggested that I "test-fire" some likely successors to the M14. Considering the immense stockpiles of NATO 7.62 ammo scattered throughout the world, we may end up with yet another 30-cal. rifle. Some promising candidates in this size are the ArmaLite AR-10 and their brand new AR-16. A marginal contender (I feel) is the Belgian FN Browning Light Assault Rifle. In line with the effort to lighten both weapon and ammo, we come up with the 223 caliber rifles, the AR-15 and newly unveiled AR-18.

First, however, let's try to learn where the M14 failed its great promise. The M14 represents a political victory but a monumental mechanical failure for the U.S. Army Ordnance. In 1955 we literally bludgeoned the 15-nation North Atlantic Treaty Organization into accepting the T65 (now 7.62 NATO), a boiled-down version of the half-century old 30-06, as the standard NATO cartridge. This course was pursued despite the insistence of countries like England that a smaller caliber, such as their 280, could perform as well and provide lighter ammunition.

The U.S. also wanted a common rifle for NATO, but Atlantic Treaty Alliance members baulked at accepting the American T44 (experimental M14), a rifle that was far from proven and is still years away from truly mass production.

Several NATO countries adopted the FN rifle. In 1954, it was designated the T48 and tested by our Ordnance, alongside the M14. Both guns were adjudged superior to the M1 Garand, but the FN was rejected in favor of the home-grown rifle. Among other advantages, the M14 was said to be, "better suited for American transition to mass production." Delays of over a year in delivery of the first M14 rifles touched off a stir in Congress in 1961. At that time, Iron Curtain countries were estimated to possess some 35 million modern, 30-shot "Avtomat Kalashnikov" AK-47 full automatic rifles, with production going full tilt in Russia, China and Czechoslovakia. Meanwhile, Belgium, England, Germany and Canada had adopted and were in full production of the FN assault rifles.

The sudden end to orders for the M14 at just under 1.4 million units has caught several major producers flatfooted, yet it comes as no real surprise. Early obsolescence of the M14 was candidly predicted in March of 1960, when General Trudeau, Chief of Army Research and Development, testified before a Congressional hearing that a replacement was already being sought for the M14. The date of expected obsolescence was 1965. He elaborated, "I think that a new-type, shorter range ammunition is possible. We should consider the design of the best weapon to fire it. I believe the weapon should be light and simple to operate."

The M14, which was originally projected as a "light rifle," eventually trimmed less than a pound from the unwieldy Garand. There is little apparent difference between the M14 that resulted from 20 years of development and $130 million in expenditures, and the original Garand prototypes of 1920. Early publicity heralded the M14 as a full-automatic rifle that would replace such special purpose weapons as the sub-machine gun and light machine gun. The M14's major failing is its lack of control-ability in full-automatic fire. Trained rifleman have told me the gun climbs so badly they can't keep 3 shots in a silhouette at 25 yards. Current issue M14's are semi-automatic. Officers control a supply of full automatic selectors, which, it is said, could be placed in the guns when needed.

Apologists for this policy say that full-automatic rifles in the hands of infantrymen pose an impossible logistical problem, the supplying of a steady stream of leaden "water" to the soldier's lethal "hoses." Statistics point up that it required

50,000 rounds of ammunition to produce one "good Commie" in Korea. Compare this with the average 29 round balls the Colonials fired per British Redcoat killed in the Revolutionary War, using muzzle-loading rifles and muskets.

Apparently the soldier values his shots more if they come one at a time. Still full-auto fire has its uses, if we can but train our GIs to recognize them. It can keep enemy heads down during flanking maneuvers, and provide small outnumbered groups with superior fire power for short periods. Air Force Manual 50-12 lists maximum rate of fire at 150 to 200 rounds per minute. USAF Tech Sergeant Vern Duchek tells me he can pour out 240 to 280 rounds per minute, including reloading time, using the AR-15. Even a squad could lay down a nearly impenetrable rain of fire at that rate — assuming they had ample ammo!

In Russia, during World War II, the vaunted Wehrmacht faced death charges lasting for hours. Eventual breakthrough often resulted in the collapse of entire German defense perimeters. At Stalingrad, such a marathon suicide charge led to the capture of 400,000 Germans. Infantry armed with full-automatic rifles could well make such an attack too costly to continue.

## M14 Rivals

The Belgian FN rifle that we rejected in favor of the M14 was designed by M. Dieudonné Siave, engineer with Fabrique Nationale d'Arms de Guerre, in Liége, and a protégé of the late John M. Browning. Originally chambered for a short 7mm cartridge, the FN was converted to fire the 7.62 NATO. A number of NATO members adopted the FN, including Germany. Germany later took in, or was taken in by, the CETME, or Gew C3, a rifle designed by German engineers, working in Spain. The CETME uses a delayed blowback action, and boasts all of the failings of that system as applied to heavy rifle calibers, especially the problem of overly violent extraction, to prevent case head separations, the chamber is fluted and ammo lubricated. No CETME was available for testing, but a semi-automatic version of the FN came to hand.

It seems remarkable that *all* of the other likely M14 replacements were designed by ArmaLite, Inc., a small independent development company in Costa Mesa, Calif. It began in 1954 with three dedicated gun buffs who believed that stable, lightweight missile-age plastics and alloys could be applied to firearms. Metallurgist George Sullivan was president, plastics expert Chuck Dorchester, vice-president, and ballistician Gene Stoner, chief engineer. ArmaLite, then a division of Fairchild Engine and Airplane Corp., soon received an R and D (research and development) contract from the Air Force for the AR-5, the 22 Hornet survival rifle.

Later, the ArmaLite trio turned their attention to regular military rifles. Uninhibited by preconceived notions of what a rifle should look like, they made their objective the producing of a practical weapon of the least possible weight. The AR-10, a 7½-pound 7.62 NATO caliber full- and semi-automatic rifle resulted. It has a European style machine gun configuration. Major metal parts such as the receiver and magazine are anodized aluminum alloy. Even the barrel of the original model was aluminum with a steel liner. Handguard and butt-stock are molded of fiberglass. To operate the action, gas is routed from a port near the muzzle through a tube atop the barrel, to enter a massive steel bolt carrier and start it rearward. As it

(above) Don Egger found the AR-15 could be readily aimed and controlled from the shoulder during full-automatic fire. Note two ejected cases in the air, one behind his ear and the other just leaving the action.

(left) The original onus laid on the AR-15 by Gen. Wm. G. Wyman was that it must "penetrate both sides of a GI helmet at 500 yards." Here's physical proof that the gun fullfills that requirement.

moves back, the carrier cuts off entry of gases and bleeds off the pressure within through escape vents. Kinetic energy carries it back, camming open the 7-lug bolt and extracting the case.

In 1956, the AR-10 was submitted to an Ordnance Board for testing at the Springfield Armory, but failed to pass the criteria set up for it. At that time, Chuck Dorchester pleaded in vain that the M14 be fired alongside, as a control. Recently released test data on the M14 show it to be markedly inferior to the AR-10 performance.

correct artillery projectile. The AR-15, a scaled-down version of the AR-10, was developed to fire the new centerfire 22.

The AR-15 went through months of Ordnance testing, alongside the Winchester 224 rifle, a modification of the M1 carbine in 1958–59. Afterwards, a review board under General Powell recommended the purchase of at least 700 AR-15s for extended field testing. Ordnance countered with a proposal to work for an "optimum round of 25 caliber," which could then be incorporated into the new rifle.

had not Air Force Chief of Staff, General Curtis LeMay come across it in 1960, and recommended the Air Force test the gun as a replacement for their antiquated M1 carbines. In a new test at Lackland AF Base, the AR-15 easily outshot both the M14 and the Russian AK-47.

Tests indicated further that training time could be cut in half with the AR-15. In a 3-week period, almost half the trainees made Expert with the AR-15 (now labeled the 5.56mm M16 by Army Ordnance), while less than one-quarter made it with the M14.

## USAF Orders AR-15 Rifles

Many of the initial AF order for 8,500 AR-15s went with Special Services to Vietnam, where they racked up an incredible record for dependability and effectiveness. An AF armorer returned to Lackland in 1963 to provide first-hand knowledge on battle maintenance problems. When asked what replacement parts were most needed, he replied, "I don't know. We haven't broken anything yet!"

The revolution in concept represented

(left) ArmaLite lineup, top to bottom; brand new AR-18, 223; prototype AR-16, 7.62 with wooden stocks — to be replaced with polycarbonate; famed AR-15, 223; note absence of openings for entrance of dirt and mud; AR-10, a truly fine military rifle, 7.62 NATO.

(below) AR-15; a trim and deadly military rifle. Bayonet and quick detachable bipod add to gun's versatility. It can fire grenades without any added attachments.

Fairchild licensed the AR-10 to Artillerie-Inrichtingen of Holland in 1957 and to Colt's Patent Fire Arms Mfg. Co. a year later. It was a Netherlands gun, with a steel barrel boosting the weight to a hair over 9 pounds, that we had for testing.

Despite Ordnance turndown, the AR-10 brought ArmaLite a reputation for functional innovation. It also brought General Wm. G. Wyman, Chief of the Continental Army Command at Fort Monroe, Va., to California in mid-1957 with a suggestion that a 22-caliber automatic rifle that could "penetrate both sides of a GI helmet at 500 yards," might prove interesting to the Army. Gene Stoner tried the 222 Remington cartridge, but found it lacking the energy required. He reamed the chamber deeper and fire-formed 222 cases to hold more powder, then designed a 55-gr. boat-tail bullet for his new "223" cartridge by scaling down a ballistically

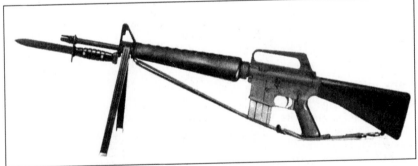

No 25 caliber cartridge ever materialized.

Eventually, a discouraged Fairchild Corp. began hurting from the $1,450,000 development cost of the AR-15, and licensed it to Colt's. Colt's found a good reception with emerging nations of the Far East, where small statured Asiatic soldiers discovered at last a rifle that made them all at least 10 feet tall. The AR-15 might have been relegated to this oriental limbo

by the AR-15 lies not so much in the rifle as in using a small-bore for a military weapon. Chuck hunters have long known the explosive destruction of high velocity small-bores, but the idea of shooting combatants with them just never caught on before. The Army made quite a fuss about not reducing lethality in adopting the AR-15. They needn't have worried. Reports from Vietnam tell of men beheaded or with arms and legs nearly shot off. Wounds that would prove minor with the 7.62 mean certain death with the 223, it is claimed, but there has been no incontrovertible proof of that flat statement. There could hardly be, by the nature of things.

Various articles have ascribed this devastating effect to the 223 bullet "tumbling" in tissue. ArmaLite Vice-President Burton T. Miller, (Col., USAF, ret.) helped conduct the original AR-15 tests. He discounts the tumbling theory, though he agrees the 223 may yaw in tissue. "There's really no mystery about the killing power of the 223," says Col. Miller. "Any varmint shooter knows that hydrostatic shock does the damage. Soon after we got the AR-15, gun buffs at Lackland AF Marksmanship School had sporting rifles chambered to the 223. During deer season, they shot numerous whitetails, with seldom a second shot required, even with full jacketed military ammo. Low neck shots invariably bloodshot meat on the off front shoulder."

Col. Miller says that exit wounds on most of the animals were relatively small, indicating the bullets stayed together. The 223 may disintegrate, though, on close range shots. During testing, I shot into gallon paint cans of water, which blew up most impressively. The lack of exit holes was explained when I found bits of jacket and core inside several of the cans.

Colonel Miller also refutes the hoary contention that light, high velocity bullets are more easily deflected than heavy, slow bullets. "I understand that the Marines constructed a deflection range at Quantico," he says, "with 50 yards of brush between the firing line and the targets.

It was virtually impossible for bullets to avoid encountering limb of varying sizes. Over a period of weeks, the AR-15 and M14 were fired side by side through this brush. The 223 scored as many hits, with no more apparent keyholes than the 7.62. At Aberdeen Proving Grounds, wooden dowels of given size and position, provide an absolutely controlled deflection test. Here, the 223 actually got more hits than the 7.62."

The 223 easily meets the original criterion laid on it, to penetrate both sides of a GI helmet at 500 yards. It also penetrates 5/16" steel plate with a 200 Brinell rating at 200 yards. During our testfiring the 223 penetrated ⅜" boiler plate at 50 yards, right alongside the 7.62, and almost got through ½" plate, cratering as deeply as the NATO round.

The 223 has the inherent accuracy that delights bench rest and varmint shooters. Col. Van Dueson, CO at the Lackland AFB Marksmanship School, has a lightweight sporter in 223 that consistently shoots under 1 inch at 200 yards. Armed forces use opens the door to cheap and plentiful 223 ammo. The 223 may not fare as well as the 7.62 in high winds, but 1000-yard tests of light machine guns in both calibers developed 50% more hits with the small-bore, perhaps because the 223 was less disrupted by recoil.

The AR-15 proved more accurate with a twist of 1–12 rather than with the bench resters' favored 1–14 twist. Colt's changed the twist to 1–12 because cold tests at 65° indicated the heavier air unstabilized 55-gr. 223 bullets from a 1–14 twist.

## AR-15 Accuracy Test

A USAF Operational Suitability Test run last year describes accuracy testing

of 40 random-chosen AR-15s, with some 10,000 rounds fired from a Mann rest, through a 100-yard tunnel. Results indicated that GI AR-15s using issue ammo could outshoot most match grade M1s and M14s. To top this, the 223 ammo used was considered inferior by its manufacturer, who promised marked improvement in future lots. Over-all average of all of the 223 guns tested with 1–12 twist was 3.21" AES (at extreme spread), in Part A of the test, and 2.85" AES in part B. Reloads of 26 grains of BL-C and 52-gr. Sierra bullets reduced groups 1 to 2 inches. Merely pulling the GI bullets and substituting Sierras cut groups 1 inch.

The AR-15 and AR-10 were products of early ArmaLite genius. They have recently come up with a couple of new weapons, the AR-16 (7.62 NATO) and the AR-18 (223), sharing the same general conformation — squarish pressed-steel receiver and trigger groups, with low-lying barrels to avoid climbing in full-automatic fire. The new AR team uses a piston and tappet rod, situated above the barrel to energize the bolt carrier, which disengages 7 locking lugs by rotating them 22.5°. Both guns sport manual charging handles.

Army Ordnance objected to the lack of a manual charging handle on the AR-15, but ArmaLite had a good reason for its absence. The AR-15 is sealed against dirt and mud by a hinged cover over the ejection port and a hollow polyethelyne muzzle plug. A charging handle slot would destroy this seal. The AR-15 goes from "buttoned up" condition into action with the first shot, camming open the ejection port cover and blowing off the plastic muzzle plug.

Don Egger fired all of the rifles prone as well as on the bench, as did the author. Guns, left to right: AR-18 with open sight, AR-15, AR-10 (firing is AR-16), FN, and another AR-18 with peep sight. All handled well.

(As we go to press, Colt's informs us that they have added a new manual bolt-forward-assist to all AR-15s going to the Army. The assist is a small knob projecting back from the right of the receiver. It can be struck with the palm. It moves only about ½". It engages one or another of 28 notches in the bolt carrier, a la ratchet, to force the bolt closed at any point where it might conceivably stick in its forward travel. The USAF has not asked for this device, considering the 8-pound forward thrust of the recoil spring sufficient to close the bolt.)

ArmaLite designed its two new rifles to attack the dirt problem from another angle. They exclude dirt and mud where feasible, but if some does get into an action, it literally chews up the foreign material and spits it back out through openings around the trigger and bolt. The bolt carrier slides on two guide rods that also carry the recoil springs, making for a self-cleaning action. So long as the ammunition remains clean, the guns will function through unbelievable sand or mud baths. In H.P. White lab tests, the AR-16 and AR-18 continued to fire with the trigger groups completely full of mud.

A recent demonstration of the AR-18 at Lorton, Va., turned out numerous interested military observers, domestic and foreign. It developed later that there was even a Communist agent in the group! After the tests, General Curtis LeMay remarked, "If you can hold the price, I think you've got something there!" Such curt praise from the General could be likened to 6 choruses of Handel's "Messiah" from the average man.

The AR-16 and AR-18 are already licensed to the West German firm Erma-Werke GMBH, of Dachau, for European distribution. Estimated tooling costs run $1.2 million, about 25% of tooling-up money for the M14 or AR-15. In 10,000 lots, unit cost will be under $60, less than half that for the M14 in like quantities. "Their low cost and ease of manufacture helps make these guns the finest military rifles of all time," says Chuck Dorchester, current ArmaLite president. "Every Free World nation, large or small, is determined to produce its own small arms. Both guns combine the extensive use of sheet metal stampings with automatic screw machine parts, designed to require a minimum of close tolerances. Small nations can virtually produce these guns in ordinary machine shops; and when the military need is met, this same tooling can literally be converted back from making swords to plowshares."

The AR-16 and AR-18 boast another military advantage, a folding stock that is practical in use and locks securely out of the way when not wanted. With the stock folded, the guns measure about 28 inches, for use in tanks, personnel carriers, etc., or for jump troops. They can be fired like machine pistols. The stock material is a new, virtually unbreakable plastic called polycarbonate. "You could drive a truck over that stock, says Chuck Dorchester, "and not hurt it any." Contrast this with the rash of broken stocks whenever paratroops jump carrying the M14s.

## Test Firing and Evaluations

Evaluating all of these rifles presented a formidable project. Actual firing required several days and over 2,000 rounds of ammo. To give *GUN DIGEST* readers an educated analysis of their military capabilities, I enlisted Don Egger, of Los Angeles, a skilled rifleman and hunter. Don completed his hitch in the Marines, where he trained with both semi- and full-automatic weapons, and was rated a Sharpshooter.

Three basic criteria determine the combat effectiveness of any military rifle. First, the weapon must function dependably, often under extremely adverse conditions. Also, it must be accurate and lethal. We tested the guns for malfunctions by deliberately firing them full-automatic until they were badly overheated, except for the civilian model FN, which was fired rapidly semi-auto. Accuracy was checked from a bench rest. Lethality of the two cartridges involved is beyond question, but we tested for penetration and disruptive effect in cans of water.

Since the AR-18 was a brand new gun, we tried it out first. We demonstrated its destructive force by reducing a concrete block wall to a rubble in a matter of minutes, using full-auto fire. In my first experience with a full-automatic rifle, I took a death grip on the AR-18. It was about like using the touch of a Mack truck driver on a power steering Cadillac. I overcontrolled grossly. Finally, I loosened my clutch on the pistol grip and let the fore-end rest on my open palm, where it vibrated gently like a foot massage machine. The effect was miraculous. I could direct a steady stream of fire wherever desired.

We tested three AR-18 rifles, one the No. 2 prototype and two chosen at random from the first production lot. All 3 functioned full-auto without a hitch, through half a case of ammo. The handguard on the prototype got too hot to hold, but chief engineer Art Miller said more vents would be added to the alumi-num heat deflector, next to the barrel, to carry off excess heat.

The first prototype AR-18 taken to the range by Col. Miller worked at full-auto straight off, which is in itself a pretty fair testimonial for the slip-stick boys at ArmaLite. A few stoppages occurred when cases spun back into the action. Moving the ejection port back slightly eliminated this problem, and the gas port was opened a little to increase the cycling rate.

Well-engineered though it was, the AR-18 did develop one bug. The flash-hider doubles as a grenade launcher, as on the AR-15, so no added attachments are required to fire the bomblike grenades. However, in test firing dummy grenades, we found the recoil shock jarred the gun open. ArmaLite added a spring-loaded crossbolt to lock the latch in place.

We then turned our attention to the AR-15, firing the same 223 round. In firing, the AR-15 matched all of the talents of the AR-18. It has a less boxy but bulkier silhouette. Handling qualities were similar with the two guns. I rather preferred the lower sights on the AR-18. The rear sight on the AR-15 provides a built in handle, but the AR-18 carries easily at the balance point, just ahead of the receiver. The AR-15 has the edge in resistance to corrosion, with its milled alloy receiver. It also has a fold-down trigger guard that allows its use with mittens. Windage adjustment on the AR-15 is effected by turning a drum with the point of a cartridge, similar to the AR-18. There were more similarities than differences between the two.

## Test Fire Report

All the guns tested had many points in common. All were gas-operated and fired from closed bolts. All had vertical pistol grips and 20-shot clips jutting down from the receivers, and safety-selectors above the pistol grips on the left side for full or semi-auto. Front sights on all of the guns were round posts, threaded so they could be rotated for elevation adjustment. Don Egger preferred the FN sight because it was the dullest and blackest of the lot. He would have liked all of the posts 1/32" wider and the peeps enlarged about the same amount. The AR-10 and AR-15 can be equipped with a special scope designed to fit a mount built into the handle. The FN has a special bolt cover for scope mounting. The AR-16 and AR-18 are being fitted with a heavy-duty 3X scope developed by Lyman, in a QD mount that will not obscure the iron sights when the scope is removed.

Bench rest accuracy with these 223 rifles was about equal, with groups running from 3 to 4½ inches. The AR-18 is potentially as accurate as the already proven AR-15. They both feature a new style of construction, using a barrel extension within the receiver to provide locking surfaces for the bolt lugs. The receiver acts merely to join the stock and barrel, and carry the bolt, being subjected to no stress. Accuracy is based almost wholly upon the barrel-ammunition combination, not on such tenuous factors as stock bedding.

Of the 7.62 rifles, the AR-10 seemed to have the best all around handling qualities, but both the AR-10 and AR-16 handled well in full-automatic fire; certainly not with the ease of the 223 rifles, but they were readily controlled for short bursts. Bench rests groups were surprisingly close to the small bores. We fired three 10-shot groups with each rifle. The averages are shown in the accompanying chart. We fired into gallon paint cans and old ammo boxes full of water with the 7.62s, and they punched neat little holes on both sides. The 223's exploded the same cans for a convincing demonstration of greater shock. It appears that 21 rounds of 223 could do far more damage than their scale balance of 10 NATO cartridges. They also cost the government 2¢ less apiece.

The FN provided some remarkable bench rest groups, using GI ammo. At 3 to 3½ inches, they were within Army standards for match guns and ammo. Prone firing with the bipod gave groups almost as good, but lowered the point of impact about 4 inches. The bipod arms fold, to nest neatly within the steel handguard on the model tested. Standard is a wooden fore-end and buttstock. I can only surmise the rifle's handling characteristics under full auto-fire, but it has a low barrel and straight line recoil, and proved controllable during very rapid semi-auto firing. An adjustable gas regulator allows the gun to be adapted to adverse conditions of cold and mud. Also, the cycling rate could be varied at will. The lower receiver is a stamping, the upper section apparently forged and milled. Two opposing screws adjust windage on the rear sight. It has a sliding ramp for ranges of 200 to 600 yards. I liked the husky charging handle on the left side.

Using my accuracy-proven Avtron chronograph, we found that American- and German-made 7.62 ammo gave about identical velocity figures. Complaints that foreign NATO ammo was not up to pressure standards, and that U.S. issue would not function in foreign guns

GUN DIGEST Editor, John T. Amber, test-firing the new AR-18 at Costa Mesa, Calif. during the recent Los Angeles meeting of the NRA. ArmaLite's vice president, Col. Miller, is explaining the operation of the weapon.

## MACHINE RIFLES and PISTOL CARBINES
### Data and Specifications

| Gun | FN Browning | AR-10 | AR-15 | AR-16 | AR-18 |
|---|---|---|---|---|---|
| Caliber | 7.62 NATO | 7.62 NATO | 223 (5.56mm) | 7.62 NATO | 223 (5.56mm) |
| Weight, lbs. [1] | 10.5 [6] | 9.12 | 6.62 | 8.75 | 6.3 |
| Over-all length | 44.5 | 41 | 39 | 41.5 (27) [5] | 38 (28¾) [5] |
| Barrel length [2] | 21-3 | 20-2 | 20-1 | 20-2 | 18¼-1 |
| Bore dia. | .2995 | .2995 | .220 | .2995 | .2190 |
| Groove dia. | .3075 | .3075 | .2245 | .3075 | .2235 |
| Rifling, twist, rate | 4, RH, 1-12 | 4, RH, 1-12 | 6, RH, 1-12 | 4, RH, 1-12 | 6, RH, 1-12 |
| Cyclic rate [3] | 650/700 | 700 | 700/800 | 650 | 750 |
| Trigger pull, lbs. | 9 | 7½ | 6½ | 7¾ | 7½ |
| Bullet wgt., type | 150-gr. BT spitzer | 150-gr. BT spitzer | 55-gr. BT spitzer | 150-gr. BT spitzer | 55-gr. BT spitzer |
| Velocity fps | 2840 | 2760 | 3199 | 2764 | 3182 |
| Sight radius | 21.77 | 20.7 | 19.94 | 22.5 | 20.125 |
| Grouping [4] | 3¼" | 3⁷⁄₁₆" | 3⅝" | 4¼" | 3¾" |

All dimensions are in inches, unless otherwise stated.
All arms tested were production type. The Browning is Belgian-made. The AR-10 is Netherlands-made. The AR-15 is the U.S. Ordnance Dept.'s. M16, Colt-made. The AR-16 and AR-18 are ArmaLite-produced.
Trigger pulls were fairly crisp except on the Browning and the AR-15.
Velocity, in feet per second, was recorded at 10' from the muzzles.

[1] With magazine empty.
[2] Second figure gives length of flash hider.
[3] Rounds per minute.
[4] The average for three 10-shot groups, center-to-center of farthest shots, at 100 yds. Slow fire, from a rest.
[5] With stock folded.
[6] Weight of standard Browning. Light version runs 8¼ lbs., bipod type 10½.

nfounded in this instance. The FN, with its extra inch of barrel, chronographed 80 fps faster than the AR-10 and AR-16.

The Colt-made AR-15 also surprised us with 129 fps more than the AR-18. We guessed that the original chamber configuration in the AR-15, rather than its 1–14 twist was the cause. To be certain, we took the gun back to ArmaLite, reamed the chamber to the new SAAMI standard, and chronographed it again. Velocity fell off to nearly equal the AR-18. The original chamber was changed when pressures ran to as high as 58,000 psi instead of Army specs of 52,000 psi. The new chamber, with 2°27' angle and a .060" lead, dropped pressures to 50,000 psi, with a corresponding drop in velocity. During AF tests, AR-15s dropped 8 primers in 1000 rounds with the old chamber, and only 1 primer in 10,000 rounds with the new chamber.

The 223 is notably easy on barrels. NATO specs call for 6,000 rounds minimum barrel life. After firing 11,000 rounds in one AR-18, most of it full-auto. ArmaLite removed and sectioned the barrel. The completely erosion-free chamber came as a surprise. Usually, gas leaks around the case and erodes the chamber neck. Rifling was scorched near the chamber, but the barrel was still shooting 3½-inch groups when it was dissected. I noted a chamfer in the front edge of the gas port, where it entered the bore. Art Miller explained that the gases speed past the port, strike the base of the bullet, and bounce back to enter the port. The hole is too small to chamfer after drilling, but the gases cut their own chamfer, stepping up the cyclic rate as much as 50 rounds per minute during the life of the barrel.

I timed field stripping and reassembly for each gun, but found little to choose between them. All were swift and easy to take down, breaking open like shotguns, with a latch or pin release. The innards literally spilled out of all of them. Average takedown time was 20 to 30 seconds, reassembly 30 to 45. The only tool required was a single cartridge.

For whatever it's worth, I'll list the guns in order of my preference: AR-18, AR-15, AR-10, AR-16 and FN. Don Egger rated them: AR-15, AR-18, AR-16, FN and AR-10. The choices were hard to make! Both Don and I thought the 223 outrated the 7.62 for over-all combat effectiveness by 2 to 1.

Among the NATO caliber rifles, I rated the FN last because of its 11½ lb. weight when loaded. A lightweight model with "Hyduminium" receiver trims about a pound. Don preferred the sights on the FN, and found its weight no handicap, thus he judged it ahead of the AR-10.

To me, the AR-10 is in a class by itself. I can't understand its rejection by Army Ordnance. The weapon provides match accuracy, and is controllable full automatic, from the shoulder or hip. On a bipod, it doubles ably as a light machine gun. The AR-10 is a steeping giant that may yet awaken.

The AR-16 retains the AR-10's favorable qualities and adds an unheard of compactness in a weapon for this potent a cartridge. Add ease and economy of manufacture, and you have an ideal rifle for Alliance nations still committed to the NATO caliber.

The AR-18 has the assets of the AR-16, with the added effectiveness of the 223 cartridge. The AR-15 has already proved its capabilities in actual battle. The FN is recognized throughout the world as a fine military weapon. Any one of the guns tested could profitably be substituted for the discredited M14.

All new Army AR-15s have Colt's new manual bolt-forward assist. 28 notches are cut on the right side of the bolt carrier. The assist moves about ½-inch, and it is used to force the bolt closed if it should stick at any point in its forward travel.

Col. Miller inspects remains of concrete block wall shot to shreds with full automatic fire from the 223 cal. AR-18. Such a wall would offer no defense to an enemy soldier.

# The Story of
# AR-10

■ Wm. B. Edwards

THE "GREAT RIFLE CONTRO-VERSY" is still a controversy. It was called just that years ago by military analyst Hanson W. Baldwin, in reference to the inability of the U.S. Ordnance Department to decide on a new infantry rifle to replace the Garand, and the term is still apt. A new rifle has stirred up the controversy again in the sacred halls of Washington, in the concrete ranges of Springfield Armory, and on the firing fronts at Aberdeen Proving Ground. This promising contender for adoption as our service rifle is the AR-10, designed by the west coast Armalite Division of Fairchild Engine & Airplane Corp., with headquarters in Hagerstown, Maryland. AR-10, weighing 6.85 pounds, is the first actually light rifle to be tested since the start of the Army's light rifle development program over a decade ago. It is the only rifle in existence which would meet the recent *Futurarmy* requirements of a seven-pound or less shoulder weapon. The Garand weighs well over nine pounds; various recent test weapons range up to 12 pounds.

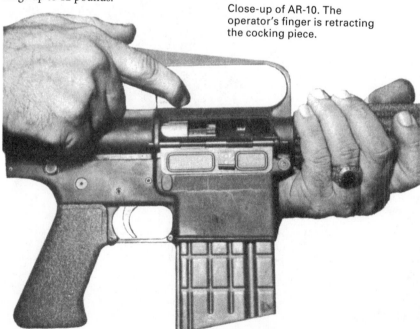

Close-up of AR-10. The operator's finger is retracting the cocking piece.

Junking the Ml Garand is long overdue. Since the first American soldier died with an empty Garand in his hands, the enemy charge signalled by the characteristic twanging sound as the Ml's clip was ejected on the last shot, this rifle has been recognized as obsolete The search for a weapon to replace it has been conducted by the small arms research and development branch of the Office of Chief of Ordnance, in cooperation with Springfield Armory and foreign and U. S. contractors. First in line was a modified Ml Garand, with a 20-shot detachable box magazine and selector switch for full-auto fire. But the modification weighed more than its prototype. Lightweight, plus firepower, and the ability to hit what was aimed at, were alt desirable. A succession of "T" (test) rifles proceeded through the model shops, from T-25, a modified Ml to T-44, a still-further modified box-magazine Ml, and the ill-fated T-47. Then came the T-48, a full-auto weapon heralded as

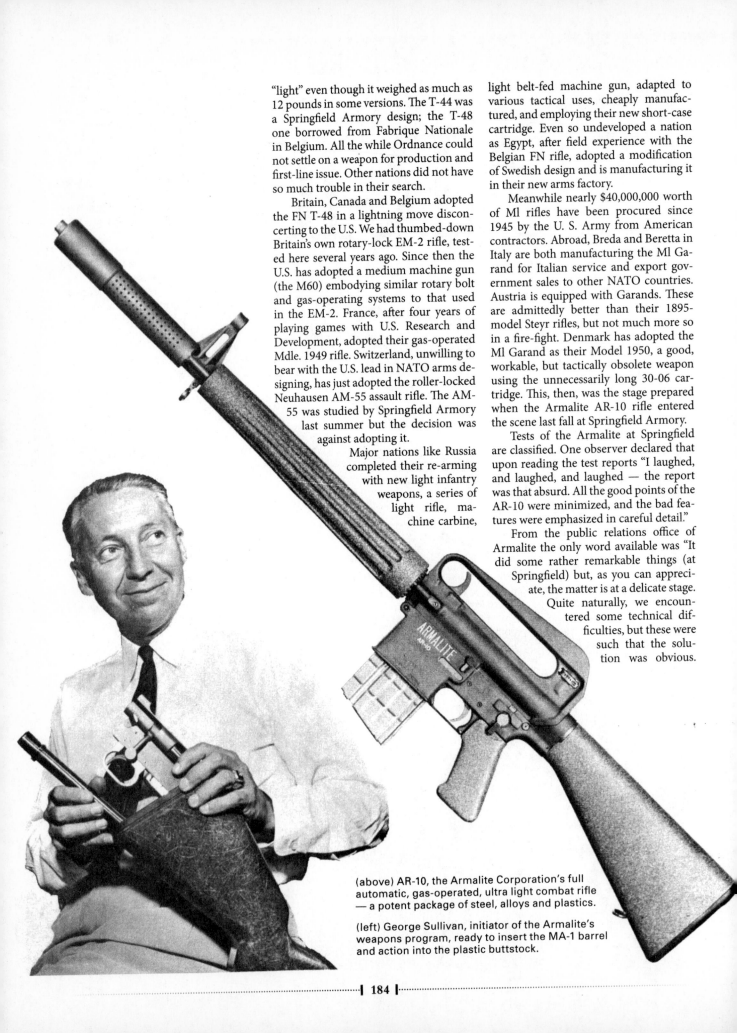

"light" even though it weighed as much as 12 pounds in some versions. The T-44 was a Springfield Armory design; the T-48 one borrowed from Fabrique Nationale in Belgium. All the while Ordnance could not settle on a weapon for production and first-line issue. Other nations did not have so much trouble in their search.

Britain, Canada and Belgium adopted the FN T-48 in a lightning move disconcerting to the U.S. We had thumbed-down Britain's own rotary-lock EM-2 rifle, tested here several years ago. Since then the U.S. has adopted a medium machine gun (the M60) embodying similar rotary bolt and gas-operating systems to that used in the EM-2. France, after four years of playing games with U.S. Research and Development, adopted their gas-operated Mdle. 1949 rifle. Switzerland, unwilling to bear with the U.S. lead in NATO arms designing, has just adopted the roller-locked Neuhausen AM-55 assault rifle. The AM-55 was studied by Springfield Armory last summer but the decision was against adopting it.

Major nations like Russia completed their re-arming with new light infantry weapons, a series of light rifle, machine carbine,

light belt-fed machine gun, adapted to various tactical uses, cheaply manufactured, and employing their new short-case cartridge. Even so undeveloped a nation as Egypt, after field experience with the Belgian FN rifle, adopted a modification of Swedish design and is manufacturing it in their new arms factory.

Meanwhile nearly $40,000,000 worth of Ml rifles have been procured since 1945 by the U. S. Army from American contractors. Abroad, Breda and Beretta in Italy are both manufacturing the Ml Garand for Italian service and export government sales to other NATO countries. Austria is equipped with Garands. These are admittedly better than their 1895-model Steyr rifles, but not much more so in a fire-fight. Denmark has adopted the Ml Garand as their Model 1950, a good, workable, but tactically obsolete weapon using the unnecessarily long 30-06 cartridge. This, then, was the stage prepared when the Armalite AR-10 rifle entered the scene last fall at Springfield Armory.

Tests of the Armalite at Springfield are classified. One observer declared that upon reading the test reports "I laughed, and laughed, and laughed — the report was that absurd. All the good points of the AR-10 were minimized, and the bad features were emphasized in careful detail."

From the public relations office of Armalite the only word available was "It did some rather remarkable things (at Springfield) but, as you can appreciate, the matter is at a delicate stage. Quite naturally, we encountered some technical difficulties, but these were such that the solution was obvious.

(above) AR-10, the Armalite Corporation's full automatic, gas-operated, ultra light combat rifle — a potent package of steel, alloys and plastics.

(left) George Sullivan, initiator of the Armalite's weapons program, ready to insert the MA-1 barrel and action into the plastic buttstock.

I can say that the gun passed tests which no other gun has undergone." What these specific tests are cannot be said until the report is published. Meanwhile, what sort of a gun is this new focal point of Ordnance controversy?

It is light — a full-scale automatic machine-rifle weighing 6.85 pounds compared with, for example, the BAR's 18–20 pounds heft. It is simple in design. Although nominally gas operated, the gas piston and tubes associated with most gas guns are dispensed with. Operating pressure is tapped from near the muzzle and conducted through a small tube to the breech. Inside the receiver, the tube passes into a channel cut in a bolt-operating slide at the rear of the actual breech bolt. The bolt, a multi-lug affair reminiscent of the Johnson short-recoil guns, locks inside a barrel collar. A stud on the bolt is cammed in a rotary fashion by a slot in the bolt operating slide. As the slide is blown to the rear by gas pressure, the bolt rotates, then withdraws, extracting the fired case and compressing the recoil spring contained in the butt stock.

The simplicity of this gas system, a decided improvement on any now in use by any army for a military rifle, accounts in part for the ridiculously low cost of the

AR-10. "In mass production we could make these to sell for about $40" was the claim of one Armalite man.

A straight-line weapon, with very high sights because the top line of the stock is on the same axis as the barrel, the AR-10 is topped by a handle big enough for Arctic mittens, moulded integral with the receiver. At the handle's rear is an adjustable aperture sight. The handle allows the gun to be held up like a big pot of coffee, and there is more similarity than that: the weight of gun complete with loaded aluminum clip magazine and 20 7.62 NATO or 308 cartridges, is just the same as a two-quart pot of coffee!

I've fired this new rifle, and it's a dream. The light weight does not cause any pronounced recoil. A light titanium can is hung on the front for a muzzle brake, and on full-auto fire the gun simply does not have any objectionable rearward motion or muzzle rise. Even without the muzzle brake, kick is much less than with some other full-auto shoulder rifles. Yet the caliber is "full power," not reduced to ease kick in any way. In spite of the fact that I am left handed, the gun is very easy to use since the operating handle is placed vertically above the receiver, like the old model Thompson, and below the sight line.

At the right, a spring loaded cover seals the ejection port from dirt, mud and rain. It flips open instantly on firing when the first shot is snapped off, but can be easily closed by the soldier during a lull in combat.

The first time I saw the AR-10 was on a wintry, raw wet day late in November, last year. In company with machine gun dealers Sam Cummings of Interarmco, Val Forgett of "Ma Hunter's," and Col. George M. Chinn, USMC, author of that monumental work, *The Machine Gun*. I had driven up from Washington to the home of Richard Boutelle, president of Fairchild Aircraft, in Hagerstown, Md.

As we stamped in Boutelle's lodge-like home, shaking rain from our coats, Col. Chinn's eyes lit on the AR-10 and several prototype rifles spread out in anticipation of our visit. "Boy," he said in his Kentucky drawl, "I'd have walked up here to see these." In working the action and noting the unusual gas operating system, Chinn observed considerable gas smudges on the left locking lugs. "You might get some pretty bad gas fouling from this," he commented. "But it would be an easy matter to take your gas off a little farther to the rear," he agreed with Boutelle, who had pointed out that this gun had been fired

(above) Iso-Cyanate foam, the plastic filter that makes the stocks light and strong, overflows the mold.

(center) Removing the AR-10 stock from the mold.

(right) MA-1, the Survival Gun, floats — barrel, action, etc., are held watertight within the hollow buttstock.

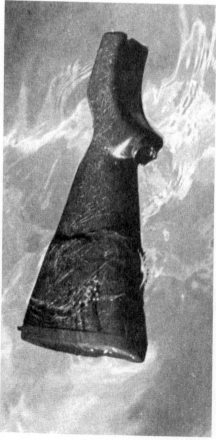

over 600 times without cleaning, and that the need for cleaning was not unknown in other gas-operated guns.

The sensational thing immediately noticed about the AR-10 was its light weight. Aluminum, magnesium, titanium, and small amounts of stainless steel plus plastic are the ingredients of AR-10. Originally planned as a stamped sheet-aluminum receiver, the AR-10 was finalized with a forged and machined receiver of high-strength alloy, possible because all the locking surfaces which take most of the beating in firing were on the stainless steel bolt head, or in the small barrel collar.

The barrel itself is a steel liner swaged in an aluminum tube fluted on the outside. Surrounding this is a thin shell of tough plastic, the front tubular handguard. Air circulates freely through this cover, keeping it cool in hot firing.

We had a chance to get AR-10 hot a few minutes later, in the back yard of Boutelle's home. Shortly the stillness of the Sabbath was shattered by the repeated "bruuup" fire of light machine guns. Cummings had brought along his FG-42 German paratroop machine rifle, a well-designed but heavy 9-pound shoulder weapon, outmoded now by light-alloy guns. Boutelle had an automatic sporting rifle of a different design, but very light weight, using plastics and aluminum. These three — the AR-10, FG-42, and the experimental sporter, performed in what may prove to be a history-making test, the first "press showing" of the Armalite weapons.

The gun has no built-in inaccuracies — it will shoot true. In every respect the AR-10 behaved well. In one test it performed better than expected — the use of too-short ammunition in full-auto fire. Loaded with 110-grain Winchester 308 stuff, the AR-10 slammed twenty shots through the chamber in one easy burst. In practically any other automatic weapon on full auto, the short-bullet rounds would have made failure to feed a certainty. The ability to use sporting ammunition in an emergency is one factor not to be over-looked in developing arms for a nation where the citizen is the soldier. Kick was negligible.

In handling, the "feel" of both AR-10 and the experimental sporter was something definitely pleasant. Reams of copy have been ground out by gun writers on the advantages of a light rifle or shotgun in the field. But the AR-10's basic principles, its alloy and plastic construction, offer the first chance ever presented to American sportsmen to get a truly light weapon. Though both Armalite weapons bulked as large as standard commercial arms, they weighed hardly as much as a boy's 22. Needless to say, Armalite got my order for the first production gun sold, right then.

There are some more gadgets in Armalite's bag of tricks. One neat trick is the MA-1 survival rifle, a stubby 22 Hornet caliber clip-fed bolt action using the alloy and plastic construction pioneered by Armalite. A sub-caliber barrel insert for 22 Long Rifle adapts the weapon to small game, while the 22 Hornet will do for some animals a little bigger. The weapon can be completely dismounted without using tools, and packed into its own buttstock, it's a mere 14" in over-all length. With the rubber cap "butt plate" in place, the whole package will *float*.

Adopted by the Air Force, the MA-1 is not in quantity production because large stocks of less efficient models of survival rifle are on hand. But Armalite feels that with 2" added to the barrel, and 2" more to the butt stock to hold it, they can sell the gun to sportsmen. The next time you capsize a canoe in white water, think how nice it would be to find your rifle, neatly put up in a watertight parcel, floating beside you.

Also almost ready for the sportsman are prototype models of conventional bolt-action sporting rifles and repeating shotguns. With barrels of the high-strength aluminum alloy developed for Armalite by Alcoa, the new rainbow-hued autoloading shotguns weigh less than 5½ pounds. Full-sized sporting rifles, built on Mauser and M722 Remington actions, with steel-lined Armalite aluminum barrels in bright anodized gold, blue and red, weigh as little as six pounds complete with 4X scopes.

The creative engineering, designing, and production of such a variety of futuristic weapons has been the result of teamwork at Armalite. Under the guidance of George Sullivan, a Los Angeles aeronautical engineer and gun hobbyist, the Armalite Division was set up as a research branch of the Fairchild Engine & Airplane Corp., in 1953. Sullivan had been experimenting with aircraft manufacturing methods in his home workshop, and believed that lighter weight guns would be better guns. His work was brought to the attention of Richard S. Boutelle, president of Fairchild, in 1953. Boutelle is a member of the "One-Shot" antelope club, and has for years enjoyed guns as a

Richard Boutelle, head of Fairchild Aircraft, submerges the MA-1 but it pops surface-ward and floats!

(above) Warren Runnals, gunsmith at Armalite, test firing the AR-10 at the company's indoor range.

(below) AR-10 in the test cradle, just after firing 600 rounds in 30 minutes.

(bottom) Stoner (left) and Dorchester waiting for the gun to cool enough for removal from the cradle.

hobby. Once when a friend asked his wife "Why don't you buy Dick a gun cabinet?" she looked around the room with its walls hung with trophies and rifles, and witheringly replied "Because we keep house in one." Sullivan's ideas and Boutelle's coincided from the first, and Fairchild funds have backed the project since then.

To work with Sullivan came Eugene Stoner, another gun crank with experience in the Marine Corps and with U.S. Army Ordnance. Stoner's design philosophy dovetailed right in with Sullivan's lightweight ideas, and the ex-Marine became Armalite's chief engineer. Coordinating all was Charles Dorchester, another member of Sullivan's team, experienced in engineering matters.

These men and their associates in the Armalite Los Angeles shop have created a new concept of weapons that is already making its effect felt throughout the world. Since their work first became known, a leading Swiss small-arms firm has become interested in the new Armalite-Alcoa alloy. Within the past few months (this past spring) the AR-10 rifle has been demonstrated with commendable success to South American countries which have wanted to obtain first-class, light, infantry rifles of modern model. The government of Israel, interested in the greatest economy with the greatest fire-power and durability in a rifle, is studying the AR-10. Meanwhile, what will its effect be with our Army Ordnance?

"We don't really want the T-48 Belgian rifle," one top Springfield Armory department head told me, "since it would mean a 100% retooling." But the T-44 is not entirely satisfactory, either. A stalemate between T-44 and T-48 has now been broken. With the Armalite entry in the great rifle controversy, the need for a decision can be postponed a little longer. Last

summer, for instance, the Swiss AM-55 assault carbine delayed the decision for a few months. Now the AR-10 must be considered. Even if no decision is made, Ordnance need not be unhappy. In the offing is a radically new system of firearm, a combination revolver-automatic with jam-proof feed and triangular cartridges, the Dardick gun. "The army is all steamed up about our gun," Dardick Corporation's ordnance consultant said.

Can it be that the Ordnance Dept. welcomes these new gun developments, welcomes them because they permit postponing any decision to adopt a new weapon? Could be. Meanwhile, we still have plenty of the Garands.

(top) Left to right — Dorchester, Stoner and Runnals checking over the AR-10 after test firing.

(bottom) Left, chief engineer Gene Stoner, and Charles Dorchester, superintendent at Armalite. The Survival Gun, broken down, left in foreground.

THE WORLD'S GREATEST GUN BOOK $15⁰⁰

# Gun Digest
## 1986/40th Annual Edition
Edited by
Ken Warner

The complete gun book, comprehensive and detailed, for all shooters—hunters, handgunners, collectors, handloaders and law enforcement officers.

# The M16A2
## New World Standard For Infantry Rifles...
### ■ C. E. Harris

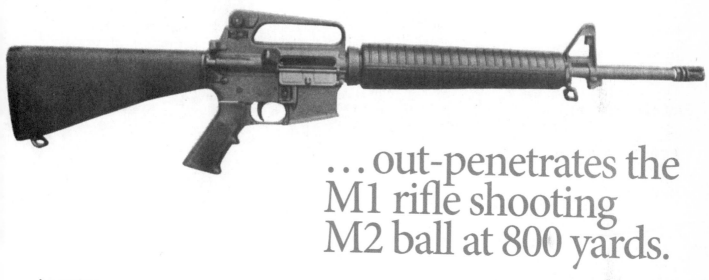

# ...out-penetrates the M1 rifle shooting M2 ball at 800 yards.

THE M16A2 is the new standard to which past and future military rifles will be compared. This second-generation 5.56mm rifle is the product of cooperation between industry and U.S. forces to develop, test and field a product-improved rifle which should meet their needs to the end of this century. The M16A2, standardized in November, 1983, is a wonderful example of how the military development and procurement system is *supposed* to work. The efficiency with which this work proceeded from concept to production and fielding is a tribute to military-industrial cooperation.

When the M16A1 rifle was first adopted by U.S. troops in 1967, the Marines were the most vocal opponent of a "small

caliber" rifle. At that time there were valid complaints about the reliability of the M16 and its M193 ammunition and its range and lethality. Although changes in the rifle and ammunition corrected the functional problems, by 1970 it was apparent the sights and the ballistics of the 55-gr. M193 cartridge reached their limits in combat at about 500 yards. To many critics, even 500 yards pushed credibility.

Adopting the 5.56mm NATO SS109/M855 cartridge in 1977 brought ammunition effective to well beyond 600 yards in lethality and accuracy and penetration. Standardization of this NATO cartridge brought a need to adapt the M16 rifle to it, and provided the opportunity to correct the known tactical deficiencies in the M16A1. The USMC Firepower Division, at Quantico, VA, was tasked with this development in cooperation with Colt Industries, under supervision of the Joint Services Small Arms Program (JSSAP).

The product-improved rifle was identified as M16A1E1 during operational testing which preceded formal type classification. Operational testing of 30 M16A1E1 rifles served to evaluate the changes and provide input for further refinements which would be incorporated

M16A2 barrel marking gives caliber and twist as "1/7."

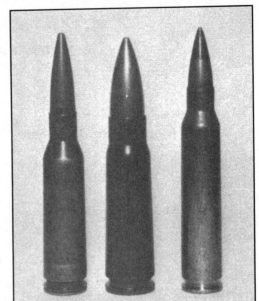

The AK74 5.45mm cartridge and the AK47 7.62mm cartridge — the competitors — are shown to the left of the 5.56mm NATO M855 cartridge, our new standard.

Production version of Colt M16A2: Obvious changes visible are heavier barrel, new muzzle-brake/compensator, improved sights and hand guard, integral brass deflector on receiver and contoured pistol grip.

in the production version of the M16A2. The Modified Operation Test (MOT) began on November 23, 1981, and was completed on December 11, 1981. Supplemental tests continued through August, 1982, to confirm the validity of some proposed improvements and to confirm their production feasibility.

The M16A2 is now in full production, having been adopted by the U.S. Marines to replace their entire complement of M16A1 rifles within the next five years. The Army has also decided to adopt the M16A2. The Canadians are also adopting it, but without the new sights or burst control, as the C7.

The test findings summarized in the MOT Final Report conclude the M16A2 performs as well or better than the M16A1 in all areas. The advantages of the M16A2 over the M16A1 are listed below:

• *Increased effectiveness:* higher hit probability, greater lethality and penetration, improved range through use of NATO standard SS109/M855 ammunition.

• *Better durability and handling* with improved, stronger handguard, and buttstock, longer buttstock, new buttcap, contoured pistol grip.

• *Reduced barrel jump and muzzle climb* during full automatic or sustained semi-automatic fire with new muzzle-brake-compensator.

• *Reduced dust signature* as well when fired over sandy or dusty ground.

• *Heavier, stronger barrel*, to resist bending, with 7-inch twist to exploit advantages of new NATO ammunition.

• *Better sights:* improved contrast and less glare with square post front sight, faster target acquisition of moving targets, better detection of targets in low light, and improved accuracy at long range by use of two optimized rear sight apertures.

• *Better fire control* and more effective use of ammunition with 3-shot burst option.

Operational firepower effectiveness was evaluated by comparing the M16A1 and M16A2 in tactical scenarios. These included base of fire, assault and coun-

terattack, ambush, long range and mid-range defensive fires, final protective fires, defense against ambush, area target suppression, and night firing.

There was no appreciable difference in base of fire effectiveness between the M16A1 and M16A2, but in the assault and counterattack, test results from the Small Arms Remoted Target System (SARTS) showed the A2 obtained a significantly greater percentage of hits in burst fire. When fired semi-automatic on the field range and Infantry Tactical Training (ITT) course simulations, no significant difference was noted. In the ambush scenario, using high volume semi-automatic fire no appreciable difference was noted. Firing in the burst mode at night the data were inconclusive, but when the same course of fire was fired in daylight on the area target suppression test, the A2 delivered 7 percent more hits at 100 meters than did the M16A1.

When firing in the burst mode at multiple targets at 100 meters the A2 gave a significantly higher number of hits, but at

Right side of receiver shows the integral brass deflector on the receiver behind the ejection port which prevents lefthanders from being struck by ejected cases. Aluminum device sandwiched between pistol grip and lower receiver inhibits inadvertent automatic in non-combat situations, such as marksmanship training, where this photo was taken.

50 meters this difference was not apparent. All persons firing the M16A1 used for comparison were firing short bursts of 2 or 3 rounds, which may or may not be what would happen in the high stress of actual combat. In the simulation of a patrol being ambushed, requiring quick reaction, immediate action and firing in bursts or automatic fire, the A2 obtained 19 percent hits, compared to only 12 percent for the M16A1.

The A2's increased ruggedness was evaluated through user assessments and inspection of rifles for damage after an exercise in which several squads conducted an operation clearing seven buildings in "combat town." Rifles were used as steps and to gain access to second stories of buildings. Each participant attacked a rubber dummy stabilized by ropes, ex-

ecuting the vertical butt stroke, smash, parry and horizontal butt stroke, in the same sequence with each weapon. Participants also fixed bayonets and attacked a simulated enemy, bayonetting and slashing it twice. The handguards of the A2 were more durable and appeared to offer better control in close combat, and for urban or builtup area operations.

Portability of each weapon was compared for tactical and non-tactical methods of carry, including the manual of arms while marching. Test participants marched to and from the range with both weapons, and carried them through the combat town course, day movement course and other subtests which included a forced march. User comments indicated no preference for carrying either the M16A1 or A2.

Vulnerability of the weapons to detection and countermeasures were assessed by comparing the noise generated when being carried, and while being operated, as well as the muzzle flash and/or dust signature produced when each weapon fired in day or night conditions. Photographic presentations of the muzzle flash or dust produced were obtained to provide an accurate assessment. Personnel in the butts also answered questionnaires assessing their ability to identify which weapons were being fired based on sounds heard in the butts.

Conclusions indicated no difference in the amount of noise generated by either weapon when being carried or operated. No difference was indicated in muzzle flash in day or night conditions. No significant dust signature was noted due to

The contoured pistol grip is intended to provide more secure grasping; backstrap is deeply grooved, and frontstrap has deep finger groove to provide secure hold. Selector lever offers choice of semi-auto or 3-shot bursts. Rear sight has minute of angle clicks for windage and elevation, matched to M855 or SS109 ammunition.

cold weather conditions, although when firing over new snow less disturbance was noted under the muzzles of the A2s. No essential difference in shape that could be used as a characteristic to identify units can be noted at any distance without the aid of binoculars or a telescope. Personnel in the butts could distinguish which ammunition was being fired at ranges beyond 600 meters, because the NATO SS109 and M855 ammunition remains supersonic to a far greater range, producing a distinct crack as it passes overhead, whereas the 55-grain M193 bullet goes subsonic shortly beyond 600 meters, producing only a muffled pop.

A limited test compared the M16A1 and the new A2 as to any interference generated while carrying the weapons caused by changes in center of gravity, or meth-

ods of carry when engaged in airborne, amphibious or helicopter operations. Participants carried both rifles in operation scenarios wearing full combat gear. There was no meaningful difference between weapons regarding their compatibility or suitability while entering or exiting landing craft, vehicles or aircraft.

The human factors evaluation, or "man-machine interface" characteristics of the two rifles were compared as they might affect operating safety (including hot or sharp parts), useability and adjustability of sights and controls in terms of speed, accessibility, and accuracy of adjustment; and recoil, as it affects recovery time, in burst fire or sustained rapid semi-automatic fire, accuracy in precision fire, comfort and confidence. The effects of the redesigned handguard and buttstock

were also evaluated as they affected accuracy, control in automatic fire and hand to hand combat.

Test participants preferred the sights on the M16A2 to those on the M16A1 because they were easier to adjust and provided a greater range of adjustment, which effectively doubles the useful engagement range of this rifle with SS109-M855-type ammunition compared to the M16A1 with M193-type ammunition. The sights on the A2 are safer to adjust when the weapon is loaded than those on the M16A1, because the front sight is not used for routine sight changes. Ranging adjustments are made on the elevation dial of the rear sight after the front sight is initially adjusted to obtain a battlesight zero. Refinements were made in the size of the front sight post and rear sight ap-

M16A2 front sight is square in cross-section with parallel sides to provide a more distinct sight picture. After first zero adjustment, rear sight offers all adjustments normally required.

The small aperture leg is used for precision daylight fire at ranges beyond 200 meters. The large aperture is used for snap shooting at ranges less than 200 meters and for low light level use near dawn or dusk. Elevation drum moves sight in minute of angle clicks.

ertures based on these tests to optimize precision of fire in daylight conditions, and target acquisition for close range snap shooting and firing in morning or evening nautical twilight conditions.

The M16A2 production sight is adjustable from 300 to 800 meters and has indexing marks on the dial and receiver which align when the sight is turned all the way down or within one click. The 300- and 800-meter settings are co-located on the same position, marked with an indexing line on the top of the dial. Remaining ranges are marked on the dial in 100m increments, i.e., 4, 5, 6, and 7. Range markings on the elevation dial align with the following detents 8/3 (800/300 meters) at 0 or 25th click, 4–3rd click, 5–7th click, 6–12th click, 7–18th click. The short range rear sight aperture is used for ranges up to 200m, has an outside diameter of .375-in. and an inside diameter of .20-in. It is marked "0–2" at the base and has a windage reference point at the top which is used for precision fire with the long range aperture.

The long range aperture is used for firing beyond 200m and has an outside diameter of .375-in. with an inside diameter of .070-in. It is marked "3–8" at the base. The rear faces of both sight apertures are concave and heavily phosphated to reduce glare. One quarter-revolution (one movement/detent) of the front sight moves point of impact approximately 1.4 MOA, one click of the elevation dial on the rear sight moves point of impact approximately 1 MOA, and one click of the windage knob on the rear sight moves point of impact approximately ½ MOA. Firing tests indicate that point of impact is not significantly different with M193 or SS109/M855 ammunition when using the same sight settings at ranges less than 500 meters.

Accuracy and penetration of the M16A1 with M193, the A2 with M193 and SS109/M855 and the Soviet AK-74 with 5.45mm Type PS ammunition were compared at ranges from 100 to 900 meters. The Soviet AK-74 was found to be reliable and accurate at short ranges, but its sights were a limiting factor beyond about 200 meters — it has a short sighting radius, open rear notch sight and no windage adjustments. The M193 ammunition was found most accurate at ranges less than 300 meters, but the SS109 most accurate at ranges beyond 500 meters. The most accurate rifle overall was the M16A2 with SS109 ammunition; the next most accurate was the M16A2 with M193, followed by the M16A1 with M193 and finally the

## Table I
## Accuracy Comparison of M16A2 vs. AK-74

| Weapon/Ammunition | Range (yds.) | | | | |
|---|---|---|---|---|---|
| M16A2 with 55-gr. M193 | 100 | 300 | 600 | 800 | 1000 |
| Mean Radius (ins.) | 1.87 | 4.18 | 13.2 | 18.3 | no hits |
| Extreme Spread (ins.) | 5.25 | 13.4 | 31.4 | 46.5 | no hits |
| Hits On "E" Silhouette 39" high x 19" wide | 20x20 | 20x20 | 11x20 | 10x20 | no hits |
| Score on NRA decimal target SR and MR | 99-6X | 93-1X | 81-1X | 79 | no hits |
| M16A2 with M855/SS109 | | | | | |
| Mean Radius (ins.) | 1.95 | 5.22 | 10.98 | 11.78 | 15.95 |
| Extreme Spread (ins.) | 5.5 | 15.75 | 32.75 | 43.0 | 73.9 |
| Hits on "E" Silhouette | 20x20 | 20x20 | 15x20 | 12x20 | 6x10 |
| Score on NRA decimal target SR and MR | 99-5X | 90-1X | 91-2X | 82-1X | 79-1X |
| AK-74 with 5.45 mm PS | | | | | |
| Mean Radius (ins.) | 1.87 | 8.47 | 15.9 | 20.3 | no hits |
| Extreme Spread (ins.) | 7.25 | 21.6 | 44.0 | 74.5 | no hits |
| Hits on "E" Silhouette | 20x20 | 17x20 | 9x20 | 7x20 | no hits |
| Score on NRA decimal target SR and MR | 99-6X | 79-0X | 69-0X | 57 | no hits |

AK-74 with Type PS ammunition. Accuracy results for the various weapons and types of ammunition tested are summarized in the accompanying tables.

In penetration tests the M16A1 rifle with M193 ammunition, the M16A2 with SS109, M855, M193 and Olin Penetrator (commercial approximation of the SS109), and the AK-74 with Type PS ammunition were fired against 3.5mm thick mild steel plates at various ranges. In addition, the 7.62mm M40A1 Remington sniper rifle with M118 Special Ball (Match, 175-2.0 gr. bullet at 2575 fps) and M80 standard Ball (148.0-2.0 bullet at 2750 fps) were fired for comparison. Maximum ranges at which penetrations of the test plate occurred were 500 yards for the M193, 600 for the AK-74 and 7.62mm M80, and 800 for the 7.62mm M118, 5.56mm SS109, M855 and Olin Penetrator. Results are summarized in an accompanying table.

The question of lethality and effectiveness of the M193 cartridge fired from the fast twist rifling in the M16A2 was of concern because existing stocks of M193 ammunition will be used until sufficient supplies of type M855 ammunition can be produced to replace it. Previous testing had already established there was no loss of precision when M193 ammunition was fired in the M16A2. However, since some nations had adopted faster twists of rifling for supposed humanitarian reasons, this factor had to be investigated. Test firings were conducted with M193 ammunition in both the M16A2 and M16A1 at ranges of 100, 300 and 500 yards, shooting into 20 percent gelatin blocks of U.S. DoD standards, 50cm thick. Testing indicated there was no significant difference in the lethality of M193 ammunition in the M16A2 as compared to the M16A1 at any range fired. The SS109/M855 was equivalent to the M193 at ranges up to 300 yards, and it was significantly more effective at longer ranges, such as 500 yards.

Brief tests were conducted to determine the compatibility of the M16A2 barrel with 22 rimfire ammunition used in the M261 Conversion Unit. This sub-caliber training device is used by Army and Air Force units for preliminary training and by reserve units not having year-round ranges. The conversion unit replaces the standard bolt carrier assembly and converts the weapon to blowback operation, firing 22 LR ammunition from 10-round magazine inserts which are loaded into standard M16 magazines. The device is made under contract to the U.S. Army by Saco Defense Systems, Inc., Saco, ME.

Familiar M16A1 features such as take-down mechanism and bolt-assist knob coexist with new things like brass deflector at right on M16A2.

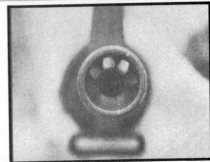

New muzzle-brake/compensator has a closed bottom to reduce dust signature produced when rifle is fired from prone position. It also dramatically improves hit probability in burst fire by reducing muzzle climb.

## Table II
### Performance Of Typical Military Rifles Against NATO 3.5mm Thick Mild Steel Test Plate

| Weapon | Cartridge | Range (yds.) | Performance* |
|---|---|---|---|
| Carbine, M1 | Ball, M1 | 100 | CP |
| | | 200 | FP |
| AKM | 7.62x39 PS (steel core) | 300 | CP |
| | | 400 | 50% CP, 50% PP |
| M16A1 | Ball, M193 | 400 | CP |
| | | 500 | 50% CP, 50% PP |
| | | 600 | FP |
| M16A2 | Ball, M855 | 600 | CP |
| | | 700 | CP |
| | | 800 | 50% CP, 50% PP |
| | | 1000 | FP |
| AK-74 | 5.45x39 PS | 600 | CP |
| | | 800 | FP |
| Rifle, M1 | Ball M2 | 500 | CP |
| | | 600 | FP |
| Rifle, M14 | Ball M80 | 700 | CP |
| | | 800 | FP |
| Rifle, M21/M40 | Ball M118 | 800 | CP |
| | | 900 | 50% CP, 50% PP |
| | | 1000 | FP |

*Explanation of terms:
   CP - complete perforation in which major portion of the projectile exits the armor
   PP - partial penetration in which a hole is generated but the major portion of the projectile does not exit the armor
   FP - failure to penetrate, the plate may be dented but is intact

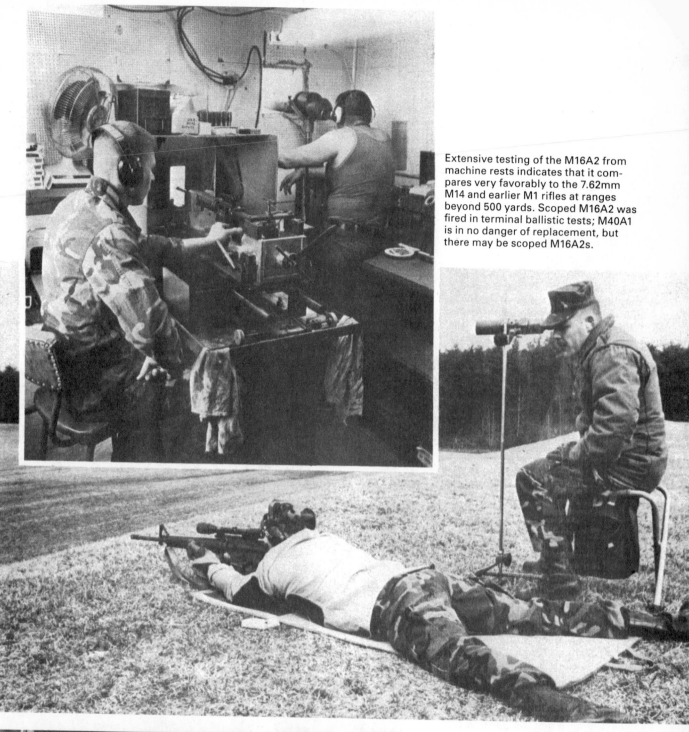

Extensive testing of the M16A2 from machine rests indicates that it compares very favorably to the 7.62mm M14 and earlier M1 rifles at ranges beyond 500 yards. Scoped M16A2 was fired in terminal ballistic tests; M40A1 is in no danger of replacement, but there may be scoped M16A2s.

(left) Writer Harris is well-known as a shooter who will shoot all of what's handy anytime there's a chance. Here he shoots an Egyptian AKM; he has fired the AR-15 and the various M16 options in about all the variations there are and created some of them himself. Indeed, the USMC officially commended Harris for his work with them on the M16A2.

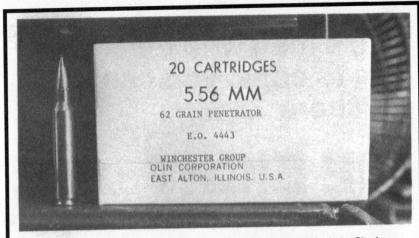

NATO 5.56mm ammunition is made in the U.S. by Olin Corp. and by Lake City Ammunition Plant. FN production is the standard by which others are compared. Ballistics are approximately 3100 fps for a 62-gr. steel core bullet from the M16A2, capable of perforating a 3.5mm steel plate at 700 yards, and capable of defeating soft body armor to 1000 yards. Accuracy of this ammunition from the M16A2 is approximately 2 minutes of angle at ranges less than 300, and about 3 minutes to 1000 yards.

The normal accuracy expected of 10-shot groups with 22 rimfire ammunition fired from the M16A1 with M261 Conversion unit is about 4 MOA at ranges up to 50 meters. Although this is about twice the dispersion of M193 or SS109 type ammunition, it is deemed adequate for training purposes. Side-by-side comparisons with two M16A2 and M16A1 upper receivers, used alternately on the same lower receivers, firing the same M261 unit showed no significant difference in precision, the mean extreme spread of ten consecutive 10-shot groups with each being 2.25-in. and 2.37-in., respectively, at 50 yards.

Testing to date indicates that the M16A2 preserves the strong points of the M16A1 system, while correcting most, if not all of its deficiencies. Since the M16A2 has been adopted by the U.S. Army and U.S. Marine Corps, as well as by the Canadian Forces, it is sure to become a new standard against which future generations of small caliber weapons will be compared.

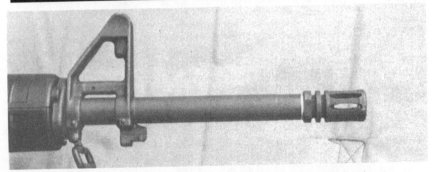

All the old infantry hardware is present — sling swivel and bayonet lug — on the M16A2 but the barrel is noticeably heavier than the M16A1 and the new muzzle brake is a boon.

# TheAR-15/M16:
# The rifle that was never supposed to be

## How the "Mattel Toy" became America's Assault Rifle.

■ Chrstopher R. Bartocci

Photos by Lawrence Ventura. Property of the Wisconsin Department of Justice, State Crime Laboratory-Milwaukee.

The M16-series rifles have served the U.S. military, law enforcement and sportsman with distinction for nearly 40 years. They have become the world's standard for comparison. Here is the latest, the M16A2 assault rifle.

IN MARCH OF 1965, the first U.S. troops landed in Vietnam. They were carrying the M14 rifle, chambered for the 7.62×51mm NATO (M80 Ball) cartridge, which had a detachable 20-round magazine and was capable of semi- and full-automatic fire. The military soon learned the M14 on full auto was extremely difficult to control; most burst fire was ineffective. As a result, many M14 rifles were issued with the selector levers removed, making the rifle effectively, an M1 Garand with a 20-round magazine. The M14 was accurate but heavy, weighing nearly nine pounds, empty. As U.S. involvement in the Vietnam War escalat-

ed, our troops encountered North Vietnamese as well as the Vietcong carrying the Soviet-designed AK47 (**A**vtomat **Ka**lashnikova model **47**), chambered for the 7.62×39mm Soviet cartridge, and had a 30-round magazine. The AK's light recoil permitted controllable, accurate full-auto bursts and American troops began to feel outgunned. The United States needed it's own assault rifle — and needed it fast.

During the early 1950s, ArmaLite, a division of Fairchild Engine and Airplane Corporation of Hollywood, California, was working on a new assault rifle. The chief engineer was Eugene M. Stoner (1922–1997), described by many as the

most gifted firearms designer since John Browning. His first attempt to create a new assault rifle was designated the AR10 (**Arma**Lite **R**ifle model **10**).

The AR-10 was the first weapon to incorporate Gene Stoner's patented (U. S. Patent No. 2,951,424) gas system. This system uses a port in the barrel to bleed gas from the fired cartridge into a tube that runs under the hand-guard, from the front sight assembly to the upper receiver and into the carrier key on the bolt carrier. The pressure gives a hammer-like blow to the bolt carrier, pushing it rearward while simultaneously unlocking the eight-lug bolt from the barrel extension. The bolt and bolt carrier, continuing to move rearward, extract and eject the spent cartridge case and the buffer and recoil/buffer spring return the bolt assembly forward, stripping a cartridge off the magazine, chambering it and locking the bolt into the barrel extension. Using expertise gained in the aircraft industry, Stoner designed the upper and lower receivers of the AR-10 to be made of lightweight aircraft aluminum.

The first AR-10 prototype, chambered for the 7.62×5 1mm NATO cartridge carried in a 20-round magazine, was completed in 1955. The rifle proved extremely accurate for a gas-operated weapon. In December 1955, the first AR10 was presented to the Infantry Board and School at Fort Benning, Georgia, by Gene Stoner and George Sullivan, an ArmaLite executive. Stoner demonstrated his new weapon concept to General William Wyman at Fort Benning on May 6th, just five days after the announcement of the adoption of the M14. Subsequently, the Board recommended further investigation into the AR-10. In 1957 General Wyman, impressed by the merits and performance of the AR-10, went to the ArmaLite Company and asked

Gene Stoner to join a weapons program, offering ArmaLite financial support for future development of ArmaLite rifles in exchange for proprietary rights to the final product. Subsequently, ArmaLite introduced a totally new concept for the modern battlefield, a 22-caliber battle rifle. As a result, the 30-caliber AR-10 was to have a short history with the U.S. military.

The AR-10, scaled down to fire the popular 222 Remington cartridge, had little recoil in semi-auto mode and was amazingly controllable on full-auto. There was heavy resistance to the radical new design from the Ordnance Corps, especially from Dr. Frederick Carten. Doctor Carten was adamantly opposed to weapons developed by commercial companies outside the Ordnance Corps and Springfield Armory, as well as guns made of aluminum and plastic.

General Wyman ordered 10 of these new rifles, along m with 100,000 rounds of ammunition, for Infantry M Board trials. ArmaLite's W focus was thus changed to the 22-caliber rifle and the AR-15 M (ArmaLite Rifle model 15) was born. In 1958, General Wyman ordered the Army to conduct the first tests on the new AR-15.

Among the changes from the AR-10 to the AR-15 were revised sights to accommodate the flatter-shooting 22-caliber cartridge; elevation to be adjusted via a threaded front post sight rather than within the rear sight, where a less expensive L-shaped peep sight was substituted. The resulting rifle was 37½ inches long and weighed an incredible 6 pounds empty; 6.12 pounds with a loaded 25-round magazine.

The AR-15 made use of high-impact fibrite stocks, pistol grips and handguards. A selector lever on the left side of the rifle could be manipulated with the shooter's right thumb without removing the hand from the pistol grip. The magazine release, on the right side of

The original AR15; the weapon configuration that Colt bought from ArmaLite. Notice the three-prong suppressor, the fibrite stock/ pistol/grip/firearm grips, the absent forward assist and the smooth bolt carrier without forward-assist grooves. This was the model used in the Department of Defense testing which launched the weapon's reputation for durability, reliability and accuracy.

The Army/Marine version adopted towards the middle of the Vietnam War to serve the U.S. Marines (until 1983) and the Army (until 1986). Note the forward assist, magazine release fence "Boss" and the "bird cage" flash suppressor. Note the 25-meter zeroing target.

the receiver, could be operated with the trigger finger; when pressed, the magazine would drop free. A fresh magazine, requiring no camming — or 'rocking' — could be inserted straight into the magazine well. This attribute contributed significantly to speedy reloading in combat situations compared to its closest rival, the AK47/AKM. These are two of the main reasons why the AR-15/M16-series rifles are considered the finest human-engineered assault rifles in the world.

A bolt catch mechanism is located on the left side of the rifle. When the last round was fired, the magazine follower would elevate the bolt catch and lock the bolt to the rear. After inserting a full magazine, the rifleman would push in on the upper portion of the bolt catch to release the bolt and load the rifle. The receivers, produced from 7075 T6 aircraft aluminum, which helps keep the rifle lightweight and dissipates heat better than conventional metals, are hard-anodized with a non-reflective matte gray weather-resistant finish.

Stoner went to Aberdeen Proving Ground for ammunition assistance. He enlisted the expertise of Robert Hutton, known as the father of the 5.56×45mm round. The pressures involved were more than the 222 Remington case could handle, so the 222 Special was developed. Sierra Bullet Co. made the 55-grain full metal jacket boat-tail bullet and the first "222 Special" ammunition was loaded by Remington Arms. This cartridge, with a muzzle velocity of 3250 fps and a maximum effective range of 460 meters, became the 5.56×45mm Ball M193/223 Remington.

Tests by the Infantry Board and School at Fort Benning went very well for the AR-15. Stoner personally delivered the weapons and conducted training and familiarization classes for all involved in the testing. In March of 1958, the Board found some "bugs" in the AR-15 system. Some of the resultant changes incorporated in the first rifles were reduction of the trigger pull to seven pounds; replacement of the one-piece handguard with a two-piece triangular handguard; magazine capacity reduced from 25 to 20 rounds and the switching of the selector lever settings. The Board found the AR-15 to be nearly three times more reliable than the M14 in the development stages. Despite the positive conclusion of the

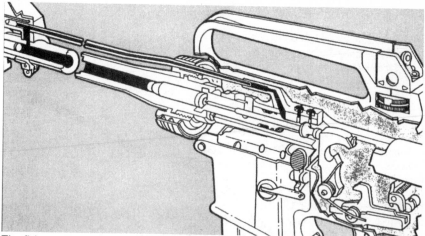

The firing sequence of Gene Stoner's design. After the hammer strikes the primer and fires the round, the bullet travels down the barrel and reaches the gas port where gas is bled into the gas tube and back into the bolt carrier assembly. The diverted gas delivers a hammer-like blow and moves the carrier to the rear, unlocking the bolt, extracting and ejecting the fired cartridge. The buffer spring returns the bolt carrier forward, chambering a fresh round and locking the bolt into the barrel extension — the rifle is now ready to fire again. *Printed with permission of Colt Firearms.*

test, Dr. Carten's report stated the AR-15 had not demonstrated sufficient technical merit and should not be developed by the Army. Accordingly, the Ordnance Corps lost interest in the AR-15.

When Bill Davis, at the time Chief of the Small Arms Branch at Aberdeen Proving Ground, first encountered the AR-15, he was quite impressed and found it had no shortcomings that would not be worked out in the normal course of development. Davis thought Carten's decision to drop the AR-15 rifle was a bad one and that the weapon held great promise.

On February 19, 1959, Colt's Patent Firearms Manufacturing Company of Hartford, Connecticut purchased the rights to the AR-15 and AR-10 from Fairchild Stratos (ArmaLite) for a lump sum of $75,000 plus a royalty of four and a half percent on all further production of the AR-15 and AR-10. Colt also paid Cooper & Macdonald (a sales group who did a lot of work in Southeast Asia) $250,000 and a one percent royalty on all production of AR-15 and AR-10 rifles.

In July of 1960, Air Force General Curtis LeMay attended a Fourth of July celebration where a Colt salesman placed three watermelons on a firing range at distances of 50, 100 and 150 yards — then gave General LeMay an AR-15 and load-

The forward assist bolt closure mechanism. The M16A1 (shown) had the *"tear drop"* style while the new M16A2 has a round button style.

Tlution of the M16 to the M16A1 is very evident when the rifles are compared side by side. The M16 (top) and the M16A1 (bottom). Note the addition of the forward bolt assist, magazine fence guard "BOSS" and the "birdcage" flash suppressor on the M16A1.

ed magazines. Following this hands-on range evaluation, General LeMay ordered 80,000 rifles on the spot. However, Congress put the General's order on hold.

Concurrently, Colt had requested a retrial from the Ordnance Corps to demonstrate improvements to the rifle. Initially the request was denied, the Ordnance Corps saying the military had no use for such a weapon. However, a request arrived at the Pentagon from Lackland Air Force Base requesting the AR-15 be qualified as a candidate to replace M2 carbines.

The combat 5.56×45mm. The M193 Ball Cartridge (left), 55-grain full metal jacket boattall bullet. The M855/SS109 Ball Cartridge (right), 62-grain full metal Jacket boattall with a hardened steel penetrator core. Identified by the green tip.

This turn of events caused Congress to investigate why the Ordnance Corps had boycotted the AR-15. Subsequently, the Ordnance Corps set up the test without delay.

The test was concluded in November 1960. Three rifles were subjected to a light machine-gun test and two to accuracy tests. There were a total of 24,443 rounds fired. One rifle in the accuracy test delivered an amazing 10-round group at 100 yards that measured only 1.5 inches; any group under six inches at 100 yards being acceptable for an assault rifle. The rifle also performed admirably in the unlubricated, dust, extreme cold and rain tests. The final results indicated the AR-15 was superior to all competitors, including the M14. The rifle was then approved for Air Force trial.

It took General LeMay three tries before his request was approved. In the summer of 1961, the Deputy Defense Secretary approved 8,500 AR-15 rifles for the Air Force, pending congressional approval … which Congress withheld. General LeMay then brought the issue to President Kennedy, without success. Finally, in May of 1962, the purchase was approved. With things warming up in Southeast Asia, the AR-15 was about to meet the Army.

Many of the U.S. advisors in Vietnam were equipped with the new AR-15 rifle. Rifles began to surface throughout Vietnam, totally outside the normal small arms procurement process. The first troops using the AR-15 under combat conditions were very enthusiastic, pre-

ferring it to all other weapons. The South Vietnamese were impressed with the rifle, as well. In December 1961, Secretary of Defense Robert McNamara authorized a purchase of 1,000 AR-15s. There was further testing (Project AGILE) to explore the compatibility of the AR-15 rifle to the smaller Vietnamese. The results indicated the AR-15 was more suitable for the South Vietnamese military than the M2 carbine. In actual combat, the new 5.56×45mm cartridge was found to be more lethal than its 30-caliber counterparts. while Project AGILE testing was being conducted, the Army completed the Hitch Report, which was a comparison of the AR-15, AK47, M14 and Ml Garand. The report concluded that the AR-15 was superior to the weapons to which it was compared.

Testing of the AR-15 weapon system had met with contempt from the Ordnance Corps. In one test in the Arctic, weapons were malfunctioning at alarming rates. As soon as Gene Stoner heard, he was on the next plane to Fort Greeley, Alaska. He found parts misaligned, front sights removed (front sights held in with taper pins have no reason to ever be removed) and replaced with pieces of welding rod. With missing and damaged parts, there was no way the weapons would function properly and, with welding rod replacing the front sight, accuracy suffered. The arctic test was, in fact, rigged to make the AR-15 look inadequate. Gene Stoner repaired all the weapons; the test resumed and the weapons performed admirably.

Fortunately, Defense Secretary Mc-

Namara was fond of the AR-15, knew the Ordnance Corps was dragging its feet on the weapon and on January 23, 1963, halted all procurements of the M14. Finally, in 1964, Defense Secretary McNamara ordered the Ordnance Corps to work with all branches of the armed forces to get the AR-15 ready for issue to all military personnel…one rifle for all branches. The Army purchased 100,000 rifles for issue to the Air Assault, Airborne, Ranger and Special Forces units.

After the AR15 — now, the M16 rifle — went into circulation, more was learned about how to improve the rifle. The rifling twist was changed from 1:14 inches to 1:12 inches. The Army wanted a manual bolt closure device added so, if the bolt failed to lock, it could be manually closed — and the forward assist assembly was born. The firing pin was lightened to prevent slam-fires (caused by the inertia of the firing pin when the bolt closed on a round). The buffer was changed from the original hollow version to one with weights in it to prevent the bolt from bouncing back when it slammed into the barrel extension.

On November 4, 1963, Colt was awarded a contract worth $13.5 million dollars for the procurement of 104,000 rifles … the legendary "One Time Buy." Of those rifles, 19,000 were M16s for the Air Force and 85,000 were the XM16E1 (with the bolt closure device/forward assist assembly) for the Army and Marines. The XM16E1 was adopted as the M16A1 rifle. Steps were taken to procure ammunition.

Procurement of the ammunition is one of the main factors in the rifle's performance early in the Vietnam War. The initial ammunition used by DOD was made to Armalite/Colt specifications that called for IMR 4475 propellant. The weapon's

The M16A1 field-stripped. The ease and simplicity of disassembly made cleaning easy. All AR-15/M16-series weapons disassemble in the same manner.

reputation for durability and reliability was based on this ammo/extruded propellant combination. However, the military wanted to standardize propellants and the propellant used in the established 7.62×51mm NATO cartridge was Ball powder manufactured by Olin Corporation. So, when ammunition was ordered, Olin's Ball powder was used for the new 5.56×45mm M193 Ball cartridge. Both powders created the desired 50,750 psi.

Ball (spherical) powder reaches its peak pressure significantly faster than extruded IMR powder. Ball powder generates larger amounts of carbon residue that clogs the gas tube and barrel port, causing the firearm to malfunction. The most serious malfunctions, during the early use of Ball powder, involved extraction problems and a significant increase in the cyclic rate of fire. Despite having this information, the Department Of Defense still approved use of Ball powder. Gene Stoner was approached by Frank Vee of the OSD Comptrol-

lers office after the package was approved and asked what he (Gene Stoner) thought of the use of Ball powder. Stoner asked, "Why are you asking me now?" Vee said, "I would have felt better if you would have approved the package." Stoner replied, "Well, now we both don't feel so good."

The "one-time buy" was now a thing of the past. The original $13.5 million contract turned into a $17,994,694.23 contract. There were an additional 33,500 rifles that went to the Air Force, 240 to the Navy and 82 to the Coast Guard. Over $517,000 worth of spare parts was ordered.

The first field performance reports, from the 5th Special Forces in Vietnam, were excellent. The rifle had been well received and was very popular, although instruction manuals were in "short supply." During the investigation by the Ichord Subcommittee of the M16 Rifle Program, Honorable Richard Ichord said — regarding the rifle's reputation with the North Vietnamese Army and Vietcong — "I understand that they refer to this rifle as 'black rifle,'…I have heard their motto is 'Beware of the units with the black rifles'… they have been possessed with deadly fear." In September 1965, General Westmoreland ordered an additional 100,000 rifles and requested all U.S. ground

The battle cartridges of the 20th Century ( left to right ): 7.62×63mm (30-06 Springfield); 8mm Mauser; 7.62×54mm Russian; 7.92×33mm Kurtz; 30 US Carbine; 7.62×51 mm NATO (308 Winchester); 7.62×39mm Soviet; 5.56×45mm NATO (223 Remington) and the 5.45×39mm Soviet.

Which is the better assault rifle? The M16A1 (top) or the AKM/AK47 (bottom)? Both are the most prolific military rifles of the last half of the 20th century; the most tested and most produced all over the world. Author feels hands-down winner is the M16 series.

forces in Vietnam be equipped with the new M16A1 rifles. Colt now signed an additional contract to deliver 25,000 rifles a month by December 1966. In 1968, GM Hydramatic Division and Harrington & Richardson were awarded second-source contracts from the Department of Defense.

Letters from the field began reporting the rifles were malfunctioning at an alarming rate, with U.S. troops found dead next to jammed M16 rifles. Spent cartridge cases were becoming lodged in the chamber and the only way to remove them was to knock them out with a cleaning rod. Requests were made for Colt to send a representative to the field to solve this problem. This turn of events was highly publicized by the media.

A representative from Colt, Mr. Kanemitsu Ito, went to Vietnam and claimed to be shocked, having never seen equipment in such poor shape. He claimed to have looked down the barrel of one rifle and not seen 'daylight' due to severe rusting and pitting. Many of the troops he spoke to said they were never trained to maintain their rifle, that the rifle was "self-cleaning" and that they had not handled an M16/M16A1 rifle until they arrived "*in-country*." Subsequently, Mr. Ito gave classes on maintenance all over South Vietnam.

Seeking an independent, unbiased report of the true field performance situation, the Ichord Congressional Subcom-

mittee selected a retired officer, Colonel Crossman, as their representative and sent him to Vietnam. In the course of his investigation, he interviewed 250 soldiers and Marines throughout South Vietnam, fully 50 percent of whom reported malfunctions with their M16/M16A1 rifles. Of these malfunctions, 90 percent were failures to extract. Colonel Crossman found 22-caliber cleaning kits in short supply and concluded many of the problems were due to lack of maintenance and cleaning. He also felt there was room for improvement in the rifle. He concluded, "It was not possible to correlate ammunition make or type with malfunctions." His findings report, dated June 16, 1967, included the statement that the rifle needed a complete overhaul in design and manufacture.

According to Gene Stoner, there were hardly any 22-caliber cleaning kits in Vietnam — and no instruction manuals. The "cleanup" began: The military developed bore and chamber cleaning brushes and began to distribute 22-caliber cleaning kits, firearm maintenance cards and instruction manuals, for the M16/M16A1 rifles.

From May 15th through August 22nd, 1967, the much-publicized Ichord Congressional Subcommittee (Honorable Richard Ichord, Chairman) investigated the history, development, testing, procurement and foreign sales of the M16 rifle. During the investigation, the subcommit-

tee visited U.S. military training installations of all branches where the committee members interviewed hundreds of Vietnam returnees on their experiences with the M16/ M16A1 rifle. They also visited South Vietnam to interview troops in combat zones. Several people were called to testify before the subcommittee. Two topics, not identified until after the subcommittee returned from Vietnam, were the propellant and high cyclic rate issues. The subcommittee would focus most of their attention on these two aspects.

Reports from Vietnam of failures to extract in the field caused the subcommittee great concern. They investigated, finding the major contributor to malfunctions was ammunition assembled using Ball powder. The change from IMR extruded powder to Ball powder in 1964 for the 5.56mm ammunition was neither justified nor supported by test data, they found. The subcommittee also found the Ball propellant sole-source position enjoyed by Olin Mathieson for many years — and their close relationship with the Army — may have influenced Army Materiel Command. They felt the AR-15/ M16 rifle, as initially developed, was an excellent and reliable weapon. Further, certain modifications made to the rifle at the insistence of the Army — also unsupported by test data — were unnecessary. For example, both the Air Force and the Marine Corps found no evidence to support the expense and possible problems of the manual bolt closure (forward assist) device.

Gene Stoner was called to testify at the congressional hearings to explain the extraction problem; he explained the failure to extract was due to the use of Ball powder.

Gene Stoner [To Mr. Bray]: "Well, the cartridge tends to stick under high residual pressure in the barrel, and of course with this too-soon action you also have a higher bolt velocity. In other words, your bolt is trying to open at higher speeds, so you have an aggravated condition where the cartridge is tending to stick in there a little longer or a little harder, and you are also giving it a harder jerk by driving the bolt faster."

Mr. Bray [To Gene Stoner]: "Then a faster rate of fire could cause that situation (failure to extract)?"

Gene Stoner [To Mr. Bray]: "This is probably one of the worst conditions you can get, by increasing the cyclic rate."

Basically, Ball propellant causes the bolt to open prematurely, before the spent cartridge case has had sufficient time to contract. The result is the extractor shears off the rim of the spent cartridge case — which sticks in the chamber. Ball and IMR powders create the same peak pressure but the Ball powder reaches its peak much faster than IMR powder, causing a significant increase in the cyclic rate of fire. Ball powder leaves significantly more fouling in the chamber and bolt assembly. Gene Stoner also pointed out the rifle had gone through more than 22 changes from his original design and neither Colt nor the Department of Defense consulted him on how some changes would impact his design.

The forward assist was one of the changes on which he was not consulted and Mr. Ichord asked Gene Stoner his opinion of the device.

Gene Stoner [To Mr. Ichord]: "I wasn't in on that, except I was told the Army insisted on it. There were reasons for it. One reason was that they felt that due to the fact that the M1, and the M14 rifle, and the carbine had always had something for a soldier to push on; that maybe this would be a comforting feeling to him, or something. I could never quite get it through my mind that it was necessary. I did not really advise it. I thought it was a mistake, myself. But I made my thought known to the people."

He explained the last thing you want to do is force a round into a dirty chamber, which quickly leads to function failures. The chamber fouling tends to embed

## Specifications Table

| | M16/M16A1 Rifles | M16A2 Rifles |
|---|---|---|
| Caliber | 5.56×45mm NATO | 5.56×45mm NATO |
| | M193 Ball | M855Ball/M 193 Ball |
| Method of Operation | Gas | Gas |
| Locking System | Rotating Bolt | Rotating Bolt |
| Type of Fire | Selective | Semi/ 3-Shot Burst |
| Weight Empty | 7 pounds | 7.9 pounds |
| Magazine Capacity | 20 & 30 Rounds | 20 & 30 Rounds |
| Barrel Length | 20 inches | 20 inches |
| Overall Length | 39 inches | 39.624 inches |
| Technical Data | Rifling: 6 grooves, right hand twist, 1 turn in 12 inches | Rifling: 6 grooves, right hand twist, 1 turn in 7 inches |
| Sights | **Front;** post with elevation adj. **Rear;** L-type aperture windage adj. only. | **Front;** post with elevation adj. **Rear;** L-type aperture adj. windage and elevation |
| Cyclic Rate | 750 to 950 RPM | 750 to 950 RPM |
| Practical Rate of Fire | 150–200 RPM, Automatic | 150–200 RPM, Automatic |
| Muzzle Velocity | M193 Ball-3,250 fps. | M193 Ball-3,250 fps. M855 Ball-3,100 fps. |
| Muzzle Energy | M193 Ball- 1,270 ft/lb | M193 Ball-1,270 ft/lb M855 Ball-1,302 ft/lb |
| Cooling | Air | Air |
| Maximum Effective | 460 Meters/ 503 yards | M193 Ball-460 meters/ 503 yards |
| Range | (Individual / Point Targets) | M855 Ball-550 meters/ 600 yards |
| | (Area Target) | M855 Ball-800 meters/ 875 yards |
| Maximum Range | 2,653 Meters/ 2,902 yards | M193Ball-2, 653 meters/ 2,902 yards |
| | | M855 Ball-3, 600 meters/ 3,935 yards |

in the soft brass cartridge case and lock it in, causing a fired cartridge case to be — literally — locked into the chamber at the moment of extraction. Gene Stoner was able to prove the rifle and ammunition combination he furnished to Armalite/Colt was a totally reliable weapon system and the change the military made, without his consent, caused the malfunctions. He told the committee he expressed these concerns to the OSD Comptrollers office and was ignored. The subcommittee ac-

cepted this as the reason for the condition.

M16 rifle project manager, Col. Yout, was of particular interest to the subcommittee. Throughout the hearing he was accused of making irresponsible decisions as to the direction of the program.

Mr. Ichord [to Col. Yout]: "We have evidence and are advised by our experts … that Ball propellant, which you apparently speak so highly of, does have an adverse affect upon the operation of the

M16 rifle. It speeded up the cyclic rate. It is dirtier burning … . When we are also advised that the Army was cautioned against making this change from IMR to Ball propellant … Naturally, we would be quite concerned. Apparently you aren't so concerned. I don't understand your explanation. I just haven't been able to understand you — but perhaps you haven't offered the information in words I can understand. Would you care to say something?" He never replied to the question.

The Army made a statement on July 27, 1967: "From the vantage point of retrospect, it has sometimes been suggested that the particular behavior of Ball propellant should have been predicted … Had the Army anticipated these developments, it is most unlikely that the course chosen in January, 1964, would have been the same. A decision to reduce the velocity requirement, and continue loading IMR4475 propellant would probably have been made instead, and development of alternate propellants could have been pursued more deliberately."

This is the closest to an admission of negligence by the Army for the decision to use Ball powder. Gene Stoner warned them long before it got to this point; who would know more about the rifle's performance and design intent than the man who designed it? In the end, the rifle was not the problem; instead, this was an ammunition-driven problem that altered the design intent of the rifle.

In August 1967, the hearings ended, and in October 1967, the subcommittee concluded, "Grave mismanagement, errors of judgment

The CAR15 (Colt Automatic Rifle 15) gained major popularity with the development of the new M4 and M4A1 carbine. Note the telescoping stock and the shorter barrel. Most CAR15 rifles were issued with a 14.5-inch barrel.

and lack of responsibility had characterized the Army's handling of the entire M16 program." They stated the officials in the Department of the Army were aware of the adverse affect of Ball propellant on

the cyclic rate of the M16 rifle as early as March 1964, yet continued to accept delivery of additional thousands of rifles that were not subjected to acceptance or endurance tests using Ball propellant. All Colt endurance testing was done using IMR 4475. The subcommittee also concluded, "The failure on the part of officials with authority in the Army to cause action to be taken to correct the deficiencies of the 5.56mm ammunition borders on criminal negligence."

The cyclic rate of the rifle was increased 10 to 15 percent (approximately 200 rounds per minute), resulting in higher stress on certain components caused by the higher velocity of the bolt carrier assembly. As a result, there were parts driven beyond their working parameters - as well as the bolt opening prematurely. Many parts were changed to more stringent specifications to help deal with the higher pressure curve and harder impact. To solve the chamber corrosion and failure-to-extract issues, all future production rifle barrels would be chrome-lined. Even though chrome-lining barrels is a military specification, Ordinance failed to require this basic requirement on the AR-15/M16 rifle system.

Chrome-lining the barrels gave three major improvements to the standard barrel. First, the chrome-lined barrel was corrosion resistant. Second, chrome is slippery in nature and assists in extraction and ejection. When chromed, the walls of the chamber are harder; sand and mud don't "iron" into them. Thirdly, chrome is 2 to 3 times harder than standard barrel steel so the barrel lasts significantly longer. The new, improved M16/M16A1

barrel assemblies would have stamped on the barrel, in front of the front sight assembly: "**C**" (Chrome Chamber Only), "**C MP B**" (Chrome Chamber, Barrel & Magnetic Resonance Tested) or "**C MP Chrome Bore**"(Chrome Chamber, Barrel & Magnetic Resonance Tested). Many experts, including Bill Davis, felt the failure to chrome the chamber was responsible for many of the early malfunctions in Vietnam.

The flash hider was changed from the early three-prong to the new "bird cage" style. The three-prong suppressor was superior to the new design, but was snagprone in the field. With these modifications in place, the M16/M16A1 rifle was "perfected" and performing to the Department of Defense acceptance standards.

## The AR15/M16 Carbines

Soon there was a demand for a smaller, more compact, version of the rifle. Early in 1966, the Army expressed interest for a carbine for its special operation units, placing an order totaling some 2,050 carbines. Lieutenant Col. Yout later ordered an additional 765 Colt "Commandos" — and a new name was coined for the carbine project. The first carbines were known as CAR15 (Colt Automatic Rifle). These first designs incorporated a 10-inch barrel and a sliding butt stock. Later the barrel was changed to 11.4 inches to permit the weapon to launch grenades. The Army signed a contract for 2,815 "Commando model" submachine guns on June 28, 1966.

As expected, the CAR15 — now the XM177E2 — successfully passed all testing phases at Aberdeen Proving Ground. However, a new problem appeared: the deafening noise and large fireball from the muzzle, thanks to the CAR15's higher cyclic rate of 700 to 1,000 rounds per minute. As a remedy, many of these rifles were equipped with 14.5-inch barrels, a practice that carried over to the M4 project of the early 1980s.

## Product Improvement (PIP)

On October 28, 1980, there was a new 5.56×45mm cartridge on the block. NATO (Northern Atlantic Treaty Organization) had adopted the Belgian-made SS109. This new bullet had two major differences from the GI 5.56×45mm M193 Ball cartridge. First, the bullet weighed 62 grains instead of 55 grains. Second, this new bullet had a hardened steel penetrator core, giving this new 5.56×45mm round better penetration at all distances than the 7.62×51mm NATO (M80 Ball) round. This new SS109 round penetrated three 3.5mm mild steel plates at 640 meters and a U.S. issue helmet at 1,300 meters.

The new 5.56×45mmNATO round revolutionized military small arms ammunition all over the world. In 1974, the Soviet Union switched from the 7.62×39mm (AK47/AKM) to the 5.45×39mm Soviet round of the new AK74 rifle. This new round was a .221-inch diameter 52-grain full metal jacket boat-tail armor-piercing bullet with a velocity of 3000fps.

The new SS109 round was more lethal than the original M193 Ball round due to the faster "spin" and fragmentation upon impact with soft tissue.

Military surgeons all over the world have asked the United Nations to ban small caliber high-velocity rounds in combat — including the 5.56×45mm and the 5.45×39mm cartridges — which they believe cause unnecessary pain and suffering.

Switzerland re-designed the M855/SS109 round with a thicker jacket to stop fragmentation upon impact.

The SR25, perhaps the most accurate autoloader on the face of the earth. Gene Stoner revives his original AR10 design, with some added features of the M16A2, to build this semi-automatic 7.62×51 mm sniper rifle.

This new cartridge, however, was significantly more accurate at longer ranges than the M193 Ball cartridge, boosting the maximum effective range to 800 meters. To accommodate this new cartridge, a new barrel twist — from 1:12 inches to 1:7 inches — was required to stabilize the heavier 62-grain bullet.

There was a catch: the SS109 ammu-

nition could not be fired accurately in an M16/M16A1 rifle due to its slower rifling twist. The bullet would not stabilize and would "keyhole" in flight. This new cartridge was about to be adopted as the M855 Ball cartridge of the U.S. military and the new PIP project would redesign the M16A1 rifle around this cartridge.

The United States Marine Corps began negotiations with Colt in January of 1980, asking for three modified rifles that would make use of the new FN SS109/XM855 cartridge and would incorporate four Marine-designated changes:

1. The sights must be adjustable to 800 meters.

2. The bullet must be accurate to 800 meters and possess the capability to penetrate all known steel helmets and body armor at 800 meters.

3. The strength of the plastic stock, pistol grip and handguards — as well as the strength of the exposed portion of the barrel — must be improved.

4. The rifle must have the full-auto capability replaced with a 3-shot burst mode.

## The Joint Services Small Arms Program (JSSAP) PIP

The first rifles arrived from Colt in November of 1981. The USMC Firepower Division at Quantico, Virginia, would lead the PIP project. On November 11th, 20 Marines and 10 soldiers from the 197th Infantry Brigade at Fort Benning, Georgia, would take 30 M16A1 rifles and 30 M16A1E1 (PIP rifles) and test them for a month. The test report was issued on December 11th and the conclusions were as follows:

• The sights were easily adjusted in the field by hand rather than with a bullet tip.

• Increased the effectiveness at long range, more so than the M16A1.

• More durable plastic furniture on the M16A1E1, for hand-to-hand combat.

• Sights were better for low-light conditions thanks to a larger-diameter (5mm) close-range aperture in the rear sight.

• Increased ammunition conservation and more effective fire with the 3-round burst than with full-auto fire.

• Utilized the XM855 NATO (SS109) ammunition, which improves the accuracy and penetration at all ranges. The product-improvement (PIP) "M16A1E1" was classified as the **M16A2** in September of 1982 and was adopted by the United States Marine Corps in November of 1983. The Marines ordered 76,000 M16A2 rifles from Colt.

The Army did not adopt the M16A2 until 1986.

## The M16A2 Rifle

There were twelve major changes from the M16A1 to the M16A2 and, although the rifles seem similar at first glance, they are two totally different weapons. Many improvements were necessary to accommodate the new M855 Ball and M856 tracer rounds. The twelve major variances between the A1 and A2 are as follows:

1. The flash suppresser of the M16A1 is now a muzzle brake/ compensator on the M16A2. Instead of having vents all around the flash suppresser, the bottom has been left solid, which reduces muzzle climb and prevents dust from flying when firing from the prone position.

2. The barrel, from the front sight assembly to the flash suppressor/compensator, is heavier. The M16A1 rifles barrels were known to bend when paratroopers landed and the barrels hit the ground. When the A1 barrels would heat up, sling tension could bend them. The new M16A2 barrels had a rifling twist of 1:7 inches to accommodate the SS109/M855 cartridge.

3. The front sight post on the M16A2 is square, contrasted to the round post of the M16A1.

4. The M16A2 handguard was redesigned to have an interchangeable, upper and lower, round ribbed handguard.

5. The slip-ring "delta ring" was redesigned and is now canted for easier removal of the hand-guards.

6. A spent shell deflector was added to the upper receiver behind the ejection port of the M16A2 to accommodate left-hand shooters and, as well, the pivot pin area of the upper receiver has been

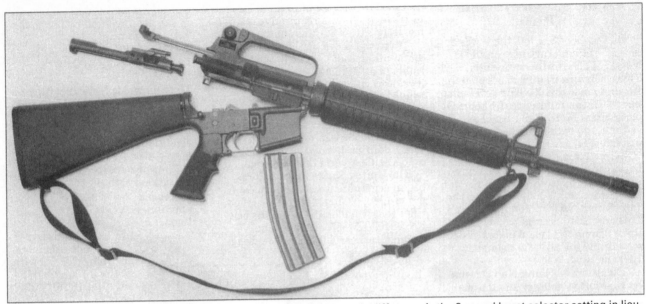

The M16A2 is mechanically identical to the M16 and the M16A1. The only difference is the 3-round burst selector setting in lieu of full-auto. All the changes were improvements to accuracy, more durable stock and grips as well as some structural reinforcements.

strengthened. The area around the buffer tube extension (takedown pin area) was strengthened to prevent cracking during hand-to-hand combat or from impact on the butt of the weapon while cushioning one's fall.

7. The rear sight was redesigned. The 1.75mm and 5mm apertures made adjustable for windage as well as elevation. The maximum elevation setting is 800 meters. There is still an "L-shaped" sight aperture, and there is a 5mm aperture battle sight effective to 200 meters.

8. The forward assist assembly was changed from the "tear drop" style of the M16A1 to the new round "button" style forward assist assembly of the M16A2.

9. The pistol grip is now made of a stronger plastic (™Zytel), and incorporates a "swell" below the middle finger position.

10. The three-shot Burst selector lever setting of the M16A2 replaced the Auto setting of the M16A1.

11. The ⅝-inch longer M16A2 stock is made from foam-filled nylon, said to be ten to twelve times stronger than the fibrite stocks of the M16 /M16A1.

12. The buttplate has been made stronger (™Zytel), and the entire buttplate is checkered. The trapdoor can be opened by hand rather requiring the tip of a cartridge.

## Critics Attack the M16A2

There were critics who still found problems with the M16A2. One of the greatest criticisms was the substitution of the Burst mode for the Automatic mode selector option. The critics reasoned the M16 rifle was adopted because U.S. troops felt outgunned by the North Vietnamese Army/Viet Cong who were equipped with full-auto AK47s. While, theoretically, the 3-round burst was more effective than full-auto fire, there was no substitute for a well-trained automatic rifleman. More recently, infantry units have noticed it takes more time to clear rooms and buildings in the MOUT (Military Operations in Urban Terrain) environment with the 3-round burst versus the full-auto mode and feel the full-auto option is desirable in those circumstances.

Not only was the conceptual validity of the three-round Burst under scrutiny, but the mechanical design as well. The burst mechanism does not recycle. If only two rounds were fired — because the trigger was not held long enough or the weapon ran out of ammunition — the next time the trigger was pulled only one round would fire.

Further, some critics found the sighting system too complex. The Canadian military addressed many of the issues brought up by American military critics. When Canada replaced their aging FN FAL 7.62mmNATO rifles, they modeled the new rifle after the M16A2. Their Diemaco-manufactured C7 was, virtually, an M16A2 that retained the rear sight and the full-auto setting of the M16A1. Some critics did not like the fact that the new M855 cartridge could not be fired in the current issue M16 /M16A1 rifles without raising concerns that the fast 1:7-inch rifling twist would more quickly burn out barrels during extended rapid fire.

## The "Shorty" Program Revisited: The M4 Carbine.

In 1994, the Army adopted the second carbine of the 20th century and the first general issue carbine since 1941, the M4, perhaps the finest carbine ever developed. They were, at first, to be used by special operation units, but then were selected for use in many other units. Deliveries began in August of 1994, from Colt's Manufacturing, for 24,000 M4 carbines contracted at $11 million; another contract followed in 1995 for 16,217 M4A1 carbines.

The M4 is basically an M16A2 with a telescoping butt stock and a 14.5-inch barrel. The barrel has the heavy profile of the M16A2 barrel with a modified groove to accommodate the M203 grenade launcher. With its 14.5-inch barrel, the M4 fires the M855 Ball round at 2900 fps. The M4 incorporates the M16A2 fully adjustable rear sight. Colt's Manufacturing claims there is little, if any, difference in accuracy at ranges up to 500-600 meters. M4 carbines can be found with either full-auto or burst settings. The M4 duplicates the reliability and accuracy of the full-size rifle and weighs only 5.65 pounds.

The M4 has two variants, the standard M4 and the M4A1. The M4A1 is identical to the M4 with the exception of its removable carrying handle, which is attached to a Picatinny Weaver rail system. This arrangement enables easy attachment of

The latest in the M16 family, the M16A2. The standard by which all assault rifles are judged. Note major changes: fully adjustable rear sight, round handguards, longer stock, finger swell on pistol grip and cartridge case deflector. Note the 25-meter zeroing target.

optical sighting systems or, by reattaching the carrying handle, use of the iron sights.

## Rebirth of the AR-10, Further Developments by Gene Stoner

The legacy of the ArmaLite rifles is far from over. The great weapons designer, Eugene Stoner, never stopped working on his AR-10 design. He, along with C. Reed Knight of Knight's Manufacturing, perfected the AR-10 and added many design features of the M16A2, to build the SR25 (Stoner Rifle Model 25). The model number comes from adding the 10 from the AR-10 and the 15 from the AR-15. Basically the SR25 looks like an M16 on steroids, beefed up to accommodate the 30-caliber round. The SR25 Match rifle is a 7.62×51mm NATO sniper rifle. Knight's Manufacturing is one of the only manufacturers that guarantee their rifle will shoot one minute of angle at 100 yards using factory 168-grain Match 7.62×51mm NATO/308 Winchester ammunition. This rifles incorporates the 5R rifling sniper barrel manufactured by Remington Arms for the M24 sniper rifle. Knight's Manufacturing is the only company to which Remington has ever sold these precision barrel blanks. The 5R rifling is designed to optimize the use of 168-grain Match 7.62×51mm NATO/308 Winchester ammunition. Many firearms experts claim the SR25 is the most accurate semiautomatic rifle in the world.

In May of 2000, the U.S. Navy SEALS adopted the SR25 — now classified as the Mk 11 Mod 0 — as a full weapons system: rifle, Leupold scope, back-up pop-up iron sights and a sound suppresser. This is a modified SR25 Match rifle, which has a 20-inch barrel instead of 24-inch barrel. Following this sale, the U.S. Army Rangers also purchased SR25 rifles.

## Production Sources of Civilian/ Military Versions of the AR-15/M16

The AR-15 rifle has been copied all over the world, in military and sporting configurations. The Canadian military adopted the C7 as its main battle rifle. The C7, literally a modified M16A2 rifle, is manufactured by Diemaco of Ontario, Canada, an unknown company to most of the world but a large player in this weapons system. Diemaco has supplied their C7 and C8 weapons systems to Denmark, Norway, New Zealand and the Netherlands. They also equip the legendary British SAS and SBS with their SFW (Special Forces Weapon), designated the British L119A1 Assault Rifle. There have also been other military copies of the M16-series rifle made by Elisco Tool Company of the Philippines and Chartered Industries of Singapore.

Currently manufacturing the M16A2 and M4 carbines for the U.S. military are Colt's Manufacturing Inc, Hartford, Connecticut, and FN Manufacturing of Columbia, South Carolina. Quality Parts/Bushmaster Firearms of Windham, Maine, have manufactured approximately 400 complete M4 carbines for the United States Department of Defense as well as an additional (approximately) 400 complete M4 upper receivers assemblies.

The semi-automatic Colt AR-15/ Sporter-series rifles have become very popular in the world of competitive shooters. Colt's Manufacturing Company, Inc., manufactures more civilian versions of the rifle than any other manufacturer, even though there are many other semi-auto clones produced. One of the finest is the XM15E2S, made by Quality Parts-Bushmaster Firearms. Some other manufacturers are Olympic Arms of Olympia, Washington, and ArmaLite, Inc., a division of Eagle Arms of Coal Valley, Illinois.

The AR-15/M16 rifle has come a long way, surviving political opposition and its troubles in Vietnam to become one of the finest military rifles ever produced, with more than 9 million M16-series rifles in service throughout the world, equipping the troops of more than 20 nations. The U.S. military has always been a military of marksmen, and the M16A2 complements this philosophy, setting a standard of accuracy very few assault rifles can match while enjoying the reputation of being the finest human-engineered assault rifle in the world. The M16-series rifle continues to be the rifle of choice of SWAT teams and police departments all over the country, and it will be the main battle rifle of the United States well into the new millennium.